A PRACTITIONER'S GUIDE TO INTERNATIONAL TAX INFORMATION EXCHANGE REGIMES

DAC6, TIEAs, MDR, CRS, and FATCA

By

Harriet Brown & Grahame Jackson

First published September 2021

by Spiramus Press Ltd
102 Blandford Street
London W1U 8AG

www.spiramus.com

ISBN

9781913507237 Paperback

9781913507244 Digital

British Library Cataloguing-in-Publication Data.

A catalogue record for this book is available from the British Library.

Printed and bound in Great Britain by Grosvenor Group (Print Services) Ltd

Contents

Acknowledgements

Many people who have helped us prepare this work deserve thanks; our long-suffering families are the first amongst them with their patience and ability to tolerate their husbands and wives shouting at their computer because of some minor point in the guidance of a far-flung country related to a vital but obscure tax information exchange agreement.

We would also like to thank those that have helped us on our way and given us the space to tackle such a broad topic, our colleagues who have encouraged us and especially those friends and helpers that have contributed by editing, and formatting and the general doing of publishing a book.

Guidance Abbreviations

We have endeavoured to confirm all the guidance we have referred to is up to date at the date of writing. However, guidance is a dynamic and changing process which can be changed without notice.

In the text we refer to various pieces of guidance using abbreviations. The abbreviations we use and the edition of the relevant guidance we are referring to are listed below. On occasion, we will use more than one term to refer to the same guidance. Where we do, all terms are listed.

The directive which gives rise to what is known as DAC6 is itself an offspring of the Council Directive 2011/16/EU of 15 February 2011 on administrative cooperation in the field of taxation and repealing Directive 77/799/EEC which we shall refer to as the 'DAC' in its overarching form and 'DAC6' when referring specifically to the amending directive Council Directive (EU) 2018/822 (DAC6) which introduced the DAC6 regime.

Abbreviation	**Date of Publishing**	**Full Title**
The HMRC Guidance IEIM	31st December 2020	International Exchange of Information Manual
The Belgian Guidance	15th June 2020	FAQ: DAC 6 – Melding Van Grensoverschrijdende Constructies Artikels 326/1 Tot 326/10 Van Het Wetboek Van Inkomstenbelastingen
The German Guidance	29th March 2021	Anwendung der Vorschriften über die Pflicht zur Mitteilung grenzüberschreitender Steuergestaltungen
The Italian Guidance	10th February 2021	Circolare No 2
The Maltese Guidance	6th January 2021	Guidelines on the Mandatory Automatic Exchange of Information in relation to Cross-Border Arrangements (S.L. 123.127)
The Irish Guidance	March 2021	EU Mandatory Disclosure of Reportable Cross-Border Arrangements Part 33-03-03

The Luxembourg Guidance	14th October 2020	'Details Concerning the implementation of the law of 25th March 2020 on Cross Border Arrangements to be subject to declaration' – Version 14th October 2020
The French Guidance	25th November 2020	Official Public Finance Bulletin BOI-CF-CPF-30-40-10-10
The Isle of Man Guidance The IoM Guidance HMRC Guidance	21st December 2017	The Common Reporting Standard Isle of Man Regulations Application of the CRS for Isle of Man Financial Institutions Guidance Note GN 53
Jersey Guidance	October 2017	The Common Reporting Standard (CRS) Automatic Exchange of Financial Account Information Guidance Notes
Bermuda Guidance	17th April 2019	The Common Reporting Standard for Automatic Exchange of Financial Account Information in Tax Matters GUIDANCE Version 2.0
Guernsey Guidance	24th December 2016	Automatic Exchange of Information ("AEOI") for the Common Reporting Standard Supplementary Guernsey Guidance Notes
Mauritian Guidance	April 2019	Implementation of CRS Guidance Notes

Introduction

Legal questions are divided into three types. Questions to which there is one valid answer, questions to which there are more than one valid answer, and questions to which there is no valid answer. Often when interpreting legislation, lawyers try to claim that their answer is the only valid answer. They often forget that truth and validity are not the same thing.

These issues are the core of debate and argument and ultimately litigation. Debate, argument and litigation are the processes we use to sort the valid answers and seek the truth (though it is doubtful that this is an aim always, or – perhaps – even frequently attained).

It is not, however, always the case that there is a single 'true' answer to any given question no matter how long we argue and debate. In these cases, the legal profession bumbles along, finding compromise and general acceptance as the foundation for many propositions, which over subsequent generations will become 'trite law'. This process is carried out every time a new area of law is created and new provisions give those of us who work in a given area fresh challenges of interpretation. This challenge of interpretation is particularly significant where international provisions are in point.

In the experience of both the authors, every new provision in the tax arena is met with cries of 'it's open to interpretation' and 'it's impossible'. The reason people respond thus is because new words are necessarily open to interpretation, no piece of legislation can be made perfectly comprehensible in exactly the way intended, to all people at all times: language does not function like that. It is the act of interpretation that begins the process of understanding; those paralysed by a lack of guidance and unable to apply their own interpretation, let alone defend it and promote it are not contributing to the process of finding the correct understanding of any given provision (though anyone who has been faced with a lengthy set of new – whether to all or merely to them – tax provisions may well have strong sympathy with such an approach).

It is with this in mind that we have approached the writing of this book. We are unafraid to take positions where questions are not clear or where answers to questions are not yet apparent, because we know that in doing so we contribute to the process, and we are confident that those positions we have taken are backed by logic, law and reason. This is of course, rather a grand way of saying both that we reserve the right to change our minds on views expressed herein and that this book DOES NOT constitute advice. You should take advice on the specific scenario in question.

You will find in here many references to guidance from national authorities (especially in the DAC6 sections). National guidance is not law. It can be wrong. Commissioners of income tax give guidance simply in their capacity as interpreters of the law. That is to say, interpreters with important stature but not definitive – and importantly who can get it wrong. The courts are the arbiters of the construction of legislation. HMRC or Irish Tax and Customs[1] do not write the law, and their guidance should not be left unchallenged where it seems to be incorrect. However, clients should be aware that there are risks to taking an alternative approach to a revenue authority (even where that interpretation is far more likely to be correct). Where we believe a piece of guidance to go beyond the text of the relevant framework documents or the relevant law, we have questioned it. This does not mean that taxpayers can ignore guidance we disagree with; they should always take relevant tax advice in their local jurisdiction. What is crucial to understand is that the patchwork of guidance and notes from tax authorities across those jurisdictions implementing the regimes we discuss, is inconsistent in its implementation and interpretation. We hope that as a result of works like ours, such inconsistencies will be exposed and resolved in the interests of taxpayers.

We also note that we refer to guidance from a mishmash of jurisdictions. We are – between us – qualified in England and Wales, Gibraltar and Jersey. We necessarily, therefore, mention the guidance in these jurisdictions. We also mention the guidance from other jurisdictions with which we are familiar through our practices. We hope to expand these references in future editions. If you would like to see the guidance from your jurisdiction covered in future editions, do please send us a link to the guidance through our publishers.

We have also discussed at length the historical context of the provisions studied in this work. Anti-avoidance tax provisions are often presented as slaying the beasts of tax avoidance or attacking the wicked. It is worth noting that, on occasion, the behaviour targeted is a creature of the actions and omissions of the states who seek to demonise the uncooperative taxpayer. Generally, in life as well as tax, if something is permitted, then it will be done by some at least. Over the last century, the jurisdictions have had many opportunities to take steps toward automatic information exchange. Their failure to do so must be considered a contributing factor in taxpayer (mis)behaviour, and thus, to give context to current debates, we have described the historical development of automatic information exchange.

[1] Or indeed the revenue authorities of Jersey, Guernsey, Isle of Man or Mauritius

1. History and Context

1.1 The historical landscape in relation to tax information exchange

There is one longstanding rule of international law relating to the international tax landscape, from which much flows and to which much of this book is a response. That rule is the Revenue Rule[1], best articulated by Viscount Simonds in *Government of India, Ministry of Finance v Taylor* [1955] AC 491:

> '... I was greatly surprised to hear it suggested that the courts of this country would and should entertain a suit by a foreign State to recover a tax. For at any time since I have had any acquaintance with the law I should have said as Rowlatt J. said in the King of the Hellenes v. Brostron: 'It is perfectly elementary that **a foreign government cannot come here - nor will the courts of other countries allow our Government to go there - and sue a person found in that jurisdiction for taxes levied and which he is declared to be liable to in the country to which he belongs**'.

This principle is far older than Viscount Simonds' articulation of it, and it may well stretch back until the late 18th century,[2] if not earlier. The principle itself flows from the concept of sovereignty: since an act of taxation is an exercise of the sovereign power of the state, no state or jurisdiction can act to enforce the sovereignty of another, without an international agreement.

For those who wish to understand the Revenue Rule in detail, there are many papers on the matter including, amongst others, *'Government of India v Taylor: The End of the Line?'* by H. Brown, co-author of this work. For our purposes, however, no detailed analysis is required beyond stating that this is the starting point and base line from which all relations between tax authorities flow. The principle being that no assistance will be given by one state, to another state in the recovery of its taxes[3].

---

[1] The principle is often also called the 'rule in *Government of India v Taylor*' from an English case that confirmed its application in England and Wales, though it is in fact much older than that case, and is also referred to in conjunction with Lord Mansfield's name. This name is best avoided; the same Lord Mansfield's name is also sometimes used to refer to the rule of evidence that—in the US at least—both husband and wife were not entitled to give testimony on the question of whether they had access to the other at the time of conception in questions of legitimacy. Thus it is unhelpful to use this nomenclature

[2] *Holman v Johnson* (1775) 1 Cowp. 341.

[3] It should be noted that the principle has been significantly curtailed by legislation and international agreement, as well as case law. It is not clear – even before such curtailment – that it would always apply in relation to exchanges of information.

1.2 International relations and the family of nations: first attempts

Prior to 1918, whilst the international relations landscape was not entirely devoid of international frameworks from which to work, the situation was primarily one of nations, large and small, working on a bilateral basis outside any wider framework. As a result of the terrible destruction this system wrought upon the world between 1914 and 1918, various leaders proposed a global organisation through which such matters could be discussed, most famously President Woodrow Wilson of the United States, in the fourteenth of his Fourteen Points:

> 14. A general association of nations must be formed under specific covenants for the purpose of affording mutual guarantees of political independence and territorial integrity to great and small states alike.[4]

This was the proposal which gave birth to the League of Nations, the often derided precursor to today's United Nations. The League was certainly an imperfect creature, but it created a precedent and ambition for a functioning global community of nations, large and small, in equality. In addition to this lofty ideal of a functioning international community, it also built institutions later absorbed by the UN into bodies such as the World Health Organisation and formed the bedrock of their work.

The League was not only active in the field of health and international relations, but also in the field of tax. In 1927 its Committee of Technical Experts on Double Taxation and Tax Evasion published a report, recommending four model conventions to the members, to assist in eliminating double taxation and tax evasion. They were:

(i) Convention on the Prevention of Double Taxation;
(ii) Convention on the Prevention of Double Taxation in the special matter of succession duties;
(iii) Convention on the Administrative Assistance in Matters of Taxation; and
(iv) Convention on Judicial Assistance on the Collection of Taxes.

This 1927 Convention of the Prevention of Double Taxation is the direct ancestor of today's Organisation for Economic Cooperation and Development Model Convention on Income and on Capital (2017), and it is by the far the most widely adopted.

The Committee of Experts was not unaware of the mountain they had to climb, and the chair of the committee expressed this in the covering letter to the 1927 report:

---

[4] President Woodrow Wilson, 8 January 1918

> … the Committee on Double Taxation and Tax Evasion is fully conscious that the work which it has just concluded is imperfect in that it does not provide solutions for all the difficulties which may arise in this very complex question. But, having regard to the diversity of the legislative systems represented in the Committee and the necessity for finding formulae capable of acceptance by everyone it will be recognised that the experts were bound to confine themselves to indicating general rules leaving particular points of difficulty to be dealt with – in the spirit of the accepted general principles – by those on whom the task of negotiating the bilateral conventions shall ultimately fall[5]

Anyone who has read the current provisions relating to international exchange of information will see that this issue – of ensuring international agreements or directives function, or come close to functioning, within the legal systems of the nations in which they are intended to be implemented – has yet to be settled. Signore D'Aroma, the chair of the Committee of Experts, would surely feel sympathy for Paolo Gentiloni[6] and his team in their efforts to draft provisions allowing the EU Member States to exchange information openly on tax-related matters. This explains why so many of the existing provisions lead to voluminous and confusing guidance. It is a difficult task, the end product of which is, by necessity, imperfect[7].

Nevertheless, a Convention on Administrative Assistance in Matters of Taxation (the '1927 Draft Convention') was produced. It was a sparse document by modern standards, running to a page and a half, and eight articles. Article 1 states:

> With a view to obtaining a better apportionment of fiscal burdens in the interest both of Governments and taxpayers, the Contracting States undertake, subject to reciprocity, to give each other administrative assistance in regard to all matters required for the purpose of tax assessment.
>
> Such assistance may consist in:
> (a) the exchange of fiscal information in either of the contracting countries. The exchange will take place following a request concerning concrete cases, or, without any special request, for the classes of particulars defined in Article 2;

---

[5] Letter Addressed by the Chairman of the Committee of Technical Experts on Double Taxation and Tax Evasion to the Chairman of the Finance Committee, 12 April 1927

[6] EU Commissioner for Economy as at July 2021

[7] This is further impacted by the difficulties inevitably plaguing all attempts to 'legislate' internationally, such as differing legal systems and the need for translation into several languages.

(b) cooperation between the administrative authorities in carrying out certain measures of procedure.[8]

What may be surprising to modern eyes is how much within this short paragraph[9] is still being implemented. It is testament to the work of the Committee that the principles and main thrust of international tax information exchange remain inherently unchanged since this report was published one April day in London in 1927. It is, perhaps, also testament to how difficult a job it is.

Those principles are:
(i) That the information exchange is to the benefit not only of governments, but also taxpayers, by ensuring all pay the correct amount of tax;
(ii) That information exchange must be reciprocal;[10]
(iii) That information should be exchanged on request;
(iv) That in some cases it should be exchanged automatically; and
(v) That only 'concrete cases' can be subject to an information request. This principle is articulated nowadays by the 'no fishing expeditions' rule.[11]

The matters related to automatic exchange of information contained in Article 2 of the 1927 Draft Convention were:
(i) Immovable property;
(ii) Mortgages and similar claims;
(iii) Industrial, commercial or agricultural undertakings;
(iv) Earned income and directors' fees;
(v) Transferable securities deposits and current accounts; and
(vi) Successions.

Those readers familiar with the provisions of the OECD Common Reporting Standards (CRS) and the US Foreign Account Tax Compliance Act (FATCA) — which are the today's automatic exchange of information provisions — will know that even if the 1927 Draft Convention was 'imperfect', it had a broader vision of what needed to be attained than either of those

[8] Article 1, 'Draft of a bilateral convention on administrative assistance in matters of taxation', League of Nations 1927

[9] This is, presumably, also the forerunner of Article 26 of the OECD Model DTA, which provides '1. The competent authorities of the Contracting States shall exchange such information as is foreseeably relevant for carrying out the provisions of this Convention or to the administration or enforcement of the domestic laws concerning taxes of every kind and description imposed on behalf of the Contracting States, or of their political subdivisions or local authorities, insofar as the taxation thereunder is not contrary to the Convention. The exchange of information is not restricted by Articles 1 and 2' – though this is arguably less relevant (and lends itself to the spontaneous exchange of information).

[10] The US FATCA Model 1B and Model 2 IGAs, as well as the underlying FATCA structure belie this principle – see Chapter 5.

[11] See Chapter 2.

provisions.[12] As with so many of the League of Nations' attempts radically to overhaul the international landscape, the constituent nations were lacking the political will to solve a problem which could only be solved by multilateral cooperation.

As the League described itself in its publication 'Powers and Duties Attributed to the League of Nations by International Treaties' in 1944:

> ... the League of Nations is not only a political institution, but an organ of international cooperation.

The automatic exchange of tax information may not be the greatest failure of the League of Nations era, but it is certainly as attributable to the failings of its members as any other. It was not impossible for members of the League to adopt a convention drafted by the Committee of Experts — that much is demonstrated by the fact that some countries entered into the Convention on the Prevention of Double Taxation that — but when it came to information exchange, they were unwilling to do so.[13]

One is forced to consider whether today's world of international finance would exist as it does, were it not for this failure to adopt the 1927 Draft Convention. Many of the international tax issues which presently exercise transparency campaigners so greatly might not have emerged. Similarly, we must ask if the global economy would have developed in such a manner as it has, at such great speed, if tax information exchange had acted as a coolant on the mobility of capital (even at the level of purely administrative requirements, the exchange envisaged by the 1927 Draft Convention would have been burdensome in a pre-computer age, quite aside from considering whether mobile capital contributes to tax evasion and avoidance). Whether or not the 1927 Draft Convention amounted to a lost opportunity, or an avoided pitfall will never be known; suffice to say the intervention of the Second World War made the matter a moot point.

1.3 After the war – lost opportunities

The beginning of the greatest bloodletting in the history of mankind interrupted (either on 7 July 1937 or 1 September 1939 depending on your perspective and historical methodology) the construction of an international tax framework. By the effective end of the war on 14 August 1945, the League

[12] Though given the administrative burden of matters under CRS and FATCA, their limited nature may be considered a blessing by busy professionals and taxpayers whose concern is primarily one of privacy, rather than taxation.

[13] It should perhaps be remembered that obligations to exchange tax information have not only increased the administrative burden for taxpayers and their advisers, but also for revenue authorities. They also pose challenges to domestic privacy laws and potentially, in some circumstances, to civil and human rights. The lack of will to move forward may be explicable by reference to such factors also.

of Nations had been replaced by the United Nations and its projects had been reassigned or terminated.

Post-World War II and in the new Cold War era, there was little (if any) political will to make the creation of an international framework for exchanging tax information a central matter in international relations. There was the matter of rebuilding a shattered global economy, of tracking and caring for millions of displaced people and of counting the dead; consequently and understandably, new attempts at a general information exchange were not high, or even present upon the list of priorities. Had there not been a post-war world to rebuild, of course, that world would still have lacked the information-technology and communications advances so crucial to the operating of today's governments and international financial institutions.

In his book *The Hidden Wealth of Nations*, Gabriel Zucman describes a joint French and US attempt in 1945 to impose upon the Swiss an exchange related to banking matters. Though whether it would have amounted to an 'exchange' in any real sense is a matter for discussion.

However, one organisation would ultimately become the focus for global tax initiatives. In 1948, the Organisation for European Economic Cooperation (OEEC) was founded, to assist in the implementation of the Marshall Plan for rebuilding the global economy. OEEC went on to become the Organisation for Economic Cooperation and Development (OECD) in 1961. In 1963, the OECD published its first Draft Double Taxation Convention on Income and Capital (the 1963 Draft Convention), descendant of the 1927 Draft Convention on the Prevention of Double Taxation and ancestor to all model conventions since. According to the OECD website, at this time only 'a few dozen tax agreements were in force' and by 2017 there were more than 3,000.

This success story for the Model Convention on Double Taxation must be tempered by the failure of the international community to adopt an updated version of the 1927 Draft Convention, thus defeating the unified approach to information exchange and to the elimination of double taxation and tax evasion adopted by the Committee of Experts in 1927.[14] The Committee of Experts explained the necessity of this dual approach in their commentary to the 1927 Draft Convention:

> From the very outset, the Committee realised the necessity of dealing with the questions of tax evasion and double taxation in co-ordination with each other. It is highly desirable that States should come to an arrangement with a view to ensuring that a taxpayer shall not be taxed on the same income by a number of different countries,

[14] Though it should be noted that the OECD Model DTA has included an information exchange article since 1963

> and it seems equally desirable that such international co-operation should prevent certain incomes from escaping taxation altogether.[15]

It is beyond the remit of this work to explore the reasons and machinations behind the international community's failure to taking this combined approach, but as history shows, its members did not. Instead, they chose to include a much-reduced information exchange requirement at Article 26(1) of the 1963 Draft Convention, stating:

> 1. The competent authorities of the Contracting States shall exchange such information as is necessary for the carrying out of this Convention and of the domestic laws of the Contracting States concerning taxes covered by this Convention insofar as the taxation thereunder is in accordance with this Convention. Any information so exchanged will be treated as secret and shall not be disclosed to any persons or authorities other than those concerned with the assessment of collection of taxes which are the subject of the Convention

There was no mention of information related to specific classes of income, nor of automatic exchange, in fact the Commentary on Article 26(1) states:

> the rule laid down in paragraph 1 of the Article presupposes that information shall be exchanged on application[16]

This was most certainly a neutering of the dual approach envisaged by the 1927 Draft Convention, even if it still allowed for exchange of information, and made vaguely encouraging indications that automatic exchange agreements existed and might 'be adopted bilaterally by Member countries'.[17]

1.4 Global economic crisis – a reawakening of awareness

By the late 1970s it was apparent that the economic landscape was changing. The post-war growth spurt had finally exhausted itself in the oil shocks of the decade's end, and the costs of the welfare states were expanding as the population began to age. The sophisticated economies of the political West began to reform their tax systems. As Sven Steinmo notes in his *Taxation and Democracy*:

> in the 1980s a huge set of remarkably diverse countries have overhauled their tax systems. In virtually all cases these tax reforms have meant lowering income and profits tax rates, cutting back tax expenditures and broadening the tax base. In each case, these overhauls have been advertised under the rubric of simplification,

---

[15] 'Commentary on the Draft of a bilateral convention on administrative assistance in matters of taxation', League of Nations 1927

[16] 'Commentary on the Draft Double Taxation Convention on income and capital', Paragraph 6 of the Commentary on Article 26, OECD 1963

[17] Ibid

> efficiency and fairness. But when one steps back and examines tax policy development around the globe in the 1980s, one sees an unmistakable trend: *Tax reform* has now come to mean the redistributing of existing tax burdens *downward*.[18]

The tax burden needed to be shifted downward, to continue to pay for the enhanced activities of a modern state. The state, in turn, took on the role of ultimate guarantor of the entire economy, a process reaching its peak in March 2020, when modern states stepped in to guarantee wages, subsidise businesses and provide a safety net to catch a rapidly failing and locked-down economy. In a sense, by turning tax into something many more people were touched by, taxation was democratised.

In parallel to the spreading of the tax burden throughout society, capital had become much more mobile by the 1980s and 90s:

> Since the mid-1970s the world economy has undergone massive changes. The expansion of world trade has been well documented. Perhaps less well understood is the striking extent to which capital has become more international, more mobile and more integrated. Such changes have substantively altered the context in which domestic tax policies are made. The result has been a crumbling of the post war consensus over taxation policy.[19]

This increased mobility of capital created an opportunity for those jurisdictions choosing to attract capital as a means to increase the prosperity of their populations. This found its expression, on a grand scale, in the phenomenon known as 'tax competition'.

> First classical tax havens target individual or corporate portfolio capital through a combination of low or even zero rates with legal provisions such as bank secrecy or trusts. The latter make it impossible for the revenue agencies entitled to tax the capital in question to trace it… Second, there is competition for so-called paper profits. Multinationals are able to shift profits from high-tax jurisdictions to low tax jurisdictions.[20]

Setting aside the author's campaigning tone, the above passage explains how and why tax competition came about. An increasingly fiscally interdependent world, coupled with increased capital mobility and a lack of international frameworks for the exchange of information made tax competition an easy means for poorer island nations to lift their populations into affluence. The plethora of exempt company or international business

[18] *Taxation & Democracy*, Steinmo, Sven. Yale University Press 1993

[19] Ibid

[20] 'The State and Tax Competition: A Normative Perspective', Dietsch, Peter, in *Taxation: Philosophical Perspectives*. Oxford University Press 2018

company tax regimes which sprung up in the 1960s and 70s shows what an attractive route this was.

The combination of an increased tax burden on the lower-earning sectors of society and reduced tax burdens on large corporates and wealthy individuals began to cause a backlash against perceived abuses. Campaign groups were set up, and pressure applied. Governments and non-governmental organisations began to agitate for multilateral reform.

In May 1996, the ministers of the member countries of the OECD asked the OECD to produce a report on potentially harmful tax practices and in 1998 the OECD published this review (the '1998 Report').[21] Two years later they introduced a blacklist system in their 2000 review 'Towards Global Tax Cooperation" (the '2000 Report').

The 1998 report contained the following recommendation.

> that countries consider undertaking co-ordinated enforcement programs (such as simultaneous examinations, specific exchange of 51 information projects or joint training activities) in relation to income or taxpayers benefiting from practices constituting harmful tax competition.[22]
>
> ...
>
> 135. The Recommendation is aimed at further developing collaboration in that respect. The efforts that will be taken under this Recommendation will typically result in countries combining their information and audit powers in order to better apply domestic tax rules vis-à-vis income from, or entities of, other countries from which such information cannot be obtained. Simultaneous examinations based upon the 1992 OECD Model Agreement should be encouraged.[23]

This is a return to the vision of the 1927 Draft Convention, of an automatic exchange of information aimed at ensuring correct tax is paid and the rules are properly respected.

From the perspective of the tax campaigner, this flurry of activity was short-lived. The United States signalled its disapproval in May 2001, when US Treasury Secretary Paul O'Neill said:

> 'I am troubled by the underlying premise that low tax rates are somehow suspect and by the notion that any country, or group of

---

[21] Organisation for Economic Cooperation and Development, 'Harmful Tax Competition: an emerging global issue', OECD Publishing 1998

[22] Chapter 3 Part III Recommendation 13 Organisation for Economic Cooperation and Development, 'Harmful Tax Competition: an emerging global issue', OECD Publishing 1998

[23] Ibid

> countries, should interfere with any other country's decision about how to structure its own tax system...'[24]

Once again, this time as a consequence of booming economic activity ensuring rising tax revenues, the political will to unify the world's tax information exchange regimes slipped away.

However, a Rubicon had been crossed, the creation of the OECD blacklist and the threat of sanctions for uncooperative jurisdictions remained, even if it was not being actively pursued. It only required another economic crisis and the end of growing tax revenues for that mechanism to be reactivated.

1.5 Tax information exchange agreements

Also as a consequence of the 1998/2000 process undertaken by the OECD, Tax Information Exchange Agreements (TIEAs) had become more commonplace. To avoid being placed on the OECD blacklist, a jurisdiction was required first to make a political commitment to the principles of transparency and effective exchange of information. Central to delivering on this commitment was a requirement for every jurisdiction to enter into a minimum number of TIEAs.

TIEAs[25] follow a model form as published by the OECD[26] and contain the following provisions:

- exchange of information on request by one contracting party that is 'foreseeably relevant' to the administration and enforcement of domestic tax laws of the Contracting Parties;
- protection of the information exchanged under the TIEA. Disclosure can be made to courts or judicial forums only for the purpose of determination of the taxation matter in question;
- the requested party must gather information even if there is no domestic relevance;
- no 'fishing expeditions'. Information requested must be specific to an identified person and be of a specific nature;
- information is defined in an expansive manner to cover banking details, ownership details of companies/persons/funds/trusts etc.
- representatives of one party may be permitted to conduct tax examinations in the territory of another party including interviews of individuals and examination of records.

The observant will notice echoes of the 1927 Draft Convention in the provisions of the TIEA, most specifically the 'no fishing expeditions' clause, guarding against blanket requests and respecting the rights of the taxpayer against intrusive and speculative requests.

---

[24] 'ONeill: OECD Tax Haven Too Broad', Anderson, Curt Associated Press, 10 May 2001 http://www.washingtonpost.com/wp-srv/aponline/20010510/aponline125928_000.htm

[25] For more information on TIEAs see Chapter 11

[26] OECD Agreement on Exchange of Information on Tax Matters

However, as a result of the United States pouring cold water on the process in 2001, fewer TIEAs were entered into than might otherwise have been expected, and political commitments remained exactly that. It was not until the near-collapse of the international banking system in 2008 and the following 'Great Recession' that the international tax system reappeared on the agenda. The vast amounts of borrowing required to support the international finance centre had once again motivated an examination of the means by which large corporates sheltered profits from tax.

The international community responded to this by calling an *ad hoc* meeting in Paris, hosted by the French and German governments, in October 2008[27] entitled the 'Conference on the Fight Against International Tax Avoidance and Evasion: Improving transparency and stepping up exchange of information in tax matters'. This conference demanded a more active approach from the OECD and the OECD Secretary General Angel Gurría articulated the connection between the 2008 financial crisis and the issue of tax avoidance and evasion:

> 'Tax may not have been one of the main issues of the crisis, but I do believe it should be an integrated part of the long-term solution. We cannot expect taxpayers to fund the bailing out of failed financial institutions and at the same time allow these institutions to facilitate offshore non-compliance by using tax havens' [28]

The G20 instructed the OECD to prepare a report for their April 2009 summit which would categorise jurisdictions in accordance with the number of TIEAs they had signed[29]. The blacklist would remain, however, a second list of those jurisdictions which had 'committed to implementing the internationally agreed standard on tax transparency' (the 'grey list') and a third list (the 'white list') would list those jurisdictions which had 'substantially implemented the standard' and entered into a minimum of 12 TIEAs.

This led to a flurry of activity, with the number of TIEAs signed globally rising from 50 in mid-2008 to 450 by mid-2010.[30]

TIEAs were undoubtedly a step forward for the international tax community and they led to small jurisdictions entering the international arena in a way

---

[27] 'The G20 and Tax Havens: Maintaining the Momentum?' (Prepared for the conference 'Governing the Global Economy: The Role of the G20', University of Toronto – Munk School of Global Affairs, 18 June 2010) Prof dr. Dries Lesage, University of Ghent

[28] Remarks by Angela Gurría, Paris 21 October 2008 www.oecd.org/general/improvingtransparencyandsteppingupexchangeofinformationintaxmatters.htm retrieved 10 January 2020

[29] 'A Progress Report On The Jurisdictions Surveyed By The OECD Global Forum In Implementing The Internationally Agreed Tax Standard', 2009

[30] A. M. Sawyer, 'The OECD's Tax Information Exchange Agreements an Example of (In)Effective Global Governance', *Journal of Applied Law and Policy*, 2011

never seen before. For example, the Chief Minister of Gibraltar signed his jurisdiction's TIEA with the United States on 31 March 2009; across the table from him sat the Secretary of the Treasury, Tim Geithner. Such a state of affairs would have been unthinkable were it not for the international tax system operating as it did in the early 21st century. However, TIEAs were far from beloved by all, and nor was the simple number count system which acted as the criterion for entry onto the grey or white lists. A.M. Sawyer summed up his objections:

> the TIEA initiative will need to undergo major revision if it is to have any realistic chance of making effective inroads to information exchange. Systematic change to the Model TIEA (and associated updating of the 600 plus individual TIEAs) appears to be most unlikely. This leaves the question open as to whether the TIEA initiative is an expensive exercise in 'window dressing' that leaves tax havens with little to fear and other countries with little to gain.[31]

Sawyer seems to be blaming those jurisdictions which he classes as 'tax havens' for the lack of effectiveness of TIEAs, however, when he wrote the above in 2011, the system designed in 1927 was still only partially implemented. The members of the Committee of Experts in 1927 had been fully aware that bilateral agreements merely allowing for exchange on demand would not suffice. It seems odd that campaigning academics such as Sawyer should have been surprised by this 82 years later. From the perspective of information exchange, TIEAs were a step in the right direction, but they were not the end of the process. They could only prove effective at tackling evasion if coupled with some kind of automatic exchange.

It was not the case that no attempt had been made to implement an automatic exchange of information impacting on those jurisdictions accused of sheltering money from taxation. The now-defunct EU Savings Directive[32] had generated much heat and light amongst banking circles but little extra revenue for the Member States, as it could not reach beyond Europe, failed to include the Swiss banking system and was targeted solely at individuals.

The first functioning automatic exchange of information regime would be imposed on the world unilaterally, not by way of a multilateral agreement. Instead, one of the only economies large enough to impose such a provision did so in order to fund its own efforts at reducing unemployment; its *modus operandi* was to target those of its citizens who were avoiding tax by using foreign bank accounts.

---

[31] Ibid

[32] Council Directive 2003/48/EC of 3 June 2003 on taxation of savings income in the form of interest payments

1.6 FATCA, CRS and real automatic exchange

The provisions of the Hiring Incentives to Restore Employment Act (HIRE) of the United States were a response to the global economic crisis of the years just prior to 2010 when HIRE was introduced. They promoted the employment of the long-term jobless, and in order to raise the relevant revenue, a sister provision known as the Foreign Account Tax Compliance Act 2010 was introduced.

FATCA contained a number of innovations, making it successful where other attempts had failed; it also capitalised on the fact that, in a world of mobile capital, every major financial institution had a presence in the United States or received payments from the United States banking system.

The innovations were:

(i) The requirement for financial institutions to report on their clients instead of placing reporting requirements on the taxpayer;
(ii) The threat of withholding taxes on all dollar payments to non-cooperative financial institutions, including payments for their clients; and
(iii) Initially FATCA did not envisage relationships between governments, it was simply a compliance matter for financial institutions, thus sidestepping prolonged negotiations.

This combination of factors meant that foreign financial institutions based in jurisdictions with banking secrecy laws pressed their governments to resolve matters for them so that they could comply with FATCA, avoid withholding tax on payments to them and also not be in breach of their local legislation (including, importantly, legislation in relation to privacy). The result was that governments had their hands forced; they caught up with the United States legislation, entering into Model Intergovernmental Agreements (IGAs) to allow FATCA to function. By the time of writing, 113 jurisdictions had entered into IGAs with the United States.[33]

The provisions of FATCA are not for discussion at this point, but any readers who have been involved in fulfilling its requirements or interpreting its Byzantine text will agree that its ambition and breadth of vision are breath-taking. If globally adopted, it will have required the classification, into one of three categories (which are still not entirely clear), of every legal entity holding an account with a financial institution[34] in the entire world. The size of this task is immense, and the achievements of financial institutions in fulfilling the requirements of FATCA in anything approaching a meaningful way, go almost entirely without recognition.

---

[33] US Treasury home.treasury.gov/policy-issues/tax-policy/foreign-account-tax-compliance-act

[34] More widely defined than those which are obviously such, and therefore, more significant in scope – see Chapter 5

The success of FATCA led to a truly multilateral project, building upon the framework FATCA established. Around the time FATCA was introduced, the OECD had also revived its Convention on Mutual Assistance in Matters of Taxation (the 'Convention on Mutual Assistance') by issuing an amending protocol. The Convention on Mutual Assistance had been ratified by only 14 nations prior to the issuing of the amending protocol on 27 May 2010. Prior to that date, it was open only to those nations who were members of the OECD or the Council of Europe. In 2010, the amending protocol opened the Convention on Mutual Assistance to non-members of those organisations on invitation.

Utilising the provisions of Article 6 of the Convention on Mutual Assistance which referred to automatic exchange of information, the OECD Common Reporting Standard was agreed and the OECD Council issued its Declaration on the Automatic Exchange of Information on Tax Matters at their meeting in May 2014 the contents of which contained the following statements:

> CONSIDERING that tax fraud and tax evasion jeopardise citizens' trust in the fairness and integrity of the tax system as a whole, thereby undermining voluntary tax compliance by all taxpayers, which is essential to effective tax administration…;
>
> MINDFUL that as the world becomes increasingly globalised it is becoming easier for all taxpayers to make, hold and manage investments through financial institutions outside of their country of residence, and that investments that are kept offshore by taxpayers may go untaxed to the extent that taxpayers fail to comply with their tax obligations to the detriment of those who pay their taxes…;
>
> NOTING that there is growing interest in many countries in the opportunities provided by reciprocal automatic exchange of information between tax authorities; and finally
>
> 1. DECLARE that we are determined to tackle cross-border tax fraud and tax evasion and to promote international tax compliance through mutual administrative assistance in tax matters and a level playing field;
> 2. CONFIRM that automatic exchange of financial account information will further these objectives particularly if the new single global standard, including full transparency on ownership interests, is implemented among all financial centres;
> 3. ACKNOWLEDGE that information exchanged on the basis of the new single global standard is subject to appropriate safeguards including certain confidentiality requirements and the requirement that information may be used only for the purposes

foreseen by the legal instrument pursuant to which it is exchanged.[35]

On 30 September 2017, 54 jurisdictions, including a number of the traditional 'tax havens' and a large number of finance centres carried out the first exchange of information under the CRS. Finally, 90 years after the Committee of Experts of the League of Nations issued their 1927 Draft Convention, real automatic exchange of information occurred. Despite all interested parties agreeing that automatic exchange was vital, it took a combination of conditions to make it possible. These included near-global economic collapse, the ability of the United States to act unilaterally, the work already carried out by the international financial institutions to satisfy FATCA, the tax reforms of the 1980s and the subsequent broadening of the tax burden, the increased mobility of capital and the opening of the OECD framework to those outside the organisation itself.

1.7 Base Erosion & Profit Shifting – the bandwagon rolls on

CRS was only one of the concurrent projects initiated by the OECD in the aftermath of what became known simply as 'the Economic Crisis'.[36] In parallel to the work on CRS, the OECD established a project known as the Base Erosion Profit Shifting project or "BEPS".

In 2017 in their 'Background Brief: Inclusive Framework on BEPS', the OECD explained the nature of the BEPS project:

> The international tax landscape has changed dramatically in recent years. With political support of G20 Leaders, the international community has taken joint action to increase transparency and exchange of information in tax matters, and to address weaknesses of the international tax system that create opportunities for BEPS. The internationally agreed standards of transparency and exchange of information in the tax area have put an end to the era of bank secrecy. With over 130 countries and jurisdictions currently participating, the Global Forum on Transparency and Exchange of Information for Tax Purposes has ensured consistent and effective implementation of international transparency standards since its establishment in 2009. At the same time, the financial crisis and aggressive tax planning by multinational enterprises (MNEs) have put BEPS high on the political agenda. With a conservatively

---

[35] Meeting of the OECD Council at Ministerial Level 'Declaration on the Automatic Exchange of Information on Tax Matters', adopted 6 May 2014.

[36] Rather like footballers who are so well known they are reduced to a single name, the 'Economic Crisis' of 2008-2013 is sufficiently famous as to require no dates or other indicators. It was, in fact, a complex chain of events precipitated by a combination of government actions, bad regulation and greed, and included several sub-crises, such as the Credit Crunch, the Euro Crisis, etc. Such bland shorthand is inadequate to convey the severity of the crisis, its impact and after-effects, some of which are still being felt at the time of writing.

> estimated annual revenue loss of USD 100 to 240 billion, the stakes are high for governments around the world. The impact of BEPS on developing countries, as a percentage of tax revenues, is estimated to be even higher than in developed countries.[37]

Estimates of lost revenue to avoidance and evasion are notoriously inaccurate and seem to vary wildly depending on how radical the agenda of the campaign group producing them is. However, the perception that 'offshore' was now a major problem and holding back the global recovery was embedded in the public psyche, worsened by journalistic publication of leaks such as the 'Panama Papers' and 'Paradise Papers'.

There are two main results of the BEPS project. The first is a list of 15 action points endorsed by the G20 at their meeting in Antalya in November 2015. It contained the following action points:

(i) Address the tax challenges of the digital economy;
(ii) Neutralise the effects of hybrid mismatch arrangements;
(iii) Strengthen CFC rules;
(iv) Limit base erosion via interest deductions and other financial payments;
(v) Counter harmful tax practices more effectively taking into account transparency and substance;
(vi) Prevent treaty abuse;
(vii) Prevent artificial avoidance of PE status;
(viii) Assure that transfer pricing outcomes are in line with value creation (action points 7, 8 and 9);
(ix) Establish methodologies to collect data and analyse BEPS and the actions to address it;
(x) Require taxpayers to disclose their aggressive tax planning arrangements;
(xi) Re-examine transfer pricing documentation;
(xii) Make dispute resolution mechanisms more effective; and
(xiii) Develop a multilateral instrument.[38]

The second main result was the establishment of the Inclusive Framework on BEPS: an international forum where OECD members and 'interested countries' can meet as equals, to discuss the aims of BEPS and how to implement the action plan. At the time of writing, 137 jurisdictions were members of the Inclusive Framework, with new members still joining. The difference in approach between the Inclusive Framework and the OECD's approach to the 1998/2000 process could not have been more stark.

In 1998 the OECD issued a report and threatened the low tax jurisdictions with 'defensive measures' if they refused to co-operate. It was a diktat

[37] 'Background Brief: Inclusive Framework on BEPS', OECD Publishing, 2017.

[38] Details of the BEPS action points can be found in many places. The authors have referred to the OECD's 'Action Plan on Base Erosion and Profit Shifting', OECD Publishing, 2013.

delivered from on high, and a diktat with which two members of the OECD (Luxembourg and Austria) refused to co-operate.

Several of the low tax jurisdictions consented to the 1998 principles, subject to the following comments, best articulated in the letter of 27 February 2002 from the then-Chief Minister of Gibraltar, Sir Peter Caruana to the OECD:

> 'those jurisdictions, including OECD Member countries [at this point Austria and Luxembourg] that fail either to make equivalent commitments or to satisfy the standards of the 1998 report will be subject to a common framework of defensive measures'; and further,
>
> 'Gibraltar will be invited to participate fully on an equal basis in any discussions in the Global Forum of OECD member countries and representative non-member countries and jurisdictions on the design of internationally accepted standards for the implementation of these and similar commitments. Gibraltar is of the view that jurisdictions generally must become increasingly integrated into the process of setting new international standards if those standards are to attract global support'[39]

Gibraltar was not alone, of course, and similar clauses are included in the letters from Guernsey, Jersey and Isle of Man and those who came after them. One can see the opening of the BEPS Inclusive Framework as the cost of cooperation. The jurisdictions being threatened with action needed a voice, and their interests had to be represented if the project was to be successful. The diplomatic compromise demanded by the finance centres was done and solidified into the Inclusive Framework. This can be seen in the following:

> Embodied in the CFA, the Inclusive Framework on BEPS makes use of this consensus-based mechanism whereby all Members participate on an equal footing[40]

1.8 EU Implementation of Action Point 12

The EU appears to perceive itself as the gold standard of anti-avoidance jurisdictions. Maybe this view is an echo of the same reasoning deployed by the 1927 Committee of Experts, that the opening of borders and facilitating of international trade can only be achieved by guarding against abuse.

The fact that the EU is a less perfect union than the United States may well explain why it guards against tax avoidance with such vigilance In the absence of an overarching 'federal' tax system, lack of harmonisation necessarily leads to tax arbitrage, which could eventually lead to the emptying of the coffers of those jurisdictions with high tax rates. In the

---

[39] Letter of the Chief Minister of Gibraltar to Secretary-General D. Johnston, OECD, 27 February 2002

[40] 'Background Brief Inclusive Framework on BEPS', OECD Publishing, 2017.

United States, such an outcome could be rectified by state-level redistribution at the federal level from federal resources.

Across the EU, even in 2021, such basic matters as the test for corporate tax residence are disparate: some countries rely on location of management and control (Malta), some on incorporation (Romania), some on a combination of both, some on a second management test known as 'Place of Effective Management'. Without standardisation, there will always be an opportunity for abuse in a zone which has as its *raison d'être* the free movement of capital at will.

As a result of this, the EU embraces OECD projects with great enthusiasm, often 'gold plating' proposals. Their response to BEPS Action Point 12 (taxpayers to disclose their aggressive tax planning arrangements) in the Directive on Administrative Cooperation in the field of taxation (Council Directive 2011/16/EU) as amended by Council Directive (EU) 2018/822 (DAC6) is the global leader in cross-border arrangement disclosure. It is unlikely to be the last word, as other jurisdictions catch up and it is clearly related to pre-existing regimes (it adopts a 'hallmark' based approach similar to the Disclosure of Tax Avoidance Schemes (DOTAS) regime in the United Kingdom[41]) but at the time of writing, it is the first fully functioning iteration of automatic exchange of aggressive arrangements and it is also the most rigorous of those proposed.

The contents of DAC6 will be discussed at great length below, but for our purposes here it is necessary only to note that DAC6 is the only cross-border regime (at the time of writing) which properly tackles the aims of Action Point 12. The Mandatory Disclosure Regime proposed by the OECD is not a comprehensive approach, dealing only with one of five categories of aggressive avoidance. It is not a comprehensive approach and will undoubtedly be expanded upon in coming years, if the OECD Inclusive Framework members mean properly to implement Action Point 12.

1.9 Mandatory Disclosure Regime (MDR)

Unable to impose a disclosure regime on its members as the EU can, by way of directive, the OECD tackled Action Point 12 in a more light-touch manner, utilising similar mechanisms to those that implemented CRS and country-by-country reporting.

On 8 March 2018, slightly before the adoption of the EU's DAC6 proposal, the OECD's Committee on Fiscal Affairs adopted the Mandatory Disclosure Rules. Their purpose and expected outcome was explained thus:

> 'The purpose of these model mandatory disclosure rules is to provide tax administrations with information on CRS Avoidance Arrangements and Opaque Offshore Structures, including the users of those Arrangements and Structures and those involved with their

[41] Though there the similarity ends – see Chapter 4

> supply. Information disclosed pursuant to the application of these model rules can be used both for compliance purposes and to inform future tax policy design. These rules should also have a deterrent effect against the design, marketing and use of arrangements covered by the rules.'[42]

This is possibly the most comprehensive and frank description of the aims of such provisions. They are four-fold:

(i) To gather information about specific schemes;
(ii) To understand who supplies such schemes;
(iii) To inform future policy; and
(iv) To deter targeted schemes.

The MDR is often considered to be 'DAC6-lite', because it has a more limited scope than that of DAC6. However, to view the MDR as a finished work would be foolish. Frameworks such as these have a wider utility once established, and once mechanisms are in place and proven to work, it is unlikely that that the OECD will stop with the current level of information exchange.

1.10 Conclusion

The work of anti-avoidance is never done; when designing mechanisms to undermine the ability of taxpayers to avoid tax, that is the principle by which tax authorities in most jurisdictions abide. However, as the 1927 Committee of Experts understood, a single jurisdiction, fighting against tax avoidance and evasion, cannot hope to succeed. The inheritors of the task of designing a functioning international tax system at the OECD similarly understand the double-edged nature of tax sovereignty:

> Taxation is at the core of countries' sovereignty, but the interaction of domestic tax rules in some cases leads to gaps and frictions. When designing their domestic tax rules, sovereign states may not sufficiently take into account the effect of other countries' rules. The interaction of independent sets of rules enforced by sovereign countries creates frictions, including potential double taxation for corporations operating in several countries. It also creates gaps, in cases where corporate income is not taxed at all, either by the country of source or the country of residence, or is only taxed at nominal rates. In the domestic context, coherence is usually achieved through a principle of matching – a payment that is deductible by the payer is generally taxable in the hands of the recipient, unless explicitly exempted. There is no similar principle of coherence at the international level, which leaves plenty of room for arbitrage by

[42] 'Model Mandatory Disclosure Rules for CRS Avoidance Arrangements and Opaque Offshore Structure', OECD Publishing, 2018.

> taxpayers, though sovereign states have co-operated to ensure coherence in a narrow field, namely to prevent double taxation.[43]

In order to identify the gaps, to close the gaps and smooth the frictions created by the lack of coherence between independent regimes, the authorities must have information, that information must flow across borders, and it must be targeted at avoidance.

The problem identified by the League of Nation Committee of Experts in 1927 endures: the free flow of capital and trade between differing tax jurisdictions produces tax arbitrage opportunities. That is inevitable. The OECD and EU have finally managed to deliver frameworks in CRS, country-by-country reporting, MDR and DAC6, which go some way to solving that problem. It is unlikely that the information generated by these frameworks will not be actioned. New proposals will follow, driving an increasing coherence within the international taxation system, which in turn, will limit opportunities for tax avoidance. This will, most likely, be coupled with a revival of the plan for a Common Consolidated Corporate Tax Base (CCCTB) in the EU.

The authors believe that the practical issues discussed below will affect the lives and jobs of many thousands of individuals across Europe and beyond. To understand the origins of such issues, and the rationale behind the provisions developed in response to them will be vital, particularly if we wish to know what might happen next. 2021 is only a single step on a long road stretching into the distance. This chapter is necessarily a summary of almost 100 years of developments, and entire books could be devoted to the history of international tax co-operation. Whilst admitting the necessary flaws and limitations of such a summary, the authors hope that the reader will gather an understanding of the context underpinning the provisions which we will discuss in detail below.

---

[43] 'Action Plan on Base Erosion and Profit Shifting', OECD Publishing, 2013

2 Types of Exchange

Verbose international pronouncements, made by very grave men and women, whilst worthily tackling the great issues of our day, are often best understood by turning to the internet. Websites representing the organisations set up by these personages often provide a better summary of their intentions, and their actions. If seeking a description of 'Exchange of Information' (one that goes further than simply 'information exchanged between tax authorities') one can do worse than to look to the OECD website, which contains the following statement:

> Exchange of information is about achieving global tax co-operation through the implementation of international tax standards and other instruments to put an end to bank secrecy and tackle tax evasion.[1]

This tells us that the 'Exchange of Information' project goes much further than simply ensuring that information is provided when requested. The OECD project aims to build frameworks in which information will be exchanged in a standard manner, which will, in turn, eliminate bank secrecy and tax evasion (for our purposes we can assume that, once again, the OECD has entirely conflated avoidance and evasion). This project is the building of international institutions and forums to ensure that exchange is efficient, long lasting and institutionalised. For the OECD, information exchange is the magic bullet, which will eradicate tax evasion across borders.

There are three broad conceptual categories of exchange of information: spontaneous exchange of information, automatic exchange of information and exchange of information on request. These are concepts, rather than specific forms of implementation, and such conceptual classes should not be confused with the specific projects or provisions, turning them from concepts into actual regimes which are implemented, and which impose obligations and liabilities on practitioners.

All of these three broad categories are subject to the requirement that they may only pass information which is 'foreseeably relevant'.[2] 'Foreseeable relevance' is the main protection afforded to taxpayers in the international exchange of information arena. The measure of 'foreseeably relevant' is discussed in the Commentary to Article 26 of the Model Convention. It is designed to prevent authorities simply embarking upon what are known as 'fishing expeditions', i.e. purely speculative efforts to cast a net across a jurisdiction, in the hope of catching a relevant tax evader without specific cause to believe the investigation will prove fruitful.

---

[1] www.oecd.org/ctp/exchange-of-tax-information/ Retrieved 27 March 2021.

[2] This language is ubiquitous: it is contained in Article 26 of the Model Convention, Article 4 of the Multilateral Convention on Mutual Assistance in Tax Matters, and also Article 1 of the EU Directive on Administrative Cooperation.

In relation to the three different types of exchange, 'foreseeable relevance' is important in the following ways:

(i) Spontaneous exchange: the exchanging authority must assess whether or not information is 'foreseeably relevant';
(ii) Automatic exchange: the information contained in the relevant data set is mandated and therefore automatically considered to be 'foreseeably relevant';
(iii) Exchange on request: the requested authority may query whether information requested is relevant, but on receipt of an explanation, it is mandated to provide the information.

2.1 Spontaneous exchange of information

The OECD Manual for the Implementation of Exchange of Information Provisions for Tax Purposes ('the Manual') states:

> Spontaneous exchange of information is the provision of information to another contracting party that is foreseeably relevant to that other party and that has not been previously requested.[3]

In other words, a tax authority should exchange information which it believes could be relevant to another tax authority. The main well-spring of this obligation on a state is that Article 26 of the OECD Model Convention contains a spontaneous exchange of information provision:

> The competent authorities of the Contracting States shall exchange such information as is foreseeably relevant for carrying out the provisions of this convention or the administration or enforcement of the domestic laws concerning taxes of every kind.[4]

This allows for all three forms of exchange (spontaneous, automatic and on request) and establishes the framework for the tests which need to be satisfied for an exchange to occur. The Commentary to Article 26 Paragraph 1 envisages that a state will spontaneously exchange when it has

> acquired through certain investigations, information which it supposes to be of interest to the other state.[5]

Article 26 is not aimed simply at the functioning of the treaty and its subject matter, but also the effective administration of 'any' domestic taxes. Thus, for example, information relevant to the inheritance tax position of a French resident should be spontaneously supplied by any authority with which

---

[3] Manual for the Implementation of Exchange of Information Provisions for Tax Purposes Module on Spontaneous Exchange of Information, Chapter 1. OECD Publishing, 2006.

[4] Article 26 Model Tax Convention on Income and Capital Condensed Version, OECD Publishing, 2017. This of course not only facilitates spontaneous exchange, but also automatic and on-request exchange; indeed the presence of an Article like Article 26 in an existing double tax convention underpins several parts of the FATCA automatic exchange regime.

[5] Commentary on Article 26 Part II Para 9 (c) Model Tax Convention on Income and Capital Condensed Version, OECD Publishing, 2017.

France has a treaty in this form, regardless of whether that treaty otherwise covers inheritance tax.[6]

As the delivering authority must initiate the exchange, this then becomes dependent upon the desire of such an authority to exchange. The delivering authority must want to 'push' information to other authorities, and in a world where economies can be impacted severely by the effectiveness of information exchange, this may well cause issues in the efficient spontaneous exchange. The OECD acknowledge this in the Manual:

> It is therefore important that local tax officials have the reflex to pass on to their competent authority information which would potentially be of use to a tax treaty partner

The contents of the Model Convention are supplemented by the provisions of the Multilateral Convention on Mutual Administrative Assistance in Tax Matters (see below), which contains the following text at Article 7:

1. A Party shall without prior request forward to another Party information of which it has knowledge in the following circumstances:
   a) The first-mentioned Party has grounds for supposing that there may be a loss of tax in the other Party;
   b) A person liable to tax obtains a reduction in or an exemption from tax in the first mentioned Party which would give rise to an increase in the tax or to liability to tax I the other party;
   c) Business dealings between a person liable to tax in a Party and a person liable to tax in another Party conducted through one or more countries in such a way that a saving in tax may result in one or other Party or in both;
   d) A Party has grounds for supposing that a saving of tax may result from the artificial transfers of profits within groups of enterprises;
   e) Information forwarded to the first-mentioned Party by the other Party has enabled information to be obtained which may be relevant in assessing liability to tax in the latter Party.
2. Each Party shall take such measures and implement such procedures as are necessary to ensure that information described in Paragraph 1 will be made available for transmission to another Party.

As an aside, the spontaneous exchange method requires a competent, proactive and diligent tax authority in all jurisdictions. It is as much the motivator for initiatives like the international tax training initiative 'Tax Inspectors Without Borders' as anything else. A common training policy

---

[6] This is not dissimilar to some other 'special provisions' found in double tax agreements based on the OECD Model.

instilling a developed country-style approach to tax inspection in developing countries is as beneficial to the Western countries driving it as it is to the developing countries at which it is aimed. As approaches become unified and consistent, it will also deliver increased revenues.

Conceptually, Article 26 mandates that the delivering authority must exchange all information which is 'foreseeably relevant'. The measure of 'foreseeably relevant' is discussed in the Commentary. It is designed to be a brake on authorities simply going on what are known as 'fishing expeditions'. That is purely speculative efforts to cast a net across a jurisdiction in the hope of catching a relevant taxpayer without any real cause for the belief the investigation will prove fruitful. However, the non-requested nature of spontaneous exchange means that the test of 'foreseeable relevance' is complex. To assess what is properly foreseeable, the delivering authority requires a knowledge of the tax law of the recipient jurisdiction and its expansive approach. This practical difficulty means that spontaneous information exchange is the most limited of the forms of exchange and is not subject to any major models or standards, such as automatic or on-request exchange. Further extensions of spontaneous exchange in such a manner – should they occur – would likely give rise to a number of concerns and, it is to be hoped, would not be implemented without much careful consideration.

2.2 Automatic exchange of information ('AEOI')

The automatic exchange of information aims to 'do what it says on the tin'. First, it seeks to receive a commitment from the relevant authorities to enter into an automatic exchange, then secondly to ensure that the exchange occurs. It is the exchange of a standardised set of information, gathered and exchanged automatically. This means that, of necessity, its ambit is greatly limited and more clearly prescribed by the various regimes when compared to the information that can or might be exchanged under either a spontaneous or on-request regime.

Most famously, the first form of what became known as AEOI was the Foreign Account Tax Compliance Act or FATCA, which the United States imposed upon the world after it became (US) law in 2010. It is, perhaps, a misnomer to call this an 'exchange', since the status of reciprocal exchange remains somewhat a matter of debate, and certain elements of the regime include no obligation for the US to provide information[7]. In some instances, the US has taken information without reciprocating, however, it did establish the model from which the OECD Common Reporting Standard was developed. At the time of writing, the US refuses to join the CRS, and the April 2019 US Government Accountability Office report on the matter stated:

> While having the United States adopt the CRS reporting system in lieu of FATCA could benefit FFIs that may otherwise have to operate two overlapping reporting systems, it would result in no additional benefit to IRS in terms of obtaining information on U.S. accounts. Additionally, it could generate additional costs and reporting burdens to US financial institutions that would need to implement systems to meet CRS requirements.[8]

Any reader who has implemented FATCA will find such reasoning at best hypocritical and at worst laughable. The US seems happy to impose costs on others, yet refuses to spend its own money to assist them.

CRS, in contrast, does amount to a proper exchange, as all participants both give and receive the same data set on all residents with accounts in their jurisdiction.[9]

The standardised data set approach has now been extended by the EU to cover arrangements exhibiting the hallmarks of aggressive tax avoidance (as in the Directive on Administrative Cooperation in Matter of Taxation version 6 (DAC6) provisions discussed below) and the OECD has sought to extend AEOI to cover those arrangements which undermine the CRS or the identification of ultimate beneficial owners (an area of overlap with DAC6). However, as we will see below, as data sets become more complex, there are inevitably problems with interpretation and implementation, which may lead to conflicting guidance and patchy reporting. Rectifying these differences is partly the ambition of this book.

The strength of AEOI as a method of exchange is that it standardises the procedure. Given an acceptably simple data set, any tax authority, however sophisticated, can gather information and exchange it.

2.3 Exchange of information on request

Exchange of information on request is a 'pull' method of exchange, in that it requires one tax authority to request information from another. Practically, one can imagine that such an information request will be made in the context of a wider investigation within a country of residence or some other jurisdiction which concerns itself with an individual's tax affairs.

Exchange on Request was the method which the international organisations chose as a lever to open up information exchange between authorities. As

[8] U.S. Govt Accountability Office, GAO-19-180, Foreign Asset Reporting: Actions Needed to Enhance Compliance Efforts, Eliminate Overlapping Requirements, and Mitigate Burdens on U.S. Persons Abroad, 33-34 (2019).

[9] However, the relevance of that information to the exchanging tax systems will depend on the tax burdens they impose; thus while equivalent exchange is achieved, it is unlikely to be of equivalent utility (and therefore may impose a disproportionate burden on one party to a particular exchange), particularly – for example – where the parties to the exchange are an onshore and offshore jurisdiction.

discussed above, around the beginning of the 21st century, the OECD pressured 'uncooperative' jurisdictions to enter into a number of tax information exchange agreements. These tax information agreements took a model form and were designed to sit between jurisdictions which did not have a double taxation agreement to allow information exchange, and were not part of any other multilateral arrangement. By 2010, it had become apparent that TIEAs needed to be supplemented by a multi-lateral approach and the OECD's long-running development of a Multilateral Convention on Mutual Administrative Assistance in Tax Matters drew to a close, with the amendment of the pre-existing convention by protocol. Over the ensuing decade, the number of jurisdictions covered by the Multilateral Convention has risen from 20 in June 2011 to 141 to date.

The framework for exchange on request is contained in Article 5 of the Convention and it provides for the following:

1) At the request of the applicant State the requested State shall provide the applicant State with any information referred to in Article 4 which concerns particular persons or transactions.
2) If the information available in the tax files of the requested State is not sufficient to enable it to comply with the request for information, that State will take all relevant measures to provide the applicant State with the information requested.

Therefore, the obligation under the Convention is not simply to exchange information but for the state to legislate for sufficient information-gathering powers. Similar language is contained in Article 1(1) and Article 5 of the Directive on Administrative Cooperation 2011/16/EU.

The requested authority has the power to request further information. However, the commentary on Article 26 of the Model Convention makes the following points at Paragraph 5:

(i) The actual relevance of the information requested is not the relevant test. If it is reasonable to believe that there is a reasonable possibility the information may be relevant at the time of request the request cannot be rejected if a definite assessment of relevance can only be made after receipt of the information;
(ii) If the circumstances that led to the request, or the relevance or the content of the request are not clear the requested authority should consult. The requested state may not decline if it receives an explanation of the relevance;
(iii) The requested State should request an explanation if it receives information which casts doubt on the relevance of the information;
(iv) The article does not require a State to provide information in regard to 'fishing expeditions'.

There is a clear tension here, between attempting to obligate uncooperative or incompetent jurisdictions, and allowing competent jurisdictions to reject applications from those who are not 'playing the game properly'. The result is unsatisfactory. It cannot be that any explanation from a requesting state is sufficient to ensure a request is fulfilled, whilst any state, simultaneously reserves the right to reject fishing expeditions. It is not beyond the whit of a tax authority indulging in 'fishing expeditions' to provide unsatisfactory explanations when challenged. Therefore, the requested state must have some right to measure the reasonableness of a request and its explanation, no matter how hard the authors of the OECD commentary have tried to make it seem as if they possess no such right.

2.4 Current examples of information exchange

This section of the current work is not intended to be a comprehensive overview of the workings of the current crop of information exchange regimes. That is for discussion later; this is simply a summary of those regimes which exist at the time of writing and which a practitioner may encounter in his or her daily practice. Many, if not all of the regimes detailed in this section have already been mentioned in either their historical context or in passing as examples of one or other of the conceptual classes of exchange detailed above.

2.4.1 Double taxation treaties

As we described above, Article 26 of the OECD Model Convention on Income and Capital contains a standard information exchange agreement which allows for automatic, spontaneous and on-request exchange of information. The Commentary to the Model Convention explains that:

> the present Article embodies the rules under which information may be exchanged to the widest possible extent

Therefore, it is clear that exchange is meant to be an expansive process and to this end, Article 26 was revised quite extensively in 2005. For example, where the 1998 Model stated that a state must exchange information 'necessary' to carrying out the provisions of the Convention or the domestic laws of the Contracting States concerning taxes covered by the Convention, the 2017 Model states that they will provide all information 'foreseeably relevant' to such implementation. This is much more expansive language. However, it is also worth noting that Article 26 retains the provision that no state shall exchange information unobtainable under the laws or in the normal course of administration of either contracting state. This is at odds with the more stringent approach taken by the OECD in the Convention on Administrative Assistance in Tax Matters, and that of the EU's Directive on Administrative Cooperation, both of which mandate that information-gathering powers should be implemented such that the objective of a full and relevant information exchange will be undertaken.[10]

As noted before, Article 26 is drafted widely enough to allow all three conceptual categories of information exchange, and exchange of all types are therefore possible under a treaty, provided it contains a substantively similar provision to Article 26 of the Model.

2.4.2 Tax Information Exchange Agreements (TIEAS)

Following on from the 1998 Report 'Harmful Tax Competition: an emerging global issue', the OECD identified the lack of a framework for international exchange of information as a major brake on anti-avoidance initiatives. The 'tax havens' needed to be tackled and the method chosen was to pressure those jurisdictions to enter into bilateral agreements with major trading partners to allow the free flow of information. Such jurisdictions generally did not enter into double taxation agreements[11] and the negotiating process for hundreds of new Double Taxation Treaties ("DTTs") was bound to take a substantial amount of time. Thus, in April 2002, the OECD released its Model Agreement on the Exchange of Information in Tax Matters (the 'Model TIEA') which became the model for hundreds of TIEAS around the world.

The Model TIEA concerns itself entirely with exchange of information on request (as explained in Paragraph 1 of the commentary Article 5 of the Model TIEA) and contains language around 'foreseeable relevance' familiar to those who know the Model Convention. As such the efficacy of a TIEA is related almost exclusively to the competence and diligence of the requesting party (assuming that all jurisdictions co-operate when requests are made). Anecdotal evidence indicates that requests are inconsistent in their quality, and that the majority of requests which fail do so, not because of uncooperative recipients, but because they either amount to little more than fishing expeditions or are unclear as to the information they seek.

2.4.3 CRS and FATCA

The OECD Common Reporting Standard and the United States FATCA are variants on the automatic exchange of information with a closed and simple data set, designed to expose the holdings of accounts by residents of one jurisdiction within another jurisdiction. In other words if, for example, a French resident should hold an account in Lichtenstein, then Lichtenstein

---

[10] Though in practice it amounts to the same thing. While Article 26 does not require any particular information-gathering framework to be in place in domestic legislation, in practice this may well be required by a party before such an Article is entered into. While the scope of information-gathering powers may therefore differ, the restriction between the two regimes is in substance the same: if information cannot be obtained domestically, it cannot be exchanged.

[11] Whether this was about avoiding information exchange or simply because – generally having simpler and less extensive tax bases – double tax arrangements are generally of less use to such jurisdictions.

will gather some pre-determined information and send it to the French authorities. The data set includes:

(i) Account holder name and address and tax identification number
(ii) Jurisdiction of residence
(iii) Date and place of birth
(iv) Controlling person (entities)
(v) Name of institution
(vi) Gross amount of interest paid
(vii) Gross amount of dividends credited
(viii) Gross amount of sale proceeds of assets held in the account
(ix) Account balance on reporting date

The data set across every jurisdiction in CRS/FATCA[12] is identical and simply mechanical, there is little-to-no room for personalisation of a report simply listing values and statuses. This benefits from simplicity, and much of the work attendant in implementation can be passed to specialist teams carrying out what is essentially a compliance function, linked to onboarding and account maintenance. It is mostly on the edges of the stretched definitions where compliance becomes more complex and interpretations less certain.

The fine details of CRS and FATCA will be discussed later, but it is worth noting here that, since the implementation of FATCA in 2016, all accounts and their holders in financial institutions (and that definition is very broad) in relevant jurisdictions have been categorised and reported on. This was a huge undertaking and one which often goes unremarked. In parallel to this, the huge volumes of data received by tax authorities are yet to be worked through properly, though anecdotally there is evidence of investigations being driven by CRS data, with the revealing of accounts and entities hitherto undetected by the relevant authorities.

2.4.4 Mandatory disclosure regime ("MDR")

The natural consequence of CRS is that taxpayers who did not want to co-operate with, or to have their information reported under the CRS (and also FATCA) to their home jurisdiction[13] developed circumventive arrangements. In response to this, the OECD developed a parallel information exchange provision known as the MDR. It takes inspiration for its form from the BEPS Action Point 12 recommendations issued by the OECD to ensure that taxpayers report their aggressive tax avoidance arrangements and covers some of the same ground as the EU's DAC6. The

[12] Though the US 'data set' in reciprocal FATCA arrangements is not the same as the non-US data set.

[13] In the context of MDR, those unwilling to report are often painted as thorough 'wronguns'. However, the position is more complicated. CRS encompasses jurisdictions whose commitments to data protection and human rights differ significantly to those driving the CRS project. In such circumstances, fear of reporting under CRS may well be a fear of misuse, rather than simply a fear of having to pay more tax.

MDR's aim is simply the reporting of CRS/FATCA avoidance and of the use of opaque structures concealing ultimate beneficial ownership. It is not a fulfilment of BEPS Action Point 12, nor is it an equivalent to the EU's DAC6; at the time of writing the only jurisdictions engaging in something approximating MDR reporting are the UK and Gibraltar in relation to the EU.[14] Both those jurisdictions have reduced their DAC6 implementation to Hallmark D (discussed below).

The MDR has at its core the same conceptual basis as CRS. That is a defined data set exchanged automatically. However, given that the data involved in an MDR report is much more expansive than a simple list of fixed data points. This means that the practicalities of an MDR report require much more free text entry than a CRS report. It includes, for example, a 'description of the arrangement'. As the MDR is not widely implemented to date, it remains to be seen what difficulties this may cause, though one can imagine a world of inconsistent reporting and vague statements, proving of little use to any authority without further investigation.

2.4.5 EU DAC6

The Directive on Administrative Cooperation version 6 or DAC6 is the EU's implementation of BEPS Action Point 12 and as yet the world's only international implementation of such.

In its form DAC6 is substantially similar to the OECD MDR, in that it requires 'intermediaries' —who either design, promote or implement, or assist in the design, promotion or implementation of arrangements exhibiting the predefined hallmarks of aggressive avoidance — to report such arrangements to the relevant authorities. It is important to understand that DAC6 does not mandate the reporting of individuals or entities, but instead of arrangements. The persons involved are not the primary focus of the reporting (though their data is shared), instead it is the characteristics of the arrangement in question. The types of arrangements which require reporting are broken down into hallmarks, falling into broad categories which can be summarised thus:

(i) Category A – Commercial characteristics seen in marketed tax avoidance scheme;
(ii) Category B – Tax structured arrangements seen in avoidance planning;
(iii) Category C – Deductible cross border payments between associated enterprises, where the recipient is located in a specified type of jurisdiction or the payment receives a special tax treatment;
(iv) Category D – arrangements which undermine automatic exchange of information and identification of ultimate beneficial owners;

[14] In Gibraltar's case, there is a specific provision which replicates DAC6 only in connection with those matters concerning both Spain and Gibraltar. This is mandated by the UK/Spain International Agreement relating to Gibraltar entered into on 4 March 2019.

(v) Category E – arrangements related to transfer pricing.

DAC6 imposes a burden of understanding on intermediaries which has not been present in any such provisions before. It suffers from the same issues as MDR. The beauty of CRS is its simplicity: it can be implemented by large teams mechanically processing data. DAC6 cannot. It requires understanding of the treatment of tax-relevant events, an understanding of the main benefits of an arrangement and an understanding of commerciality — none of which are required by CRS. It also suffers from inconsistent implementation across the EU, as will become apparent in the sections of this book concerning the various sets of available guidance, and their tendency to prove both contradictory and unhelpful.

Regardless of these issues, it seems inevitable that some form of provision which has grown out of DAC6 shall be extended to cover the other OECD countries. Whether the US chooses to co-operate or not is yet to be seen, but that will not prevent a form of implementation.

2.4.6 Country by country reporting

These are not the only information exchange regimes relevant to tax. Country by country reporting (CbC) is of particular relevance to large organisations.

CbC is part of the OECD's BEPS Action Plan 13. Its aim is to ensure tax authorities have visibility of the revenue, income, tax paid and accrued, employment, capital, retained earnings, tangible assets and activities of large organisations. 'Large organisations' in this context means multinationals with revenue in excess of €750 million. Thus it applies to a relatively narrow proportion of businesses, and is less far-reaching in terms of the number of organisations and individuals it effects.

CbC reporting requires the making of an annual return, which gives details of its financial statement by reference to jurisdictions. We hope to cover CbC in greater detail in future editions.

3 Interpretation

3.1 Introductory principles

3.1.1 Rules of interpretation[1]: introduction

This is an area that rightly deserves a book of its own[2] and we merely outline what are most likely to be the most relevant rules for the purposes of interpreting legislation and agreements dealing with international information exchange.

However, we note one thing in relation to the interpretation of legal provisions generally. Tax is an unusual area of the law where solicitors, barristers, accountants and other tax professionals bring to bear their unique skill-sets on a single set of provisions or facts; none of us has all of the skills of any of the others. The different knowledge and experience held by each of these professions means they are well-placed to deal with different aspects of taxation. We would suggest that interpretation of legislation is an area uniquely suited to the knowledge, experience and skill-set of lawyers (barristers and solicitors) and would caution against interpretation being relied upon where it has not been confirmed by a lawyer.

We are also mindful of the difficulty of tackling such a subject; in *Taxation of Non-Residents and Foreign Domiciliaries*, Appendix 6 James Kessler QC says:

> However most of the principles of interpretation can only be expressed at a high level of generality which makes their application doubtful and their usefulness to the practitioner questionable. In short, as Voltaire is said to have observed, language is difficult to put into words

Consequently, we treat the subject of interpretation, both of national and international provisions with a large degree of caution. You should too!

The rules of statutory interpretation are largely provided in case law, not statute. The following are likely to be particularly relevant. We note that the principles discussed are largely done so by reference to English law and the law of Gibraltar. This is because these are the jurisdictions in relation to which we have the most experience, knowledge and qualification. Some of

---

[1] The terms 'interpret' and 'construe' are often used interchangeably, and we do so here. However, some commentators have suggested that there is a distinction (see *Driedger on the Construction of Statutes* 3rd edn, 1994, p xiv) such that 'interpretation' should be used to determine what the legislature meant to refer to and 'construction' to determine the purpose it meant to accomplish. Yet it remains the case that we use the terms interchangeably in this text, and consider that we are in good company in doing so; Jeremy Bentham also declined to draw a distinction between the terms (see Bentham *A Comment on the Commentaries* 1928, ed Everett, p 99).

[2] And, of course, many have been written. We would recommend consulting those texts for a fuller understanding of this subject. We set out some of them in outline here because judgments dealing with the interpretation of international provisions tend to discuss interpretation with the domestic position as a point of contradistinction.

these principles may also apply in other jurisdictions, but you should always take local law advice.

3.2 National provisions

3.2.1 Context of interpretation

The context in which the need to interpret arises is also frequently relevant (both in the context of national and international provisions). Provisions usually need to be interpreted in one of two circumstances:

(i) where the aim is to understand the meaning of legislation which is unclear or – more likely – the application of which is unclear in the facts of the instant case (non-contentious interpretation); and

(ii) where the taxpayer and HMRC each contend for a different legal meaning of the enactment in its application to the facts of the case (contentious interpretation).

Interpretation is often simpler in the latter case, with each party putting forward the construction for which it contends. Thus, it is essential – in both contentious and non-contentious interpretation – that where a particular meaning is asserted, this is expressed clearly. For example, in *Secretary, Department of Social Security v Clear* [1991] 23 ALD 22 (at paragraph 27),[3] the appellate court granted the appeal where a literal interpretation was rejected, simply on the basis that the outcome of such an interpretation would have been unfair. The tribunal was criticised for failing to put forward 'a construction of language, however slight or tenuous, which could be preferred to the obvious and literal meaning'.

Similarly, in *Chilcott v Commissioners for HM Revenue and Customs* [2011] STC 456, [2010] EWCA Civ 1538, Sedley L.J. was acerbic in his criticism of a case that failed to provide an alternative interpretation of ICTA, section 144A, saying (at paragraph 28):

> I would add it has been a new experience, for me at least, to listen to an argument that, although the words of the statute are plain and unambiguous, they should be construed as not meaning what they say, without any proposed remedial or alternative construction being put forward. It was only when prompted by the court that Mr Yerbury took the point that 'shall' in s 144A should be construed as if it were 'may'. Although this without doubt reflects the logic of his foundational argument that the section is capable of operating very unfairly, it involves not construing but upending both Parliament's words and their manifest intent, which is not merely to encourage compliance but to secure it by prescribed means. Without any authority or principle to support it, the argument does not begin to stand up.

---

[3] an Australian case.

This should, perhaps, be axiomatic, but in interpreting provisions it is not sufficient to say that they should not operate in a certain way. One must also be able to state in what way they should operate, why and by what that particular construction is supported.

In the case of ambiguity, it is probable that the different possible meanings are both grammatically possible. However, it is possible – particularly in cases similar to *Chilcott* where it cannot be said that the provision is ambiguous, but it is considered that the strict grammatical interpretation leads to an unfair or illogical result – that the non-grammatical construction may be strained. This is discussed further below, and is one area in which the construction of national and international provisions is likely to differ.

3.2.2 Starting point

The ordinary, everyday meaning of the words in question will usually be the correct starting point. This, however, will not always be the interpretation that is ultimately found to be correct. In *West (Inspector* of *Taxes) v Trennery*[4] [2005] STC 214, [2005] UKHL 5 (at paragraph 10) Lord Millett (coming down on the side of a broader interpretation) gave four reasons as to why the construction of the provision purely grammatically was rejected, saying:

> This is a possible way of reading the subsection, but I have no doubt that the Court of Appeal (Kennedy, Jonathan Parker and Longmore LJJ) (see [2003] EWCA Civ 1792, [2004] STC 170) were right to reject it. The subsection is concerned with the extraction of value from a settlement for the benefit of the settlor or his spouse before the year in which a chargeable gain accrues to the trustees of the settlement. On the taxpayer's construction the subsection catches the extraction of value in the form of income but not of capital. **It is impossible to ascribe to Parliament so capricious an intention, which not only leaves a gaping hole in the protection which the section is intended to afford the revenue but makes no sense**. It is **more natural, as well as making more sense**, to read the subsection as referring to
> (i) income from that property or

[4] This case was about TCGA, section 77(2). At the relevant time this provided that a settlor should be regarded as having an interest in a settlement, if any property which might at any time be comprised in the settlement, or any derived property was, or would, or might become, payable to or applicable for the benefit of the settlor or his spouse in any circumstances whatsoever, or the settlor or his spouse enjoyed a benefit deriving directly or indirectly from any property which was comprised in the settlement or any derived property. Section 77(8) provided that 'derived property' in relation to any property, meant income from that property or any other property directly or indirectly representing proceeds of, or of income from, that property or income therefrom. The taxpayer contended that the subsection merely extends the scope of the section to income. 'Derived property', he submitted, means income from (i)that property... or (ii)any other property...

(ii) any other property directly or indirectly representing proceeds from, or income of, that property or
(iii) income therefrom

(Emphasis added)

3.2.3 Uncertainty

Uncertainty arises in one of two ways. First, where the words are generally uncertain and secondly, where their application to certain facts is uncertain (this scenario arises frequently in relation to deeming provisions). In *Pearson v IRC* [1981] A.C. 753 Lord Dilhorne (in considering the provisions of the Finance Act 1975, Sch 5, para 3(1)) distinguished between the two types of ambiguity:

> I do not think the words 'interest in possession in settled property' are… open to divers meanings. It is the determination of the application of those words to particular circumstances which gives rise to difficulty.

This clearly indicates the difficulty in determining ambiguity where it arises in relation to a specific set of facts. Ambiguity may be resolved by considering it in light of opposing constructions of the enactment on the particular facts of the case. If there is no clearly preferable construction, other measures must be applied.

These are often rules applied as a primary aid to interpretation in an international context.

3.3 International provisions: other than EU provisions

It is generally necessary to apply a different approach to international provisions; thus the domestic rules of statutory interpretation should not be strictly applied or (perhaps) applied at all. It can be seen that international agreements such as Double Taxation Agreements (DTAs), TIEAs and multilateral instruments are not merely creatures of statute (being international treaties, by and large, they could not be so) and their terms (both at creation and subsequent variation) are highly susceptible to the political climate.

Thus, a more purposive and nuanced approach to interpretation is often justified. There are also other factors likely to have greater relevance in the context of international provisions, such as commentary. In this section, therefore, we start by discussing the different approach to interpretation of international provisions and case law in this respect, before moving on to discuss the place of additional aids to interpretation, such as commentary.

INTERPRETATION

In *The Vienna Rules on Treaty Interpretation Before Domestic Courts*[5] Bjorge discusses three types of interpretation.[6]

(i) Objective interpretation (i.e. the meaning of the words);
(ii) Subjective interpretation (i.e. the intention of the parties); and
(iii) Teleological/purposive interpretation (i.e. the purpose of the document).

The starting point should usually be the Vienna Convention on the Interpretation of Treaties. This is even the case where one party to the agreement in question is not a signatory to the Vienna Convention. This is because the rules of interpretation found therein are also rules of customary international law.[7] Article 31 provides:

> 1. A treaty shall be interpreted in good faith in accordance with the ordinary meaning to be given to the terms of the treaty in their context and in the light of its object and purpose.
> 2. The context for the purpose of the interpretation of a treaty shall comprise, in addition to the text, including its preamble and annexes:
>   a) any agreement relating to the treaty which was made between all the parties in connection with the conclusion of the treaty;
>   b) any instrument which was made by one or more parties in connection with the conclusion of the treaty and accepted by the other parties as an instrument related to the treaty.
> 3. There shall be taken into account, together with the context:
>   a) any subsequent agreement between the parties regarding the interpretation of the treaty or the application of its provisions;
>   b) any subsequent practice in the application of the treaty which establishes the agreement of the parties regarding its interpretation;
>   c) any relevant rules of international law applicable in the relations between the parties.
> 4. A special meaning shall be given to a term if it is established that the parties so intended

Article 31(1) does not help us distinguish between the different types of interpretation, apparently advocating for adopting all three approaches.[8]

---

[5] [2015] LQR 78

[6] See also TFD, paragraph 71.8 – where James Kessler QC discusses these approaches in greater detail and sets out the three-pronged approach adopted above.

7 See for example, *Anson v HMRC* [2015] STC 1777 at [54].

[8] In this respect James Kessler QC says (TFD, paragraph 71.8) 'This is no different from the approach to UK's statutory interpretation; and generally, while there are differences between

The remaining paragraphs set out what constitutes the 'context' of a treaty, which comprises:

(i) The treaty's preamble and annexes;
(ii) Any agreement in connection with the conclusion of the treaty; and
(iii) Any instrument (whether unilateral or otherwise) made by parties to the treaty in connection with its conclusion.

In effect, these must be taken into account – this is mandatory, not optional. In addition to this contemporaneous context, the treaty also specifies that the following must also be taken into account in interpreting a treaty:

(i) Subsequent agreements in relation to the interpretation of the treaty, and application of its provisions;
(ii) Subsequent practice of the parties in the application of the treaty; and
(iii) Applicable rules of international law.

Article 32 of the Vienna Convention goes on to discuss aids to interpretation (i.e. matters which can be taken into consideration, but in relation to which it is not mandatory to take into consideration). It provides:

> Recourse may be had to supplementary means of interpretation, including the preparatory work of the treaty and the circumstances of its conclusion, in order to confirm the meaning resulting from the application of article 31, or to determine the meaning when the interpretation according to article 31:
> a) leaves the meaning ambiguous or obscure; or
> b) leads to a result which is manifestly absurd or unreasonable

Domestic case law has generally considered that a broader approach to interpretation is necessary than is the case for domestic legislation. For example, in *James Buchanan & Co. Ltd. v. Babco Forwarding & Shipping (U.K.) Ltd.* [1978] A.C. 141, 152, Lord Wilberforce notes that interpretation of international provisions should be 'unconstrained by technical rules of English law, or by English legal precedent, but on broad principles of general acceptation.'

In *UBS AG v Revenue and Customs Commissioners* [2007] STC 588, the English Court of Appeal had to consider the interpretation of a DTA between the UK and Switzerland, which was based on the OECD Model DTA (on income and capital). Arden LJ explained (at paragraph 61):

> … On questions of interpretation of the OECD convention, the commentary published with it is of persuasive value: see per Mummery J in IRC v Commerzbank AG…
>
> Article 23 forms part of an international treaty between the United Kingdom and Switzerland. Accordingly, **it must be interpreted in**

---

treaty interpretation and UK statutory interpretation, they do not seem to me to be fundamental'.

> **the manner applicable to such treaties and this means, among other things, that it should be interpreted in the light of its object and purpose**: see generally per Mummery J in IRC v Commerzbank AG, approved by this court in Memec plc v IRC... the court must **seek out the meaning of the general provisions** in art 23(2), **giving each phrase its proper effect and consider whether art 23(2) has effect in relation to the particular provision of domestic law in issue**...
>
> (Emphasis added)

The following approach recommended itself to the English Court of Appeal in *Commerzbank*:

(1) look first for a clear meaning of the words used in the relevant article of the convention, bearing in mind that 'consideration of the purpose of an enactment is always a legitimate part of the process of interpretation'... A strictly literal approach to interpretation is not appropriate in construing legislation which gives effect to or incorporates an international treaty;

(2) The process of interpretation should take account of the fact that 'The language of an international convention has not been chosen by any domestic legislative body and is designed to be construed by a much wider and more varied judicial audience than law which deals with the merely domestic;

(3) the essential aim in the construction of treaties is the search for the real intention of the contracting parties in using the language employed by them;

(4) 'supplementary means of interpretation' can be used, however, subsequent commentaries on a convention or treaty have persuasive value only, depending on the cogency of their reasoning. Similarly, decisions of foreign courts on the interpretation of a convention or treaty text depend for their authority on the reputation and status of the Court in question. None of these is a substitute for a proper consideration of the treaty in question's terms.

The dicta in *IRC v Commerzbank* has been quoted with approval in a number of other cases on DTAs, including by the Court of Appeal in *HMRC v Smallwood* [2010] STC 2045 and the High Court in *Revenue and Customs Commissioners v Ben Nevis (Holdings) Limited* [2012] STC 2157.

It is probable that in the application of treaties like the OECD Model Tax Convention on Income and Capital, we may place too much importance on the commentaries (which presumably come under preparatory work of the treaty and are therefore within Article 32 of the Vienna Convention) and insufficient on the context, as mandated by Article 31. However, there is case law that could be argued to support an alternative view. Before considering this, we must ask: what is meant by commentaries? The OECD has produced model terms, both for DTAs and TIEAs and now of course MDR. They also produce a commentary on each set of model terms.

In its introduction to the OECD model MDR, the OECD explains:

> The purpose of these model mandatory disclosure rules is to provide tax administrations with information on CRS Avoidance Arrangements and Opaque Offshore Structures, including the users of those Arrangements and Structures and those involved with their supply. Information disclosed pursuant to the application of these model rules can be used both for compliance purposes and to inform future tax policy design. These rules should also have a deterrent effect against the design, marketing and use of arrangements covered by the rules.

Increasingly jurisdictions rely on model terms and this appears to be the case in relation to MDR. So how far can they be used in interpreting actual legislation? The New Zealand Court of Appeal held in *Commissioner of Inland Revenue v JFP Energy Inc* [1990] 3 NZLR 536:

> The OECD Convention rules have an international currency used as they are by and in countries throughout the world and accordingly the language of the rules should be construed on broad principles of general acceptance and have an appropriate regard to the Commentary.

While Arden LJ[9] gives general principles of interpretation, she subsequently sounds a note of caution for those looking to adopt the same principles of interpretation established in relation to DTAs in relation to other treaties. She continues (at paragraph 63):

> When interpreting a double tax convention, it is important to recall that **double tax treaties are generally the subject of hard bargaining between contracting states** (as to this, see the comments of Lord Walker of Gestingthorpe in the Pirelli case…), and that contracting states have their own reasons for entering into such treaties. For instance, a contracting state may take into account considerations of its own fiscal policy. In so doing, it would be open to it to take the view (for example) that it should confer generous tax benefits on non-residents with a view to encouraging investment in its own state. But, likewise, it might take the contrary view that it did not wish to encourage investment (for example) by an enterprise resident in the other contracting state which carried on business within its own jurisdiction, but made losses, and thus paid no tax. These are not questions for the court interpreting the treaty, but

---

[9] See *UBS*

> underscore the need for the court to interpret the treaty and any implementing legislation with attention to its precise terms.
>
> (Emphasis added)

These considerations seem unlikely to apply to MDR, which generally appears to be following the general pattern of the OECD Model. Consequently, while general guidance on interpretation established in cases on DTAs may be helpful, it should not in our view be carried too far. However, where an actual agreement or set of provisions deviates from the OECD Model, it is probable that this will be significant and the reason for such deviation should be identified and its impact in interpretation considered.

3.4 Interpretation of EU provisions[10]

There are numerous sources of EU law that must be considered in interpreting EU law (like the DAC). These range from the EU Treaties, a source firmly rooted in 'international legislation' to the opinions and judgments of the CJEU. We consider – briefly – each of these in turn, before discussing how we should interpret the DAC in light of them.

3.4.1 The treaties

There are numerous treaties making up EU law. These can be divided into three groups:

(i) founding treaties;
(ii) accession treaties; and
(iii) other treaties.

The founding treaties are the Treaty on European Union, the Treaty Establishing the European Economic Community, the Treaty Establishing the European Atomic Energy Community and the Treaty Establishing the European Coal and Steel Community (the Treaties).

The accession treaties are the treaties by which the Member States joined the European Union. These include numerous protocols which set the parameters by which the acceding State's accession and membership is governed. In relation to the UK, the relevant treaty is the Accession of Denmark, Ireland and the United Kingdom 1972 and its withdrawal under the Agreement on the withdrawal of the United Kingdom of Great Britain and Northern Ireland from the European Union and the European Atomic Energy Community, of 24 January 2020. In relation to the UK, the Act of Accession 1972 and the European Union (Withdrawal Agreement) Act 2020 are also relevant.

The other treaties of the EU are a miscellaneous collection of treaties which are not founding treaties or accession treaties. They include the Charter of

---

[10] For detailed consideration of this subject in the context of tax, see Mullan and Brown *The Interaction Of EU Treaty Freedoms & The UK Tax Code*, Key Haven Publications, 2011.

Fundamental Rights of the European Union, Treaty of Lisbon amending the Treaty on European Union, the Treaty establishing the European Economic Community and the Treaty establishing a Constitution for Europe.

It is now expressly provided that the TEU and the TFEU[11] have the same legal value and constitute the treaties on which the EU is founded.[12]

3.4.2 Regulations

In addition to the EU treaties, there are two further types of EU legislation: regulations and directives. It is important to understand how these types of legislation are implemented in the Member States, particularly the directives, because the DAC is implemented by way of directive.

The Council of Ministers and the Commission, and the European Parliament acting jointly with the Council, are empowered to issue regulations in order to carry out their tasks. Regulations set out the reasoning upon which they are based, and refer to any proposals or opinions obtained. They are published in the Official Journal of the Communities, and enter into force on either the date specified in them or on the twentieth day following their publication.

Under Article 288, TFEU regulations have general application. They are also directly applicable.

The scope or interpretation of a regulation is left to the CJEU, although it is possible for supplementary regulations to define the scope of regulations or interpret earlier regulations. Member States do, however, retain some legislative powers. First, they may impose penalties.[13] Secondly, they may introduce reasonable and non-discriminatory time limits,[14] but only where relevant time limits are not set out in the regulations. Thirdly, they may issue administrative regulations in order to preserve the effect of Community provisions.

3.4.3 Directives

Directives require implementation by the Member States pursuant to Article 288 TFEU. Thus the implementation of directives leaves a greater degree of choice to the Member State implementing them than Regulations, which are directly applicable in the form set out. This means that there arises the possibility for divergence and possible differences in the national enacting

---

[11] One of the confusing aspects arising from the case law is that the Article numberings of treaty provisions, particularly those on freedoms of movement, have changed. The numbering of the treatie s was changed by the Treaty of Rome, with effect from 29 December 2006. The Treaty of Lisbon again changed the numbering and naming of the treaties with effect from 1 December 2009.

[12] Article 1(2) TFEU

[13] See C 40/69 *Hauptzollamt Hamburg v Bollman*

[14] See C 33/76 *Rewe v Landwirtschaftskammer Saarland*

legislation. However, it will be of paramount importance to consider the domestic legislation in question as the starting point.

This has, and will undoubtedly continue to give rise to difficulties because there is scope for a lacuna to develop between the 'true meaning' of the directive and the meaning of the provision enacting the directive. The CJEU has addressed the possibility of aggrieved parties falling into the gap between the meaning of the directive and the wording used to implement it in national law — by allowing that they may invoke the obligation imposed by the directive (which is binding as to effect).[15]

Certain principles as to when a directive will be treated as being directly effective have been developed by the CJEU and can be summarised as follows:

(i) When having regard to the terms of a directive, the nature, general scheme and wording of the provisions in question must be considered to determine if the provision is capable of directly affecting the relationship between a Member State and its citizens.[16]
(ii) A Member State may not rely on unimplemented directives against its own citizens.[17]
(iii) Where the time limit for implementation by a Member State has elapsed and the directive remains unimplemented, then unconditional and sufficiently precise provisions of a directive may be relied upon by an individual.[18]
(iv) Where a Member State has failed correctly to implement a directive, an individual can rely on unconditional and sufficiently precise provisions of a directive against the Member State.[19]

3.4.4 Conflicts between EU and domestic law

The Treaties were originally silent on the point of supremacy of law (and institutions) between Members States and the bodies of the EU. This point was decided in *Costa*[20] where it was held that law stemming from the EC Treaty could not be overridden by domestic provisions.

Thus, where there is a conflict between an EU provision and a national law provision of a Member State (including a constitutional provision of a Member State[21]) the Community provisions take precedence. Further in *Costa* it was held that every national court had to apply Community law in its entirety, protect the rights conferred by the Treaties and set aside any

[15] C 41/74 *Van Duyn*
[16] C41/74 *Van Duyn*
[17] C148/78 *Ratti*
[18] C8/81 *Becker*
[19] C283/94 *Denkavit*
[20] C6/64 *Costa v ENEL*
[21] C11/70 *Internationale Handelsgesellscahft*

provisions of national law (whether predating the introduction of the Treaties or otherwise) which were contrary to EU law.

The Treaty of Lisbon introduced provision that Member States are required to provide remedies sufficient to ensure effective legal protection in the fields covered by Union law. This provided a legislative statement of the Principle of Effectiveness previously developed by the CJEU. This was explicitly recognised by the Courts of England and Wales in *Factortame.*[22]

3.5 Guidance generally

Guidance, whether domestic or international, is likely only to be persuasive, unless it is given a special status in domestic legislation. This is sometimes done, but is generally problematic.[23] The weight given to guidance will – unfortunately – vary dependent on the facts of the instance case.

The OECD often relies quite heavily on guidance to elucidate, or even build on the meaning of the terms of its Model agreements. This is problematic when provisions based on those models are adopted in domestic legislation and agreements between jurisdictions. Specific examples of the issues this can cause are discussed throughout the substantive chapters of this book.

---

[22] *R v Secretary for State of Transport ex parte Factortame Limited* [1990] 2 AC 85

[23] See in this respect Guernsey's implementation of the MDR

4 Disclosure of Tax Avoidance Schemes ('DOTAS')

4.1 An introduction

It may seem odd that a book ostensibly about tax information exchange should feature a section about DOTAS, which is not an exchange of information regime, but a UK-centric reporting regime for domestic use. However, in its historical context, one cannot avoid consideration of DOTAS. Exhibiting several characteristics shared with MDR and DAC6, at the time of its introduction in 2004, DOTAS marked a radical departure, and met with the criticism (indeed, cry of outrage) that it was mandating a breach of client-attorney privilege. Any conversation with a solicitor or barrister who was in practice when DOTAS was introduced will demonstrate the great discomfort with which the proposal was met. As ever with lawyers who feel deeply about such things, and propose that the regulations should be undermined, the objections slowly melted away as the practitioners remembered that compliance with the law is a basic precursor to being a lawyer.

That such conversations occurred demonstrates the limited efficacy of civil disobedience, when led by people with a duty to abide by the law. However, the greater significance is that DOTAS represented a departure, being the first time that lawyers and accountants became, in effect, part of the tax compliance framework, rather than advisers acting in the best interests of their clients. It was the first such regime in a major international jurisdiction and since its introduction in 2004, it has been expanded to cover many forms of taxation. It now amounts to three separate regimes, those being the VAT Disclosure Regime (VATDR), the Disclosure of Avoidance Schemes of VAT and other indirect taxes regime (DASVOIT) and the Disclosure of Tax Avoidance Schemes (including the Apprenticeship Levy) (DOTAS). Here we will concern ourselves only with DOTAS, and within DOTAS, only its scope and hallmarks. We will further only concern ourselves with the core of DOTAS, and not the peripheral elements around Annual Tax on Enveloped Dwellings (ATED), National Insurance Contributions (NIC) and Inheritance Tax (IHT) nor will we enter into a highly detailed discussion of the foregoing, as its inclusion is more for completeness and context, than the reviewing of international exchange regimes. Rather than attempt an analysis of the entirety of DOTAS and its related schemes, which would demand an entire work in themselves, we will focus on those areas which overlap with DAC6 and other similar regimes.

4.2 Scope

DOTAS has a wide scope and covers arrangements or schemes which relate to:

(i) Income tax, Corporation tax

(ii) Capital Gains Tax

(iii) National Insurance Contributions

(iv) Stamp Duty Land Tax

(v) Annual Tax on Enveloped Dwellings
(vi) Inheritance Tax; and
(vii) The Apprenticeship Levy

4.3 What arrangements need reporting?

HMRC's approach to defining which arrangements are reportable seems to be based on an understanding that all the taxes are different in scope, and that therefore the definitions of arrangement or schemes which require reporting are slightly different. However, the core principles of them all are summed up in the HMRC Guidance at paragraph 2.3.2 in the section on Income Tax, Corporation Tax and Capital Gains Tax:

> A tax arrangement should be disclosed where:
> (i) it will, or might be expected to, enable any person to obtain a tax advantage
> (ii) that tax advantage is, or might be expected to be, the main benefit or one of the main benefits of the arrangement
> (iii) it is a hallmarked scheme by being a tax arrangement that falls within any description (the 'hallmarks') prescribed in the relevant regulations[1]

Once again, the attentive reader will notice similarities with the provisions of DAC6. In the second and third limbs of the requirements for disclosure here we have the Main Benefit Test and the concept of hallmarks. In the first limb (that is the expectation of a tax advantage), we see an echo of the first limb of the UK's now aborted implementation of the Main Benefit Test.

4.4 Who reports?

As to those on whom an obligation is placed, the obligation to report falls firstly on those defined as 'promoters' and in certain circumstances, on the taxpayer themselves.

A promoter is defined in s307 of the Finance Act 2004, which states that a person is a promoter if, in the ordinary course of a relevant business, they:
(i) are to any extent responsible for the design of a scheme;
(ii) make a scheme available for implementation by others;
(iii) organise or manage the implementation of a scheme; or
(iv) make a firm approach to another person with a view to making a scheme available for implementation by that person or others.

Those familiar with the provisions of both DAC6 and the OECD MDR, which are discussed in great depth below, will recognise this form of provision. The aim is to convert professionals into information providers. The basis for this approach seems to be that taxpayers are reluctant to report on themselves, while practitioners value their practicing certificates and insurance cover to

[1] HMRC Disclosure of Tax Avoidance Schemes: Guidance para 2.3.2 HMRC 2021.

an extent that makes them far more likely to be compliant, as well as far better equipped with knowledge and expertise to understand the rules, no matter how byzantine. Unlike DAC6, however, an adviser must also be carrying on a relevant business that is:

(i) a business involving provision of services relating to tax (or where applicable National Insurance contributions); or
(ii) a business carried on by a bank or a securities house.

This extra layer of requirements does narrow the burden of obligations and could be considered helpful (one of the criticisms of DAC6 is that it may or may not catch many entities and individuals who have never previously been caught in a similar net), however, any layer of complexity confuses matters. The authors favour simplicity and the certainty it gives. DOTAS is a highly complex regime, and this is only one example of that complexity.

4.4.1 Designing Schemes

Those who are 'to any extent' responsible for the design of a scheme are obliged to report. Except, of course, those who are exempt. There are three exemptions for reporting if one is solely involved in the design of a scheme and does not make the scheme available for implementation, or organise or manage it:

(i) The Benign Test. This exemption from obligation to report hinges on the person in question being 'involved in the design' by giving tax advice but also not being 'responsible for the design'. That may seem nonsensical, but the aim is to make exempt those who give secondary tax advice which is not primarily related to the act of designing, but without which the design cannot be completed. HMRC guidance states:

> For example, a promoter may seek advice from an accounting or law firm on whether two companies are 'connected' for any purpose of the Taxes Acts. Provided the advice goes no further than explaining the interpretation of words used in tax legislation, it would be benign, as would advice on general compliance requirements, and so on.

On the other hand, if the advice given seeks to highlight opportunities to exploit the relevant provisions, then it is not benign advice.[2]

(ii) The Non-adviser Test. The Non-adviser Test is closely related to, but distinct from the Benign Test. Whereas the Benign Test looks at tax advice, the Non-adviser Test exempts those who give connected, but non-tax-related advice, such as: company law advice, or property advice, or other advice which is not tax related, yet without which the scheme could not be designed.

---

[2] HMRC Disclosure of Tax Avoidance Schemes: Guidance para 3.4.1 HMRC 2021.

(iii) The Ignorance Test. The Ignorance Test applies where a person could not reasonably be expected to know that the scheme is a disclosable scheme or cannot reasonably be expected to have sufficient information to comply with a reporting obligation.

4.4.2 Making Schemes available for implementation

HMRC's guidance explains that in order to make a scheme available for implementation the following must be true:

(i) the scheme is fully designed

(ii) it is capable of implementation in practice

(iii) he/she communicates information about the scheme to potential clients suggesting that they consider entering into transactions forming part of the scheme[3]

The scheme is available for implementation only when it is actually ready to go. A design which requires a taxpayer to build the scheme themselves by incorporating companies, or arranging loans, etc. is not available for implementation. The HMRC guidance uses the example of a scheme which requires a loan: in such a case, the scheme is not available for implementation until the financing has been sourced and funds are ready to be lent.

The aim of this limb of the test is not to catch advisers, they would be obliged to report under the 'designing schemes' limb. Instead, this is aimed at facilitators such as company incorporation agents, fiduciaries and general consultants.

4.4.3 Making a firm approach to another

The final type of 'promoter' is defined in s307 (1)(a) of the Finance Act 2004:

> in relation to a notifiable proposal, if, in the course of a relevant business, the person ("P")—
>
> (i)...
>
> ii) makes a firm approach to another person ("C") in relation to the notifiable proposal with a view to P making the notifiable proposal available for implementation by C or any other person.

This type of promoter was introduced in 2010 because of practitioners hedging around the definition of making schemes available and gaining as much time as possible prior to the scheme being 'capable of implementation in practice'. Instead of implementation, it is focussed on making a firm approach to a client to propose implementation. Of course, this is DOTAS after all, so there are multiple layers of tests to be met prior to reporting. First, three tests must be met:

(i) P 'makes a marketing contact' with another person (C) in relation to the scheme; and

---

[3] HMRC Disclosure of Tax Avoidance Schemes: Guidance para 3.5 HMRC 2021.

(ii) at the time of the marketing contact, the scheme is 'substantially designed'; and
(iii) P makes the marketing contact with a view to P making the scheme available for implementation by C or any other person.

These three tests in turn have layers of tests to ascertain if they are met. HMRC's guidance is lengthy and complex and we can at best summarise it. In essence test (i) 'making a marketing contact' is met thus:

P makes a marketing contact with C if P:
(i) communicates information about the scheme to another person, C;
(ii) the communication is made with a view to C (or any other person) entering into transactions forming part of the arrangements;
(iii) the information communicated includes an explanation of any tax advantage that a person might be expected to obtain from using the arrangements.

For a marketing contact to be made, it is sufficient for the information communicated about the scheme to indicate the nature of the tax advantages that might be obtained by persons using the scheme. In order for there to be a marketing contact, it is not necessary for the information communicated to explain how the scheme works.[4]

Test (ii) is explained at paragraph 3.6.2 of the HMRC Guidance:

> The statutory test is that a scheme is substantially designed at any time if, at that time, the nature of the transactions to form part of the scheme has been sufficiently developed that it would be reasonable to believe that a person who wishes to obtain the tax advantage communicated might enter into either:
> i) transactions of the nature developed at the time
> ii) transactions not substantially different from those developed at the time[5]

Test (iii) is explained at paragraph 3.6.3 as:

> The test is that a person makes a marketing contact with a view to making the scheme available (that is, they are making a marketing contact with a view to obtaining clients who will buy the scheme from them).[6]

4.4.4 Introducers

Helpfully (or unhelpfully, depending on your perspective) as well as being extended to insert the type of promoter (those who make firm approaches to another with a view to the implementation of a scheme) DOTAS was extended in 2010 to cover a second class of person with a reporting

[4] HMRC Disclosure of Tax Avoidance Schemes: Guidance para 3.6.1 HMRC 2021.
[5] HMRC Disclosure of Tax Avoidance Schemes: Guidance para 3.6.2 HMRC 2021.
[6] HMRC Disclosure of Tax Avoidance Schemes: Guidance para 3.6.3 HMRC 2021.

obligation. The Finance Act 2010 introduced the category of 'Introducer' to those who have a reporting obligation. An introducer is defined in Finance Act 2004 s307(1A) as:

> For the purposes of this Part a person is an introducer in relation to a notifiable proposal if the person makes a marketing contact with another person in relation to the notifiable proposal[7]

See above for the definition of 'marketing contact'.

Despite the complexity of the definition and the extensive guidance around what amounts to a 'marketing contact', an introducer is simply someone who markets an arrangement without designing it or implementing it. An example would be a financial adviser who markets tax-beneficial schemes, which are then implemented by an insurance company or a lawyer and were previously designed by some other person.

It is tempting to see a parallel between a DOTAS introducer and a 'service provider' in connection with DAC6. However, that is a false equivalence; a service provider, for DAC6 purposes, is actively involved in implementation, while an introducer is simply a marketeer. In a DAC6 environment, a person who meets the DOTAS definition of 'introducer' would qualify as a 'promoter', as they would be involved in the marketing of the arrangement.

4.5 Hallmarks

As with DAC6 a scheme is only reportable if it exhibits one of the predefined hallmarks which require reporting. HMRC themselves admit that not all those arrangements exhibiting hallmarks are unacceptable, and that unnecessary reporting is a natural consequence of the approach:

> The absence of a hallmark should not be regarded as an indicator that arrangements not caught constitute practices that are acceptable to HMRC.
>
> Similarly, we do not regard all arrangements that include or meet a hallmark description as practices that are unacceptable to us – whilst we have tried to keep burdens to a minimum, you may have to tell us about schemes that may not be considered to be avoidance.[8]

In a similar approach to the provisions of Article 27(2) of the DAC[9] which mandates a two-year review of the effectiveness of the DAC6 Hallmarks, HMRC state in their guidance:

---

[7] Finance Act 2004 s307(1A).

[8] HMRC Disclosure of Tax Avoidance Schemes: Guidance para 7.1 HMRC 2021.

[9] Article 27 (2) Council Directive 2011/16/EU.

> It is expected that the range of hallmarks will change over time, such as to test perceived changes in the avoidance marketplace or the effectiveness of a counter-avoidance measure.[10]

This dynamic approach in both DAC6 and DOTAS shows us that these provisions are as much about establishing frameworks as they are about specific behaviours on the part of tax advisers.

The DOTAS hallmarks are complex and multi-layered, and a detailed analysis of all of them is beyond the remit of this work, but we will discuss the general characteristics of those hallmarks which display a similarity to the DAC6 hallmarks, or exhibit features of special interest.

4.5.1 Hallmark 1 'Confidentiality'

Hallmark 1 concerns itself with those schemes whereby a promoter would wish certain elements of the scheme to be kept confidential, either from other promoters, or HMRC itself. It cannot be engaged where there is no promoter.

Hallmark 1 is divided into two sub-hallmarks, first that of confidentiality regarding other promoters (Hallmark 1a), and secondly regarding HMRC (Hallmark 1b).

Hallmark 1a targets those schemes where a promoter would reasonably wish to protect the operation of the scheme from his competitors, on the basis that such confidentiality would protect those arrangements which are novel and innovative and would thus automatically also be of interest to HMRC.

HMRC's guidance goes into some detail as to questions the promoter should ask itself about how a hypothetical promoter would behave. This seems overly complex and unhelpful. Ultimately it boils down to 'would you want your competitor to know about this?' If the answer is 'no', then the scheme is reportable.

Hallmark 1b works in a similar way, except that, instead of hypothetical questions about hypothetical promoters' desire to protect their new ideas, the promoter must ask the same question of HMRC. Would the promoter want HMRC to know how his scheme works? If the answer is 'no', then the scheme is reportable.

4.5.2 Hallmark 2 'Confidentiality with no promoter'

As Hallmark 1 applies solely to those arrangements with a promoter, there is by necessity a sister hallmark, performing a similar task to Hallmark 1, except that there is no promoter.

Hallmark 2 applies solely where the intended user is a 'large' business, where the scheme or arrangement gives rise to a tax advantage. HMRC summarise the test which a user should apply to itself for Hallmark 2 thus:

(i) do I wish to keep confidential from HMRC? [or]

---

[10] HMRC Disclosure of Tax Avoidance Schemes: Guidance para 7.1 HMRC 2021.

(ii) would any user wish to keep confidential from HMRC?

(iii) the way any element of the arrangements (including the way they are structured) gives rise to and secures the expected tax advantage …

(iv) …at any time following the material date?

Is a reason for doing so to:

(i) facilitate the repeated or continued use of that element, in the future?

(ii) reduce the risk that HMRC might open an enquiry into any return or account that I am required to make?

(iii) reduce the risk that HMRC might withhold some or all of a repayment sought in a claim outside a return, in respect of relief for losses under section 261B Taxation of Chargeable Gains Act 1992 (trade loss treated as capital loss) or Part 4 Income Tax Act 2007 (loss relief)?[11]

HMRC's guidance insists on using this form of hypothetical questions concerning the state of mind of a reasonable but hypothetical user. The authors feel that it complicates matters and sheds little light, despite obviously being designed to assist the taxpayer. As with Hallmark 1b, it hinges on whether the user wishes to keep the way in which the scheme saves tax away from the 'prying' eyes of HMRC.

This hallmark does beg the question 'is there any tax planning which is not reportable?'. In practical terms, no taxpayer would want to volunteer information about mechanisms to HMRC for fear that a report would bring about an investigation, no matter how ordinary and everyday that planning might be. It seems that the drafters of this hallmark do not quite inhabit the mindset of the taxpayers, the majority of whom believe that never engaging with HMRC is the best course of action to avoid an inquisitive investigation.

4.5.3 Hallmark 3 – Premium fee

Hallmark 3 could be understood as similar to or related to the DAC6 hallmark Category A2, the hallmark which hinges on whether a fee element is related, either to gaining a tax advantage, or the quantum of that advantage. Instead, here DOTAS takes a more complex approach. This is not about what fee is actually charged, instead it is articulated thus in Regulation 8 of Tax Avoidance Schemes (Prescribed Descriptions of Arrangements) Regulations 2006 (SI 2006/1543):

> 1. Arrangements are prescribed if they are such that it might reasonably be expected that a promoter or person connected with a promoter of arrangements that are the same as, or substantially similar to, the arrangements in question, would, but for the requirements of these Regulations, be able to obtain a premium fee from a person experienced in receiving services of the type being provided.

---

[11] HMRC Disclosure of Tax Avoidance Schemes: Guidance para 7.4 HMRC 2021.

In other words, just as with Hallmark 1 and 2 the intermediary must work out what a hypothetical client would do in relation to a hypothetical intermediary. Would such a client pay a 'premium' for the advice?

This, of course, means that one should consider what a 'premium' amounts to. HMRC do spend some time discussing this, explaining that:

> Our assumption is that where a client regards the advice as valuable and not generally available he would be prepared to pay a premium for it. Equally, by contrast, if similar advice was available elsewhere the client would be unwilling to pay more than a normal fee for it.[12]

This would seem to indicate that advice must be innovative and hard to find, and that as a result of this scarcity, a premium would be chargeable even if it is not actually paid.

HMRC go on to explain that the premium must be charged in connection with the tax advantage. They provide an exemplary list of factors where, if the premium is solely attributable, it will not amount to a 'premium' for the purposes of the hallmark.

- the adviser's location: for example, fees could be expected to be higher in London
- the urgency of the advice: a fee that is higher due to the adviser having to give the advice urgently is not a premium fee for that reason alone
- the size of the transaction: if a large amount is at stake on a deal, the tax adviser may increase his fee to reflect the greater level of exposure
- the skill or reputation of the adviser – some advisers normally charge more for advice than others to reflect the perceived higher quality of advice they offer
- the scarcity of appropriately skilled staff: some areas of tax advice are more complex and fees may be higher to reflect this
- the number of users who sign up for a scheme: in some schemes, for example, certain salary sacrifice schemes, the size of the fee depends upon the number of employees who take up the scheme[13]

From this it is clear that any premium (if any) must be linked to the nature of the advice and its scarcity, and that scarcity must be created by its innovative nature.

As mentioned before, HMRC's guidance in this arena rests on the unsatisfactory basis of professionals imagining some hypothetical world, in which hypothetical versions of themselves provide advice to similarly hypothetical clients. This overlooks the diversity, both of advisers and

[12] HMRC Disclosure of Tax Avoidance Schemes: Guidance para 7.5.3 HMRC 2021.

[13] Ibid

advisees. What may be 'innovative' and worthy of a premium to a family solicitor in Hartlepool may well not be innovative and worthy of a premium to a specialist tax adviser in Manchester or Leeds, and may be positively ordinary to a 'big four' accountant in London. This subjectivity has one, particularly unsatisfactory outcome. Those with inexperienced advisers, taking a conservative approach, will be reported more often than those whose advisers are experienced. Their experience, moreover, is already worthy of a premium.

4.5.4 Hallmark 5 – Standardised tax products

As with Hallmark 3 and Category A(2) of DAC6, Hallmark 5 has as its sister hallmark Category A (3) that is the standardised products hallmark.

Under Regulation 10 of Tax Avoidance Schemes (Prescribed Descriptions of Arrangements) Regulations 2006 (SI 2006/1543) an arrangement is prescribed if:

2 (a) the arrangements have standardised, or substantially standardised, documentation —
- (i) the purpose of which is to enable the implementation, by the client, of the arrangements; and
- (ii) the form of which is determined by the promoter, and not tailored, to any material extent, to reflect the circumstances of the client;

(b) a client must enter into a specific transaction or series of transactions; and

(c) that transaction or that series of transactions are standardised, or substantially standardised in form.[14]

Therefore, the arrangement must have at its core standard documentation, which does not require major customisation or consultation with the client; there must a pre-ordained transaction or set of transactions, and that transaction itself must be standard.

It is worthy of note that the requirement for standard documentation and that for standard transactions is separated.

Regulation 11 provides us with a lengthy list of exempted arrangements which are described in the HMRC guidance:

> Under subsection 2, the following arrangements are excepted from being prescribed under regulation 10:
> - a) arrangements which consist solely of one or more plant or machinery leases (see regulation 14)
> - b) an enterprise investment scheme (Part 5 ITA 2007 and schedule 5B to the Taxation of Chargeable Gains Act 1992)

[14] Regulation 10 (2)(a) of Tax Avoidance Schemes (Prescribed Descriptions of Arrangements) Regulations 2006 (SI 2006/1543).

c) arrangements using a venture capital trust (Part 6 ITA 2007)
d) arrangements qualifying under the corporate venturing scheme (see schedule 15 to the Finance Act 2000)
e) arrangements qualifying for community investment tax relief (see schedules 16 and 17 to the Finance Act 2002), [Now Part 7 ITA 2007 and Part 7 of the Corporation Tax Act 2010]
f) an account which satisfies the conditions in the Individual Savings Account Regulations 1998
g) an approved share incentive plan (see Chapter 6 of Part 7 of, and schedule 2 to, ITEPA 2003)
h) approved share option scheme (see Chapter 7 of Part 7 of, and schedule 3 to, ITEPA 2003)
i) an approved CSOP scheme (see Chapter 8 of Part 7 of, and schedule 4 to, ITEPA 2003)
j) the grant of one or more qualifying options which meet the requirements of schedule 5 to ITEPA 2003 (enterprise management incentives):
    - together only with such other steps as are reasonably necessary in all the circumstances for the purposes of facilitating it, or
    - which fall to be notified to the Board in accordance with Part 7 of that schedule
k) a registered pension scheme (see section 150(2) of the Finance Act 2004)
l) an overseas pension scheme in respect of which tax relief is granted in the United Kingdom under section 615 of ICTA 1988 (exemption from tax for superannuation payments in respect of persons not resident in the United Kingdom or in respect of trades carried on wholly or partly outside the United Kingdom)
m) a pension scheme which is a relevant non-UK pension scheme within the meaning given by paragraph 1(5) of schedule 34 to the Finance Act 2004)
n) a scheme to which section 731 of ITTOIA 2005 applies (periodical payments of personal injury damages)
o) arrangements which would be prescribed by regulation 19 but for regulation 21 (Code of Practice on Taxation for Banks)

This seems to amount to an attempt by the legislation to carve out those things which are standardised but are also acceptable to HMRC. It will be noted that the approved exceptions are all the creatures of statutory rules, such as approved share option plans, or ISAs.

When explaining how to apply the statutory test, the HMRC guidance becomes very complex, and it is a prime example of seemingly simple-enough legislation being immensely complicated by expansive and exhaustive guidance.

To exhibit the hallmark, an arrangement must pass four tests.

Test 1
Are the arrangements made generally available?

Ultimately, despite HMRC's guidance discussing the bespoke nature of non-standard advice and the nature of marketing, this test boils down to the following statement:

> Subject to the other tests and exceptions, the hallmark will apply to any 'tax product' that a promoter makes available for 2 or more persons to implement.[15]

At this point it is suitable to introduce the concept of the 'informed observer', a hypothetical individual who will be engaged in ascertaining whether the next three tests are met. HMRC describe the 'informed observer' thus:

> An informed observer is to be contrasted with an 'uninformed observer' but isn't an 'expert' or necessarily a tax practitioner. The informed observer is independent, has all relevant information about the scheme and has sufficient knowledge to understand both the scheme and the relevant statutory context.[16]

Tests 2, 3 and 4 will only be met if the informed observer agrees they are met.

Test 2
Is the documentation standardised?

HMRC's guidance is quite clear as to this test. If the informed observer would reasonably believe that the documentation was standard or substantially standardised then it is met. They state:

> As a minimum this will mean that standardised contracts, agreements or other written understandings between the parties to the arrangements are provided by the promoter to the person or persons implementing the arrangements. Instructions on how to implement the scheme might, typically, also be included, as may a copy of Counsel's Opinion.

For this hallmark to apply, the arrangements will also commit users to enter into either a specific standardised (or substantially standardised) transaction, or more usually a number of specific transactions, comprising the scheme.

For example, a person entering into the scheme may be required to join a specific partnership, take out a specific loan from a specific provider, buy a specific financial instrument, etc.[17]

---

[15] HMRC Disclosure of Tax Avoidance Schemes: Guidance para 7.6.4 HMRC 2021.
[16] HMRC Disclosure of Tax Avoidance Schemes: Guidance para 7.6.5 HMRC 2021.
[17] HMRC Disclosure of Tax Avoidance Schemes: Guidance para 7.6.6 HMRC 2021.

As with the DAC6 Category A Hallmark 2, this hallmark is not simply designed to catch any arrangement which simply uses precedent-based documentation, it is designed to catch what is described as 'plug and play' arrangements. The imposition of the informed observer as the test by which we measure the standardisation is effective, whilst complex. The nature of the legal profession is that all documents feature a measure of standardisation. In the experience of the authors, no single document is ever drafted from a blank piece of paper, and if it has been then it will undoubtedly contain unnecessary errors.

Test 3
Are the arrangements a tax product?

Rather unhelpfully, this test is divided into two sub-tests, either of which can be met for an arrangement to be described as a 'tax product'.

a) Is the main purpose of the arrangement to obtain a tax advantage? Note that the sole purpose must be a tax advantage which is a narrower test than the DAC6 'the, or one of the main benefits' test, note also 'purpose' rather than 'benefit'; and
b) would the person or persons who entered into the arrangements be unlikely to do so, if it were not for the expectation of obtaining a tax advantage?

In (a) one is required to have as one's main purpose the gaining of a tax advantage and in (b) one is asked whether one would not enter into the arrangement if there was no advantage. Both tests are sides of the same coin and seek to establish intention. One in a positive way and one by reference to a negative test. In the authors' view, little but complexity has been added by HMRC's decision to split the test into two sub-tests. It is simple, if the tax advantage to be gained is sufficient to motivate one to enter into the arrangement, then the test is met.

Test 4
Does the arrangement fall into a Regulation 11 exception? (See above.)

4.5.5 Hallmark 6 Loss schemes

Regulation 12 states:

> Arrangements are prescribed if:
> (a) the promoter expects more than one individual to implement the same, or substantially the same, arrangements
> (b) an informed observer (having studied the arrangements and aving regard to all relevant circumstances) could reasonably be expected to conclude that:
> (i) the main benefit or one of the main benefits which could be expected to accrue to some or all of the individuals participating in the arrangements is the provision of losses
> (ii) the arrangements (including the way they are structured) contain an element which is, or elements which are, unlikely

to have been entered into by the individuals concerned were it not for the provision of those losses

(iii) those individuals would be expected to use those losses to reduce their liability to income tax or capital gains tax[18]

The hallmark is designed to catch all those multi-faceted arrangements which artificially create losses for use against income or gains. Although superficially similar to Category B Hallmark 1 (acquisition of loss-making entities) of DAC 6, Hallmark 6 is a much wider net than Category B 1, which limits itself to the acquisition of loss-making entities.

For the hallmark to be met, the arrangement must be made available to more than one individual (mirroring the nature of Hallmark 5), and secondarily the informed observer must believe:

a) the, or one of the, main benefits is a tax advantage available to someone (note rather than the 'purpose' test used for the standardised documents hallmark discussed above), this is an articulation of the same main benefit test contained in DAC6;
b) that the arrangement would not exist commercially if tax were not a consideration;
c) that the participants' income or gain will be reduced as a result of the arrangement.

If, and only if, those tests are met, the hallmark is in place.

4.5.6 Hallmark 7 Leasing arrangements

Regulation 13 states:

(1) Arrangements are prescribed if:
(a) the arrangements include a plant or machinery lease
(b) one of the additional conditions is met (see regulation 15)
(c) the relevant value condition is met (see regulation 16), and
(d) the lease is not a short-term lease (see regulation 17)

(2) But arrangements are not prescribed by this regulation if:
(a) no person is a promoter in relation to them, and
(b) the tax advantage which may be obtained under the arrangements is intended to be obtained by an individual or a business which is a small or medium-sized enterprise.

This regulation is the finest example of unclear DOTAS drafting that can be envisaged. The test itself is almost entirely devoid of information as to how the test can be met. Other than grasping the fact that a plant or machinery lease is required, a casual reader would have no hope of understanding the provision.

[18] Regulation 12 of Tax Avoidance Schemes (Prescribed Descriptions of Arrangements) Regulations 2006 (SI 2006/1543).

Firstly, there must be a lease or plant hire, secondly that lease must meet an 'additional condition' (of which there are three), then a minimum value must be met, and the lease must be over a short term. Finally, there must be a promoter, and individuals or small-to-medium enterprises are carved out of scope.

The additional conditions are as follows:

a) one party must make a claim for capital allowances, and another party must be outside the scope of corporation tax;
b) the lessor must have the risk of non-payment of lease payments removed from him/her by virtue of a money debt;
c) does the arrangement include a sale and finance leaseback, or a lease and finance leaseback (with some guidance around where the sale and leaseback is a bona fide property transaction)

In addition to this, at Regulation 13(1)(c) there is a value condition. The lease arrangement must be for a high value lease, which is described as;

> Facilities to lease assets with an individual value of £10 million or to the aggregate value of at least £25 million are caught by this test even if there is no guarantee that the £25 million threshold will be reached and should be disclosed when the facilities are made available.[19]

In addition, the lease must not be a short-term lease (Regulation 13(1)(d)). A short-term lease is defined in the guidance thus:

> A short-term lease is one whose term is 2 years or less but does not include leases that:
> (i) contain an option allowing the lessee to extend the lease beyond 2 years
> (ii) at the time of inception, other arrangements have been entered into that contemplate an extension beyond 2 years
> (iii) are incepted on or after 1 August 2006 with the intention that the assets be leased under it to one or more other persons such that the aggregate term exceeds 2 years.[20]

In addition there must be a promoter, and the tax advantage must fall to a large enterprise.

After reading such guidance one is compelled to consider whether HMRC should simply publish a flow chart and have done with textual guidance. There is much to be admired in the linguistic acrobatics of those attempting accurately to describe these provisions, but it is doubtful whether it is helpful to anyone other than the most qualified of specialists.

---

[19] HMRC Disclosure of Tax Avoidance Schemes: Guidance para 7.8.4 HMRC 2021.

[20] HMRC Disclosure of Tax Avoidance Schemes: Guidance para 7.8.5 HMRC 2021.

The observant reader will have noticed that as we move through the hallmarks of the DOTAS regime, they seem to be gathering complexity. As we move to the last two hallmarks, this trend does not abate.

4.5.7 Hallmark 8 Employment income provided through third parties

Regulation 18 states:

> (1) Arrangements are prescribed if:
> (a) Conditions 1 and 2 are met and Condition 3 is not met, or
> (b) Conditions 1, 2 and 3 are met and at least one of 4 and 5 is met
>
> (2) Condition 1 is met if the arrangements involve at least one of the following:
> (a) a relevant third person taking a relevant step under section 554B
> (b) any person taking a relevant step under section 554C or 554D, or
> (c) B taking a step under section 554Z18 or 554Z19
>
> (3) Condition 2 is met if the main benefit, or one of the main benefits, of the arrangements is that an amount that would otherwise count as employment income under section 554Z2(1) is reduced or eliminated.
>
> (4) Condition 3 is met if, by reason of at least one of sections 554E to 554X or regulations made under section 554Y, Chapter 2 of Part 7A does not apply.
>
> (5) Condition 4 is met if the arrangements involve one or more contrived or abnormal steps without which the main benefit in paragraph (3) would not be obtained.
>
> (6) Condition 5 is met if the arrangements involve:
> (a) a relevant step being treated as taking place, and
> (b) Chapter 2 of Part 7A applying as a consequence of sub-paragraph (a)
>
> (7) In this regulation:
> (a) references to sections or Parts are to those in ITEPA unless otherwise stated
> (b) 'B' has the meaning given for Part 7A by sections 554A(1)(a) and 554Z17(7) read together
> (c) 'contrived or abnormal' has the same meaning as in section 207 of the Finance Act 2013, and
> (d) 'relevant third person' has the same meaning as in section 554A(7)

It has often been commented on that the Shipping Forecast on Radio 4[21] has a gentle soporific effect similar to whale music; the words lose meaning, especially to the non-seafarer and one becomes lulled by their poetic rhythm and cadence. Regulation 18 exhibits similar characteristics, though one is forced to conclude that there was little original meaning for the words to lose and certainly no poetry. No matter, we must try to understand its effect.

Regulation 18 is engaged if Conditions 1 and 2 but not 3 are met and also if 1, 2 and 3 are met, and also if either 4 or 5 is met.

Condition 1
Earmarking

If an employer takes steps to earmark a sum to fulfil an undertaking defined by reference to ss554B, 554C, 554D and 554Z18 and 554Z19 of Income Tax (Earnings and Pensions) Act 2003 (ITEPA).

Condition 2
Main benefit

The main benefit, or one of the main benefits is a reduction of employment income.

Condition 3
Disapplication of Chapter 2 Part 7A of ITEPA

The provisions of Chapter 2, which deem the sums subject to the steps taken at Condition 1 to be taxable income, are disapplied by virtue of the statutory exemptions from such deeming provisions.

If Condition 3 is met (i.e. the statutory exemptions from the deeming provisions are being met), then the hallmark may still be engaged if either Condition 4 or 5 are met.

Condition 4
Abnormal steps

If the arrangement features one or more abnormal or contrived steps and those steps are the triggers for the benefit accrued.

Condition 5
Relevant step triggers Chapter 2 Part 7A ITEPA

If a relevant step is being taken and the effect of that step is to force application of the deeming provisions in Chapter 2 Part 7A of ITEPA. This

---

[21] The authors apologise for this Anglo-centric reference. The Shipping Forecast is a long-running late-night weather forecast for the shipping industry, broadcast on the BBC's talk radio channel, Radio 4. It has a following far in excess of its utility to fishermen and tanker captains with their high-tech equipment, but like so much of the British establishment it remains, shorn of its original purpose, yet cherished, while periodic proposals to remove it provoke much fury from middle England.

condition is deliberately designed to exclude manipulation of what is known as the 'fall back' charge, a secondary layer of anti-avoidance.

HMRC's guidance is as technical as the regulation itself and adds more words to an already opaque set of information. These highly technical provisions take the form of flowcharts, but without the underlying information regarding, for example, the provisions of s554B of ITEPA, they are simply a set of instructions, adding no insight as to their intention or purpose.

Ultimately this hallmark is designed to cast a light on those arrangements which transfer value to employees in ways that lower the value of their taxable income, whilst avoiding the deeming provisions in Chapter 2 which would otherwise make that transfer of value part of their taxable income.

4.5.8 Hallmark 9 Financial products

Regulation 19 states:

(1) Subject to regulation 21, arrangements are prescribed if:
- (a) condition 1 is met, and
- (b) it would be reasonable to expect an informed observer (having studied the arrangements and having regard to all relevant circumstances) to conclude that:
  - (i) condition 2 is met, and
  - (ii) either condition 3 or condition 4 is met

(2) Condition 1 is that the arrangements include at least one financial product specified in regulation 20(1) (a 'specified financial product').

(3) Condition 2 is that the main benefit, or one of the main benefits, of including a specified financial product in the arrangements is to create a tax advantage.

(4) Condition 3 is that a specified financial product included in the arrangements contains at least one term which is unlikely to have been entered into by the persons concerned, were it not for the tax advantage.

(5) Condition 4 is that the arrangements involve one or more contrived or abnormal steps without which the tax advantage could not be obtained.

(6) For the purposes of this regulation, condition 3 is treated as not having been met if:
- (a) the specified financial product includes a term requiring that it is held for a minimum period of time before it is redeemed and:
  - (i) section 135 or 136 of the Taxation of Chargeable Gains Act 1992 applies to the specified financial product, and
  - (ii) condition 3 is met only by virtue of that term, or

(b) the specified financial product includes a term whereby the issuing company can secure that the date for redemption falls before the end of the permitted period and:

(i) but for that term, the specified financial product would be an equity note, and

(ii) condition 3 is met only by virtue of that term.

(7) In paragraph (6)(b) 'equity note' and 'the permitted period' have the meanings given by section 1016 of the Corporation Tax Act 2010.

(8) For the purposes of condition 4 a step is not to be treated as being contrived or abnormal if:

(a) that step involves only the transfer of an asset to which the condition in paragraph 15A(2)(b) of schedule 7AC to the Taxation of Chargeable Gains Act 1992 applies, or

(b) that step involves only the issue of shares and:

(i) that step is taken to eliminate or substantially reduce the economic risk of holding a loan relationship or a derivative contract, or part of such a loan relationship or a derivative contract, which is attributable to fluctuations in exchange rates, and

(ii) the shares are treated for accounting purposes as a liability of the company in accordance with generally accepted accounting practice.

(9) For the purposes of this regulation, neither condition 3 nor condition 4 is treated as having been met if:

(a) the specified financial product includes a term providing for conversion into, or redemption in, a currency other than sterling, and

(b) both condition 3 and condition 4 are met only by virtue of that term.

Once again we are confronted with the form 'if condition 1 and condition 2…etc' so beloved of the drafters of DOTAS, coupled with the hypothetical informed observer.

The essential form of the hallmark is that:

If there is a financial product (condition 1) and it is reasonable to conclude the main benefit test is met (condition 2) and either, the product contains a term which would not be entered into without the tax advantage (condition 3) or there are contrived steps which trigger the tax advantage (condition 4) then the hallmark is engaged.

The financial products in question are listed in regulation 20:

(1) The financial products specified in this paragraph are:

(a) a loan

(b) a share

(c) a derivative contract within the meaning given by section 576 of the Corporation Tax Act 2009

(d) a repo in respect of securities within the meaning given by section 263A(A1) of the Taxation of Chargeable Gains Act 1992

(e) a creditor repo, creditor quasi-repo, debtor repo or a debtor quasi- repo (within the meanings given by sections 543, 544, 548 and 549 of the Corporation Tax Act 2009 respectively)

(f) a stock lending arrangement within the meaning given by section 263B(1) of the Taxation of Chargeable Gains Act 1992

(g) an alternative finance arrangement within Chapter 6 of Part 6 of the Corporation Tax Act 2009 or Part 10A of ITA 2007

(h) a contract which, whether alone or in combination with one or more other contracts:

(i) is in accordance with generally accepted accounting practice required to be treated as a loan, deposit or other financial asset or obligation, or

(ii) would be required to be so treated by the person entering into the arrangements, were that person a company to which the Companies Act 2006 applies.

(2) Paragraph (1) does not specify a financial product held within an account which satisfies the conditions in regulation 4 of the Individual Savings Account Regulations 1998.[22]

What is considered to be 'contrived or abnormal' is not defined in the legislation. However, the HMRC guidance urges the informed observer to 'reach his or her conclusions after having studied the arrangements and having regard to all relevant circumstances, including commercial rationale and HMRC guidance'[23]. It further elaborates by directing the reader to the examples of abnormal and contrived steps which are detailed in the guidance to the General Anti-Avoidance Rule (GAAR). Therefore, the usage in relation to DOTAS is firmly entrenched within the wider tradition of anti-avoidance.

4.6 Conclusion

In the days of Microsoft DOS and the cumbersome technology of the early 1990s, a popular saying was 'never buy Version One of anything'. DOTAS was introduced in the early 2000s, and it has clearly been subject to patches and redrafts in an attempt to massage an old and creaky framework into a modern streamlined form. Such efforts are almost always unsuccessful. Anyone with a basic understanding of both provisions can see the similarities between DAC6 and DOTAS. They follow the same form, and apart from some variations in language, impose obligations on similar

---

[22] Regulation 20 of Tax Avoidance Schemes (Prescribed Descriptions of Arrangements) Regulations 2006 (SI 2006/1543).

[23] HMRC Disclosure of Tax Avoidance Schemes: Guidance para 7.10.7 HMRC 2021.

individuals. The draftsmen of DAC6 have learnt from the byzantine drafting of DOTAS, and no matter how imperfect DAC6 may be, it is a far simpler and more easily understood provision than DOTAS.

DOTAS is littered with inconsistent applications of main benefit or main purpose tests, there are highly technical references to other highly technical provisions in other Acts. In an effort to legislate for every scenario and every reasonable exception to every scenario, the provision has become almost unfathomable and most likely unworkable for the average practitioner. This is most clearly demonstrated by reports that only 16 schemes were reported under DOTAS in 2018[24], and of those, only 5 were proactively reported. Perhaps if the provisions were simpler, the number of reports would be higher, and well-meaning and hardworking practitioners would live a little less in fear of this labyrinthine provision.

---

[24] 'HMRC Cracks down on tax avoidance scheme promoters amid loan charge row' B Smith *Civil Service World* 24th October 2019.

5 Foreign Account Tax Compliance Act - FATCA

5.1 FATCA and other regimes

As stated elsewhere, FATCA is a regime that is not dissimilar to CRS.[1] However, CRS is a completely separate regime, which nonetheless shares features with FATCA. This is illustrated by the OECD which says[2]:

> The Common Reporting Standard, with a view to maximising efficiency and reducing cost for financial institutions, draws extensively on the intergovernmental approach to implementing FATCA. While the intergovernmental approach to FATCA reporting does deviate in certain aspects from the CRS, the differences are driven by the multilateral nature of the CRS system and other US specific aspects, in particular the concept of taxation on the basis of citizenship and the presence of a significant and comprehensive FATCA withholding tax…

Thus, it is important to consider CRS and FATCA in conjunction with each other and neither one separately (though, as acknowledged in the above quote, the USA 'beat the OECD to the punch' in getting its automatic exchange provisions in place[3]), in particular it may be helpful to consider CRS in the light of FATCA. In any event – as should become apparent in the course of this Chapter – despite being separate, the regimes do interact. Consequently, it is necessary to be aware of one in the context of the other. This is best illustrated by considering practical examples, which we do in the remainder of this Chapter.

5.2 FATCA, MDR and DAC6

CRS interacts with MDR and DAC6; indeed a significant aim of MDR is to identify and prevent measures adopted to avoid CRS reporting. As we have previously stated, it is difficult, if not impossible to understand or apply MDR without understanding CRS, because the MDR is heavily weighted towards identifying those arrangements intended to avoid application of CRS as is DAC6, Hallmark D. In this sense, FATCA is not encompassed in MDR. If you take steps to avoid FATCA reporting, which are not otherwise caught, MDR should not be in point. This is consistent with the approach of the USA, which has been to adopt its own approach to international exchange of tax information and is, therefore, not included.

This does not, however, mean that FATCA has no relevance to MDR. It is particularly relevant in one context: will transactions that involve moving Financial Assets outside of the scope of CRS, or structures designed to hold Financial Assets outside of CRS because they are moved to or held in the

---

[1] Indeed, some commentators refer to CRS as 'GATCA' – which is intended to mean 'global FATCA'. However, this is a misnomer and we do not adopt the terminology here.

[2] At paragraph 5 of the Introduction to CRS

[3] For more on the history of CRS and FATCA and the design and implementation of the two regimes

USA be subject to MDR? This is a thorny issue. However, it should be noted that despite the wholly separate approach, the different information regimes cannot be considered in isolation from FATCA.

5.3 What is FATCA?[4]

FATCA is – unsurprisingly – an automatic exchange of information regime, under which (very broadly) information on US taxpayers is provided to the US IRS (in a number of ways – see further below). The US Department of Treasury explains that 'FATCA was enacted in 2010 by Congress to target noncompliance by US taxpayers using foreign accounts'[5]. It goes on to say:

> FATCA requires foreign financial institutions (FFIs) to report to the IRS information about financial accounts held by US taxpayers, or by foreign entities in which US taxpayers hold a substantial ownership interest. FFIs are encouraged to either directly register with the IRS to comply with the FATCA regulations (and FFI agreement, if applicable) or comply with the FATCA Intergovernmental Agreements (IGA) treated as in effect in their jurisdictions

FATCA is designed to promote cross-border tax compliance by implementing an international standard for the automatic exchange of information related to US taxpayers, and requires tax authorities to obtain detailed account information for US taxpayers on an annual basis.

FATCA's primary (or only?) aim is to increase transparency for the IRS in relation to 'US persons' investing and earning income through non-US institutions. While the primary goal is to gain information about US persons, FATCA imposes (as a last resort) tax withholding where the applicable documentation and reporting requirements are not met.

It is fair to say that, when it was announced, the FATCA regime caused widespread consternation and concern; this was in part due to the way it intended to be implemented. After much dissatisfaction, FATCA has largely been implemented through 'intergovernmental agreements'. These are bilateral agreements, based on one of two (or three) model agreements

---

[4] This is a question with both a practical answer and a 'proper' answer. The 'proper' answer is that in 2009, the USA enacted the Foreign Account Tax Compliance Act 2009 - www.congress.gov/bill/111th-congress/house-bill/3933/text). In 2010, the USA further enacted the Hiring Incentives to Restore Employment Act. This included provisions addressing foreign account tax compliance. This was intended to improve taxpayer compliance by providing new administrative measures promoting identification of, and deterrence from, offshore tax abuse. This domestic provision adopted the language of FATCA. In addition to FATCA itself, the US legislation consists of further US Treasury Regulations (www.irs.gov/businesses/corporations/fatca-regulations-and-other-guidance).

[5] home.treasury.gov/policy-issues/tax-policy/foreign-account-tax-compliance-act

between the US and the implementing country[6]. Many, if not most, jurisdictions have signed up to such an agreement.

Where there is no such agreement in place, there are many consequences. It was initially intended that such IGAs should not be in place, and instead that non-US Financial Institutions should enter into agreements directly with the IRS to report the required information. The penalty for failure to do so was a 30% withholding tax on payments of US -source income to such institutions (so that their use became much less attractive).

HMRC explain the regime in the following way:[7]

> In 2010 the United States of America enacted the Foreign Account Tax Compliance Act provisions (FATCA) which are contained in the HIRE Act 2010. These provisions are aimed at reducing tax evasion by US citizens and entities.
>
> FATCA requires Financial Institutions outside the USA to pass information about their USA customers to the US tax administration, the Internal Revenue Service. The legislation allows for a 30% withholding tax to be applied to the US source income of any non-US Financial Institution that fails to comply with this requirement. This caused a number of issues for UK Financial Institutions, not least of which was how they could comply with the requirements of FATCA without breaching data protection restrictions.
>
> On 12 September 2012, the UK and the USA signed a Treaty to implement FATCA in the UK – 'The UK-US Agreement to Improve International Tax Compliance and to Implement FATCA' (the US IGA). Legislation at section 222 Finance Act 2013 provides HM Treasury with powers to make regulations to give effect to this and other similar agreements. The US IGA was brought into force by the International Tax Compliance (United States of America) Regulations 2014, which were subsequently incorporated into the International Tax Compliance Regulations 2015 (SI 2015/878). These regulations impose obligations on UK Financial Institutions to identify, capture and report information to HMRC on financial accounts held by US citizens and entities. Provided these Financial Institutions comply with the requirements of the legislation they will not be subject to the 30% withholding tax on US source income

This also accurately summarises the UK domestic regime.

---

[6] Of course, such agreements also must be given force of law through enactment into the domestic legislation of the jurisdiction in question.

[7] IEIM400040: www.gov.uk/hmrc-internal-manuals/international-exchange-of-information/ieim400040

5.4 Purpose

The broad aim of tax information exchange is to help fight against tax evasion and protect the integrity of national tax systems. The problems that such regimes – including FATCA – seek to address can be summarised as the following:

(i) the concealment of offshore assets, and failure to provide information about them to national tax authorities was too readily achieved; and

(ii) the costs, time, and complexity of conducting checks in relation to offshore income and gains was prohibitive for national revenue authorities[8].

(iii) The impact of tax evasion and, to a lesser, but still significant extent, tax avoidance is difficult to measure. Because both avoidance and evasion rely on the use of finan cial secrecy, assets and movements of value flows are concealed. The IMF's Fiscal Affairs Department, however, estimated in 2015 total tax losses at over $400 billion for OECD member states, as a result of the use of tax havens[9]. This represents the higher end of the estimates available, but on any basis, the problem was one that required attention.

HMRC describe it in the following way at IEIM100010[10]:

> In the ever-increasing multinational world of business and finance, where people, businesses, investments, and transactions frequently reach across international borders, HMRC need to be able to obtain information from overseas to help in our compliance and other activities. Exchange of Information with other tax authorities is an essential way of increasing tax transparency and cooperation between jurisdictions. It is a two-way process: we receive useful information for our work and, in turn, we provide other jurisdictions with information we either hold as a tax authority or can obtain with our information powers.

The OECD itself explains the importance of information exchange thus[11]:

> As the world becomes increasingly globalised and cross-border activities become the norm, tax administrations need to work together to ensure that taxpayers pay the right amount of tax to the right jurisdiction. A key aspect for making tax administrations ready for the challenges of the 21st century is equipping them with the

---

[8] It should be noted that one of the issues of information exchange is the impact of the principle in *Government of India v Taylor* [1955] AC 491, which is now largely dealt with in this respect by domestic legislation allowing exchange of information. See further – Brown *Government of India v Taylor*: The End of the Line? [2019] 1 JGLR 35

[9] The effect of one country's tax system on another. See *Base Erosion, Profit Shifting and Developing Countries* by Ernesto Crivelli, Ruud De Mooij and Michael Keen, IMF, 2015

[10] www.gov.uk/hmrc-internal-manuals/international-exchange-of-information/ieim100010

[11] http://www.oecd.org/tax/automatic-exchange/

necessary legal, administrative and IT tools for verifying compliance of their taxpayers. Against that background, the enhanced co-operation between tax authorities through AEOI is crucial in bringing national tax administration in line with the globalised economy.

There are three recognised methods of exchanging tax information: exchange on request, spontaneous exchange, and automatic exchange. CRS is a system of automatic exchange. The other two types of exchange require different specific provisions. These are provided for under bilateral agreements and under multilateral treaties and are (sadly) beyond the scope of this book.

5.5 Implementation: introduction

A brief word on the implementation of FATCA: the implementation may be different, dependent on the approach of the jurisdiction in question. In the first instance, most jurisdictions have entered into an IGA. Here the process will largely be dictated by the type of IGA entered into[12] and the matter is relatively straightforward. A sizeable minority of jurisdictions have not engaged with FATCA, and have no IGA. Generally, these are not jurisdictions commonly dealt with in the financial services or private client regime, though there are many notable exceptions, including Belize, Monaco and Russia. In such countries, the position expressed above is likely to apply.

In the remainder of this Chapter, we consider the three separate approaches and how they are applied.

5.6 Model 1 IGAs: Introduction

The Model 1 IGA is the most commonly adopted. However, this itself has several iterations. In relation to agreements that were 'reached in substance' prior to 30 June 2014, there are:[13]

(i) Reciprocal Model 1A Agreement, Preexisting TIEA or DTC;
(ii) Nonreciprocal Model 1B Agreement, Preexisting TIEA or DTC; and
(iii) Nonreciprocal Model 1B Agreement, No TIEA or DTC.

The same three options are available – though different – where the agreement was reached 'in substance' on, or after 1 July 2014. Thus there are six different Model 1 IGAs. It can also seen from this, that to have a reciprocal Model 1A agreement, it is necessary to have a preexisting TIEA (tax information exchange agreement) or DTC (double tax convention).

However, having compared the Model Agreements for the pre- and post-June 2014 agreement 'in substance', there appear to be very few relevant changes. Those that we find are highlighted below.

---

[12] The types are based on IGA Model 1A, Model 1B or Model 2. These are discussed in detail below.

[13] home.treasury.gov/policy-issues/tax-policy/foreign-account-tax-compliance-act

5.7 Terminology: introduction

The terminology used in both Model 1 IGAs is substantively similar. It is also substantively similar to that used in a Model 2 IGA. Understanding the terminology is essential to understanding how FATCA applies, and to whom it applies.

In what follows, we refer primarily to a Model 1A IGA, however we note wherever there are differences with the Model 1B IGA.

Finally, the structure of the FATCA Model IGAs requires some introduction. The defined terms are scattered through the body of the agreements and two Annexes: 'Annex I' and 'Annex II', with seemingly little thought or order as to what is included in which part[14]. Thus, it is necessary to consider both the body of the IGAs and the various Annexes in order to understand what comes within each definition. This is, perhaps, not ideal, but it is the status quo.

One saving grace is that there are only two 'Annex Is' and two 'Annex IIs' as opposed to six (as there are with IGAs). There is an Annex I1 and II for all Model 1 agreements and an Annex I and II for all Model 2 agreements.

Also noteworthy in this respect is that the IGA definitions are not static. There remains an option to use US Treasury Regulation definitions. Article 4(7) provides:

> 7. Coordination of Definitions with US Treasury Regulations. Notwithstanding Article 1 of this Agreement and the definitions provided in the Annexes to this Agreement, in implementing this Agreement, [FATCA Partner] may use, and may permit [FATCA Partner] Financial Institutions to use, a definition in relevant US Treasury Regulations in lieu of a corresponding definition in this Agreement, provided that such application would not frustrate the purposes of this Agreement.

Little commentary has been given on the expression 'such application would not frustrate the purpose of this Agreement'[15]. This is – we believe – inviting concerned parties to apply a purposive approach to the definitions and to adopt whichever is preferable. This means that it is also necessary to consider the definitions in US Treasury Regulations. These are considered in places below. This does add to the complexity of the situation; it may be that an 'in principle' decision can be made to use one or the other, though this may not always be possible or helpful in practice. One cannot be criticised simply for sticking to the IGA definitions, and this may, in practice, be the

---

[14] Neither author of this book is qualified to advise on the law of any part of the USA. This may be a quirk of US drafting with which we are unfamiliar and more comprehensible to those trained in this style of drafting. Unfortunately, it leaves us, in this edition, unable to shed further light.

[15] A similar expression is used in relation to CRS and the application of FATCA definitions

simpler and surer approach. However, where necessary, we tackle the US Treasury Regulation definitions (albeit from the perspective of the unqualified).

5.8 Terminology: Financial Institutions

This is a key definition. This is because it is by reference to status as a Financial Institution (reporting or nonreporting) that reporting requirements are set, and by which status is ultimately determined. This is because an 'NFFE'[16] - any Non-US Entity that is not an FFI as defined in relevant US Treasury Regulations, and also includes any Non- US Entity that is resident [Partner Jurisdiction] and that is not a Financial Institution – is also defined by reference to 'Financial Institution'. Thus, it can be seen that the term is key to the whole structure and operation of FATCA.

The term 'Financial Institution'[17] means a Custodial Institution, a Depository Institution, an Investment Entity, or a Specified Insurance Company. It should be noted that this is not very different to the definition in CRS so far.

In this respect HMRC says[18]:

> There are four categories of Financial Institution common to both the FATCA and CRS agreements –
> i) Custodial Institution [see IEIM400640]
> ii) Depository Institution [see IEIM400740]
> iii) Investment Entity [IEIM400760], and
> iv) Specified Insurance Company [IEIM400840]
>
> Under the US FATCA Regulations, other definitions of Financial Institution exist but these are not Reporting Financial Institutions for FATCA purposes

This is not as helpful as it might be, since the distinction between Reporting and Nonreporting Financial Institutions have not been discussed at that point in the IEIM. HMRC then continue[19]:

> Each category of Financial Institution is determined by set criteria. Where an entity does not meet the definition of financial institution in any of the categories then it will be classified as Non-Financial Entity (NFE) [see IEIM404040] or, for FATCA purposes, a Non-Financial Foreign Entity (NFFE). Throughout this guidance references to NFE should be read as including a reference to NFFE unless otherwise specified.

---

[16] Annex I(VI)(B)(2)

[17] Article 1(1)(g)

[18] See IEIM400600: www.gov.uk/hmrc-internal-manuals/international-exchange-of-information/ieim400610

[19] Ibid

> Where an entity falls within the definition of one of the above categories the Financial Institution will be classified either as a Reporting Financial Institution or a Nonreporting Financial Institution (NRFI). The definition of NRFI varies between the regimes such that a NRFI for FATCA may be a Reporting Financial Institution for the CRS. The definitions of NRFI for each regime can be found at [see IEIM400920] onwards

This highlights a difference in terminology: CRS references NFEs, whereas FATCA references NFFEs. This is not material, though as highlighted below, there are some distinctions between what is encompassed in the definition of NFE for CRS purposes, and what within NFFEs for FATCA purposes.

The term 'Custodial Institution'[20] means any entity that holds, as a substantial portion of its business, financial assets for the account of others. An entity holds financial assets for the account of others as a substantial portion of its business, if the entity's gross income attributable to the holding of financial assets and related financial services equals or exceeds 20 percent of the entity's gross income during the shorter of, either: (i) the three-year period that ends on 31 December (or the final day of a non-calendar year accounting period) prior to the year in which the determination is being made; or (ii) the period during which the entity has been in existence.

In relation to central securities depositories, HMRC say[21]:

> In the UK a Central Securities Depository (CSD) will not be treated as maintaining financial accounts. The participants of UK securities settlement systems that hold interests recorded in the CSD are either Financial Institutions in their own right, or they access the system through a Financial Institution (a sponsor), or are not subject to reporting obligations. It is these Financial Institutions that maintain the accounts and it is these participants and/or sponsors that are responsible for undertaking any reporting obligations.
>
> For example, members of the CREST securities settlement system (CREST system) operated by Euroclear UK & Ireland Limited (EUI), or the Financial Institution that accesses the CREST system on their behalf, are responsible for i) ensuring that the relevant member is compliant and ii) any reporting required by the agreement in respect of securities held by means of the CREST system. EUI acting as the CSD is not required to undertake any due diligence and reporting required by the agreement in respect of such securities.

---

[20] Article 1(1)(h)

[21] IEIM400680: www.gov.uk/hmrc-internal-manuals/international-exchange-of-information/ieim400680

> This treatment will also apply to a UK entity which is a direct or indirect subsidiary used solely to provide services ancillary to the business operated by that CSD or CSD Related Entity.
>
> The relationship between the securities settlement system and its participants is not a financial account and accordingly the CSD and any CSD Related Entity is not required to undertake any reporting required in connection with interests held by, or on behalf of, participants.
>
> Notwithstanding the foregoing, the CSD may act as a third-party service provider [see IEIM402000] and report on behalf of such participants in respect of reportable interests.

A 'Related Entity' is defined in Article 1(1)(jj), which provides:

> An Entity is a 'Related Entity' of another Entity if either Entity controls the other Entity, or the two Entities are under common control. For this purpose, control includes direct or indirect ownership of more than 50 percent of the vote or value in an Entity. Notwithstanding the foregoing, [FATCA Partner] may treat an Entity as not a Related Entity of another Entity if the two Entities are not members of the same expanded affiliated group as defined in section 1471(e)(2) of the US Internal Revenue Code

Section 1471(e)(2) provides:

> For purposes of this section, the term 'expanded affiliated group' means an affiliated group as defined in section 1504(a), determined —
>
> (A) by substituting 'more than 50 percent' for 'at least 80 percent' each place it appears, and
> (B) without regard to paragraphs (2) and (3) of section 1504(b).
>
> A partnership or any other entity (other than a corporation) shall be treated as a member of an expanded affiliated group if such entity is controlled (within the meaning of section 954(d)(3)) by members of such group (including any entity treated as a member of such group by reason of this sentence).

However, Jersey Guidance says[22]:

> Such institutions could include brokers, custodial banks, nominee companies (see 3.12) and clearing organisations. Insurance brokers do not hold assets on behalf of clients and so should not fall within the scope of this provision. An execution-only broker that simply executes trading instructions, or receives and transmit such instructions to another executing broker will not hold assets for the

[22] www.gov.je/TaxesMoney/InternationalTaxAgreements/IGAs/Pages/UnitedStatesIGA.aspx

> account of others and should not fall to be custodial institutions (although it is possible that they could be an investment entity).

Thus attention should be paid to the domestic legislation and the domestic guidance. HMRC go on to discuss the definition of Custodial Institution in the context of trusts (though we agree with HMRC that it is far more probable that trusts will usually be Investment Entities or NFFEs – see further below). They say[23]:

> Trusts are treated as entities by all of the agreements for automatic exchange of information.
>
> A trust can be either a financial institution or a Non-Financial Entity. Where a trust meets one of the definitions for being a Financial Institution [see IEIM400600] it is most likely to be an Investment Entity [see IEIM400760] but it may, alternatively, meet the requirements for being a Custodial Institution [see IEIM400640].
>
> For example, shares held in trust may be in a Custodial Account [see IEIM402200] and therefore subject to reporting by the trust as the Custodial Institution that holds the account. This may be the case where a trust such as an Employee Benefit Trust continues to hold financial assets, such as shares, for an employee after they have been granted.
>
> Where an Employee Benefit Trust holds shares for the future benefit of employees, but the shares are not allocated, then under most circumstances this right to a future allocation would not fall to be a custodial account. Similarly, when shares are allocated and the trustee is directed to transfer the assets as soon as reasonably possible to the beneficiary, a broker, a custodian, etc., then the trust will not be treated as maintaining a financial account for the duration of time it takes to complete the transfer.

In relation to 'fund nominees', HMRC characterise them as 'distributors in the chain of legal ownership'. They say[24]:

> Distributors that hold legal title to assets on behalf of customers and are part of the legal chain of ownership of interests in Collective Investment Schemes are Financial Institutions. In most cases they will be Custodial Institutions because they will be holding assets on behalf of others.
>
> Fund nominees, fund intermediaries and fund platforms will nevertheless still be Financial Institutions because they would

[23] IEIM400640: www.gov.uk/hmrc-internal-manuals/international-exchange-of-information/ieim400700

[24] IEIM400720: www.gov.uk/hmrc-internal-manuals/international-exchange-of-information/ieim400720

otherwise be within the definition of Investment Entity [see IEIM400760]. In this case, the financial accounts will be those maintained by the distributor, and the distributor will be responsible for ensuring it meets its obligations in respect of those accounts.

Fund nominees, fund intermediaries and fund platforms should be treated as Custodial Institutions, unless specific factors indicate that their businesses are better characterised as falling within the definition of an Investment Entity. Normally, the primary business of a fund nominee, fund intermediary or fund platform will be to hold financial assets for the account of others.

For the purpose of aggregating accounts [see IEIM403560] to determine whether any preexisting custodial accounts are high value accounts [see IEIM402900], a Custodial Institution will need to consider all the financial accounts held with them by each customer even though the underlying interests are in different Collective Investment Schemes

This is a good example of the scope of FATCA, and indeed CRS (since we consider the position would be similar). While certain fund nominees appear – in HMRC's view – to fall outside the definition of Custodial Institution, they remain Financial Institutions and potentially (or probably) within scope, on the basis that they are Investment Entities.

The term 'Depository Institution'[25] means any entity that accepts deposits in the ordinary course of a banking or similar business. The definition of a 'banking or similar business' is contained in the US Treasury Regulations, section 1.1471-5(e)(2)[26]. An entity is considered to be engaged in a banking or similar business if, in the ordinary course of its business with customers, the entity accepts deposits or other similar investments of funds and regularly engages in one or more of the following activities:

(i) Makes personal, mortgage, industrial or other loans or provides other extensions of credit
(ii) Purchases, sells, discounts or negotiates accounts receivable, instalment obligations, notes, drafts, cheques, bills of exchange, acceptances or other evidences of indebtedness;
(iii) Issues letters of credit and negotiates drafts drawn thereunder;
(iv) Provides trust or fiduciary services;
(v) Finances foreign exchange transactions; or
(vi) Enters into, purchases, or disposes of finance leases or leased assets.

---

[25] Article 1(1)(i)

[26] HMRC also assert that this definition applies for CRS purposes.

HMRC say[27]:

> HMRC will regard a person carrying out an activity in the UK that is a regulated activity for the purposes of the Financial Services and Markets Act 2000 by virtue of Article 5 of the Financial Services and Markets Act 2000 (Regulated Activities) Order 2001 (accepting deposits) as a Depository Institution.
>
> Entities within this definition will include entities regulated in the UK as a savings or commercial bank, a credit union, industrial and provident societies and building societies. In considering Article 5, HMRC will apply the relevant exclusions contained therein – for example, insurance brokers and solicitors would not be expected to fall within this definition. However in considering whether an entity is conducting banking or similar business, it will be the actual activities that the entity carries out that will be determinative.
>
> ...
>
> Entities that solely provide asset-based finance services, such as a factoring or invoice discounting business, or which accept deposits from persons solely as collateral or security pursuant to a sale or lease of property, a loan secured by property or a similar financing arrangement, between such entity and the person making the deposit, will not be Depository Institutions.
>
> Entities that facilitate money transfers by instructing agents to transmit funds, including the provision of merchant's payments accounts, but do not finance the transactions, will not be considered to be engaged in banking or similar business, as this is not seen as accepting deposits.

Jersey confirms in its Guidance that, similar to the UK, Depository Institution includes all entities regulated under the Banking Business (Jersey) Law 1991 (if they undertake one of the listed activities)[28]. It goes on to say:

> The following would not be expected to fall within this definition:
>
> - Insurance brokers.
> - Solicitors/Advocates.
> - Factoring or invoice discounting businesses.
> - Entities that complete money transfers by instructing agents to transmit funds.
> - Entities that solely provide asset-based finance services or that accept deposits solely from persons as collateral or security

[27] IEIM400740: www.gov.uk/hmrc-internal-manuals/international-exchange-of-information/ieim400740

[28] Paragraph 3.8

pursuant to; a sale or lease of property; a loan secured by property; or similar financing arrangements, between that entity and the person making the deposit.

The term 'Investment Entity'[29] means any entity that conducts as a business (or is managed by an entity that conducts as a business) one or more of the following activities or operations for or on behalf of a customer:

(i) trading in money market instruments (cheques, bills, certificates of deposit, derivatives, etc.); foreign exchange; exchange, interest rate and index instruments; transferable securities; or commodity futures trading;
(ii) individual and collective portfolio management; or
(iii) otherwise investing, administering, or managing funds or money on behalf of other persons.

The definition then clarifies that this definition is to be interpreted in a manner consistent with similar language in the definition of 'financial institution' in the Financial Action Task Force Recommendations. It can also be seen that – in common with CRS – an entity can be an Investment Entity by way of being a 'managed by' Investment Entity. HMRC describes such an entity as:[30]

> An entity will be an investment entity if it is managed by a Financial Institution [see IEIM400600] and meets the financial assets test as described below.
>
> An entity is managed by a Financial Institution if that Financial Institution performs, either directly or through another service provider, any of the activities described in the section above (activity based investment entity) on behalf of the entity. An entity is not regarded as managed by a financial institution if that Financial Institution does not have discretionary authority to manage the entity's assets either in whole or in part.
>
> An entity may be managed by a mix of other entities and individuals. If one of the entities so involved in the management of the entity is a Financial Institution within the meaning of the agreements then the entity meets the requirements for being managed by a Financial Institution.
>
> ~~An entity meets the financial assets test if its gross income is primarily attributable to investing, reinvesting or trading in financial assets. This is a similar test to that in the section above requiring that~~

---

[29] Article 1(1)(j)

[30] IEIM 400770: www.gov.uk/hmrc-internal-manuals/international-exchange-of-information/ieim400770

~~at least 50% of its income is attributable to investing, reinvesting or trading in financial assets in the shorter of:~~

~~The three year period ending on 31 December in the year preceding that in which its status as in investment entity is to be determined; or~~

~~The period in which the entity has been in existence.~~

The struck through portion of the extract from the HMRC Manual should not be applicable to FATCA, which does not contain an asset test. The Jersey Guidance discusses the overlap between FATCA and CRS in relation to Investment Entities, while noting that there is a difference between the two. It says:[31]

> Although Investment Entity is clearly defined in the IGA, the definitions in the US Treasury Regulations and the Common Reporting Standard (CRS) are different. Since the CRS has become the global standard, and is substantially similar to the US Treasury Regulations definition, this has also been included in the Jersey Regulations. Entities have a choice of which definition to apply.
>
> An Investment Entity does not include any entity that is an Active NFFE because it meets any of the criteria in section 11.3 subparagraphs d) through to g)

In relation to the 'managed by' Investment Entity, the Jersey Guidance says:

> For the purposes of the 'managed by' test under the IGA definition, a distinction should be made between one entity 'managing' another and one entity 'administering' another. For instance, the following services provided by an entity to another will not constitute the latter entity being 'managed by' the former:
>
> - Provision of co-secretary and/or company secretarial services
> - Provision of registered office
> - Preparation of final financial statements (from company books and
> - records)
> - Preparation of Tax and/or VAT returns
> - Provision of bookkeeping services including budgeting and cash-flow forecasts.
> - Where a Jersey company's directors are employees of a Jersey TCSP which itself is a Financial Institution and the Jersey company is administered by that Jersey TCSP Financial Institution, the Jersey company may be treated as being managed by a Financial Institution and so be an Investment Entity itself.

[31] At paragraph 3.9

The Jersey Guidance then goes on to discuss the CRS definition of 'Investment Entity'. It is suggested that this is of greater assistance than the HMRC Guidance on this point, which does not distinguish between the two, though this is – for trust companies and private client practitioners – likely to be one of the most important definitions in FATCA.

However, the HMRC Guidance goes on to give a number of examples that are potentially helpful. They start with the basic definition,[32] giving the following example:

> Advice Co Ltd, provides advice on and discretionary management of securities held by a number of clients. The securities meet the definition for being financial assets. Almost 80% of the gross income of Advice Co Ltd for the last three years has come from providing such services. Advice Co Ltd primarily conducts a business of managing financial assets on behalf of clients and is, therefore, an Investment Entity

It then goes on to consider the situation of an entity that is carrying on a business managed by a Financial Institution, saying:

> Investment Fund X primarily invests in equities on behalf of customers. Fund X is managed by Invest Co Ltd, a Financial Institution. Fund X was formed two years ago since which it has earned 90% of its income from these activities. Fund X is an Investment Entity because it primarily conducts as a business one or more of the relevant activities or operations for or on behalf of a customer. It is not relevant that it is managed by a Financial Institution as it is an Investment Entity by virtue of its business activities

This is correct. In relation to a 'managed by' Investment Entity, HMRC say:

> Investment Partnership LLP is a vehicle set up to invest its members' contributions in financial assets, it invests in its own right and has no customers. The LLP is managed by Invest Co Ltd, a Financial Institution. The LLP has been investing for several years and its income is derived exclusively from its investment activities. As the LLP is managed by a Financial Institution and at least 50% of its income in the last three years is primarily attributable to investing, reinvesting or trading in financial assets it will be an Investment Entity.

Again, the reference to 50% of income is not relevant to FATCA, only CRS. HMRC then go on to make the point about whether the residence of the managing Financial Institution is relevant, saying:

---

[32] IEIM400780

> The facts are the same as in the example above, except that Investment Partnership LLP is managed by Invest Co GmbH, a German Financial Institution. The fact that the LLP is managed by a Financial Institution resident in another jurisdiction does not alter its status. It will be an Investment Entity, because it is managed by a Financial Institution and more than 50% of its gross income is primarily attributable to investing, reinvesting or trading in financial assets

This is probably an oversimplification (certainly for CRS if not for FATCA) since the residence of the entity may be impacted by its management. This is discussed in greater detail in the chaprter on CRS (being primarily of relevance for CRS).

HMRC then go on to consider the distinction between entities managed by individuals and those managed by other entities, saying:

> **Family trust managed by an individual**
> … if Ben managed the assets of a family trust, the trust would not be an Investment Entity as it is not primarily conducting as a business one or more of the relevant activities or operations for or on behalf of a customer, and although its gross income is primarily attributable to investing, reinvesting, or trading in financial assets, it is not an entity that is managed by a Financial Institution (because Ben, as an individual, cannot be a Financial Institution). (Note: in practice, a trust holding assets on behalf of a family arrangement will typically appoint a company or partnership to manage its assets but some family trusts may instead appoint a suitably qualified individual).
>
> **Family trust with a corporate trustee**
> The ABC family trust's gross income is primarily attributable to investing, reinvesting or trading in financial assets. The trust was set up on the advice of a law firm and that firm's own corporate trustee is the trustee of the trust. The corporate trustee acts for the law firm's clients without itself charging any fees to the clients. Even though the corporate trustee does not charge, it is a Financial Institution by virtue of being an Investment Entity. Its Related Entity (the law firm) is charging the clients for the corporate trustee's services of managing assets, the corporate trustee therefore primarily conducts as a business, for or on behalf of a customer, the prescribed activities. This in turn means that the ABC family trust is also an Investment Entity

This is uncontroversial. HMRC do note another essential difference between FATCA and CRS[33]:

[33] IEIM400790

FATCA only

Under the FATCA agreement with the USA all charities are excluded from reporting under the exemption for non-profit organisations [see IEIM401000]

The term 'Specified Insurance Company' means any Entity that is an insurance company (or the holding company of an insurance company) that issues, or is obligated to make payments with respect to, a Cash Value Insurance Contract or an Annuity Contract.

This requires some further explanation. 'Insurance Contract' means a contract (other than an Annuity Contract) under which the issuer agrees to pay an amount upon the occurrence of a specified contingency involving mortality, morbidity, accident, liability, or property risk. An 'Annuity Contract' means a contract under which the issuer agrees to make payments for a period of time determined in whole or in part by reference to the life expectancy of one or more individuals. The term also includes a contract that is considered to be an Annuity Contract in accordance with the law, regulation, or practice of the jurisdiction in which the contract was issued, and under which the issuer agrees to make payments for a term of years.

A 'Cash Value Insurance Contract' means an Insurance Contract (other than an indemnity reinsurance contract between two insurance companies) that has a Cash Value greater than $50,000. 'Cash Value' means the greater of (i) the amount that the policyholder is entitled to receive upon surrender or termination of the contract (determined without reduction for any surrender charge or policy loan), and (ii) the amount the policyholder can borrow under or regarding the contract. Notwithstanding the foregoing, the term 'Cash Value' does not include an amount payable under an Insurance Contract as:

(i) a personal injury or sickness benefit or other benefit providing indemnification of an economic loss incurred upon the occurrence of the event insured against;

(ii) a refund to the policyholder of a previously paid premium under an Insurance Contract (other than under a life insurance contract) due to policy cancellation or termination, decrease in risk exposure during the effective period of the Insurance Contract, or arising from a redetermination of the premium due to correction of posting or other similar error; or

(iii) a policyholder dividend based upon the underwriting experience of the contract or group involved

The term 'Reporting Financial Institution' means a Reporting [FATCA Partner] Financial Institution or a Reporting US Financial Institution, as the context requires.

The term 'Reporting [FATCA Partner] Financial Institution' means any [FATCA Partner] Financial Institution that is not a Nonreporting [FATCA

Partner] Financial Institution, while the term 'Reporting US Financial Institution'[34] means:

(i) any Financial Institution that is resident in the United States, but excluding any branch of such Financial Institution that is located outside the United States, and
(ii) any branch of a Financial Institution not resident in the United States, if such branch is located in the United States, provided that the Financial Institution or branch has control, receipt, or custody of income with respect to which information is required to be exchanged under subparagraph (2)(b) of Article 2 of this Agreement

The term 'Nonreporting [FATCA Partner] Financial Institution' means any [FATCA Partner] Financial Institution, or other Entity resident in [FATCA Partner], that is described in Annex II as a Nonreporting [FATCA Partner] Financial Institution or that otherwise qualifies as a deemed-compliant FFI or an exempt beneficial owner under relevant US Treasury Regulations [in effect on the date of signature of this Agreement]. The footnote to the Model 1A IGA explains:

> Some of our partner jurisdictions have expressed the need for a static definition of Nonreporting FATCA Partner Financial Institution, even though we believe that a dynamic approach is preferred to provide flexibility. The bracketed language has been included to accommodate jurisdictions that have a need for a static definition.

This is another example of where it will be important for the terms of the individual agreement, and domestic provisions, to be considered. Nonreporting FIs are discussed in detail in Annex II.

Finally, an FI can be a 'Nonparticipating Financial Institution'. This means a nonparticipating FFI, as that term is defined in relevant US Treasury Regulations, but does not include a [FATCA Partner] Financial Institution or other Partner Jurisdiction Financial Institution other than a Financial Institution treated as a Nonparticipating Financial Institution pursuant to subparagraph 2(b) of Article 5 of this Agreement or the corresponding provision in an agreement between the United States and a Partner Jurisdiction

The US Treasury Regulations define a nonparticipating FFI[35] as:

> Nonparticipating FFI. The term nonparticipating FFI means an FFI other than a participating FFI, a deemed-compliant FFI, or an exempt beneficial owner

[34] This is one of the definitions that is not repeated in the FATCA Model 1B IGA, which is not reciprocal – i.e. there is no obligation for the US to provide information to the partner jurisdiction – so such term is not required.

[35] 26 CFR, paragraph 1.1471-1(82)

The meaning of participating FFI is set out above. A deemed-compliant FFI[36] is:

> Deemed-compliant FFI. The term deemed-compliant FFI means an FFI that is treated, pursuant to section 1471(b)(2) and 1.1471-5(f), as meeting the requirements of section 1471(b). The term deemed-compliant FFI also includes a QI37 branch of a US financial institution that is a reporting Model 1 FFI

This is clearly not the 'whole story' in relation to deemed-compliant FFIs. The sections of the CFR mentioned provide[38]:

(f) ***Deemed-compliant FFIs.*** The term *deemed-compliant FFI* includes a registered deemed-compliant FFI (as defined in paragraph (f)(1) of this section), a certified deemed-compliant FFI (as defined in paragraph (f)(2) of this section), a nonreporting IGA FFI (as defined in § 1.1471-1(b)(83)), and, to the extent provided in paragraph (f)(3) of this section, an owner-documented FFI. A deemed-compliant FFI will be treated pursuant to section 1471(b)(2) as having met the requirements of section 1471(b). A deemed-compliant FFI that complies with the due diligence and withholding requirements applicable to such entity as provided in this paragraph (f) will also be deemed to have met its withholding obligations under sections 1471(a) and 1472(a). For this purpose, an intermediary or flow-through entity that has a residual withholding obligation under § 1.1471-2(a)(2)(ii) must fulfill such obligation to be considered a deemed-compliant FFI.

(1) ***Registered deemed-compliant FFIs.*** A registered deemed-compliant FFI means an FFI that meets the procedural requirementsdescribed in paragraph (f)(1)(ii) of this section and that either is described in any of paragraphs (f)(1)(i)(A) through (F) of this section or is treated as a registered deemed-compliant FFI under a Model 2 IGA. A registered deemed-compliant FFI also includes any FFI, or branch of an FFI, that is a reporting Model 1 FFI that complies with the registration requirements of a Model 1 IGA.

(i) ***Registered deemed-compliant FFI categories -***

(A) ***Local FFIs.*** An FFI is described in this paragraph (f)(1)(i)(A) if the FFI meets the following requirements.

(1) The FFI is licensed and regulated as a financial institution under the laws of its country of incorporation or

[36] 26 CFR, paragraph 1.1471-1(27)

[37] QI is – as far as we as non-US lawyers understand it – a sort of domestic FATCA. It is not discussed further in this text.

[38] 1.1471-5(f)

organization (which must be a FATF-compliant jurisdiction at the time the FFI registers for deemed-compliant status).

(2) The FFI does not have a fixed place of business outside its country of incorporation or organization. For this purpose, a fixed place of business does not include a location that is not advertised to the public and from which the FFI performs solely administrative support functions.

(3) The FFI does not solicit customers or account holders outside its country of incorporation or organization. For this purpose, an FFIwill not be considered to have solicited customers or account holders outside its country of incorporation or organization merely because it operates a Web site, provided that the Web site does not specifically indicate that the FFI maintains accounts for or provides servicesto nonresidents, and does not otherwise target or solicit U.S. customers or account holders. An FFI will also not be considered to have solicited customers or account holders outside its country of incorporation or organization merely because it advertises in print media or on a radio or television station that is distributed or aired primarily within its country of incorporation or organization but is also incidentally distributed or aired in other countries, provided that the advertisement does not specifically indicate that the FFI maintains accounts for or provides services to nonresidents and does not otherwise target or solicit U.S. customers or account holders.

(4) The FFI is required under the laws of its country of incorporation or organization to identify resident account holders for purposes of either information reporting or withholding of tax with respect to accounts held by residents or is required to identify resident accountsfor purposes of satisfying such country's AML due diligence requirements.

(5) At least 98 percent of the accounts by value maintained by the FFI as of the last day of the preceding calendar year are held by residents (including residents that are entities) of the country in which the FFI is incorporated or organized. An FFI that is incorporated or organized in a member state of the European Union may treat account holders that are residents (including residents that are entities) of other member states of the European Union as residents of the country in which the FFI is incorporated or organized for purposes of this calculation.

(6) By the later of June 30, 2014, or the date it registers as a deemed-compliant FFI, the FFI implements policies and procedures, consistent with those set forth for a

participating FFI under § 1.1471-4(c), to monitor whether the FFI opens or maintains an accountfor a specified U.S. person who is not a resident of the country in which the FFI is incorporated or organized (including a U.S. personthat was a resident when the account was opened but subsequently ceases to be a resident), an entity controlled or beneficially owned (as determined under the FFI's AML due diligence) by one or more specified U.S. persons that are not residents of the country in which the FFI is incorporated or organized, or a nonparticipating FFI. Such policies and procedures must provide that if any such account is discovered, the FFI will close such account, transfer such account to a participating FFI, reporting Model 1 FFI, or U.S. financial institution, or withhold and report on such account as would be required under § 1.1471-4(b) and (d) if the FFI were a participating FFI.

(7) With respect to each preexisting account held by a nonresident of the country in which the FFI is organized or held by an entity, the FFI reviews those accounts in accordance with the procedures described in § 1.1471-4(c) applicable to preexisting accounts to identify any U.S. account or account held by a nonparticipating FFI, and certifies to the IRS that it did not identify any such account as a resultof its review, that it has closed any such accounts that were identified or transferred them to a participating FFI, reporting Model 1 FFI, or U.S. financial institution, or that it agrees to withhold and report on such accounts as would be required under § 1.1471-4(b) and (d)if it were a participating FFI. Such certification must be submitted by the due date of the FFI's first certification of compliance required under paragraph (f)(1)(ii)(B) of this section.

(8) In the case of an FFI that is a member of an expanded affiliated group, each FFI in the group is incorporated or organized in the same country and, with the exception of any member that is a retirement plan described in § 1.1471-6(f), meets the requirements set forth in this paragraph (f)(1)(i)(A) and the procedural requirements of paragraph (f)(1)(ii) of this section.

(9) The FFI does not have policies or practices that discriminate against opening or maintaining accounts for individuals who are specified U.S. persons and who are residents of the FFI's country of incorporation or organization.

(B) ***Nonreporting members of participating FFI groups.*** An FFI that is a member of a participating FFI group is described in this paragraph (f)(1)(i)(B) if it meets the following requirements.

(1) By the later of June 30, 2014, or the date it registers with the IRS pursuant to paragraph (f)(1)(ii) of this section, the FFIimplements policies and procedures to ensure that within six months of opening a U.S. account or an account held by a recalcitrant account holder or a nonparticipating FFI, the FFI either transfers such account to an affiliate that is a participating FFI, reporting Model 1 FFI, or U.S. financial institution, closes the account, or becomes a participating FFI.

(2) The FFI reviews its accounts that were opened prior to the time it implements the policies and procedures (including time frames) described in paragraph (f)(1)(i)(B)(*1*) of this section, using the procedures described in § 1.1471-4(c) applicable to preexisting accountsof participating FFIs, to identify any U.S. account or account held by a nonparticipating FFI. Within six months of the identification of any account described in this paragraph, the FFI transfers the account to an affiliate that is a participating FFI, reporting Model 1 FFI, or U.S. financial institution, closes the account, or becomes a participating FFI.

(3) By the later of June 30, 2014, or the date it registers with the IRS pursuant to paragraph (f)(1)(ii) of this section, the FFIimplements policies and procedures to ensure that it identifies any account that becomes a U.S. account or an account held by a recalcitrant account holder or a nonparticipating FFI due to a change in circumstances. Within six months of the date on which the FFIfirst has knowledge or reason to know of the change in the account holder's chapter 4 status, the FFI transfers any such account to an affiliate that is a participating FFI, reporting Model 1 FFI, or U.S. financial institution, closes the account, or becomes a participating FFI.

(C) ***Qualified collective investment vehicles.*** An FFI is described in this paragraph (f)(1)(i)(C) if it meets the following requirements.

(1) The FFI is an FFI solely because it is an investment entity, and it is regulated as an investment fund either in its country of incorporation or organization or in all of the countries in which it is registered and all of the countries in which it operates. A fund will be considered to be regulated as an investment fund under this paragraph if its manager is regulated with respect to the investment fund in all of the countries in which the investment fund is registered and in all of the countries in which the investment fund operates.

(2) Each holder of record of direct debt interests in the FFI in excess of $50,000, of any direct equity interests in the FFI (for

examplethe holders of its units or global certificates), and of any other account holder of the FFI is a participating FFI, a registered deemed-compliant FFI, a retirement plan described in § 1.1471-6(f), a non-profit organization described in paragraph (e)(5)(vi) of this section, a U.S. person that is not a specified U.S. person, a nonreporting IGA FFI, or an exempt beneficial owner. Notwithstanding the prior sentence, an FFI will not be prohibited from qualifying as a qualified collective investment vehicle solely because it has issued interestsin bearer form provided that the FFI ceased issuing interests in such form after December 31, 2012, retires all such interests upon surrender, and establishes policies and procedures to redeem or immobilize all such interests prior to January 1, 2017, and that prior to payment the FFI documents the account holder in accordance with the procedures set forth in § 1.1471-4(c) applicable to accountsother than preexisting accounts and agrees to withhold and report on such accounts as would be required under § 1.1471-4(b) and (d)if it were a participating FFI. For purposes of this paragraph (f)(1)(i)(C), an FFI may disregard equity interests owned by specified U.S. persons acquired with seed capital within the meaning of paragraph (i)(4) of this section if the specified U.S. person is described in paragraph (i)(3)(i) and (ii) of this section (substituting the term *U.S. person* for the terms *FFI* and *member*), and the specified U.S. person neither has held, nor intends to hold, such interest for more than three years.

(3) In the case of an FFI that is part of an expanded affiliated group, all other FFIs in the expanded affiliated group are participating FFIs, registered deemed-compliant FFIs, sponsored FFIs described in paragraph (f)(1)(i)(F)(1) or (2) of this section, nonreporting IGAFFIs, or exempt beneficial owners.

(D) ***Restricted funds.*** An FFI is described in this paragraph (f)(1)(i)(D) if it meets the following requirements.

(1) The FFI is an FFI solely because it is an investment entity, and it is regulated as an investment fund under the laws of its country of incorporation or organization (which must be a FATF-compliant jurisdiction at the time the FFI registers for deemed-compliant status) or in all of the countries in which it is registered and in all of the countries in which it operates. A fund will be considered to be regulated as an investment fund for purposes of this paragraph if its manager is regulated with respect to the fund in all of the countries in which the investment fund is registered and in all of the countries in which the investment fund operates.

(2) Interests issued directly by the fund are redeemed by or transferred by the fund rather than sold by investors on any secondary market. Notwithstanding the prior sentence, an FFI will not be prohibited from qualifying as a restricted fund solely because it issuedinterests in bearer form provided that the FFI ceased issuing interests in bearer form after December 31, 2012, retires all such interestsupon surrender, and establishes policies and procedures to redeem or immobilize all such interests prior to January 1, 2017, and that prior to payment the FFI documents the account holder in accordance with the procedures set forth in § 1.1471-4(c) applicable to accounts other than preexisting accounts and agrees to withhold and report on such accounts as would be required under § 1.1471-4(b) and (d) if it were a participating FFI. For purposes of this paragraph (f)(1)(i)(D), interests in the FFI that are issued by the fund through a transfer agent or distributor that does not hold the interests as a nominee of the account holder will be considered to have been issued directly by the fund.

(3) Interests that are not issued directly by the fund are sold only through distributors that are participating FFIs, registered deemed-compliant FFIs, nonregistering local banks described in paragraph (f)(2)(i) of this section, or restricted distributors described in paragraph (f)(4) of this section. For purposes of this paragraph (f)(1)(i)(D) and paragraph (f)(4) of this section, a distributor means an underwriter, broker, dealer, or other person who participates, pursuant to a contractual arrangement with the FFI, in the distribution of securities and holds interests in the FFI as a nominee.

(4) The FFI ensures that by the later of December 31, 2014, or six months after the date the FFI registers as a deemed-compliant FFI, each agreement that governs the distribution of its debt or equity interests prohibits sales and other transfers of debt or equity interests in the FFI (other than interests that are both distributed by and held through a participating FFI) to specified U.S. persons, nonparticipating FFIs, or passive NFFEs with one or more substantial U.S. owners. In addition, by that date, the FFI's prospectus and all marketing materials must indicate that sales and other transfers of interests in the FFI to specified U.S. persons, nonparticipating FFIs, or passive NFFEs with one or more substantial U.S. owners are prohibited unless such interests are both distributed by and held through a participating FFI.

(5) The FFI ensures that by the later of December 31, 2014, or six months after the date the FFI registers as a deemed-

compliant FFI, each agreement entered into by the FFI that governs the distribution of its debt or equity interests requires the distributor to notify the FFI of a change in the distributor's chapter 4 status within 90 days of the change. The FFI must, with respect to any distributor that ceases to qualify as a distributor identified in paragraph (f)(1)(i)(D)(*3*) of this section, terminate its distribution agreement with the distributor, or cause the distribution agreement to be terminated, within 90 days of the notification of the distributor's change in status and, with respect to all debt and equity interests of the FFI issued through that distributor, redeem those interests, convert those interests to direct holdings in the fund, or cause those interests to be transferred to another distributor identified in paragraph (f)(1)(i)(D)(*3*) of this section within six months of the distributor's change in status.

(6) With respect to any of the FFI's preexisting direct accounts that are held by the beneficial owner of the interest in the FFI, the FFIreviews those accounts in accordance with the procedures (and time frames) described in § 1.1471-4(c) applicable to preexisting accounts to identify any U.S. account or account held by a nonparticipating FFI. Notwithstanding the previous sentence, the FFI will not be required to review the account of any individual investor that purchased its interest at a time when all of the FFI's distribution agreements and its prospectus contained an explicit prohibition of the issuance and/or sale of shares to U.S. entities and U.S. resident individuals. An FFI will not be required to review the account of any investorthat purchased its interest in bearer form until the time of payment, but at such time will be required to document the account in accordance with procedures set forth in §1.1471-4(c) applicable to accounts other than preexisting accounts. The FFI is required to certify to the IRS either that it did not identify any U.S. account or account held by a nonparticipating FFI as a result of its review or, if any such accounts were identified, that the FFI will either redeem such accounts, transfer such accounts to an affiliate or other FFI that is a participating FFI, reporting Model 1 FFI, or U.S. financial institution, or withhold and report on such accounts as would be required under § 1.1471-4(b) and (d) if it were a participating FFI. Such certification must be submitted to the IRS by the due date of the FFI's first certification of compliance required under paragraph (f)(1)(ii)(B) of this section.

(7) By the later of June 30, 2014, or the date that it registers as a deemed-compliant FFI, the FFI implements the policies and procedures described in § 1.1471-4(c) to ensure that it either -

(i) Does not open or maintain an account for, or make a withholdable payment to, any specified U.S. person, nonparticipating FFI, or passive NFFE with one or more substantial U.S. owners and, if it discovers any such accounts, closes all accounts for any such personwithin six months of the date that the FFI had reason to know the account holder became such a person; or

(ii) Withholds and reports on any account held by, or any withholdable payment made to, any specified U.S. person, nonparticipating FFI, or passive NFFE with one or more substantial U.S. owners to the extent and in the manner that would be required under § 1.1471-4(b) and (d) if the FFI were a participating FFI.

(8) For an FFI that is part of an expanded affiliated group, all other FFIs in the expanded affiliated group are participating FFIs, registered deemed-compliant FFIs, sponsored FFIs described in paragraph (f)(1)(i)(F)(*1*) or (*2*) of this section, nonreporting IGA FFIs, or exempt beneficial owners.

(E) ***Qualified credit card issuers and servicers.*** An FFI is described in this paragraph (f)(1)(i)(E) if the FFI meets the following requirements.

(1) The FFI is an FFI solely because it is an issuer or servicer of credit cards that accepts deposits, on its own behalf or, in the case of a servicer, on behalf of a credit card issuer, only when a customer makes a payment in excess of a balance due with respect to the credit card account and the overpayment is not immediately returned to the customer.

(2) By the later of June 30, 2014, or the date it registers as a deemed-compliant FFI, the FFI implements policies and procedures to either prevent a customer deposit in excess of $50,000 or to ensure that any customer deposit in excess of $50,000 is refunded to the customer within 60 days. For this purpose, a customer deposit does not refer to credit balances to the extent of disputed charges but does include credit balances resulting from merchandise returns.

(F) ***Sponsored investment entities and controlled foreign corporations.*** An FFI is described in this paragraph (f)(1)(i)(F) if the FFIis described in paragraph (f)(1)(i)(F)(*1*) or (*2*) of this section and the sponsoring entity meets the requirements of paragraph (f)(1)(i)(F)(*3*) of this section.

(1) An FFI is a sponsored investment entity described in this paragraph (f)(1)(i)(F)(*1*) if -

(i) It is an investment entity that is not a QI, WP (except to the extent permitted in the WP agreement), or WT; and

(ii) An entity, other than a nonparticipating FFI, has agreed with the FFI to act as a sponsoring entity for the FFI.

(2) An FFI is a sponsored controlled foreign corporation described in this paragraph (f)(1)(i)(F)(2) if the FFI meets the following requirements -

(i) The FFI is a controlled foreign corporation as defined in section 957(a) that is not a QI, WP, or WT;

(ii) The FFI is wholly owned, directly or indirectly, by a U.S. financial institution that agrees with the FFI to act as a sponsoring entityfor the FFI; and

(iii) The FFI shares a common electronic account system with the sponsoring entity that enables the sponsoring entity to identify all account holders and payees of the FFI and to access all account and customer information maintained by the FFI including, but not limited to, customer identification information, customer documentation, account balance, and all payments made to the account holder or payee.

(3) A sponsoring entity described in paragraph (f)(1)(i)(F)(*1*)(*ii*) or (f)(1)(i)(F)(2)(*ii*) of this section meets the requirements of this paragraph (f)(1)(i)(F)(*3*) if the sponsoring entity -

(i) Is authorized to act on behalf of the FFI (such as a fund manager, trustee, corporate director, or managing partner) to fulfill all due diligence, withholding, and reporting responsibilities that the FFI would have assumed if it were a participating FFI;

(ii) Has registered with the IRS as a sponsoring entity;

(iii) Has registered the FFI with the IRS by the later of January 1, 2017, or the date that the FFI identifies itself as qualifying under this paragraph (f)(1)(i)(F);

(iv) Agrees to perform, on behalf of the FFI, all due diligence, withholding, reporting, and other requirements that the FFI would have been required to perform if it were a participating FFI;

(v) Identifies the FFI in all reporting completed on the FFI's behalf to the extent required under §§ 1.1471-4(d)(2)(ii)(C) and 1.1474-1;

(vi) Complies with the verification procedures described in paragraph (j) of this section; and

(vii) Has not had its status as a sponsoring entity revoked.

(4) The IRS may revoke a sponsoring entity's status with respect to one or more sponsored FFIs based on the provisions of

paragraphs (k)(2), (3), and (4) of this section (describing notice of event of default, remediation, and termination procedures) if there is an event of default as defined in paragraph (k)(1) of this section.

(5) A sponsoring entity is not liable for any failure to comply with the obligations contained in paragraph (f)(1)(i)(F)(3) of this section unless the sponsoring entity is a withholding agent that is separately liable for the failure to withhold on or report with respect to a payment made by the sponsoring entity on behalf of the sponsored FFI. A sponsored FFI will remain liable for any failure of its sponsoring entity to comply with the obligations contained in paragraph (f)(1)(i)(F)(3) of this section that the sponsoring entity has agreed to undertake on behalf of the FFI, even if the sponsoring entity is also a withholding agent and is itself separately liable for the failure to withhold on or report with respect to a payment made by the sponsoring entity on behalf of the sponsored FFI. The same tax, interest, or penalties, however, shall not be collected more than once.

(ii) ***Procedural requirements for registered deemed-compliant FFIs.*** A registered deemed-compliant FFI described in paragraph (f)(1)(i)(A) through (E) of this section may use one or more agents to perform the necessary due diligence to identify its account holders and to take any required action associated with obtaining and maintaining its deemed-compliant status. The FFI, however, remains responsible for ensuring that the requirements for its deemed-compliant status are met. Unless otherwise provided in this section, a registered deemed-compliant FFI described in paragraph (f)(1)(i)(A) through (E) of this section is required to -

(A) Register with the IRS pursuant to procedures prescribed by the IRS and agree to comply with the terms of its registered deemed-compliant status.

(B) Have its responsible officer certify, on or before July 1 of the calendar year following the end of each certification period, that all of the requirements for the deemed-compliant status claimed by the FFI have been satisfied during the certification period. The responsible officer may certify collectively for the FFI's expanded affiliated group that all of the requirements for the deemed-compliant status claimed by each member of the expanded affiliated group that is a registered deemed-compliant FFI (other than a member that is a reporting Model 1

FFI or deemed-compliant FFI under an applicable Model 1 IGA) have been satisfied. The certification must be made on the form and in the manner prescribed by the IRS. The first certification period begins on the later of the date the FFI registers as a deemed-compliant FFI and is issued a GIIN, or June 30, 2014, and ends at the close of the third full calendar year following that date. Each subsequent certification period is the three calendar year period following the previous certification period.

(C) Maintain in its records the confirmation from the IRS of the FFI's registration as a deemed-compliant FFI and GIIN or such other information as the IRS specifies in forms or other guidance; and

(D) Agree to notify the IRS if there is a change in circumstances that would make the FFI ineligible for the deemed-compliant status for which it has registered, and to do so within six months of the change in circumstances unless the FFI is able to resume its eligibility for its registered-deemed compliant status within the six month notification period.

We set this out for completeness, though do not propose to delve further into the US legislation (since we are not qualified to do so). Instead we consider the like definition in the Model 1 IGA itself. Annex II effectively contains a number of provisions that treat certain entities as Deemed-Compliant FFIs. These are the following:

i) Small or Limited Scope Financial Institutions that Qualify as Deemed-Compliant FFIs:[39]
   a. Financial institutions with a local client base (see Annex II, III(A) for the requirements in this respect);
   b. Local banks (Annex II, III(B));
   c. Financial Institutions with only low value accounts (Annex II<, III(C));
   d. Qualified credit card issuers (Annex II, III(D));
ii) Investment Entities qualifying as Deemed-Compliant FFIs:[40]
   a. Trustee-Documented Trusts (Annex II, IV(A));
   b. Sponsored Investment Entities and Controlled Foreign Corporations (Annex II, IV(B));
   c. Sponsored closely held investment vehicles (Annex II, IV(C));
   d. Investment advisers and investment managers (Annex II, IV(D));
   e. Collective investment vehicles (Annex II, IV(E)).

[39] Annex II, III

[40] Anex II, IV

This category requires further consideration, since it contains the definitions of certain deemed-compliant entities that are likely to occur – or be useful – on a regular basis. Additionally, such entities are subject to 'special rules' found in Annex II, IV(F).

A 'Trustee-Documented Trust' is a trust established under the laws of [FATCA Partner] to the extent that the trustee of the trust is a Reporting US Financial Institution, Reporting Model 1 FFI, or Participating FFI and reports all information required to be reported pursuant to the Agreement with respect to all US Reportable Accounts of the trust. This definition allows a trustee – in effect – to be the reporting entity for a trust that would otherwise be a Reporting FI itself. Thus the trust itself does not have to report, all of the reporting requirements are complied with and a certain degree of administrative burden is reduced for trustees of multiple trusts (such as trust companies).

In respect of a Trustee-Documented Trust as a Nonreporting Financial Institution, HMRC say:[41]

> Trustee-documented trusts are Nonreporting Financial Institutions (NRFI) for both regimes.
>
> A trustee-documented trust is a trust that is a Financial Institution [see IEIM400600] where the trustee of the trust is itself a Reporting Financial Institution [see IEIM402100] and reports all the information required in respect of the Reportable Accounts [see IEIM401520] of the trust. In such a case, the trust itself becomes a Nonreporting Financial Institution and the trustee Financial Institution must report the information that the trust would otherwise have reported. Therefore, when registering a trustee-documented trust on the HMRC portal, the trustee is the reporting Financial Institution, not the trust.
>
> For FATCA reporting, the GIIN used will be that of the trustee, acting in its capacity as trustee.
>
> The trustee must identify, when reporting, the trustee-documented trust in respect of which it fulfils the reporting and due diligence obligations. This should be done by including the trust name in the account number or account identifier section when completing the return for the trust on the HMRC portal. For an xml report the trust name should be included in the account number or account identifier field of the schema

In relation to Sponsored Investment Entities Annex II, IV(B) provides:

---

41 IEIM400990

A Financial Institution described in subparagraph B(1) or B(2) of this section having a sponsoring entity that complies with the requirements of subparagraph B(3) of this section.

1. A Financial Institution is a sponsored investment entity if (a) it is an Investment Entity established in [FATCA Partner] that is not a qualified intermediary, withholding foreign partnership, or withholding foreign trust pursuant to relevant US Treasury Regulations; and (b) an Entity has agreed with the Financial Institution to act as a sponsoring entity for the Financial Institution.

2. A Financial Institution is a sponsored controlled foreign corporation if (a) the Financial Institution is a controlled foreign corporation[6] organized under the laws of [FATCA Partner] that is not a qualified intermediary, withholding foreign partnership, or withholding foreign trust pursuant to relevant US Treasury Regulations; (b) the Financial Institution is wholly owned, directly or indirectly, by a Reporting US Financial Institution that agrees to act, or requires an affiliate of the Financial Institution to act, as a sponsoring entity for the Financial Institution; and (c) the Financial Institution shares a common electronic account system with the sponsoring entity that enables the sponsoring entity to identify all Account Holders and payees of the Financial Institution and to access all account and customer information maintained by the Financial Institution including, but not limited to, customer identification information, customer documentation, account balance, and all payments made to the Account Holder or payee.

3. The sponsoring entity complies with the following requirements:
   a) The sponsoring entity is authorized to act on behalf of the Financial Institution (such as a fund manager, trustee, corporate director, or managing partner) to fulfill applicable registration requirements on the IRS FATCA registration website;
   b) The sponsoring entity has registered as a sponsoring entity with the IRS on the IRS FATCA registration website;
   c) If the sponsoring entity identifies any US Reportable Accounts with respect to the Financial Institution, the sponsoring entity registers the Financial Institution pursuant to applicable registration requirements on the IRS FATCA registration website on or before the later of December 31, 2015 and the date that is 90 days after such a US Reportable Account is first identified;
   d) The sponsoring entity agrees to perform, on behalf of the Financial Institution, all due diligence, withholding, reporting, and other requirements that the Financial

Institution would have been required to perform if it were a Reporting [FATCA Partner] Financial Institution;7

e) The sponsoring entity identifies the Financial Institution and includes the identifying number of the Financial Institution (obtained by following applicable registration requirements on the IRS FATCA registration website) in all reporting completed on the Financial Institution's behalf; and

f) The sponsoring entity has not had its status as a sponsor revoked

Thus, a similar position to that of a Trustee-Documented Trust can be achieved for non-trust entities where they enter into an agreement with a sponsor. In this respect, the Jersey Guidance explains[42]:

> This category consolidates the due diligence, reporting and withholding for a group of Financial Institutions into, for example, trustee, fund manager, fund administrator, general partner, corporate director, transfer agent, company service provider or US financial institution (with regard to its controlled foreign corporations), being the Sponsoring Entity. A sponsored investment entity is an entity that has a contractual arrangement for its due diligence and reporting responsibilities to be carried out by a sponsoring entity. A Sponsoring Entity does not need to be a Financial Institution[43].
>
> The Sponsoring Entity must register with the IRS and must register each of the Sponsored Investment Entities that it manages, to the extent that the Sponsored Investment Entities hold Reportable Accounts.
>
> The Sponsoring Entity must undertake all of the FATCA compliance, such as account identification and documentation, on behalf of the Sponsored Investment Entities for which it acts, or where appropriate it can use a third party to undertake the obligations on its behalf. The Sponsoring Entity will need to ensure that new investors in the Sponsored Investment Entities that it manages are appropriately documented for FATCA purposes.
>
> Where a Sponsoring Entity acts on behalf of a range of Sponsored Investment Entities, the classification of an account as a New Account or a Preexisting Account can be done by reference to whether the account is new to the Sponsoring Entity (e.g. the fund manager) and not the Sponsored Investment Entity (e.g. the fund). This will avoid the need for a Sponsoring Entity to have to obtain

---

[42] At paragraph 4.2.1

[43] We are not sure that this is correct; however, it is unlikely to arise regularly in practice so we do not consider it further.

documentation from the same account holder repeatedly, where that account holder is invested in more than one of the Sponsored Investment Entities managed by that Sponsoring Entity...

A Jersey Sponsoring Entity will report on all Reportable Accounts held by the Sponsored Investment Entities that it sponsors. If the Sponsoring Entity ceases to be authorised by the Sponsored Investment Entity, and it is not replaced with another such arrangement, the obligations will become the obligations of the Sponsored Investment Entity...

The 'Special Rules' in question are the following:[44]

The following rules apply to an Investment Entity:

1) With respect to interests in an Investment Entity that is a collective investment vehicle described in paragraph E of this section, the reporting obligations of any Investment Entity (other than a Financial Institution through which interests in the collective investment vehicle are held) shall be deemed fulfilled.
2) With respect to interests in:
    a) An Investment Entity established in a Partner Jurisdiction that is regulated as a collective investment vehicle, all of the interests in which (including debt interests in excess of $50,000) are held by or through one or more exempt beneficial owners, Active NFFEs described in subparagraph B(4) of section VI of Annex I, US Persons that are not Specified US Persons, or Financial Institutions that are not Nonparticipating Financial Institutions; or
    b) An Investment Entity that is a qualified collective investment vehicle under relevant US Treasury Regulations;

    the reporting obligations of any Investment Entity that is a [FATCA Partner] Financial Institution (other than a Financial Institution through which interests in the collective investment vehicle are held) shall be deemed fulfilled.

3) With respect to interests in an Investment Entity established in [FATCA Partner] that is not described in paragraph E or subparagraph F(2) of this section, consistent with [for Model 1A and Model 1B Nonreciprocal IGAs: paragraph 3 of Article 5][for Model 1B Standalone IGA: paragraph 4 of Article 5] of the Agreement, the reporting obligations of all other Investment Entities with respect to such interests shall be deemed fulfilled if the information required to be reported by the first-mentioned Investment Entity pursuant to the Agreement with respect to such interests is reported by such Investment Entity or another person.

---

44 Annex II, IV(F)

4) An Investment Entity established in [FATCA Partner] that is regulated as a collective investment vehicle shall not fail to qualify under paragraph E or subparagraph F(2) of this section, or otherwise as a deemed-compliant FFI, solely because the collective investment vehicle has issued physical shares in bearer form, provided that:
   a) The collective investment vehicle has not issued, and does not issue, any physical shares in bearer form[45] after December 31, 2012;
   b) The collective investment vehicle retires all such shares upon surrender;
   c) The collective investment vehicle (or a Reporting [FATCA Partner] Financial Institution) performs the due diligence procedures set forth in Annex I and reports any information required to be reported with respect to any such shares when such shares are presented for redemption or other payment; and
   d) The collective investment vehicle has in place policies and procedures to ensure that such shares are redeemed or immobilized as soon as possible, and in any event prior to January 1, 2017.

An exempt beneficial owner is one which:

> Exempt beneficial owner. The term exempt beneficial owner means any person described in 1.1471-6(b) through (g) or that is otherwise treated as an exempt beneficial owner pursuant to a Model 1 IGA or Model 2 IGA.

The relevant US legislation[46] provides:

> (b) Any foreign government, any political subdivision of a foreign government, or any wholly owned agency or instrumentality of any one or more of the foregoing. Solely for purposes of this section and except as provided in paragraph (h) of this section, the term any foreign government, any political subdivision of a foreign government, or any wholly owned agency or instrumentality of any one or more of the foregoing means only the integral parts, controlled entities, and political subdivisions of a foreign sovereign.
>
> (1) Integral part. Solely for purposes of this paragraph (b), an integral part of a foreign sovereign is any person, body of persons, organization, agency, bureau, fund,

[45] Bearer shares have long – and with some justification – been treated with suspicion. Thus it is unsurprising to see that they are given a special, less favourable, status in FATCA and indeed in other AEOI regimes.

[46] CFR, 1.1471-6(b) – (g)

instrumentality, or other body, however designated, that constitutes a governing authority of a foreign country. The net earnings of the governing authority must be credited to its own account or to other accounts of the foreign sovereign, with no portion inuring to the benefit of any private person as defined in paragraph (b)(3) of this section. An integral part does not include any individual who is a sovereign, official, or administrator acting in a private or personal capacity. All the facts and circumstances will be taken into account in determining whether an individual is acting in a private or personal capacity.

(2) Controlled entity. Solely for purposes of this paragraph (b), a controlled entity means an entity that is separate in form from a foreign sovereign or that otherwise constitutes a separate juridical entity, provided that -

(i) The entity is wholly owned and controlled by one or more foreign sovereigns directly or indirectly through one or more controlledentities;

(ii) The entity's net earnings are credited to its own account or to other accounts of one or more foreign sovereigns, with no portion of its income inuring to the benefit of any private person as defined in paragraph (b)(3) of this section; and

(iii) The entity's assets vest in one or more foreign sovereigns upon dissolution.

(3) Inurement to the benefit of private persons. Solely for purposes of this paragraph (b) -

(i) Income does not inure to the benefit of private persons if such persons (within the meaning of section 7701(a)(1)) are the intended beneficiaries of a governmental program carried on by a foreign sovereign, and the program activities constitute governmental functions under the regulations under section 892.

(ii) Income is considered to inure to the benefit of private persons if such income benefits -

(A) Private persons through the use of a governmental entity as a conduit for personal investment;

(B) Private persons through the use of a governmental entity to conduct a commercial business, such as a commercial banking business, that provides financial services to private persons; or

(C) Private persons who divert such income from its intended use by exerting influence or control through means explicitly or implicitly approved of by the foreign sovereign.

(c) Any international organization or any wholly owned agency or instrumentality thereof. Except as provided in paragraph (h) of this section, the term any international organization or any wholly owned agency or instrumentality thereof means any entity described in section 7701(a)(18). The term also includes any intergovernmental or supranational organization -

(1) That is comprised primarily of foreign governments;

(2) That is recognized as an intergovernmental or supranational organization under a foreign law similar to 22 U.S.C. 288-288f or that has in effect a headquarters agreement with a foreign government; and

(3) Whose income does not inure to the benefit of private persons under the principles of paragraph (b)(3)(ii) of this section, as applied to the intergovernmental or supranational organization in place of the government or governmental entity.

(d) Foreign central bank of issue -

(1) In general. Solely for purposes of this section and except as provided in paragraph (h) of this section, the term foreign central bank of issue means an institution that is by law or government sanction the principal authority, other than the government itself, issuing instruments intended to circulate as currency. Such an institution is generally the custodian of the banking reserves of the country under whose law it is organized.

(2) Separate instrumentality. A foreign central bank of issue may include an instrumentality that is separate from a foreign government, whether or not owned in whole or in part by a foreign government. For example, foreign banks organized along the lines of, and performing functions similar to, the Federal Reserve System qualify as foreign central banks of issue for purposes of this section.

(3) Bank for International Settlements. The Bank for International Settlements is a foreign central bank of issue for purposes of this section.

(4) Income on certain transactions. Solely for purposes of determining whether an entity is an exempt beneficial owner of a paymentunder this paragraph (d), a foreign central bank of issue is a beneficial owner with respect to income earned on cash and securities, including cash and securities held as collateral or securities held in connection with a securities lending transaction, held by the foreign central bank of issue in the ordinary course of its operations as a central bank of issue.

(e) Governments of U.S. territories. Except as provided in paragraph (h) of this section, whether a person or entity constitutes a government of a U.S. territory for purposes of this section is determined by applying principles analogous to those set forth in paragraph (b) of this section.

(f) Certain retirement funds. A fund is described in this paragraph (f) if it is described in paragraphs (f)(1) through (6) of this section. In addition, if a withholding agent may treat a withholdable payment as made to a payee that is a retirement fund in accordance with § 1.1471-3, then the withholding agent may also treat such retirement fund as the beneficial owner of the payment. See § 1.1471-3(d)(9)(ii).

(1) Treaty-qualified retirement fund. A fund established in a country with which the United States has an income tax treaty in force, provided that the fund is entitled to benefits under such treaty on income that it derives from sources within the United States (or would be entitled to such benefits if it derived any such income) as a resident of the other country that satisfies any applicable limitation on benefitsrequirement, and is operated principally to administer or provide pension or retirement benefits;

(2) Broad participation retirement fund. A fund established to provide retirement, disability, or death benefits, or any combination thereof, to beneficiaries that are current or former employees (or persons designated by such employees) of one or more employers in consideration for services rendered, provided that the fund -

(i) Does not have a single beneficiary with a right to more than five percent of the fund's assets;

(ii) Is subject to government regulation and provides annual information reporting about its beneficiaries to the relevant tax authorities in the country in which the fund is established or operates; and

(iii) Satisfies one or more of the following requirements -

(A) The fund is generally exempt from tax on investment income under the laws of the country in which it is established or operates due to its status as a retirement or pension plan;

(B) The fund receives at least 50 percent of its total contributions (other than transfers of assets from accounts described in § 1.1471-5(b)(2)(i)(A) (referring to retirement and pension accounts), from retirement and pension accounts described in an applicable Model 1 or Model 2 IGA, or from other retirement funds described in this paragraph

(f) or in an applicable Model 1 or Model 2 IGA) from the sponsoring employers;

(C) Distributions or withdrawals from the fund are allowed only upon the occurrence of specified events related to retirement, disability, or death (except rollover distributions to accounts described in § 1.1471-5(b)(2)(i)(A) (referring to retirement and pension accounts), to retirement and pension accounts described in an applicable Model 1 or Model 2 IGA, or to other retirement funds described in this paragraph (f) or in an applicable Model 1 or Model 2 IGA), or penalties apply to distributions or withdrawals made before such specified events; or

(D) Contributions (other than certain permitted make-up contributions) by employees to the fund are limited by reference to earned income of the employee or may not exceed $50,000 annually.

(3) Narrow participation retirement funds. A fund established to provide retirement, disability, or death benefits to beneficiaries that are current or former employees (or persons designated by such employees) of one or more employers in consideration for prior servicesrendered, provided that -

(i) The fund has fewer than 50 participants;

(ii) The fund is sponsored by one or more employers and each of these employers are not investment entities or passive NFFEs;

(iii) Employee and employer contributions to the fund (other than transfers of assets from other retirement plans described in paragraph (f)(1) of this section, from accounts described in § 1.1471-5(b)(2)(i)(A) (referring to retirement and pension accounts), or retirement and pension accounts described in an applicable Model 1 or Model 2 IGA) are limited by reference to earned income and compensation of the employee, respectively;

(iv) Participants that are not residents of the country in which the fund is established or operated are not entitled to more than 20 percent of the fund's assets; and

(v) The fund is subject to government regulation and provides annual information reporting about its beneficiaries to the relevant tax authorities in the country in which the fund is established or operates.

(4) Fund formed pursuant to a plan similar to a section 401(a) plan. A fund formed pursuant to a pension plan that would

meet the requirements of section 401(a), other than the requirement that the plan be funded by a trust created or organized in the United States.

(5) Investment vehicles exclusively for retirement funds. A fund established exclusively to earn income for the benefit of one or more retirement funds described in paragraphs (f)(1) through (5) of this section or in an applicable Model 1 or Model 2 IGA, accounts described in § 1.1471-5(b)(2)(i)(A) (referring to retirement and pension accounts), or retirement and pension accounts described in an applicable Model 1 or Model 2 IGA.

(6) Pension fund of an exempt beneficial owner. A fund established and sponsored by an exempt beneficial owner described in paragraph (b), (c), (d), or (e) of this section or an exempt beneficial owner (other than a fund that qualifies as an exempt beneficial owner) described in an applicable Model 1 or Model 2 IGA to provide retirement, disability, or death benefits to beneficiaries or participants that are current or former employees of the exempt beneficial owner (or persons designated by such employees), or that are not current or former employees, but the benefits provided to such beneficiaries or participants are in consideration of personal services performed for the exempt beneficial owner.

(7) Example. FP, a foreign pension fund established in Country X, is generally exempt from income taxation in Country X, and is operated principally to provide retirement benefits in such country. The U.S.-Country X income tax treaty is identical in all material respects to the 2006 U.S. model income tax convention. FP is a resident of Country X under Article 4(2)(a) and a qualified person under Article 22(2)(d) of the U.S.-Country X income tax treaty. Therefore, FP is a pension fund described in paragraph (f)(1) of this section.

(g) Entities wholly owned by exempt beneficial owners. A person is described in this paragraph (g) if it is an FFI solely because it is an investment entity, each direct holder of an equity interest in the investment entity is an exempt beneficial owner described in paragraph (b), (c), (d), (e), (f), or (g) of this section or an exempt beneficial owner described in an applicable Model 1 or Model 2 IGA, and each direct holderof a debt interest in the investment entity is either a depository institution (with respect to a loan made to such entity), an exempt beneficial owner described in paragraph (b), (c), (d), (e), (f), or (g) of this section, or an exempt beneficial owner described in an applicable Model 1 or Model 2 IGA

The Model 1 IGA treats the following as Exempt Beneficial Owners[47]:

A. **Governmental Entity.** The government of [FATCA Partner], any political subdivision of [FATCA Partner] (which, for the avoidance of doubt, includes a state, province, county, or municipality), or any wholly owned agency or instrumentality of [FATCA Partner] or any one or more of the foregoing (each, a '[FATCA Partner] Governmental Entity'). This category is comprised of the integral parts, controlled entities, and political subdivisions of [FATCA Partner]

1. An integral part of [FATCA Partner] means any person, organization, agency, bureau, fund, instrumentality, or other body, however designated, that constitutes a governing authority of [FATCA Partner]. The net earnings of the governing authority must be credited to its own account or to other accounts of [FATCA Partner], with no portion inuring to the benefit of any private person. An integral part does not include any individual who is a sovereign, official, or administrator acting in a private or personal capacity.

2. A controlled entity means an Entity that is separate in form from [FATCA Partner] or that otherwise constitutes a separate juridical entity, provided that:
   a) The Entity is wholly owned and controlled by one or more [FATCA Partner] Governmental Entities directly or through one or more controlled entities;
   b) The Entity's net earnings are credited to its own account or to the accounts of one or more [FATCA Partner] Governmental Entities, with no portion of its income inuring to the benefit of any private person; and
   c) The Entity's assets vest in one or more [FATCA Partner] Governmental Entities upon dissolution.

3. Income does not inure to the benefit of private persons if such persons are the intended beneficiaries of a governmental program, and the program activities are performed for the general public with respect to the common welfare or relate to the administration of some phase of government. Notwithstanding the foregoing, however, income is considered to inure to the benefit of private persons if the income is derived from the use of a governmental entity to conduct a commercial business,

---

[47] Annex II, I

such as a commercial banking business, that provides financial services to private persons

B. **International Organization.** Any international organization or wholly owned agency or instrumentality thereof. This category includes any intergovernmental organization (including a supranational organization) (1) that is comprised primarily of non-US governments; (2) that has in effect a headquarters agreement with [FATCA Partner]; and (3) the income of which does not inure to the benefit of private persons.

C. **Central Bank.** An institution that is by law or government sanction the principal authority, other than the government of [FATCA Partner] itself, issuing instruments intended to circulate as currency. Such an institution may include an instrumentality that is separate from the government of [FATCA Partner], whether or not owned in whole or in part by [FATCA Partner]

These categories are likely to be of only tangential interest to most. However, they do demonstrate the circularity of the FATCA definitions, since these are partially or wholly covered by CFR.

A further category of Exempt Beneficial Owners is found in Annex II, which provides:

A. **Treaty-Qualified Retirement Fund.** A fund established in [FATCA Partner], provided that the fund is entitled to benefits under an income tax treaty between [FATCA Partner] and the United States on income that it derives from sources within the United States (or would be entitled to such benefits if it derived any such income) as a resident of [FATCA Partner] that satisfies any applicable limitation on benefits requirement, and is operated principally to administer or provide pension or retirement benefits.][3]

B. **Broad Participation Retirement Fund.** A fund established in [FATCA Partner] to provide retirement, disability, or death benefits, or any combination thereof, to beneficiaries that are current or former employees (or persons designated by such employees) of one or more employers in consideration for services rendered, provided that the fund:

1. Does not have a single beneficiary with a right to more than five percent of the fund's assets;
2. Is subject to government regulation and provides annual information reporting about its beneficiaries to the relevant tax authorities in [FATCA Partner]; and
3. Satisfies at least one of the following requirements:

a) The fund is generally exempt from tax in [FATCA Partner] on investment income under the laws of [FATCA Partner] due to its status as a retirement or pension plan;

b) The fund receives at least 50 percent of its total contributions (other than transfers of assets from other plans described in paragraphs A through D of this section or from retirement and pension accounts described in subparagraph A(1) of section V of this Annex II) from the sponsoring employers;

c) Distributions or withdrawals from the fund are allowed only upon the occurrence of specified events related to retirement, disability, or death (except rollover distributions to other retirement funds described in paragraphs A through D of this section or retirement and pension accounts described in subparagraph A(1) of section V of this Annex II), or penalties apply to distributions or withdrawals made before such specified events; or

d) Contributions (other than certain permitted make-up contributions) by employees to the fund are limited by reference to earned income of the employee or may not exceed $50,000 annually, applying the rules set forth in Annex I for account aggregation and currency translation.

C. <u>**Narrow Participation Retirement Fund**</u>. A fund established in [FATCA Partner] to provide retirement, disability, or death benefits to beneficiaries that are current or former employees (or persons designated by such employees) of one or more employers in consideration for services rendered, provided that:

1. The fund has fewer than 50 participants;
2. The fund is sponsored by one or more employers that are not Investment Entities or Passive NFFEs;
3. The employee and employer contributions to the fund (other than transfers of assets from treaty-qualified retirement funds described in paragraph A of this section or retirement and pension accounts described in subparagraph A(1) of section V of this Annex II) are limited by reference to earned income and compensation of the employee, respectively;
4. Participants that are not residents of [FATCA Partner] are not entitled to more than 20 percent of the fund's assets; and
5. The fund is subject to government regulation and provides annual information reporting about its beneficiaries to the relevant tax authorities in [FATCA Partner].

D. **Pension Fund of an Exempt Beneficial Owner.** A fund established in [FATCA Partner] by an exempt beneficial owner to provide retirement, disability, or death benefits to beneficiaries or participants that are current or former employees of the exempt beneficial owner (or persons designated by such employees), or that are not current or former employees, if the benefits provided to such beneficiaries or participants are in consideration of personal services performed for the exempt beneficial owner.

E. **Investment Entity Wholly Owned by Exempt Beneficial Owners.** An Entity that is a [FATCA Partner] Financial Institution solely because it is an Investment Entity, provided that each direct holder of an Equity Interest in the Entity is an exempt beneficial owner, and each direct holder of a debt interest in such Entity is either a Depository Institution (with respect to a loan made to such Entity) or an exempt beneficial owner.

Thus it can be seen that these categories are of potential broader relevance. HMRC say[48]:

FATCA

Under the US IGA, retirement funds are defined by reference to the UK/US Double Taxation Agreement. Pension scheme is defined as any plan, scheme, fund, trust or other arrangement established in the UK which is:

1) Generally exempt from income taxation in the UK; and
2) Operated principally to administer or provide pension or retirement benefits or to earn income for the benefit of one or more such arrangements.

This will include all UK pension schemes or other arrangements registered with HMRC under Part 4 of the Finance Act 2004, including those deemed registered by HMRC. The Pension Protection Fund is also listed as a NRFI.

Pension funds or pension schemes covered by IRS Announcement 2005-30, 2005-1 C.B. 988, on the Mutual Agreement on UK Pension Agreements are also included. Details of these can be found at http://www.irs.gov/irb/2005-18_IRB/ar10.html#d0e1440

Finally, to round off the definitions in relation to Financial Institutions:

(o) The term 'Reporting [FATCA Partner] Financial Institution' means any [FATCA Partner] Financial Institution that is not a Nonreporting [FATCA Partner] Financial Institution.

---

[48] IEIM400920:

(p) The term 'Reporting US Financial Institution' means (i) any Financial Institution that is resident in the United States, but excluding any branch of such Financial Institution that is located outside the United States, and (ii) any branch of a Financial Institution not resident in the United States, if such branch is located in the United States, provided that the Financial Institution or branch has control, receipt, or custody of income with respect to which information is required to be exchanged under subparagraph (2)(b) of Article 2 of this Agreement.

(q) The term 'Nonreporting [FATCA Partner] Financial Institution' means any [FATCA Partner] Financial Institution, or other Entity resident in [FATCA Partner], that is described in Annex II as a Nonreporting [FATCA Partner] Financial Institution or that otherwise qualifies as a deemed-compliant FFI or an exempt beneficial owner under relevant US Treasury Regulations [in effect on the date of signature of this Agreement.

In addition, Article 4(3) provides:

> Specific Treatment of [FATCA Partner] Retirement Plans. The United States shall treat as deemed-compliant FFIs or exempt beneficial owners, as appropriate, for purposes of sections 1471 and 1472 of the US Internal Revenue Code, [FATCA Partner] retirement plans described in Annex II. For this purpose, a [FATCA Partner] retirement plan includes an Entity established or located in, and regulated by, [FATCA Partner], or a predetermined contractual or legal arrangement, operated to provide pension or retirement benefits or earn income for providing such benefits under the laws of [FATCA Partner] and regulated with respect to contributions, distributions, reporting, sponsorship, and taxation

Finally (in this respect), Article 4(4) provides:

> Identification and Treatment of Other Deemed-Compliant FFIs and Exempt Beneficial Owners. The United States shall treat each Nonreporting [FATCA Partner] Financial Institution as a deemed-compliant FFI or as an exempt beneficial owner, as appropriate, for purposes of section 1471 of the US Internal Revenue Code.

Here it is helpful to remember that a Nonreporting Financial Institution is not one that simply doesn't report but one that is not required to report. This is how such Financial Institutions are not pulled into the US withholding regime.

5.9 NFFE

The term an 'NFFE' means any Non-US Entity that is not an FFI as defined in relevant US Treasury Regulations, and also includes any Non-US Entity that is resident in the United Kingdom or other Partner Jurisdiction and that is not a Financial Institution.

A 'Passive NFFE' means any NFFE that is not an Active NFFE.

An 'Active NFFE' means any NFFE that meets any of the following criteria:

(i) less than 50 percent of the NFFE's gross income for the preceding calendar year or other appropriate reporting period is passive income and less than 50 percent of the assets held by the NFFE during the preceding calendar year or other appropriate reporting period are assets that produce or are held for the production of passive income;

(ii) the stock of the NFFE is regularly traded on an established securities market or the NFFE is a Related Entity of an Entity the stock of which is traded on an established securities market;

(iii) the NFFE is not yet operating a business and has no prior operating history, but is investing capital into assets with the intent to operate a business other than that of a Financial Institution; provided, that the NFFE shall not qualify for this exception after the date that is 24 months after the date of the initial organization of the NFFE;

(iv) a charity.

5.10 Financial accounts

The term 'Financial Account' means an account maintained by a Financial Institution, and includes:

(i) in the case of an Entity that is a Financial Institution solely because it is an Investment Entity, any equity or debt interest (other than interests that are regularly traded on an established securities market) in the Financial Institution;

(ii) in the case of a Financial Institution not described in subparagraph 1(s)(1) of this Article, any equity or debt interest in the Financial Institution (other than interests that are regularly traded on an established securities market), if (i) the value of the debt or equity interest is determined, directly or indirectly, primarily by reference to assets that give rise to US Source Withholdable Payments, and (ii) the class of interests was established with a purpose of avoiding reporting in accordance with this Agreement; and

(iii) any Cash Value Insurance Contract and any Annuity Contract issued or maintained by a Financial Institution, other than a noninvestment-linked, nontransferable immediate life annuity that is issued to an individual and monetizes a pension or disability benefit provided under an account that is excluded from the definition of Financial Account in Annex II.

HMRC explain[49]:

> A financial account is an account maintained by a Financial Institution. Only accounts that fall within any of the 5 categories of financial account defined by the automatic exchange of information agreements need to be reviewed. Where such an account is held by

[49] IEIM401500

a Reportable Person [see IEIM402010] it becomes a Reportable Account [see IEIM401520]

These five types of account are:

(i) Depository Accounts ('includes any commercial, checking, savings, time, or thrift account, or an account that is evidenced by a certificate of deposit, thrift certificate, investment certificate, certificate of indebtedness, or other similar instrument maintained by a Financial Institution in the ordinary course of a banking or similar business. A Depository Account also includes an amount held by an insurance company pursuant to a guaranteed investment contract or similar agreement to pay or credit interest thereon');

(ii) Custodial Accounts ('means an account (other than an Insurance Contract or Annuity Contract) for the benefit of another person that holds any financial instrument or contract held for investment (including, but not limited to, a share or stock in a corporation, a note, bond, debenture, or other evidence of indebtedness, a currency or commodity transaction, a credit default swap, a swap based upon a nonfinancial index, a notional principal contract, an Insurance Contract or Annuity Contract, and any option or other derivative instrument)');

(iii) Cash Value Insurance Contract;

(iv) Annuity Contract ('means a contract under which the issuer agrees to make payments for a period of time determined in whole or in part by reference to the life expectancy of one or more individuals. The term also includes a contract that is considered to be an Annuity Contract in accordance with the law, regulation, or practice of the jurisdiction in which the contract was issued, and under which the issuer agrees to make payments for a term of years'); and

(v) Equity or debt interest (where 'Equity Interest' 'means a contract under which the issuer agrees to make payments for a period of time determined in whole or in part by reference to the life expectancy of one or more individuals. The term also includes a contract that is considered to be an Annuity Contract in accordance with the law, regulation, or practice of the jurisdiction in which the contract was issued, and under which the issuer agrees to make payments for a term of years').

Thus it can be seen that the definition of Financial Account extends far beyond what one would normally consider to be an account, particularly in relation to an 'equity or debt interest' in an Investment Entity. In relation to this category of 'account' HMRC say:

> Equity and debt interests are financial accounts only to the extent that they are interests in an Investment Entity[50].
>
> Where an entity is an Investment Entity solely because it acts on behalf of a customer by investing, managing or administering

[50] IEIM400760

financial assets in the name of the customer, the debt and equity interests in the Investment Entity are not financial accounts provided it only renders investment advice to, or manages portfolios for, the customer.

An equity interest may vary depending on the nature of the Investment Entity. In the case of an Investment Entity that is a partnership an equity interest is either a capital or profits interest in the partnership.

In the case of a trust an equity interest is any interest held by a person who is treated as a settlor or beneficiary of all or any part of the trust, or any other natural person exercising ultimate effective control over the trust [see IEIM403400].

A Reportable Person [see IEIM403440] will be treated as being a beneficiary of a trust if such a person has the right to receive a mandatory distribution from the trust. This distribution can be received either directly or indirectly, for example through a nominee; or

Receives a discretionary payment from the trust. Again this receipt can be either directly or indirectly from the trust

This extract – which we consider to be broadly accurate – highlights the broad scope of the treatment of trusts.

The Model 1A IGA continues:

Notwithstanding the foregoing, the term 'Financial Account' does not include any account that is excluded from the definition of Financial Account in Annex II. For purposes of this Agreement, interests are 'regularly traded' if there is a meaningful volume of trading with respect to the interests on an ongoing basis, and an 'established securities market' means an exchange that is officially recognized and supervised by a governmental authority in which the market is located and that has a meaningful annual value of shares traded on the exchange. For the purposes of this subparagraph 1(s), an interest in a Financial Institution is not 'regularly traded' and shall be treated as a Financial Account if the holder of the interest (other than a Financial Institution acting as an intermediary) is registered on the books of such Financial Institution. The preceding sentence will not apply to interests first registered on the books of such Financial Institution to July 1, 2014, and with respect to interests first registered on the books of such Financial Institution on or after July 1, 2014, a Financial Institution is not required to apply the preceding sentence prior to January 1, 2016.

The term 'Equity Interest' means, in the case of a partnership that is a Financial Institution, either a capital or profits interest in the partnership.

The term 'Equity Interest' means, in the case of a trust that is a Financial Institution, an Equity Interest is considered to be held by any person treated as a settlor or beneficiary of all or a portion of the trust, or any other natural person exercising ultimate effective control over the trust. A Specified US Person shall be treated as being a beneficiary of a foreign trust if such Specified US Person has the right to receive directly or indirectly (for example, through a nominee) a mandatory distribution or may receive, directly or indirectly, a discretionary distribution from the trust.

The term 'Controlling Persons' means the natural persons who exercise control over an entity. In the case of a trust, such term means the settlor, the trustees, the protector (if any), the beneficiaries or class of beneficiaries, and any other natural person exercising ultimate effective control over the trust, and in the case of a legal arrangement other than a trust, such term means persons in equivalent or similar positions.

Accounts excluded from being Financial Accounts pursuant to Annex II[51] are the following:

A. Certain Savings Accounts

1. Retirement and Pension Account. A retirement or pension account maintained in [FATCA Partner] that satisfies the following requirements under the laws of [FATCA Partner].
   a) The account is subject to regulation as a personal retirement account or is part of a registered or regulated retirement or pension plan for the provision of retirement or pension benefits (including disability or death benefits);
   b) The account is tax-favored (i.e., contributions to the account that would otherwise be subject to tax under the laws of [FATCA Partner] are deductible or excluded from the gross income of the account holder or taxed at a reduced rate, or taxation of investment income from the account is deferred or taxed at a reduced rate);
   c) Annual information reporting is required to the tax authorities in [FATCA Partner] with respect to the account;
   d) Withdrawals are conditioned on reaching a specified retirement age, disability, or death, or penalties apply to withdrawals made before such specified events; and
   e) Either (i) annual contributions are limited to $50,000 or less, or (ii) there is a maximum lifetime contribution limit to the account of $1,000,000 or less, in each case applying the rules set forth in Annex I for account aggregation and currency translation.

2. Non-Retirement Savings Accounts. An account maintained in [FATCA Partner] (other than an insurance or Annuity Contract)

[51] Annex II, V

that satisfies the following requirements under the laws of [FATCA Partner].

a) The account is subject to regulation as a savings vehicle for purposes other than for retirement;
b) The account is tax-favored (i.e., contributions to the account that would otherwise be subject to tax under the laws of [FATCA Partner] are deductible or excluded from the gross income of the account holder or taxed at a reduced rate, or taxation of investment income from the account is deferred or taxed at a reduced rate);
c) Withdrawals are conditioned on meeting specific criteria related to the purpose of the savings account (for example, the provision of educational or medical benefits), or penalties apply to withdrawals made before such criteria are met; and
d) Annual contributions are limited to $50,000 or less, applying the rules set forth in Annex I for account aggregation and currency translation.

B. Certain Term Life Insurance Contracts

A life insurance contract maintained in [FATCA Partner] with a coverage period that will end before the insured individual attains age 90, provided that the contract satisfies the following requirements:

1. Periodic premiums, which do not decrease over time, are payable at least annually during the period the contract is in existence or until the insured attains age 90, whichever is shorter;
2. The contract has no contract value that any person can access (by withdrawal, loan, or otherwise) without terminating the contract;
3. The amount (other than a death benefit) payable upon cancellation or termination of the contract cannot exceed the aggregate premiums paid for the contract, less the sum of mortality, morbidity, and expense charges (whether or not actually imposed) for the period or periods of the contract's existence and any amounts paid prior to the cancellation or termination of the contract; and
4. The contract is not held by a transferee for value.

C. Account Held by an Estate

An account maintained in [FATCA Partner] that is held solely by an estate if the documentation for such account includes a copy of the deceased's will or death certificate.

D. Escrow Accounts

An account maintained in [FATCA Partner] established in connection with any of the following:

1. A court order or judgment.
2. A sale, exchange, or lease of real or personal property, provided that the account satisfies the following requirements:
   a) The account is funded solely with a down payment, earnest money, deposit in an amount appropriate to secure an obligation directly related to the transaction, or a similar payment, or is funded with a financial asset that is deposited in the account in connection with the sale, exchange, or lease of the property;
   b) The account is established and used solely to secure the obligation of the purchaser to pay the purchase price for the property, the seller to pay any contingent liability, or the lessor or lessee to pay for any damages relating to the leased property as agreed under the lease;
   c) The assets of the account, including the income earned thereon, will be paid or otherwise distributed for the benefit of the purchaser, seller, lessor, or lessee (including to satisfy such person's obligation) when the property is sold, exchanged, or surrendered, or the lease terminates;
   d) The account is not a margin or similar account established in connection with a sale or exchange of a financial asset; and
   e) The account is not associated with a credit card account.
3. An obligation of a Financial Institution servicing a loan secured by real property to set aside a portion of a payment solely to facilitate the payment of taxes or insurance related to the real property at a later time.
4. An obligation of a Financial Institution solely to facilitate the payment of taxes at a later time.

E. Partner Jurisdiction Accounts

An account maintained in [FATCA Partner] and excluded from the definition of Financial Account under an agreement between the United States and another Partner Jurisdiction to facilitate the implementation of FATCA, provided that such account is subject to the same requirements and oversight under the laws of such other Partner Jurisdiction as if such account were established in that Partner Jurisdiction and maintained by a Partner Jurisdiction Financial Institution in that Partner Jurisdiction

5.11 Financial assets

In relation to Financial Assets, the Implementation Handbook says:

> The definition of Financial Asset in the Standard is consistent with the current US FATCA Regulations except that nondebt direct investments in real property have been specifically excluded from the Standard as a clarification. Jurisdictions could adopt the

approach in the Standard and rely on it for purposes of both the Standard and the Model 1 FATCA IGA.[52]

This could, of course, result in domestic rules requiring an excess of reporting in relation to FATCA. It will be necessary to consult the domestic rules where there is a concern of excess FATCA reporting (and indeed, the USA is unlikely to accept that OECD guidance on the CRS is in any way conclusive of what should be reported under FATCA).

5.12 Obligations (other than reporting) under FATCA

Under the Model 1A IGA, the reporting requirements for the US and the 'FATCA Partner Jurisdiction' are not identical. They are, however, extremely similar. Annex I, I(A) provides:

> [FATCA Partner] shall require that Reporting [FATCA Partner] Financial Institutions apply the due diligence procedures contained in this Annex I to identify US Reportable Accounts and accounts held by Nonparticipating Financial Institutions

The reporting requirements in Annex I do not extend merely to reporting, there is also an obligation for Financial Institutions to conduct certain reviews and identification. These differ, depending on the type of account. This is generally based on the 'risk profile' of the account in question. This is best illustrated by considering the different provisions. The types of accounts considered are:

(i) Preexisting individual accounts;[53]
(ii) New individual accounts;
(iii) Preexisting entity accounts; and
(iv) New entity accounts.

Before going on to discuss the individual procedures, it is important to note that each category is further broken down into subcategories based on the value of the Account in question. However, the identification of the value of such accounts is not straightforward. There are some requirements for aggregation of values. These are found in Annex I, VI, C. In relation to Individual Accounts, this provides:

> **1. Aggregation of Individual Accounts.** For purposes of determining the aggregate balance or value of Financial Accounts held by an individual, a Reporting [FATCA Partner] Financial Institution is required to aggregate all Financial Accounts maintained by the Reporting [FATCA Partner] Financial Institution, or by a Related Entity, but only to the extent that the Reporting [FATCA Partner] Financial Institution's computerised systems link the Financial Accounts by reference to a data element, such as client

---

[52] Page 129

[53] The procedure for preexisting accounts is different in the Model IGAs in relation to the period after 1 July 2014.

> number or taxpayer identification number, and allow account balances or values to be aggregated. Each holder of a jointly held Financial Account shall be attributed the entire balance or value of the jointly held Financial Account for purposes of applying the aggregation requirements described in this paragraph 1.

In relation to Entity Accounts, it provides:

> **2. Aggregation of Entity Accounts**. For purposes of determining the aggregate balance or value of Financial Accounts held by an Entity, a Reporting [FATCA Partner] Financial Institution is required to take into account all Financial Accounts that are maintained by the Reporting [FATCA Partner] Financial Institution, or by a Related Entity, but only to the extent that the Reporting [FATCA Partner] Financial Institution's computerised systems link the Financial Accounts by reference to a data element, such as client number or taxpayer identification number, and allow account balances or values to be aggregated

There is also an additional rule in relation to 'Relationship Managers':[54]

> **3. Special Aggregation Rule Applicable to Relationship Managers.** For purposes of determining the aggregate balance or value of Financial Accounts held by a person to determine whether a Financial Account is a High Value Account, a Reporting [FATCA Partner] Financial Institution is also required, in the case of any Financial Accounts that a relationship manager knows, or has reason to know, to be directly or indirectly owned, controlled, or established (other than in a fiduciary capacity) by the same person, to aggregate all such accounts

These rules should be taken into account whenever applying the limits in the identification of Reportable Accounts.

5.13 Identification of preexisting accounts: individual accounts

In relation to preexisting individual accounts, in most jurisdictions that have adopted FATCA these are now primarily of historic interest. However, they are included here, both because they remain potentially relevant for jurisdictions newly adopting a Model IGA and where there was a failure to comply upon initial adoption of FATCA. There is also, in some cases – see further below – an ongoing obligation in relation to the identification of such accounts, which may render these rules relevant on an ongoing basis.

Preexisting individual accounts are further broken down into categories based on their values. In relation to certain preexisting individual accounts, these were not required to be reviewed, identified or reported:

---

[54] This term appears not to be defined anywhere in the IGA or Annexes.

Unless the Reporting [FATCA Partner] Financial Institution elects otherwise, either with respect to all Preexisting Individual Accounts or, separately, with respect to any clearly identified group of such accounts, where the implementing rules in [FATCA Partner] provide for such an election, the following Preexisting Individual Accounts are not required to be reviewed, identified, or reported as US Reportable Accounts:

1. Subject to subparagraph E(2) of this section, a Preexisting Individual Account with a balance or value that does not exceed $50,000 as of June 30, 2014.
2. Subject to subparagraph E(2) of this section, a Preexisting Individual Account that is a Cash Value Insurance Contract or an Annuity Contract with a balance or value of $250,000 or less as of June 30, 2014.
3. A Preexisting Individual Account that is a Cash Value Insurance Contract or an Annuity Contract, provided the law or regulations of [FATCA Partner] or the United States effectively prevent the sale of such a Cash Value Insurance Contract or an Annuity Contract to US residents (e.g., if the relevant Financial Institution does not have the required registration under US law, and the law of [FATCA Partner] requires reporting or withholding with respect to insurance products held by residents of [FATCA Partner]).
4. A Depository Account with a balance of $50,000 or less

These are low value accounts that were considered to be low risk (or having information in relation to them was perhaps to be considered low reward). However, care should be taken and domestic legislation and guidance taken into account, since the domestic rules or guidance may still require or recommend that such accounts be reported locally[55].

In relation to preexisting individual accounts with a balance/value exceeding $50,000 (unless a Cash Value Insurance Contract or Annuity Contract, where the value is $250,000) but not exceeding $1,000,000, the following is required:

1. **Electronic Record Search**. The Reporting [FATCA Partner] Financial Institution must review electronically searchable data maintained by the Reporting [FATCA Partner] Financial Institution for any of the following US indicia:
    a) Identification of the Account Holder as a US citizen or resident;
    b) Unambiguous indication of a US place of birth;

[55] See, for example, www.gov.uk/guidance/automatic-exchange-of-information-financial-institutions#penalties

c) Current US mailing or residence address (including a US post office box);
d) Current US telephone number;
e) Standing instructions to transfer funds to an account maintained in the United States;
f) Currently effective power of attorney or signatory authority granted to a person with a US address; or
g) An 'in-care-of' or 'hold mail' address that is the sole address the Reporting [FATCA Partner] Financial Institution has on file for the Account Holder. In the case of a Preexisting Individual Account that is a Lower Value Account, an 'in-care-of' address outside the United States or 'hold mail' address shall not be treated as US indicia.

2. If none of the US indicia listed in subparagraph B(1) of this section are discovered in the electronic search, then no further action is required until there is a change in circumstances that results in one or more US indicia being associated with the account, or the account becomes a High Value Account described in paragraph D of this section.

3. If any of the US indicia listed in subparagraph B(1) of this section are discovered in the electronic search, or if there is a change in circumstances that results in one or more US indicia being associated with the account, then the Reporting [FATCA Partner] Financial Institution must treat the account as a US Reportable Account unless it elects to apply subparagraph B(4) of this section and one of the exceptions in such subparagraph applies with respect to that account.

4. Notwithstanding a finding of US indicia under subparagraph B(1) of this section, a Reporting [FATCA Partner] Financial Institution is not required to treat an account as a US Reportable Account if:

a) Where the Account Holder information unambiguously indicates a US place of birth, the Reporting [FATCA Partner] Financial Institution obtains, or has previously reviewed and maintains a record of:
(1) A self-certification that the Account Holder is neither a US citizen nor a US resident for tax purposes (which may be on an IRS Form W-8 or other similar agreed form);

(2) A non-US passport or other government-issued identification evidencing the Account Holder's citizenship or nationality in a country other than the United States; and

(3) A copy of the Account Holder's Certificate of Loss of Nationality of the United States or a reasonable explanation of:
   (a) The reason the Account Holder does not have such a certificate despite relinquishing US citizenship; or
   (b) The reason the Account Holder did not obtain US citizenship at birth.

b) Where the Account Holder information contains a current US mailing or residence address, or one or more US telephone numbers that are the only telephone numbers associated with the account, the Reporting [FATCA Partner] Financial Institution obtains, or has previously reviewed and maintains a record of:
(1) A self-certification that the Account Holder is neither a US citizen nor a US resident for tax purposes (which may be on an IRS Form W-8 or other similar agreed form); and
(2) Documentary evidence, as defined in paragraph D of section VI of this Annex I, establishing the Account Holder's non-US status

c) Where the Account Holder information contains standing instructions to transfer funds to an account maintained in the United States, the Reporting [FATCA Partner] Financial Institution obtains, or has previously reviewed and maintains a record of:
(1) A self-certification that the Account Holder is neither a US citizen nor a US resident for tax purposes (which may be on an IRS Form W-8 or other similar agreed form); and
(2) Documentary evidence, as defined in paragraph D of section VI of this Annex I, establishing the Account Holder's non-US status

d) Where the Account Holder information contains a currently effective power of attorney or signatory authority granted to a person with a US address, has an 'in-care-of' address or 'hold mail' address that is the sole address identified for the Account Holder, or has one or more US telephone numbers (if a non-US telephone number is also associated with the account), the Reporting [FATCA Partner] Financial Institution obtains, or has previously reviewed and maintains a record of:
(1) A self-certification that the Account Holder is neither a US citizen nor a US resident for tax purposes (which may be on an IRS Form W-8 or other similar agreed form); or

(2) Documentary evidence, as defined in paragraph D of section VI of this Annex I, establishing the Account Holder's non-US status

Documentary evidence that is 'acceptable' is set out in VI, E, which provides:

D. Documentary Evidence. For purposes of this Annex I, acceptable documentary evidence includes any of the following:

1. A certificate of residence issued by an authorized government body (for example, a government or agency thereof, or a municipality) of the jurisdiction in which the payee claims to be a resident.
2. With respect to an individual, any valid identification issued by an authorized government body (for example, a government or agency thereof, or a municipality), that includes the individual's name and is typically used for identification purposes.
3. With respect to an Entity, any official documentation issued by an authorized government body (for example, a government or agency thereof, or a municipality) that includes the name of the Entity and either the address of its principal office in the jurisdiction (or US Territory) in which it claims to be a resident or the jurisdiction (or US Territory) in which the Entity was incorporated or organized.
4. With respect to a Financial Account maintained in a jurisdiction with anti-money laundering rules that have been approved by the IRS in connection with a QI agreement (as described in relevant US Treasury Regulations), any of the documents, other than a Form W-8 or W-9, referenced in the jurisdiction's attachment to the QI agreement for identifying individuals or Entities.
5. Any financial statement, third-party credit report, bankruptcy filing, or US Securities and Exchange Commission report.

This review etc. had to be conducted prior to 30 June 2016. Where there is a change of circumstances, additional steps apply[56]:

1. Review of Preexisting Individual Accounts that are Lower Value Accounts for US indicia must be completed by June 30, 2016.
2. If there is a change of circumstances with respect to a Preexisting Individual Account that is a Lower Value Account that results in one or more US indicia described in subparagraph B(1) of this section being associated with the account, then the Reporting [FATCA Partner] Financial Institution must treat the account as

[56] Annex I, C

a US Reportable Account unless subparagraph B(4) of this section applies.

3. Except for Depository Accounts described in subparagraph A(4) of this section, any Preexisting Individual Account that has been identified as a US Reportable Account under this section shall be treated as a US Reportable Account in all subsequent years, unless the Account Holder ceases to be a Specified US Person.

There is a further enhanced review procedure for higher value accounts. Annex I, D provides:

> **Enhanced Review Procedures for Preexisting Individual Accounts With a Balance or Value That Exceeds $1,000,000 as of June 30, 2014, or December 31 of 2015 or Any Subsequent Year ('High Value Accounts').**
>
> 1. **Electronic Record Search.** The Reporting [FATCA Partner] Financial Institution must review electronically searchable data maintained by the Reporting [FATCA Partner] Financial Institution for any of the US indicia described in subparagraph B(1) of this section.
> 2. **Paper Record Search.** If the Reporting [FATCA Partner] Financial Institution's electronically searchable databases include fields for, and capture all of the information described in, subparagraph D(3) of this section, then no further paper record search is required. If the electronic databases do not capture all of this information, then with respect to a High Value Account, the Reporting [FATCA Partner] Financial Institution must also review the current customer master file and, to the extent not contained in the current customer master file, the following documents associated with the account and obtained by the Reporting [FATCA Partner] Financial Institution within the last five years for any of the US indicia described in subparagraph B(1) of this section:
>   a) The most recent documentary evidence collected with respect to the account;
>   b) The most recent account opening contract or documentation;
>   c) The most recent documentation obtained by the Reporting [FATCA Partner] Financial Institution pursuant to AML/KYC Procedures or for other regulatory purposes;
>   d) Any power of attorney or signature authority forms currently in effect; and
>   e) Any standing instructions to transfer funds currently in effect.

Additionally, however, in relation to preexisting accounts there is an exception to the duty to perform the paper record search in Annex I, D(2) where:

Exception Where Databases Contain Sufficient Information. A Reporting [FATCA Partner] Financial Institution is not required to perform the paper record search described in subparagraph D(2) of this section if the Reporting [FATCA Partner] Financial Institution's electronically searchable information includes the following:

a) The Account Holder's nationality or residence status;
b) The Account Holder's residence address and mailing address currently on file with the Reporting [FATCA Partner] Financial Institution;
c) The Account Holder's telephone number(s) currently on file, if any, with the Reporting [FATCA Partner] Financial Institution;
d) Whether there are standing instructions to transfer funds in the account to another account (including an account at another branch of the Reporting [FATCA Partner] Financial Institution or another Financial Institution);
e) Whether there is a current 'in-care-of' address or 'hold mail' address for the Account Holder; and
f) Whether there is any power of attorney or signatory authority for the account.

Finally, there is an additional requirement to treat any High Value Account (i.e. those in excess of $1,000,000) as a US Reportable Account where the following condition is met:

Relationship Manager Inquiry for Actual Knowledge. In addition to the electronic and paper record searches described above, the Reporting [FATCA Partner] Financial Institution must treat as a US Reportable Account any High Value Account assigned to a relationship manager (including any Financial Accounts aggregated with such High Value Account) if the relationship manager has actual knowledge that the Account Holder is a Specified US Person.

Where US Indicia are found the following applies:

Effect of Finding US Indicia.

a) If none of the US indicia listed in subparagraph B(1) of this section are discovered in the enhanced review of High Value Accounts described above, and the account is not identified as held by a Specified US Person in subparagraph D(4) of this section, then no further action is required until there is a change in circumstances that results in one or more US indicia being associated with the account.
b) If any of the US indicia listed in subparagraph B(1) of this section are discovered in the enhanced review of High Value Accounts described above, or if there is a subsequent change in circumstances that results in one or more US indicia being associated with the account, then the Reporting [FATCA

Partner] Financial Institution must treat the account as a US Reportable Account unless it elects to apply subparagraph B(4) of this section and one of the exceptions in such subparagraph applies with respect to that account

US Indicia in Annex I, B are the following:

(i) Identification of the Account Holder as a US citizen or resident;
(ii) Unambiguous indication of a US place of birth;
(iii) Current US mailing or residence address (including a US post office box);
(iv) Current US telephone number;
(v) Standing instructions to transfer funds to an account maintained in the United States;
(vi) Currently effective power of attorney or signatory authority granted to a person with a US address; and
(vii) An 'in-care-of' or 'hold mail' address that is the sole address the Reporting [FATCA Partner] Financial Institution has on file for the Account Holder[57].

Annex I, E provides additional procedures for High Value Accounts, providing:

1. If a Preexisting Individual Account is a High Value Account as of June 30, 2014, the Reporting [FATCA Partner] Financial Institution must complete the enhanced review procedures described in paragraph D of this section with respect to such account by June 30, 2015. If based on this review such account is identified as a US Reportable Account on or before December 31, 2014, the Reporting [FATCA Partner] Financial Institution must report the required information about such account with respect to 2014 in the first report on the account and on an annual basis thereafter. In the case of an account identified as a US Reportable Account after December 31, 2014 and on or before June 30, 2015, the Reporting [FATCA Partner] Financial Institution is not required to report information about such account with respect to 2014, but must report information about the account on an annual basis thereafter.
2. If a Preexisting Individual Account is not a High Value Account as of June 30, 2014, but becomes a High Value Account as of the last day of 2015 or any subsequent calendar year, the Reporting [FATCA Partner] Financial Institution must complete the enhanced review procedures described in paragraph D of this section with respect to such account within six months after the last day of the calendar year in which the account becomes a

---

[57] However, in the case of a Preexisting Individual Account that is a Lower Value Account, a non-US 'in-care-of' address or any 'hold mail' address is not to be treated as a US Indicia.

High Value Account. If based on this review such account is identified as a US Reportable Account, the Reporting [FATCA Partner] Financial Institution must report the required information about such account with respect to the year in which it is identified as a US Reportable Account and subsequent years on an annual basis, unless the Account Holder ceases to be a Specified US Person.

3. Once a Reporting [FATCA Partner] Financial Institution applies the enhanced review procedures described in paragraph D of this section to a High Value Account, the Reporting [FATCA Partner] Financial Institution is not required to re-apply such procedures, other than the relationship manager inquiry described in subparagraph D(4) of this section, to the same High Value Account in any subsequent year.
4. If there is a change of circumstances with respect to a High Value Account that results in one or more US indicia described in subparagraph B(1) of this section being associated with the account, then the Reporting [FATCA Partner] Financial Institution must treat the account as a US Reportable Account unless it elects to apply subparagraph B(4) of this section and one of the exceptions in such subparagraph applies with respect to that account.
5. A Reporting [FATCA Partner] Financial Institution must implement procedures to ensure that a relationship manager identifies any change in circumstances of an account. For example, if a relationship manager is notified that the Account Holder has a new mailing address in the United States, the Reporting [FATCA Partner] Financial Institution is required to treat the new address as a change in circumstances and, if it elects to apply subparagraph B(4) of this section, is required to obtain the appropriate documentation from the Account Holder

Thus – and while it should come as no surprise – there is an ongoing obligation. This is not only in relation to High Value Accounts (thought the section heading in this respect is misleading since it mentions only High Value Accounts), but also in relation to other accounts that become High Value Accounts. Thus, there remains an ongoing duty in relation to such accounts, which is somewhat poorly defined.

There is a further exception, however, in relation to preexisting individual accounts, which provides:

F. Preexisting Individual Accounts That Have Been Documented for Certain Other Purposes. A Reporting [FATCA Partner] Financial Institution that has previously obtained documentation from an Account Holder to establish the Account Holder's status as neither a US citizen nor a US resident in order to meet its obligations under a qualified intermediary, withholding foreign partnership, or withholding foreign trust agreement with the IRS, or to fulfill its obligations under chapter 61 of Title 26 of the United States Code, is not required to perform the procedures described in subparagraph B(1) of this section with respect to Lower Value Accounts or subparagraphs D(1) through D(3) of this section with respect to High Value Accounts

5.14 Identification of preexisting accounts: preexisting entity accounts

These are dealt with in Annex I, Part IV. This explains:

> Preexisting Entity Accounts. The following rules and procedures apply for purposes of identifying US Reportable Accounts and accounts held by Nonparticipating Financial Institutions among Preexisting Accounts held by Entities ('Preexisting Entity Accounts')

It continues:

> A. **Entity Accounts Not Required to Be Reviewed, Identified or Reported.** Unless the Reporting [FATCA Partner] Financial Institution elects otherwise, either with respect to all Preexisting Entity Accounts or, separately, with respect to any clearly identified group of such accounts, where the implementing rules in [FATCA Partner] provide for such an election, a Preexisting Entity Account with an account balance or value that does not exceed $250,000 as of June 30, 2014, is not required to be reviewed, identified, or reported as a US Reportable Account until the account balance or value exceeds $1,000,000

Thus account balance prior to 30 June 2014 is relevant: accounts below the threshold at this date do not become reviewable, identifiable or reportable even if they exceed the $250,000 threshold until they exceed the second threshold of $1,000,000. It is not clear why entity accounts are thought to be less at risk of abuse than individual accounts and so meriting a higher initial threshold.

This requirement is supplemented by B, which states:

> B. **Entity Accounts Subject to Review.** A Preexisting Entity Account that has an account balance or value that exceeds $250,000 as of June 30, 2014, and a Preexisting Entity Account that does not exceed $250,000 as of June 30, 2014 but the account balance or value of which exceeds $1,000,000 as of the last day of 2015 or any subsequent calendar year, must be reviewed in accordance with the procedures set forth in paragraph D of this section.

However, before we get to paragraph D, Annex I clarifies what accounts will be reportable in paragraph C, which says:

> C. **Entity Accounts With Respect to Which Reporting Is Required.** With respect to Preexisting Entity Accounts described in paragraph

> B of this section, only accounts that are held by one or more Entities that are Specified US Persons, or by Passive NFFEs with one or more Controlling Persons who are US citizens or residents, shall be treated as US Reportable Accounts. In addition, accounts held by Nonparticipating Financial Institutions shall be treated as accounts for which aggregate payments as described in subparagraph 1(b) of Article 4 of the Agreement are reported to the [FATCA Partner] Competent Authority

There is no equivalent paragraph in relation to preexising individual accounts. This is probably because the aim of the procedure in each case is to identify the underlying US citizens and residents with ultimate ownership (though not in a "traditional" common law sense); this is more straightforward where those individuals are the direct owner of the Account in question. Thus, reportable preexisting entity accounts are restricted to those:

i) Held by one or more Entities that are Specified US Persons[58]; or
ii) Held by Passive NFFEs with one or more US citizen or resident Controlling Persons.

The review process for preexisting entity accounts is undoubtedly complex. Annex I, IV(D) begins by explaining:

> D. **Review Procedures for Identifying Entity Accounts With Respect to Which Reporting Is Required.** For Preexisting Entity

[58] 'Specified US Person' means (see the IGA, Article 1(1)(ff)): '... a US Person, other than: (i) a corporation the stock of which is regularly traded on one or more established securities markets; (ii) any corporation that is a member of the same expanded affiliated group, as defined in section 1471(e)(2) of the US Internal Revenue Code, as a corporation described in clause (i); (iii) the United States or any wholly owned agency or instrumentality thereof; (iv) any State of the United States, any US Territory, any political subdivision of any of the foregoing, or any wholly owned agency or instrumentality of any one or more of the foregoing; (v) any organization exempt from taxation under section 501(a) of the US Internal Revenue Code or an individual retirement plan as defined in section 7701(a)(37) of the US Internal Revenue Code; (vi) any bank as defined in section 581 of the US Internal Revenue Code; (vii) any real estate investment trust as defined in section 856 of the US Internal Revenue Code; (viii) any regulated investment company as defined in section 851 of the US Internal Revenue Code or any entity registered with the US Securities and Exchange Commission under the Investment Company Act of 1940 (15 USC. 80a-64); (ix) any common trust fund as defined in section 584(a) of the US Internal Revenue Code; (x) any trust that is exempt from tax under section 664(c) of the US Internal Revenue Code or that is described in section 4947(a)(1) of the US Internal Revenue Code; (xi) a dealer in securities, commodities, or derivative financial instruments (including notional principal contracts, futures, forwards, and options) that is registered as such under the laws of the United States or any State; (xii) a broker as defined in section 6045(c) of the US Internal Revenue Code; or (xiii) any tax-exempt trust under a plan that is described in section 403(b) or section 457(g) of the US Internal Revenue Code'. This is undoubtedly unhelpful to those lawyers trying to decipher the IGA in 'FATCA Partner' jurisdictions. Hopefully if you are dealing with such an entity you will know, or it will be necessary to take legal advice on the position from the relevant US perspective.

Accounts described in paragraph B of this section, the Reporting [FATCA Partner] Financial Institution must apply the following review procedures to determine whether the account is held by one or more Specified US Persons, by Passive NFFEs with one or more Controlling Persons who are US citizens or residents, or by Nonparticipating Financial Institutions:

1. Determine Whether the Entity Is a Specified US Person.

a) Review information maintained for regulatory or customer relationship purposes (including information collected pursuant to AML/KYC Procedures) to determine whether the information indicates that the Account Holder[59] is a US Person. For this purpose, information indicating that the Account Holder is a US Person includes a US place of incorporation or organization, or a US address.

b) If the information indicates that the Account Holder is a US Person, the Reporting [FATCA Partner] Financial Institution must treat the account as a US Reportable Account unless it obtains a self-certification from the Account Holder (which may be on an IRS Form W-8 or W-9, or a similar agreed form), or reasonably determines based on information in its possession or that is publicly available, that the Account Holder is not a Specified US Person…

Subparagraph (D) continues:

2. Determine Whether a Non-US Entity Is a Financial Institution.

a) Review information maintained for regulatory or customer relationship purposes (including information collected pursuant to AML/KYC Procedures) to determine whether the information indicates that the Account Holder is a Financial Institution.

b) If the information indicates that the Account Holder is a Financial Institution, or the Reporting [FATCA Partner] Financial Institution verifies the Account Holder's Global Intermediary Identification Number on the published IRS FFI list, then the account is not a US Reportable Account…

Thus this aims to reduce any double reporting where two Financial Institutions are separately obliged to report on the same preexisting entity account. Subparagraph (D) then goes on to consider the position for Non-Participating Financial Institutions, providing:

---

[59] IGA, Article 1(dd) defines Account Holder.

Determine Whether a Financial Institution Is a Nonparticipating Financial Institution Payments to Which Are Subject to Aggregate Reporting Under Subparagraph 1(b) of Article 4 of the Agreement.

a) Subject to subparagraph D(3)(b) of this section, a Reporting [FATCA Partner] Financial Institution may determine that the Account Holder is a [FATCA Partner] Financial Institution or other Partner Jurisdiction Financial Institution if the Reporting [FATCA Partner] Financial Institution reasonably determines that the Account Holder has such status on the basis of the Account Holder's Global Intermediary Identification Number on the published IRS FFI list or other information that is publicly available or in the possession of the Reporting [FATCA Partner] Financial Institution, as applicable. In such case, no further review, identification, or reporting is required with respect to the account.

b) If the Account Holder is a [FATCA Partner] Financial Institution or other Partner Jurisdiction Financial Institution treated by the IRS as a Nonparticipating Financial Institution, then the account is not a US Reportable Account, but payments to the Account Holder must be reported as contemplated in subparagraph 1(b) of Article 4 of the Agreement.

c) If the Account Holder is not a [FATCA Partner] Financial Institution or other Partner Jurisdiction Financial Institution, then the Reporting [FATCA Partner] Financial Institution must treat the Account Holder as a Nonparticipating Financial Institution payments to which are reportable under subparagraph 1(b) of Article 4 of the Agreement, unless the Reporting [FATCA Partner] Financial Institution:

(1) Obtains a self-certification (which may be on an IRS Form W-8 or similar agreed form) from the Account Holder that it is a certified deemed-compliant FFI, or an exempt beneficial owner, as those terms are defined in relevant US Treasury Regulations; or

(2) In the case of a participating FFI or registered deemed-compliant FFI, verifies the Account Holder's Global Intermediary Identification Number on the published IRS FFI list…

Again, subparagraph (a) is aimed at reduction of double reporting and allows a simple exclusion on the basis of the existence of a GIIN for the Account Holder Matters then become more complex. Paragraph (D) continues to consider the position in relation to NFFEs, providing:

Determine Whether an Account Held by an NFFE Is a US Reportable Account. With respect to an Account Holder of a Preexisting Entity Account that is not identified as either a US Person or a Financial Institution, the Reporting [FATCA Partner] Financial Institution must identify (i) whether the Account Holder has Controlling Persons, (ii) whether the Account Holder is a Passive NFFE, and (iii) whether any of the Controlling Persons of the Account Holder is a US citizen or resident. In making these determinations the Reporting [FATCA Partner] Financial Institution must follow the guidance in subparagraphs D(4)(a) through D(4)(d) of this section in the order most appropriate under the circumstances.

a) For purposes of determining the Controlling Persons of an Account Holder, a Reporting [FATCA Partner] Financial Institution may rely on information collected and maintained pursuant to AML/KYC Procedures.
b) For purposes of determining whether the Account Holder is a Passive NFFE, the Reporting [FATCA Partner] Financial Institution must obtain a self-certification (which may be on an IRS Form W-8 or W-9, or on a similar agreed form) from the Account Holder to establish its status, unless it has information in its possession or that is publicly available, based on which it can reasonably determine that the Account Holder is an Active NFFE.
c) For purposes of determining whether a Controlling Person of a Passive NFFE is a US citizen or resident for tax purposes, a Reporting [FATCA Partner] Financial Institution may rely on:
   (1) Information collected and maintained pursuant to AML/KYC Procedures in the case of a Preexisting Entity Account held by one or more NFFEs with an account balance or value that does not exceed $1,000,000; or
   (2) A self-certification (which may be on an IRS Form W-8 or W-9, or on a similar agreed form) from the Account Holder or such Controlling Person in the case of a Preexisting Entity Account held by one or more NFFEs with an account balance or value that exceeds $1,000,000.
d) If any Controlling Person of a Passive NFFE is a US citizen or resident, the account shall be treated as a US Reportable Account

The first step is to identify three things:

(i) Whether the Account Holder has Controlling Persons;
(ii) Whether the Account Holder is a passive NFFE; and
(iii) Whether any of the Account Holder or its Controlling Persons is a US resident or citizen.

This must be done by reference to the remainder of D(4). It clarifies that it does not have to be done in the order set out in that subparagraph but instead in the order appropriate in the circumstances. Thus, one can take steps to determine whether the Account Holder is a passive NFFE before identifying its Controlling Persons, if any. Again, self-certification is important in this process.

Annex I also specifies a timescale for review, with IV(E) stating:

> E. **Timing of Review and Additional Procedures Applicable to Preexisting Entity Accounts.**
>
> 1. Review of Preexisting Entity Accounts with an account balance or value that exceeds $250,000 as of June 30, 2014 must be completed by June 30, 2016.
> 2. Review of Preexisting Entity Accounts with an account balance or value that does not exceed $250,000 as of June 30, 2014, but exceeds $1,000,000 as of December 31 of 2015 or any subsequent year, must be completed within six months after the last day of the calendar year in which the account balance or value exceeds $1,000,000.
> 3. If there is a change of circumstances with respect to a Preexisting Entity Account that causes the Reporting [FATCA Partner] Financial Institution to know, or have reason to know, that the self-certification or other documentation associated with an account is incorrect or unreliable, the Reporting [FATCA Partner] Financial Institution must redetermine the status of the account in accordance with the procedures set forth in paragraph D of this section

5.15 Obligations in relation to new accounts: new individual accounts

It should be noted in this respect that 'new accounts' are not simply accounts that are newly opened – though these are of course subject to the relevant requirements for new accounts – but also applies to any account opened on or after 1 July 2014, irrespective of when the relevant IGA came into force between the parties:

> III. New Individual Accounts. The following rules and procedures apply for purposes of identifying US Reportable Accounts among Financial Accounts held by individuals and opened on or after July 1, 2014 ('New Individual Accounts')

Initially, Annex I, Part III effectively removes certain limited accounts from the identification process altogether, subject to domestic legislation electing not to take advantage of this position, saying:

> A. **Accounts Not Required to Be Reviewed, Identified, or Reported.** Unless the Reporting [FATCA Partner] Financial Institution elects otherwise, either with respect to all New Individual Accounts or, separately, with respect to any clearly identified group of such accounts, where the implementing rules in [FATCA Partner] provide

for such an election, the following New Individual Accounts are not required to be reviewed, identified, or reported as US Reportable Accounts:

1. A Depository Account unless the account balance exceeds $50,000 at the end of any calendar year or other appropriate reporting period.
2. A Cash Value Insurance Contract unless the Cash Value exceeds $50,000 at the end of any calendar year or other appropriate reporting period

Of course, such accounts will still have to be kept under a certain degree of review because their value will have to be assessed on at least an annual basis (though see further below) to ensure that they remain under $50,000. Two further points should be noted. First, the only accounts that are removed from this process are low value Cash Value Insurance Contracts and Depository Accounts.

Secondly, because some jurisdictions may consider it preferable not to permit an election by Financial Institutions to remove such accounts from the process, it will be essential to check the national rules in question, to ensure that such accounts remain subject to this exception under the domestic legislation.

Part III continues:

> B. **Other New Individual Accounts.** With respect to New Individual Accounts not described in paragraph A of this section, upon account opening (or within 90 days after the end of the calendar year in which the account ceases to be described in paragraph A of this section), the Reporting [FATCA Partner] Financial Institution must obtain a self-certification, which may be part of the account opening documentation, that allows the Reporting [FATCA Partner] Financial Institution to determine whether the Account Holder is resident in the United States for tax purposes (for this purpose, a US citizen is considered to be resident in the United States for tax purposes, even if the Account Holder is also a tax resident of another jurisdiction) and confirm the reasonableness of such self-certification based on the information obtained by the Reporting [FATCA Partner] Financial Institution in connection with the opening of the account, including any documentation collected pursuant to AML/KYC Procedures.

The introduction to B makes several important points:

(i) The requirement to continue to review excepted accounts within paragraph A requires an annual review, since when the value of such an account exceeds the $50,000 there is only 90 days from the end of the calendar year in which the amount is exceeded in which to obtain the self-certification;

(ii) A US citizen is a resident of the US even where they are resident in another place (this is broadly consistent with the approach in the US double tax treaties); and

(iii) The Financial Institution cannot simply rely on the self-certification; the self-certification itself must enable the Financial Institution to confirm the reasonableness of the self-certification by cross reference (we infer) with the information needed and obtained by the Financial Institution to open the account in question, including AML/KYC documents[60].

Paragraph B then continues:

> 1. If the self-certification establishes that the Account Holder is resident in the United States for tax purposes, the Reporting [FATCA Partner] Financial Institution must treat the account as a US Reportable Account and obtain a self-certification that includes the Account Holder's US TIN (which may be an IRS Form W-9 or other similar agreed form).
>
> 2. If there is a change of circumstances with respect to a New Individual Account that causes the Reporting [FATCA Partner] Financial Institution to know, or have reason to know, that the original self-certification is incorrect or unreliable, the Reporting [FATCA Partner] Financial Institution cannot rely on the original self-certification and must obtain a valid self-certification that establishes whether the Account Holder is a US citizen or resident for US tax purposes. If the Reporting [FATCA Partner] Financial Institution is unable to obtain a valid self-certification, the Reporting [FATCA Partner] Financial Institution must treat the account as a US Reportable Account.

Thus, where the Financial Institution comes to an awareness that the self-certification is incorrect or unreliable, the default position is to treat the account as a US Reportable Account.

5.16 Obligations in relation to new accounts: new entity accounts

In this respect the relevant rules are found in Annex I, V, which states:

> New Entity Accounts. The following rules and procedures apply for purposes of identifying US Reportable Accounts and accounts held by Nonparticipating Financial Institutions among Financial Accounts held by Entities and opened on or after July 1, 2014 ('New Entity Accounts')

---

[60] Additionally, Annex I, VI(A) provides: 'A. **Reliance on Self-Certifications and Documentary Evidence**. A Reporting [FATCA Partner] Financial Institution may not rely on a self-certification or documentary evidence if the Reporting [FATCA Partner] Financial Institution knows or has reason to know that the self-certification or documentary evidence is incorrect or unreliable.'

Again, it should be noted that 'new' in this context simply means accounts opened after 30 June 2014 not merely accounts that are new in the everyday sense of the word. V continues:

> Entity Accounts Not Required to Be Reviewed, Identified or Reported. Unless the Reporting [FATCA Partner] Financial Institution elects otherwise, either with respect to all New Entity Accounts or, separately, with respect to any clearly identified group of such accounts, where the implementing rules in [FATCA Partner] provide for such election, a credit card account or a revolving credit facility treated as a New Entity Account is not required to be reviewed, identified, or reported, provided that the Reporting [FATCA Partner] Financial Institution maintaining such account implements policies and procedures to prevent an account balance owed to the Account Holder that exceeds $50,000

This is not dissimilar to the rules in relation to new individual accounts, although the categories of cases are more obscurely drafted, and are probably narrower. Thus, most new entity accounts will need to be reviewed. V continues:

> **B. Other New Entity Accounts.** With respect to New Entity Accounts not described in paragraph A of this section, the Reporting [FATCA Partner] Financial Institution must determine whether the Account Holder is: (i) a Specified US Person; (ii) a [FATCA Partner] Financial Institution or other Partner Jurisdiction Financial Institution; (iii) a participating FFI, a deemed-compliant FFI, or an exempt beneficial owner, as those terms are defined in relevant US Treasury Regulations; or (iv) an Active NFFE or Passive NFFE.
>
> 1. Subject to subparagraph B(2) of this section, a Reporting [FATCA Partner] Financial Institution may determine that the Account Holder is an Active NFFE, a [FATCA Partner] Financial Institution, or other Partner Jurisdiction Financial Institution if the Reporting [FATCA Partner] Financial Institution reasonably determines that the Account Holder has such status on the basis of the Account Holder's Global Intermediary Identification Number or other information that is publicly available or in the possession of the Reporting [FATCA Partner] Financial Institution, as applicable.
> 2. If the Account Holder is a [FATCA Partner] Financial Institution or other Partner Jurisdiction Financial Institution treated by the IRS as a Nonparticipating Financial Institution, then the account is not a US Reportable Account, but payments to the Account Holder must be reported as contemplated in subparagraph 1(b) of Article 4 of the Agreement.
> 3. In all other cases, a Reporting [FATCA Partner] Financial Institution must obtain a self-certification from the Account

Holder to establish the Account Holder's status Based on the self-certification, the following rules apply:

a) If the Account Holder is a Specified US Person, the Reporting [FATCA Partner] Financial Institution must treat the account as a US Reportable Account.

b) If the Account Holder is a Passive NFFE, the Reporting [FATCA Partner] Financial Institution must identify the Controlling Persons as determined under AML/KYC Procedures, and must determine whether any such person is a US citizen or resident on the basis of a self-certification from the Account Holder or such person. If any such person is a US citizen or resident, the Reporting [FATCA Partner] Financial Institution must treat the account as a US Reportable Account.

c) If the Account Holder is: (i) a US Person that is not a Specified US Person; (ii) subject to subparagraph B(3)(d) of this section, a [FATCA Partner] Financial Institution or other Partner Jurisdiction Financial Institution; (iii) a participating FFI, a deemed-compliant FFI, or an exempt beneficial owner, as those terms are defined in relevant US Treasury Regulations; (iv) an Active NFFE; or (v) a Passive NFFE none of the Controlling Persons of which is a US citizen or resident, then the account is not a US Reportable Account, and no reporting is required with respect to the account.

d) If the Account Holder is a Nonparticipating Financial Institution (including a [FATCA Partner] Financial Institution or other Partner Jurisdiction Financial Institution treated by the IRS as a Nonparticipating Financial Institution), then the account is not a US Reportable Account, but payments to the Account Holder must be reported as contemplated in subparagraph 1(b) of Article 4 of the Agreement

5.17 Reporting under a Model 1A IGA

While there are effectively two sets of obligations on Reporting Financial Institutions under FATCA – the first to identify (and monitor) accounts and the second to report, these are (somewhat confusingly) not all contained together. As we have previously stated, the layout of FATCA may appear confusing to those not used to American-style drafting[61] and this is another unfortunate quirk. The reporting obligations are contained in the body of the IGA itself at Article 2, while the requirements for identification are included in Annex I (as set out at length above).

---

[61] Indeed, it may appear confusing to those raised in this tradition, but we are not able to comment on such a proposition, neither author having been so raised.

Article 2 explains:

> 1. Subject to the provisions of Article 3 of this Agreement, each Party shall obtain the information specified in paragraph 2 of this Article with respect to all Reportable Accounts and shall annually exchange this information with the other Party on an automatic basis pursuant to the provisions of Article [] of the [Convention/TIEA]

This explains the prerequisite to have certain international provisions already in place for FATCA to function; the basis for exchange is found not in the rules in the IGA but in the exchange provisions in either a TIEA or a double taxation convention.[62] The IGA itself simply sets the parameters of what is to be exchanged, and when. The 'gateway' through which this information passes is the TIEA or double tax convention.

Article 2 continues to provide what must be reported by the 'FATCA Partner':

> 2. The information to be obtained and exchanged is:
>
> a) In the case of [FATCA Partner] with respect to each US Reportable Account of each Reporting [FATCA Partner] Financial Institution:
>
> (1) the name, address, and US TIN of each Specified US Person that is an Account Holder of such account and, in the case of a Non-US Entity that, after application of the due diligence procedures set forth in Annex I, is identified as having one or more Controlling Persons that is a Specified US Person, the name, address, and US TIN (if any) of such entity and each such Specified US Person;
>
> (2) the account number (or functional equivalent in the absence of an account number);
>
> (3) the name and identifying number of the Reporting [FATCA Partner] Financial Institution;
>
> (4) the account balance or value (including, in the case of a Cash Value Insurance Contract or Annuity Contract, the Cash Value or surrender value) as of the end of the relevant calendar year or other appropriate reporting period or, if the account was closed during such year, immediately before closure;
>
> (5) in the case of any Custodial Account:
>
> (A) the total gross amount of interest, the total gross amount of dividends, and the total gross amount of

[62] This is just one of the very many reasons why exchange of information provisions in these types of agreement form a crucial part of the exchange process; none of the mechanisms discussed can be considered in isolation from such provisions.

other income generated with respect to the assets held in the account, in each case paid or credited to the account (or with respect to the account) during the calendar year or other appropriate reporting period; and

(B) the total gross proceeds from the sale or redemption of property paid or credited to the account during the calendar year or other appropriate reporting period with respect to which the Reporting [FATCA Partner] Financial Institution acted as a custodian, broker, nominee, or otherwise as an agent for the Account Holder;

(6) in the case of any Depository Account, the total gross amount of interest paid or credited to the account during the calendar year or other appropriate reporting period; and

(7) in the case of any account not described in subparagraph 2(a)(5) or 2(a)(6) of this Article, the total gross amount paid or credited to the Account Holder with respect to the account during the calendar year or other appropriate reporting period with respect to which the Reporting [FATCA Partner] Financial Institution is the obligor or debtor, including the aggregate amount of any redemption payments made to the Account Holder during the calendar year or other appropriate reporting period

The first four elements apply to all accounts. Article 2(2) then goes on to set out specific additional provisions for each type of account. Thus, for all accounts, the following basic information must be provided:

(i) the name, address, and US TIN of each Specified US Person that is an Account Holder;
(ii) for a Non-US Entity[63] that, after application of the due diligence procedures set forth in Annex I, is identified as having one or more Controlling Persons that is a Specified US Person, the name, address, and US TIN (if any) of such entity and each such Specified US Person;
(iii) Account number or functional equivalent;[64]
(iv) the name and identifying number of the Reporting Financial Institution;

[63] This is added as if as an afterthought to the main provision about Account Holders. In practice, identifying Controlling Persons of such entities will be of immense importance.

[64] Again, the 'functional equivalent' appears as an unimportant afterthought; given the breadth of the meaning assigned to 'Account'many Accounts will be required to be identified by a functional equivalent.

(v) the account balance or value[65] at the end of the calendar year/reporting period or at closure, where appropriate.

There are then three separate sets of additional criteria: for Custodial Accounts, Depository Accounts and all other accounts. In relation to Custodial Accounts, in addition to the above:

(i) Total gross interest, dividends and other income paid or credited to the Account in the relevant reporting period; and
(ii) Total gross sale or redemption proceeds of property paid or credited to the Account.

In relation to Depository Accounts, it is simply required to report the gross amount of income paid or credited in the reporting period. In relation to all other Accounts, it is necessary to report total gross amount paid or credited to the Account Holder where the Reporting Financial Institution is the obligor/debtor.

Article 2 then moves on to discuss what a Reporting US Financial Institution will have to report to the FATCA Partner. It provides:

> b) In the case of the United States, with respect to each [FATCA Partner] Reportable Account of each Reporting US Financial Institution:
> (1) the name, address, and [FATCA Partner] TIN of any person that is a resident of [FATCA Partner] and is an Account Holder of the account;
> (2) the account number (or the functional equivalent in the absence of an account number);
> (3) the name and identifying number of the Reporting US Financial Institution;
> (4) the gross amount of interest paid on a Depository Account;
> (5) the gross amount of US source dividends paid or credited to the account; and
> (6) the gross amount of other US source income paid or credited to the account, to the extent subject to reporting under chapter 3 of subtitle A or chapter 61 of subtitle F of the US Internal Revenue Code

This bears some comparison with what is being supplied to the US This looks somewhat simpler and less extensive, however, in practice it is considered not to be very different. In relation to the basic information in both cases:

[65] For a Cash Value Insurance Contract or Annuity Contract, this includes the Cash Value or surrender value.

In relation to Account Holders, this is the same, since it is necessary to provide the TIN of any Account Holder resident in the FATCA Partner:[66]

(i) The key difference here is in relation to Entities, where there is no requirement to identify Controlling Persons of Entity Account Holders and report on them. Thus, the position is not equivalent for an Entity, but to give an example, it could be considered equivalent for an individual Account Holder;
(ii) The remaining general requirements are broadly similar; and
(iii) It is difficult to say whether or not the types of income on which it is necessary to report are equivalent, since this is – again unhelpfully – done by reference to the US Internal Revenue Code. The Chapters of the IRC referred to are entitled 'withholding of tax on non-resident aliens and foreign corporations' and 'information and returns'. Unfortunately, a discussion of what remains reportable under these Chapters is beyond the scope of this book but this highlights an additional difficulty; where the scope of the reporting is by reference to US provisions, this makes it difficult for those operating in the non-US FATCA Partner to operate the provisions. In this case, this is a more minor concern, since this is information to be reported by US Financial Institutions. However, it does leave the non-US adviser with the difficult job of explaining what will be reported on by a US Financial Institution.

However, the Model 1A IGA itself acknowledges that the level of exchange is not reciprocal. Article 6(1) says:

> 1. Reciprocity. The Government of the United States acknowledges the need to achieve equivalent levels of reciprocal automatic information exchange with [FATCA Partner]. The Government of the United States is committed to further improve transparency and enhance the exchange relationship with [FATCA Partner] by pursuing the adoption of regulations and advocating and supporting relevant legislation to achieve such equivalent levels of reciprocal automatic information exchange

Despite this, we do continue to take the view that the functional reciprocity of the level of exchange (and its equivalence with CRS) should be considered on a case-by-case basis, not simply on whether the requirements – in the case of reciprocity – and the equivalence – in the case of CRS – are identical overall. In our view in both circumstances, the correct question is whether or not in the individual circumstances there is equivalence.

---

[66] While in addition to this the FATCA Partner is required to provide name and address, it is suggested that this is unlikely to be functionally different provided that the TIN can be used to identify this information by the FATCA Partner.

5.18 Model 1A IGA: withholding and penalties

Some jurisdictions have introduced their own regimes in relation to penalties for failure to comply, with the domestic legislation enacting FATCA into national law.[67] These are – at present – beyond the scope of this book, however, they should be borne in mind and are another example of why it is always important to consult, not only the relevant IGA but also the domestic provisions and guidance. As can be seen from the UK Regulations cited above, the domestic penalties, though capable in aggregate of being large, are relatively minor in relation to minor infractions. The main 'penalty' in this respect is the application of withholding tax.

The IGA, Article 4 provides:

> 1. <u>**Treatment of Reporting [FATCA Partner] Financial Institutions.**</u> Each Reporting [FATCA Partner] Financial Institution shall be treated as complying with, and not subject to withholding under, section 1471 of the US Internal Revenue Code if [FATCA Partner] complies with its obligations under Articles 2 and 3 of this Agreement with respect to such Reporting [FATCA Partner] Financial Institution, and the Reporting [FATCA Partner] Financial Institution:
>
> a) identifies US Reportable Accounts and reports annually to the [FATCA Partner] Competent Authority the information required to be reported in subparagraph 2(a) of Article 2 of this Agreement in the time and manner described in Article 3 of this Agreement;
>
> b) for each of 2015 and 2016, reports annually to the [FATCA Partner] Competent Authority the name of each Nonparticipating Financial Institution to which it has made payments and the aggregate amount of such payments;
>
> c) complies with the applicable registration requirements on the IRS FATCA registration website;
>
> d) to the extent that a Reporting [FATCA Partner] Financial Institution is (i) acting as a qualified intermediary (for purposes of section 1441 of the US Internal Revenue Code) that has elected to assume primary withholding responsibility under chapter 3 of subtitle A of the US Internal Revenue Code, (ii) a foreign partnership that has elected to act as a withholding foreign partnership (for purposes of both sections 1441 and 1471 of the US Internal Revenue Code), or (iii) a foreign trust that has elected to act as a withholding foreign trust (for purposes of both sections 1441 and 1471 of the US Internal Revenue Code), withholds 30 percent of any US Source Withholdable Payment to any Nonparticipating Financial Institution; and

[67] See, for example, the UK International Tax Compliance Regulations 2015, Regulations 13 – 22.

> e) in the case of a Reporting [FATCA Partner] Financial Institution that is not described in subparagraph 1(d) of this Article and that makes a payment of, or acts as an intermediary with respect to, a US Source Withholdable Payment to any Nonparticipating Financial Institution, the Reporting [FATCA Partner] Financial Institution provides to any immediate payor of such US Source Withholdable Payment the information required for withholding and reporting to occur with respect to such payment
>
> Notwithstanding the foregoing, a Reporting [FATCA Partner] Financial Institution with respect to which the conditions of this paragraph 1 are not satisfied shall not be subject to withholding under section 1471 of the US Internal Revenue Code unless such Reporting [FATCA Partner] Financial Institution is treated by the IRS as a Nonparticipating Financial Institution pursuant to subparagraph 2(b) of Article 5 of this Agreement

Thus from this Article the following is apparent:

(i) The 'default position' is that withholding is applicable but Article 4 of the Model 1A IGA removes this withholding for Reporting Financial Institutions;

(ii) However, to obtain this treatment, it is necessary for the Reporting Financial Institution to comply with Article 2 and 3 and also the additional requirements in Article 4.

Provided that the Reporting Financial Institution is complying with all its underlying obligations, this should not pose an additional difficulty: the purpose of the IGA is to remove (a) the requirement to register with the IRS for individual Financial Institutions; and (b) the application of withholding tax, thus it is considered that Article 4(1) does not impose any additional requirement to avoid withholding.

Article 4 continues, in relation to 'recalcitrant accounts':

> 2. **Suspension of Rules Relating to Recalcitrant Accounts.** The United States shall not require a Reporting [FATCA Partner] Financial Institution to withhold tax under section 1471 or 1472 of the US Internal Revenue Code with respect to an account held by a recalcitrant account holder (as defined in section 1471(d)(6) of the US Internal Revenue Code), or to close such account, if the US Competent Authority receives the information set forth in subparagraph 2(a) of Article 2 of this Agreement, subject to the provisions of Article 3 of this Agreement, with respect to such account

A recalcitrant account holder is defined as follows:

> The term 'recalcitrant account holder' means any account holder which—

(A) fails to comply with reasonable requests for the information referred to in subsection (b)(1)(A) or (c)(1)(A), or

(B) fails to provide a waiver described in subsection (b)(1)(F) upon request.

Again, to a non-US audience this does not, perhaps, add much. However, since no withholding is required, it may be the case that this does not really matter (since lack of withholding should be the default).

Article 4(5) discusses Related Entities and Branches that are Nonparticipating Financial Institutions. It provides:

> 5. **Special Rules Regarding Related Entities and Branches That Are Nonparticipating Financial Institutions**. If a [FATCA Partner] Financial Institution, that otherwise meets the requirements described in paragraph 1 of this Article or is described in paragraph 3 or 4 of this Article, has a Related Entity or branch that operates in a jurisdiction that prevents such Related Entity or branch from fulfilling the requirements of a participating FFI or deemed-compliant FFI for purposes of section 1471 of the US Internal Revenue Code or has a Related Entity or branch that is treated as a Nonparticipating Financial Institution solely due to the expiration of the transitional rule for limited FFIs and limited branches under relevant US Treasury Regulations, such [FATCA Partner] Financial Institution shall continue to be in compliance with the terms of this Agreement and shall continue to be treated as a deemed-compliant FFI or exempt beneficial owner, as appropriate, for purposes of section 1471 of the US Internal Revenue Code, provided that:
>
> a) the [FATCA Partner] Financial Institution treats each such Related Entity or branch as a separate Nonparticipating Financial Institution for purposes of all the reporting and withholding requirements of this Agreement and each such Related Entity or branch identifies itself to withholding agents as a Nonparticipating Financial Institution;
>
> b) each such Related Entity or branch identifies its US accounts and reports the information with respect to those accounts as required under section 1471 of the US Internal Revenue Code to the extent permitted under the relevant laws pertaining to the Related Entity or branch; and
>
> c) such Related Entity or branch does not specifically solicit US accounts held by persons that are not resident in the jurisdiction where such Related Entity or branch is located or accounts held by Nonparticipating Financial Institutions that are not established in the jurisdiction where such Related Entity or branch is located, and such Related Entity or branch is not used by the [FATCA Partner] Financial Institution or any other Related Entity to circumvent the obligations under this

> Agreement or under section 1471 of the US Internal Revenue Code, as appropriate

Thus, withholding should only arise in rare circumstances where the Financial Institution is in a Model 1A IGA (and is compliant).

5.19 Model 1B IGA: differences

In addressing the situation under the other Model IGAs, we consider these in comparison to the Model 1A IGA. In this respect, the Model 1B IGA does not differ significantly and in particular the Annexes are the same (i.e. there is only one Model 1 Annex I and one Model 1 Annex II).

However, there are two iterations of Model 1B itself: one for those jurisdictions with an existing DTC or TIEA, and one for those jurisdictions without an existing DTC or TIEA. We start by comparing the Model 1B IGA for countries with an existing DTC or TIEA.

In the first instance, the recitals are slightly different, omitting any mention of 'compliance through mutual assistance in tax matters' and instead referencing 'international tax compliance'. The Model 1B IGA also omits, for obvious reasons, the following words:

> Whereas, the Government of the United States of America collects information regarding certain accounts maintained by US financial institutions held by residents of [FATCA Partner] and is committed to exchanging such information with the Government of [FATCA Partner] and pursuing equivalent levels of exchange, provided that the appropriate safeguards and infrastructure for an effective exchange relationship are in place

References to 'Reporting Financial Institution' (Model 1A IGA, Article 1(1)(n)), 'Nonreporting FATCA Partner Financial Institution' (Model 1A IGA, Article 1(1)(q)) and 'Reporting US Financial Institution' (Model 1A IGA, Article 1(1)(p)) are omitted. This is because the there is only one type of Reporting Financial Institution under the nonreciprocal model: a FATCA Partner Financial Institution. Thus all reference to a Reporting Financial Institution in the Model 1B are to a Reporting FATCA Partner Institution.

(i) In a similar vein, the term 'US Reportable Account' is the only definition of a Reportable Account in the Model 1B IGA ('Reportable Account' and 'FATCA Partner Reportable Account' are omitted; they are simply not needed since there will be no reporting, except on US accounts). The definition of a U.. Reportable Account is the same as that in the Model 1A IGA. Thus, even while there is no reciprocity under Model 1B, the same level of exchange to the USA is required.

(ii) Again, there is no definition of 'FATCA Partner TIN' (one is not required, since it will not be reported by the US).

(iii) Article 2 addresses only obligations to obtain and exchange information on US Reportable Accounts, and thus omits Articles 2(2)(b) and alters the wording of Article 2 generally so that it only applies to US

Reportable Accounts. Again, the obligations in relation to US Reportable Accounts remain the same as under the Model 1A IGA.

(iv) Importantly in Article 3 of the Model 1B IGA, the following subparagraphs are omitted:

8. Following entry into force of this Agreement, each Competent Authority shall provide written notification to the other Competent Authority when it is satisfied that the jurisdiction of the other Competent Authority has in place (i) appropriate safeguards to ensure that the information received pursuant to this Agreement shall remain confidential and be used solely for tax purposes, and (ii) the infrastructure for an effective exchange relationship (including established processes for ensuring timely, accurate, and confidential information exchanges, effective and reliable communications, and demonstrated capabilities to promptly resolve questions and concerns about exchanges or requests for exchanges and to administer the provisions of Article 5 of this Agreement). The Competent Authorities shall endeavor in good faith to meet, prior to September 2015, to establish that each jurisdiction has such safeguards and infrastructure in place.

9. The obligations of the Parties to obtain and exchange information under Article 2 of this Agreement shall take effect on the date of the later of the written notifications described in paragraph 8 of this Article. Notwithstanding the foregoing, if the [FATCA Partner] Competent Authority is satisfied that the United States has the safeguards and infrastructure described in paragraph 8 of this Article in place, but additional time is necessary for the US Competent Authority to establish that [FATCA Partner] has such safeguards and infrastructure in place, the obligation of [FATCA Partner] to obtain and exchange information under Article 2 of this Agreement shall take effect on the date of the written notification provided by the [FATCA Partner] Competent Authority to the US Competent Authority pursuant to paragraph 8 of this Article.

10. This Agreement shall terminate on September 30, 2015, if Article 2 of this Agreement is not in effect for either Party pursuant to paragraph 9 of this Article by that date

There is no wording covering the same matters in the Model 1B IGA. In fact, Article 6 is greatly simplified in the Model 1B IGA, providing only:

> **1. Treatment of Passthru Payments and Gross Proceeds**. The Parties are committed to work together, along with Partner Jurisdictions, to develop a practical and effective
>
> Model 1B IGA Nonreciprocal, Preexisting TIEA or DTC alternative approach to achieve the policy objectives of foreign passthru payment and gross proceeds withholding that minimizes burden.

> **2. Documentation of Accounts Maintained as of the Determination Date**. With respect to US Reportable Accounts maintained by a Reporting [FATCA Partner] Financial Institution as of the Determination Date, [FATCA Partner] commits to establish, by January 1, 2017, for reporting with respect to 2017 and subsequent years, rules requiring Reporting [FATCA Partner] Financial Institutions to obtain the US TIN of each Specified US Person as required pursuant to subparagraph 2(a) of Article 2 of this Agreement

Turning to the Model 1B IGA for jurisdictions that do not have a preexisting DTC or TIEA, this is most straightforwardly compared to the Model 1B IGA for jurisdictions with an existing DTC or TIEA with the USA.

Again, many of the differences between the two Model 1B IGAs simply reflect that there is a different basis for the two agreements. In the early provisions the references to an existing agreement are removed. While this is simple, it is important; the fundamental basis of the exchange of information is different; the 'power' to exchange is not contained in a preexisting agreement. Instead this is found in Article 2. In the Model 1B IGA, where there is no preexisting agreement, it states:

> 1. Subject to the provisions of Article 3 of this Agreement, [FATCA Partner] shall obtain the information specified in paragraph 2 of this Article with respect to all US Reportable Accounts and shall annually exchange this information with the United States on an automatic basis
>
> …

Thus this contains a simple obligation and power to engage in automatic exchange. There is also a mutual agreement process. Model 1B IGA (no preexisting agreement), Article 8 provides:

> 1. Where difficulties or doubts arise between the Parties regarding the implementation, application, or interpretation of this Agreement, the Competent Authorities shall endeavor to resolve the matter by mutual agreement.
> 2. The Competent Authorities may adopt and implement procedures to facilitate the implementation of this Agreement.
> 3. The Competent Authorities may communicate with each other directly for purposes of reaching a mutual agreement under this Article.

Article 9 contains a duty of confidentiality (not included in the IGAs for jurisdictions with a preexisting agreement), providing:

> 1. The [FATCA Partner] Competent Authority shall treat any information received from the United States pursuant to Article 5 of this Agreement as confidential and shall only disclose such

information as may be necessary to carry out its obligations under this Agreement. Such information may be disclosed in connection with court proceedings related to the performance of the obligations of [FATCA Partner] under this Agreement.

2. Information provided to the US Competent Authority pursuant Articles 2 and 5 of this Agreement shall be treated as confidential and may be disclosed only to persons or authorities (including courts and administrative bodies) of the Government of the United States concerned with the assessment, collection, or administration of, the enforcement or prosecution in respect of, or the determination of appeals in relation to, US federal taxes, or the oversight of such functions. Such persons or authorities shall use such information only for such purposes. Such persons may disclose the information in public court proceedings or in judicial decisions. The information may not be disclosed to any other person, entity, authority, or jurisdiction. Notwithstanding the foregoing, where [FATCA Partner] provides prior, written consent, the information may be used for purposes permitted under the provisions of a mutual legal assistance treaty in force between the Parties that allows for the exchange of tax information

5.20 Model 2: differences

The differences between Model 2 and Model 1 IGAs are more significant. In essence, a Model 2 IGA confers similar protection from withholding, but via a quite different mechanism. As we have seen, Financial Institutions in Model 1 IGA jurisdictions are exempt from FATCA withholding on payments they receive, and are not required to withhold amounts for purposes of FATCA on payments they make because of the agreement for the competent authorities of the 'FATCA Partner' to exchange information. As stated, a Model 2 IGA provides a similar protection from withholding, however, here is it because the Financial Institutions in that jurisdiction are required to register with the US IRS and comply with the terms of their agreement to register.

This is a significantly different mechanism, and therefore, the Model 1 and Model 2 IGAs contain more significant differences than the Model 1A and 1B IGAs. Thus, while we still draw a comparison between the two types of agreement, we also simply consider the Model 2 IGA on its own terms. Importantly, however, so far as possible, the defined terminology is the same between the two types of IGA. This is significantly helpful, since if you are familiar with a Model 1 IGA, you will have little difficulty in understanding, and little recourse to, the definitions in the Model 2 IGA.

There are, however, a couple of exceptions to the protection from withholding for Financial Institutions in a Model 2 IGA jurisdiction (these are sometimes referred to as 'residual' and while this term is not inapposite, it is unofficial). These withholding obligations are generally imposed under the agreements between the IRS and the Financial Institution and amount to:

(i) when the Financial Institution makes payments under an obligation in relation to dividends paid on US equities; and
(ii) when the Financial Institution acts as an intermediary, and an underlying payer of a US source 'withholdable payment' fails to withhold in accordance with FATCA.

These are discussed in more detail below. Turning therefore to the preamble, this outlines the different mechanism, saying:

> Whereas, the Government of [FATCA Partner] is supportive of the underlying policy goal of FATCA to improve tax compliance;
> Whereas, FATCA has raised a number of issues, including that [FATCA Partner] financial institutions may not be able to comply with certain aspects of FATCA due to domestic legal impediments;
> Whereas, intergovernmental cooperation to facilitate FATCA implementation would address these issues and reduce burdens for [FATCA Partner] financial institutions;
> Whereas, the Parties desire to conclude an agreement to provide for cooperation to facilitate the implementation of FATCA based on direct reporting by [FATCA Partner] financial institutions to the US Internal Revenue Service, supplemented by the exchange of information upon request pursuant to the [Convention/TIEA], and subject to the confidentiality and other protections provided for therein, including the provisions limiting the use of the information exchanged under the [Convention/TIEA];

This is a usefully concise description of the key differences between Model 1 and Model 2 IGAs. As stated above, the definitions are largely similar. The Model 2 IGA does have a number of 'new' terms that are not required to implement the Model 1 IGAs (as well as omitting some terms that are not required, but these are not listed here). Article 1(1)(h) provides that 'Foreign Reportable Amount' means a payment of fixed or determinable annual or periodical income that would be a withholdable payment if it were from sources within the United States.

The definitions relating to accounts are also different. In particular 'Financial Account' is defined in Article 1(1)(u) as follows:

> The term 'Financial Account' has the meaning set forth in relevant US Treasury Regulations, but does not include any account that is excluded from the definition of Financial Account in Annex II.

Additionally – and since the Model 2 IGA requires individual Financial Institutions to enter into agreements, a definition of 'FFI Agreement' is also essential. Article 1(1)(v) provides:

> The term 'FFI Agreement' means an agreement that sets forth the requirements, consistent with this Agreement, for the Reporting

[FATCA Partner] Financial Institution to be treated as complying with the requirements of section 1471(b) of the US Internal Revenue Code

'Cash Value Insurance Contract' and 'Annuity Contract' are defined by reference to the US Treasury Regulations in the Model 2 IGA (see Article 1(1)(x)). CFR, paragraph 1.1471-5(b)(2)(vii) provides:

(vii) Cash value insurance contract -

(A) In general. The term cash value insurance contract means an insurance contract (other than an indemnity reinsurance contractbetween two insurance companies and a term life insurance contract described in paragraph (b)(2)(ii) of this section) that has an aggregate cash value greater than $50,000 at any time during the calendar year, applying the rules set forth in paragraph (b)(4)(iii) of this section. A participating FFI may elect to disregard the $50,000 threshold in the preceding sentence by reporting all contracts with a cash value greater than zero.

(B) Cash value. Except as otherwise provided in paragraph (b)(3)(vii)(C) of this section, the term cash value means any amount (determined without reduction for any charge or policy loan) that -

(1) Is payable under the contract to any person upon surrender, termination, cancellation, or withdrawal; or

(2) Any person can borrow under or with regard to (for example, by pledging as collateral) the contract.

(C) Amounts excluded from cash value. Cash value does not include an amount payable -

(1) Solely by reason of the death of an individual insured under a life insurance contract;

(2) As a personal injury or sickness benefit or a benefit providing indemnification of an economic loss incurred upon the occurrence of the event insured against;

(3) As a refund of a previously paid premium (less cost of insurance charges whether or not actually imposed) under an insurance contract (other than a life insurance or annuity contract) due to cancellation or termination of the contract, decrease in risk exposure during the effective period of the contract, or arising from the correction of a posting or similar error with regard to the premium for the contract; or

(4) As a policyholder dividend (other than a termination dividend) provided that the dividend relates to an insurance contract under which the only benefits payable are described in paragraph (b)(3)(vii)(C)(2) of this section.

(5) As a return of an advance premium or premium deposit for an insurance contract for which the premium is payable at

> least annually if the amount of the advance premium or premium deposit does not exceed the next annual premium that will be payable under the contract
>
> ...

It is not clear why this definition is preferred to that found in the Model 1 IGA, though it may be because the definition in the Model 1 IGA includes reference to values of such accounts that are related solely to reporting by Reporting Financial Institutions, so that the definition is otiose.

Similarly in relation to 'Annuity Contract', CFR, Paragraph 1.1471-5(1)(C)(iv) provides:

> **(iv) Insurance and annuity contracts.** A contract issued or maintained by an insurance company, a holding company (as described in paragraph (e)(5)(i)(C) of this section) of an insurance company, or a financial institution described in paragraphs (e)(1)(i), (ii), (iii), or (v)of this section, if the contract is a cash value insurance contract (as defined in paragraph (b)(3)(vii) of this section) or an annuity contract.

Article 2 of the Model 2 IGA provides:

1. Directive to [FATCA Partner] Financial Institutions. [FATCA Partner] shall direct and enable all Reporting [FATCA Partner] Financial Institutions to:
   a) register on the IRS FATCA registration website with the IRS within 90 days of the Determination Date, and comply with the requirements of an FFI Agreement, including with respect to due diligence, reporting, and withholding;
   b) with respect to Financial Accounts maintained by Reporting [FATCA Partner] Financial Institutions as of the Determination Date identified as US Accounts,
      (i) request from each Account Holder the Account Holder's US TIN and consent to report [and simultaneously inform the Account Holder in writing that, if the US TIN and consent are not given, (1) aggregate information about the account shall be reported to the IRS, (2) information about the account may give rise to a group request by the IRS for specific information about the account, (3) in such case, the account information shall be transmitted to the [FATCA Partner] tax administration, and (4) the [FATCA Partner] tax administration may exchange this information with the IRS in accordance with paragraph 2 of this Article];
      (ii) report annually to the IRS, in the time and manner required by an FFI Agreement and relevant US

Treasury Regulations, the aggregate information required with respect to Nonconsenting US Accounts;

c) with respect to accounts of, or obligations to, Nonparticipating Financial Institutions that exist as of the Determination Date, and in connection with which the Reporting [FATCA Partner] Financial Institution expects to pay a Foreign Reportable Amount,
   (i) with respect to calendar years 2015 and 2016, request from each such Nonparticipating Financial Institution the Nonparticipating Financial Institution's consent to report [and simultaneously inform the Nonparticipating Financial Institution in writing that, if such consent is not given, (1) aggregate information about Foreign Reportable Amounts paid to the Nonparticipating Financial Institution shall be reported to the IRS, (2) such information may give rise to a group request by the IRS for specific information about the account or obligation, (3) in such case, the information about the account or obligation shall be transmitted to the [FATCA Partner] tax administration, and (4) the [FATCA Partner] tax administration may exchange this information with the IRS in accordance with paragraph 2 of this Article];7
   (ii) with respect to calendar years 2015 and 2016, report to the IRS the number of nonconsenting Nonparticipating Financial Institutions to which Foreign Reportable Amounts were paid during the year and the aggregate value of all such payments no later than March 15 of the year following the year to which the information relates;

d) with respect to New Accounts identified as US Accounts, obtain from each Account Holder consent to report, consistent with the requirements of an FFI Agreement, as a condition of account opening; and

e) with respect to new accounts opened by, or obligations entered into with, a Nonparticipating Financial Institution after the Determination Date, and in connection with which the Reporting [FATCA Partner] Financial Institution expects to pay a Foreign Reportable Amount, obtain from each such Nonparticipating Financial Institution consent to report, consistent with the requirements of an FFI Agreement, as a condition of opening the account, or entering into the obligation

Thus it can be seen that the Model 2 IGA process is the following:

(i) The jurisdiction in question will have to – in effect – legislate for all Financial Institutions to register with the IRS;

(ii) The Financial Institutions will have to register with the IRS;

(iii) The Financial Institution in question will have to request the information in Article 2(1)(b) from its Account Holders and inform them of the consequences if the relevant details and consent are not provided (also in Article 2(1)(b)(i));

(iv) The Financial Institutions must report annually to the IRS under the terms of their FFI Agreement; and

(v) Provide certain information in relation to anticipated payments to Nonparticipating Financial Institutions.

In relation to the exchange of information, Article 2(2) provides:

> **Exchange of Information**
>
> a) In the context of FATCA implementation, the US Competent Authority may make group requests to the [FATCA Partner] Competent Authority based on the aggregate information reported to the IRS pursuant to the directive described in subparagraphs 1(b)(ii) and 1(c)(ii) of this Article, for all the information about Nonconsenting US Accounts and Foreign Reportable Amounts paid to Nonparticipating Financial Institutions that the Reporting [FATCA Partner] Financial Institution would have had to report under an FFI Agreement had it obtained consent. Such requests shall be made pursuant to Article 8 of the [Convention/TIEA] and shall apply to information for the time period beginning on or after the date of signature of this Agreement.
>
> b) The information requested pursuant to subparagraph 2(a) of this Article shall be considered information that [may be relevant]/[is foreseeably relevant]/[is necessary] for carrying out the administration or enforcement of the domestic laws of the United States concerning taxes covered by the [Convention/TIEA] and under which taxation is not contrary to the [Convention/TIEA], without regard to whether the Reporting [FATCA Partner] Financial Institution or another party has contributed to noncompliance of the taxpayers in the group request.
>
> c) The [FATCA Partner] Competent Authority shall, within six months of the receipt of the group request, provide the US Competent Authority with all such requested information in the same format in which the information would have been reported if it had been reported directly to the IRS by the Reporting [FATCA Partner] Financial Institution. The [FATCA Partner] Competent Authority shall notify the US Competent Authority and the relevant Reporting [FATCA Partner] Financial Institution if there will be any delay in the exchange of the requested information. In such case, the provisions of

subparagraph 2(b) of Article 3 of this Agreement shall apply with respect to the Reporting [FATCA Partner] Financial Institution, and the [FATCA Partner] Competent Authority must exchange the requested information with the US Competent Authority as soon as possible.

d) Notwithstanding subparagraph 2(c) of this Article, the [FATCA Partner] Competent Authority is not required to obtain and exchange the US TIN of the Account Holder of a Nonconsenting US Account if such US TIN is not in the records of the Reporting [FATCA Partner] Financial Institution. In such a case, the [FATCA Partner] Competent Authority shall obtain and include in the exchanged information the date of birth of the relevant person, if the Reporting [FATCA Partner] Financial Institution has such date of birth in its records

Model 2 IGAs also have somewhat different Annexes, so when dealing with a Model 2 IGA, these should be checked carefully.

5.21 No IGA and withholding

In some jurisdictions, there will be no IGA in place. In these circumstances, the US Treasury Regulations (CFR) will usually apply.

6 CRS

6.1 What is CRS?

The OECD explains the rationale for CRS in the following way:

> As the world has become increasingly globalised, it is easier for all taxpayers to make, hold and manage investments through financial institutions outside of their country of residence. Vast amounts of money are kept offshore and go untaxed to the extent that taxpayers fail to comply with tax obligations in their home jurisdiction. Offshore tax evasion is a serious problem for jurisdictions all over the world, OECD and non-OECD, small and large, developing and developed. Countries have a shared interest in maintaining the integrity of their tax systems. Co-operation between tax administrations is critical in the fight against tax evasion and in protecting the integrity of tax systems. A key aspect of that co-operation is exchange of information

This explains the background to CRS (and indeed all AEoI regimes) but not, perhaps, what CRS is. This is – in fact – an argument about the etymology of the phrase 'what is CRS'? Is it the process that it uses, or the purpose that that process seeks to embody? It is, perhaps, not necessary to answer such a question in a practitioner text like this; however, it has arisen as a debate between the authors and so it is, perhaps, one worth consideration. On the one hand, the purpose of CRS – to combat international tax evasion and avoidance – is essential to understanding the CRS, since a purposive approach to interpretation is of paramount importance in the context of international provisions. On the other hand, maybe it is simpler to try to understand CRS as a regime which seeks to identify accounts held by financial institutions for non-residents[1].

Perhaps the answer is a combination of the two. CRS – and indeed other automatic exchange of information regimes – seek to provide a global information base without using a 'request mechanism'[2] of basic information about taxpayers. This is done through the mechanism of identifying three key elements:

(i) Financial Institutions (which are not merely things like banks, but cover a wide variety of vehicles potentially used not only in tax planning but also in estate and business planning, such as trusts);
(ii) Accounts (which, again, are not restricted to things like bank accounts proper, but more akin to assets generally); and
(iii) Controlling Persons (broadly speaking the natural ultimate beneficial owners of the 'Accounts', but also wider classes which can include

---

[1] At least one of us believes that this is not helpful, since none of the terms in the preceding sentence that are used in the CRS actually bears any close resemblance to the terms as used in everyday life.

[2] This is the preserve, though not exclusive, of tax information exchange agreements.

settlors of trusts and protectors – so perhaps those who to a large extent come within the natural meaning of 'controlling persons', though this is itself an over-simplification. Fuller analysis of the meaning of 'Controlling Persons' can be found below).

Reports are made by Financial Institutions on the Controlling Persons, and their accounts. They are made – in the case of CRS – usually to the revenue authority in the jurisdiction of residence. The Implementation Handbook describes it this way[3]:

> In broad terms, financial institutions report information to the tax administration in the jurisdiction in which they are located. The information consists of details of financial assets they hold on behalf of non-resident taxpayers, and the income derived therefrom. The tax administrations then exchange that information with the jurisdiction(s) of residence of the taxpayer.
>
> This process requires: rules on the collection and reporting of information by financial institutions; IT and administrative capabilities in order to receive and exchange the information; a legal instrument providing for information exchange between the jurisdictions; and measures to ensure the highest standards of confidentiality and data safeguards

6.2 A (brief) background

CRS is one of several automatic exchange of information (AEoI) regimes. In the International Exchange Manual HMRC explain[4]:

> Globalisation of the financial sector now makes it much easier for individuals and entities to hold money and assets outside of their jurisdiction of tax residence. While the great majority comply with their tax obligations, some will use the availability of offshore financial structures to evade tax.
>
> Automatic exchange of financial account information is about improving transparency in the fight against tax evasion and in so doing, protecting the integrity of the tax systems of the participating jurisdictions. The UK is party to a number of international agreements designed to provide tax administrations with details of financial accounts and assets, owned by individuals and entities that are resident for tax purposes in their jurisdiction, but which are held by financial institutions in the other territory.
>
> For this to work, the UK Government has introduced legislation that imposes obligations on the UK financial sector to review and collect details of accounts held by persons that are tax resident elsewhere and report this to HMRC for onward transmission under the

[3] Page 7

[4] at IEIM400020

exchange of information articles in the various treaties and conventions to which the UK is party. In return, those jurisdictions supply HMRC with similar information on UK tax resident individuals and entities holding accounts with their Financial Institutions.

The UK now has legislation in place for automatic exchange of financial account information under four different regimes:

- The United States Foreign Account Tax Compliance Act – FATCA [see IEIM400040]
- The Crown Dependencies and Gibraltar Regulations – CDOT[5] [see IEIM400060]
- The Common Reporting Standard developed by the OECD – CRS [see IEIM400080]
- The EU Directive on Administrative Cooperation in Tax Matters – DAC [see IEIM400100]

The UK is also party to a number of non-reciprocal automatic exchange of information agreements, under which the UK receives information, but is not obliged to report to the other jurisdictions.

All these regimes are discussed in this book, save for CDOT since it is now of historical interest only.

6.3 Purpose

The broad aim of CRS is to help fight against tax evasion (and avoidance), and protect the integrity of national tax systems. The problem that CRS seeks to address is, broadly, the following:

(i) the concealment of offshore assets, and failure to provide information about them to national tax authorities was too readily achieved; and

(ii) the costs, time, and complexity of conducting checks in relation to offshore income and gains was prohibitive for national revenue authorities[6].

The impact of tax evasion and, to a lesser but still significant extent, tax avoidance is difficult to measure. Because both avoidance and evasion rely on the use of financial secrecy, assets and movements of value flows are concealed. The IMF's Fiscal Affairs Department, however, estimated in 2015 total tax losses at over $400 billion for OECD member states, as a result of

---

[5] Now defunct: fully superseded by reporting under CRS for 2017 reporting onwards

[6] It should be noted that one of the issues of information exchange is the impact of the principle in *Government of India v Taylor* [1955] AC 491, which is now largely dealt with in this respect by domestic legislation allowing exchange of information. See further – Brown *Government of India v Taylor*: The End of the Line?

the use of tax havens[7]. This represents the higher end of the estimates available, but on any basis, the problem was one that required attention.

HMRC describe it in the following way at IEIM100010[8]:

> In the ever increasing multinational world of business and finance, where people, businesses, investments, and transactions frequently reach across international borders, HMRC needs to be able to obtain information from overseas to help in our compliance and other activities. Exchange of Information with other tax authorities is an essential way of increasing tax transparency and co-operation between jurisdictions. It is a two-way process: we receive useful information for our work and, in turn, we provide other jurisdictions with information we either hold as a tax authority or can obtain with our information powers.

The OECD itself explains the importance of information exchange in the following way[9]:

> As the world becomes increasingly globalised and cross-border activities become the norm, tax administrations need to work together to ensure that taxpayers pay the right amount of tax to the right jurisdiction. A key aspect in making tax administrations ready for the challenges of the 21st century is equipping them with the necessary legal, administrative and IT tools for verifying compliance of their taxpayers. Against that background, the enhanced co-operation between tax authorities through AEOI is crucial in bringing national tax administration in line with the globalised economy.

There are three recognised methods of exchanging tax information: exchange on request, spontaneous exchange, and automatic exchange. CRS is a system of automatic exchange. The other two types of exchange require different specific provisions. These are provided for under bilateral agreements and under multilateral treaties and are (sadly) beyond the scope of this book.

6.4 CRS and other regimes

While CRS is a regime in its own right, it also interacts – in particular – with two other regimes. The first of these is FATCA. In relation to FATCA, CRS is a separate regime, however, it shares many features with FATCA. This is illustrated by the OECD who say:

---

[7] The effect of one country's tax system on another. See *Base Erosion, Profit Shifting and Developing Countries* by Ernesto Crivelli, Ruud De Mooij and Michael Keen, IMF, 2015

[8] www.gov.uk/hmrc-internal-manuals/international-exchange-of-information/ieim100010

[9] http://www.oecd.org/tax/automatic-exchange/

> The Common Reporting Standard, with a view to maximising efficiency and reducing cost for financial institutions, draws extensively on the intergovernmental approach to implementing FATCA. While the intergovernmental approach to FATCA reporting does deviate in certain aspects from the CRS, the differences are driven by the multilateral nature of the CRS system and other US specific aspects, in particular the concept of taxation on the basis of citizenship and the presence of a significant and comprehensive FATCA withholding tax. Given these features, that the intergovernmental approach to FATCA is a pre-existing system with close similarities to the CRS, and the anticipated progress towards widespread participation in the CRS, it is compatible and consistent with the CRS for the United States to not require the look through treatment for investment entities in Non-Participating Jurisdictions

Thus, it is important to consider CRS and FATCA in conjunction with each other and not either one in a vacuum (though as acknowledged in the above quote – and since the USA 'beat the OECD to the punch' with getting its automatic exchange provisions in place), in particular it may be helpful to consider CRS in the light of FATCA. This is discussed in further detail in this Chapter.

In addition, CRS interacts with MDR. Indeed, at least one of us can regularly be heard to explain that it is not possible to understand or apply MDR without understanding CRS, because the MDR is heavily weighted towards identifying arrangements intended to avoid application of CRS as is part of DAC6 (Hallmark D). Whilst CRS is a topic in its own right, one must understand that it fits into a framework of numerous provisions which interact and rely upon each other. MDR is a nonsense without CRS, and CRS is potentially avoidable without MDR.

The provisions that most closely interact with CRS are MDR, Rule 1.1 and DAC6, Hallmark D. The former is the rule requiring disclosure of CRS avoidance arrangements, and the latter is the specific hallmark concerning automatic exchange of information and beneficial ownership (or at least part of it). Hallmark D is – in effect – the incorporation of the MDR into DAC6 and European law.

MDR, Rule 1.1 provides:

> A 'CRS Avoidance Arrangement' is any Arrangement for which it is reasonable to conclude that it is designed to circumvent or is marketed as, or has the effect of, circumventing CRS Legislation or exploiting an absence thereof, including through:
>
> (a) the use of an account, product or investment that is not, or purports not to be, a Financial Account, but has features that are substantially similar to those of a Financial Account;

(b) the transfer of a Financial Account, or the monies and/or Financial Assets held in a Financial Account to a Financial Institution that is not a Reporting Financial Institution, or to a jurisdiction that does not exchange CRS information with all jurisdictions of tax residence of a Reportable Taxpayer;

(c) the conversion or transfer of a Financial Account, or the monies and/or Financial Assets held in a Financial Account, to a Financial Account that is not a Reportable Account;

(d) the conversion of a Financial Institution into a Financial Institution that is not a Reporting Financial Institution, or into a Financial Institution that is resident in a jurisdiction that does not exchange CRS information with all jurisdictions of tax residence of a Reportable Taxpayer;

(e) undermining or exploiting weaknesses in the due diligence procedures used by Financial Institutions to correctly identify:
  (i) an Account Holder and/or Controlling Person; or
  (ii) all the jurisdictions of tax residence of an Account Holder and/or Controlling Person;

(f) allowing, or purporting to allow:
  (i) an Entity to qualify as an Active NFE;
  (ii) an investment to be made through an Entity without triggering a reporting obligation under the CRS Legislation; or
  (iii) a person to avoid being treated as a Controlling Person; or

(g) classifying a payment made for the benefit of an Account Holder or Controlling Person as a payment that is not reportable under CRS Legislation;

where it is reasonable to conclude that such Arrangement is designed to circumvent or is marketed as, or has the effect of, circumventing CRS Legislation or exploiting an absence thereof.

For the purposes of this Rule 1.1, an Arrangement is not considered to have the effect of circumventing CRS Legislation solely because it results in non-reporting under the relevant CRS Legislation, provided that it is reasonable to conclude that such non-reporting does not undermine the policy intent of such CRS Legislation.

Similarly, DAC6, Hallmark D provides (so far as is relevant):

1. An arrangement which may have the effect of undermining the reporting obligation under the laws implementing Union legislation or any equivalent agreements on the automatic exchange of Financial Account information, including agreements with third countries, or which takes advantage of the absence of such legislation or agreements. Such arrangements include at least the following:

(a) the use of an account, product or investment that is not, or purports not to be, a Financial Account, but has features that are substantially similar to those of a Financial Account;

(b) the transfer of Financial Accounts or assets to, or the use of jurisdictions that are not bound by the automatic exchange of Financial Account information with the State of residence of the relevant taxpayer;

(c) the reclassification of income and capital into products or payments that are not subject to the automatic exchange of Financial Account information;

(d) the transfer or conversion of a Financial Institution or a Financial Account or the assets therein into a Financial Institution or a Financial Account or assets not subject to reporting under the automatic exchange of Financial Account information;

(e) the use of legal entities, arrangements or structures that eliminate or purport to eliminate reporting of one or more Account Holders or Controlling Persons under the automatic exchange of Financial Account information;

(f) arrangements that undermine, or exploit weaknesses in, the due diligence procedures used by Financial Institutions to comply with their obligations to report Financial Account information, including the use of jurisdictions with inadequate or weak regimes of enforcement of anti-money-laundering legislation or with weak transparency requirements for legal persons or legal arrangements

Consequently, to consider whether an arrangement is caught by Hallmark D or Rule 1.1, it is necessary to understand how CRS works and its purposes. It is a nonsense to suppose that one can understand whether there is a DAC6 or MDR reporting requirement because of a CRS avoidance-related arrangement, if the person applying the criteria does not know, to give a few – but by no means all – examples:

(i) When something will be a Financial Account;
(ii) What Financial Accounts are Reportable and which are not;
(iii) What is meant by a 'Financial Institution' and a 'Reporting Financial Institution';
(iv) What are the relevant due diligence procedures for identifying any category of Account Holders or Controlling Persons;
(v) When something will have the effect of circumventing CRS legislation; and
(vi) What non-reporting will undermine the policy intent of CRS.

Since MDR, Rule 1.1 and DAC6, Hallmark D both represent a 'broad spectrum' approach to identifying attempts to undermine or circumvent CRS, it is necessary to have an understanding of that regime further informed by the understanding of CRS itself. Consequently, and unfortunately, there is much of CRS that must be considered in the context of MDR (and DAC6, Hallmark D). Thus, the aim of this Chapter is to give a broad understanding of CRS and its mechanisms and policy aims so that you can not only apply that regime properly but are also able to apply the MDR and DAC6 avoidance rules by reference to the relevant parts of CRS.

6.5 Scope and comparison with FATCA

The scope of CRS is, in effect, worldwide. As of August 2020, there are over 4,200 bilateral exchange relationships activated with respect to more than 100 jurisdictions committed to the CRS[10,11].

The most notable 'hold out' is the USA, which has its own automatic exchange mechanism under FATCA (which most other countries have also adopted[12]). However, in relation to FATCA, the OECD say:

> The Common Reporting Standard, with a view to maximizing efficiency and reducing cost for financial institutions, draws extensively on the intergovernmental approach to implementing FATCA. While the intergovernmental approach to FATCA reporting does deviate in certain aspects from the CRS, the differences are driven by the multilateral nature of the CRS system and other US specific aspects, in particular the concept of taxation on the basis of citizenship and the presence of a significant and comprehensive FATCA withholding tax …

However, caution is advised. While the CRS Implementation Handbook used to take a more laidback approach to crossover with the definitions used in FATCA[13] and ensuring that there was continuity between the two, the

---

[10] www.oecd.org/tax/automatic-exchange/international-framework-for-the-crs/

[11] 'Activated exchange relationships' can be found here: http://www.oecd.org/tax/automatic-exchange/international-framework-for-the-crs/exchange-relationships/ Activated exchange relationships can be sorted and displayed from both the perspective of a particular sending jurisdiction ('FROM') or a particular receiving jurisdiction ('TO'). For each exchange relationship, the legal basis and, where appropriate, the effective date and/or the activation date are shown. In case a relationship is non-reciprocal in nature, it will, for the non-reciprocal jurisdiction, be shown in the 'FROM' column, but not in the 'TO' column. The number in brackets behind each jurisdiction in the drop-down menu indicates the total number of bilateral exchange relationships currently activated with respect to that jurisdiction.

[12] In one of four variants: Model IA IGA, Model IB IGA, Model II IGA, or with no IGA (where financial institutions exchange information directly with the American IRS). The relevance of these distinctions is discussed further below.

[13] The Implementation Handbook previously provided:

Definition of Investment Entity

The definition of Investment Entity in Article 1,1, j) of the Model 1 FATCA IGA differs from the definition of Investment Entity in Section VIII, A, 6 of the Standard. While the wording of the definition of Investment Entity may differ between the Model 1 FATCA IGA and the Standard, the Standard was designed to achieve an equivalent outcome to that achieved through the

adoption of this has been mitigated against in domestic legislation by the OECD Global Forum Secretariat. The Implementation Handbook now says, in relation to the definition of investment entity[14]:

> **Definition of Investment Entity**
> The definition of Investment Entity in Article 1,1, j) of the Model 1 FATCA IGA differs from the definition of Investment Entity in Section VIII, A, 6 of the Standard.
>
> The definition of Investment Entity in Article 1(1)(j) of the Model 1 FATCA IGA cannot be used for CRS purposes on its own, as it is less prescriptive than the definition of Investment Entity in Section VIII(A) (6). However, the definitions of the Model 1 FATCA IGA and the CRS can be read consistently. For example, the CRS definition includes a gross income test to determine whether an Entity is treated as primarily conducting as a business one or more of the activities described in subparagraph A(6)(a), or an Entity's gross income is primarily attributable to investing, reinvesting, or trading in Financial Assets for purposes of subparagraph A(6)(b), and could be used to interpret the less prescriptive aspects of the Model 1 FATCA IGA definition. The CRS definition is in fact based on the definition of Investment Entity in the US FATCA regulations, which may be used to interpret the Model 1 FATCA IGA definition

Example
Jersey received the ire of the OECD Global Forum Secretariat, in relation to taking the former guidance in the Implementation Handbook to heart in its own guidance. The Jersey Guidance interpreted the previous approach in the Implementation Handbook as follows[15]:

> The CRS Implementation Handbook in Section III compares the Standard with the FATCA Model 1 IGA. This is indicative of where the IGA Guidance may continue to be relied upon without affecting the purpose of the CRS.

In our view, this was an oversimplification. The Handbook does not state – and has never stated – that Part III can be used to indicate when it is appropriate to continue to rely on FATCA definitions in the context of CRS. In fact, the Implementation Handbook, paragraph 296 (now) says:

> ... [t]he comparisons provided below focus on the differences in wording between the FATCA Model 1 IGA and the CRS, and aim to

---

Model 1 FATCA IGA. Jurisdictions should therefore be able to rely on the approach in the Standard for purposes of both the Standard and the Model 1 FATCA IGA

[14] Page 127

[15] Paragraph 3.1, October 2016 edition

assist jurisdictions in identifying where those differences can be overcome and where the differences cannot be aligned.

Jersey appears to agree. In its guidance, it now says:[16]

3.1. The CRS Implementation Handbook in Section III compares the Standard with the FATCA Model 1 IGA. In the previous editions of the Guidance Notes, it was suggested that this was indicative of where the IGA Guidance might continue to be relied upon without affecting the purpose of the CRS. This is no longer the case.

3.2. The 2015 CRS Regulations have been assessed by the OECD Global Forum Secretariat as part of a general review of the legislation of all committed jurisdictions, designed to give the jurisdictions advance warning of where their legislation is not thought to be fit for purpose, so that the necessary amendments can be made before a comprehensive review of CRS compliance is undertaken in two or three years' time. The Assessment, which has been approved by the Global Forum AEOI Working Group, concluded that while Regulation 1(5) [of the Jersey domestic regulations implementing CRS] stated that in the Regulations a word or expression which is defined in the CRS has that meaning, there was an exception allowing Reporting Financial Institutions to use as an alternative a definition in any other international governmental agreement. The assessors have recommended that Jersey should ensure that only the defined terms in Section VIII of the CRS and its Commentary are being implemented by the Reporting Financial Institutions as required under the Standard.

3.3. The conclusion of the Secretariat is that there is no situation where it is possible to use a non-CRS Standard definition for the Standard. Therefore, allowing FIs to supplement definitions in the CRS Standard based on their interpretation of what might or might not undermine the purposes of the AEOI Standard, was assessed to be a gap.

3.4. The CRS Regulations therefore have been amended to substitute for Regulation 1(5) the following –'(5) A word or expression used in these Regulations which is defined in the CRS has the meaning given in the CRS'17. Now only the CRS definitions can

---

[16] Paragraph 3.1 and 3.2, October 2017 edition

[17] Regulation 1(5) previously provided:

(5) In these Regulations, a word or expression which is defined in the CRS has that meaning **except to the extent that a reporting financial institution may use as an alternative a definition in any other international governmental agreement if –**

(a) **Jersey and a participating jurisdiction is, or has been, a party to that other agreement**; and

> be used. However, the amendment to the Regulations is not retrospective in its effect. Accordingly, if a FI has taken an informed view, in the reporting in 2017 of information on 2016 financial accounts, that the use of definitions in the IGA Guidance Notes does not frustrate the purposes of the CRS, this will be accepted as being in compliance with the Regulations

Similarly HMRC say:[18]

> The Common Reporting Standard (CRS) is the result of the drive by the G20 nations to develop a global standard for the automatic exchange of financial account information. Developed by the OECD, the CRS aims to maximise efficiency and reduce costs for Financial Institutions by drawing heavily on the approach taken to implementing FATCA.
>
> There are some distinct differences between the two systems, driven to a large extent by the multilateral nature of the CRS compared to FATCA and the US specific features of FATCA, such as tax residency in the USA including citizenship, and the FATCA withholding tax which introduces additional features into the reporting process that are not needed when implementing the CRS

The scope of CRS is wide, and unfortunately while it must be managed alongside the separate FATCA regime, a uniform approach cannot be taken to determining the appropriate status of entities and accountholders. This undoubtedly imposes an additional burden on Financial Institutions and professionals, but with the OECD's approach increasingly moving away from alignment with FATCA, there is little to be done.

6.6 Implementation: introduction

A brief word on the implementation of CRS. The subject probably merits more than a brief word, since it is somewhat opaque, however, this topic is primarily of interest to the governments and civil servants of the countries that have to implement it (while correct and effective implementation will arise in the practitioner context rarely, it is unlikely to be a 'bread and butter' topic for most) and so receives no more than brief consideration here.

The CRS itself is not an international agreement –multilateral or bilateral – rather it is a set of rules that individual countries commit to implement in their domestic legislation. Most countries do this by use of secondary

---

(b) **that other agreement provides for the automatic exchange of tax information, in so far as such use would not frustrate the purposes of the Agreement**
(Emphasis added).

[18] IEIM400080

legislation[19] and once such secondary legislation is enacted, there should then be an obligation on – for example – Financial Institutions to comply with the requirements. This is how the competent authority (usually the revenue authority of the jurisdiction in question) will obtain the information that it needs to exchange.

The basis on which the competent authority becomes obliged to exchange such information is more complex. First, there is the Multilateral Convention On Mutual Administrative Assistance In Tax Matters. This is an international agreement to which OECD members are party. The MCAA is described by HMRC as follows[20]:

> The OECD facilitate the MCAAs for the Common Reporting Standard and Country by Country Reporting. Both of these MCAAs are linked to the Multilateral Convention on Mutual Administrative Assistance in Tax Matters, which acts as the formal Governmental agreement and legal gateway.
>
> Competent Authorities sign the MCAAs, and then notify the OECD Coordinating Body when they have implemented the necessary steps to implement the Agreement, and also which other jurisdictions they wish to exchange with. This facilitates a streamlined process for the creation of thousands of bilateral Competent Authority Agreements amongst the signatories

The MCMAA provides the 'legal gateway' for the exchange of information with other countries, such information being that obtained by the application of CRS in domestic law. The MCAAs mentioned refer to multilateral competent authority agreements.

Similarly, the preface to the MCMAA itself explains:

> Over twenty-five years ago, the OECD and the Council of Europe jointly launched an ambitious project: the development of a multilateral convention to facilitate administrative co-operation among our member countries so that they could more effectively counter international tax evasion and other forms of non-compliance. That work culminated in January 1988 with the opening for signature of the Multilateral Convention in Mutual Administrative Assistance in Tax Matters.
>
> Today *[1 June 2011]* marks an important new beginning for the Convention and for the global campaign against tax evasion as we open the Convention to all countries and amend its provisions to

---

[19] See, for example, the UK International Tax Compliance Regulations 2015 and the Jersey Taxation (Implementation) (International Tax Compliance) (Common Reporting Standard) (Jersey) Regulations 2015

[20] See IEIM230210

> reflect modern international standards of exchange of information for tax purposes.
>
> As amended, the Convention has the potential to become the leading global instrument for tax co-operation around the world. It is the most comprehensive multilateral instrument available in this area. The Convention not only provides for exchange of information (with express provisions on exchange of information on request, spontaneous and automatic), it also includes assistance in recovery, the service of documents and can facilitate joint audits. This type of multilateral co-operation can also benefit businesses by reducing compliance costs and levelling the playing field

Not all of the MCMAA is relevant to CRS. Of particular relevance is Article 4, which provides:

> 1. The Parties shall exchange any information, in particular as provided in this section, that is foreseeably relevant for the administration or enforcement of their domestic laws concerning the taxes covered by this Convention.
> 2. Deleted.
> 3. Any Party may, by a declaration addressed to one of the Depositaries, indicate that, according to its internal legislation, its authorities may inform its resident or national before transmitting information concerning him, in conformity with Articles 5 and 7.

Article 6 provides:

> With respect to categories of cases and in accordance with procedures which they shall determine by mutual agreement, two or more Parties shall automatically exchange the information referred to in Article 4

This is rather an 'outline' sketch of the legal gateway. There are also other possible legal gateways. The Implementation Handbook, paragraph 77 says:

> 77. Other alternative legal instruments that can provide legal basis for information exchange under the Standard include Double Tax Treaties ('DTTs') or Tax Information Exchange Agreements ('TIEAs') as long as these allow the automatic exchange of information. For instance, it should be noted that automatic exchange goes beyond the OECD standard model TIEA, so it would need to be specifically included to allow for the TIEA to be used for exchanges under the Standard that may be achieved by inserting the language of Article 5A of the OECD Model Protocol. Further examples include the amended EU Directive on Administrative Cooperation ('DAC2'), agreements between the EU and third countries as well as other bilateral agreements, such as the UK-CDOT agreements that regulate exchanges

between the UK and its crown dependencies and overseas territories

The basis by which various jurisdictions effectively commit to CRS may vary (though we are unaware of any exchange which occurs outside the MCMAA or CAAs). To facilitate automatic exchange of information, it is necessary for there to be a more detailed framework, the legal gateway being roughly drawn in a variety of ways (the matter of most importance is the Standard itself, rather than the enabling instrument. There is nothing in the provisions of the OECD Model Convention which mandates the CRS as a form of automatic exchange, instead it allows it by its general language). This is found in the MCAA (and the CAA), though may also be found elsewhere. In this respect, the Implementation Handbook, paragraph 76 notes:

> 76. The more detailed procedures regulating the modalities of the exchange are then set out in the Multilateral Competent Authority Agreement on Automatic Exchange of Financial Account Information ('MCAA'), which was specifically drafted for the purposes of enabling the automatic exchange of information pursuant to the Standard within the framework of the Convention and is based on the Model CAA contained in the Standard...

The Model CAA is not an international agreement, agreements based on it have to be implemented between countries. This has led to the large-scale adoption of the MCAA. The important element in determining with which other jurisdictions your jurisdiction will exchange information is whether there is an 'activated exchange relationship' under the MCAA. These are in essence relationships between countries that have agreed to start exchanging information, and the OECD keeps an updated record of them, available to the public. At December 2020, there were over 4,400[21] activated exchange relationships[22].

In IEIM230200 HMRC explain:

> Competent Authority Agreements (CAAs) are agreements between Competent Authorities and can cover a wide range of situations. For exchange of information, such agreements are linked to a particular international exchange instrument, and set out the way in which a particular type of information will be exchanged. Competent Authority Agreements are a type of Memorandum of Understanding.

[21] See www.oecd.org/tax/automatic-exchange/international-framework-for-the-crs/exchange-relationships/, which is updated from time to time.

[22] However, for more details of the 'active' relationships see www.oecd.org/tax/automatic-exchange/international-framework-for-the-crs/exchange-relationships/

Competent Authority Agreements are used to set out formally the way in which Competent Authorities intend to exchange certain information. They will detail, for example, the type of information exchanged, when and how it will be exchanged, and any conditions or prerequisites to the exchange. They will also set out the underlying purpose for making the exchange

6.7 Implementation: competent authority agreements

Unfortunately, once again, the nature of CAAs is not straightforward. Most exchange relationships will be under the MCAA, and that is what we focus on here. However, it is not the only possible CAA (i.e. the basis for actual automatic exchange between two countries). The Implementation Handbook, paragraph 78 explains:

> 78. In addition to the international legal instrument for exchanges of tax information, automatic exchange relationships typically require an additional administrative agreement between Competent Authorities that further sets out the details of the information to be exchanged, as well as the timing and the operational modalities for the automatic exchanges. The Standard therefore contains a Model CAA with three options developed to suit the different exchange relationship scenarios. The first Model CAA is a bilateral and reciprocal model. It is designed to be used in conjunction with Article 26 of the OECD Model Tax Convention. The second Model CAA is a non-reciprocal model provided for use where appropriate (e.g., where a jurisdiction does not have an income tax). The third Model CAA is designed as an umbrella agreement intended to operationalise a multilateral legal instrument such as the Convention. The third approach, i.e. a multilateral agreement between Competent Authorities, which has taken shape in form of the MCAA mentioned above, is by far the most popular as it significantly reduced the time and resources necessary to negotiate multiple bilateral agreements. If only a bilateral approach were available for the implementation of the international legal framework for CRS exchanges, this would have required over 5000 bilateral negotiations between the current 102 committed jurisdictions, whereas under the multilateral approach each committed jurisdiction would only sign one agreement

This does not mean that there are no bilateral CAAs, or other approaches adopted. For example, the UK has or has had (out of 67 activated exchange relationships) the following non-MCAA relationships: with Gibraltar,

Guernsey, Isle of Man and Jersey (under CDOT) and with Hong Kong and Singapore (under bilateral CAAs)[23].

The MCAA remains the primary method of implementing the CRS (exchange relationships are 'activated' when the countries in question notify the OECD that they have reached agreement on activating the relationship, broadly speaking[24]). Some form of CAA is likely to be required, to ensure that the exchange of information can operate lawfully.

The CAA included with the CRS is in fact a model bilateral CAA. This is now of lesser relevance and here we focus on the MCAA (which is found in Annex 1 to the CRS[25]). The preamble to the MCAA explains:

1. This document is a multilateral version of the Model Competent Authority Agreement. The legal basis is Article 6 of the Convention on Mutual Administrative Assistance in Tax Matters which specifically provides that two or more Parties can mutually agree to exchange information automatically. The actual exchange of the information itself will be on a bilateral basis.
2. The main changes to adapt the bilateral Model CAA to a multilateral model are additions to the preamble, generic definitions for Jurisdiction and the term 'Common Reporting Standard', the effective date in paragraph 1 of Section 7 including a procedure for jurisdictions to join after the Agreement is in effect, and sending notices to the Secretariat of the Co-ordinating Body of the Convention. In addition the multilateral model contemplates jurisdictions participating on both a reciprocal and nonreciprocal basis (see paragraph 1 of Section 2). Jurisdictions sending information but not receiving information would be listed in Annex A

The key provisions of the MCAA are those that address the type of information to be exchanged, as well as those on the manner and timing of exchange. Section 2, Article 1 provides:

---

[23] See www.oecd.org/tax/automatic-exchange/international-framework-for-the-crs/exchange-relationships/ . CDOT relationships are now managed under the CRS framework and, therefore, we do not cover CDOT in this edition.

[24] The Implementation Handbook, paragraph 81 explains: 'Although the MCAA is a multilateral agreement, exchange relationships under the Standard require that both jurisdictions provide a subsequent notification stating that they wish to exchange with each other. This is necessary since the MCAA is a framework agreement, and it does not become operational until domestic legislation is in place and the requirements on confidentiality and data protection are met'.

[25] Annex 2 is a non-reciprocal model MCAA. This allows for exchange in one direction only. This is most commonly relevant where there is no income tax in one of the jurisdictions in question, and thus no use for CRS information in that jurisdiction.

1. Pursuant to the provisions of Article 6 and 22 of the Convention and subject to the applicable reporting and due diligence rules consistent with the Common Reporting Standard, each Competent Authority will annually exchange with the other Competent Authorities on an automatic basis the information obtained pursuant to such rules and specified in paragraph 2. Notwithstanding the foregoing sentence the Competent Authorities of the Jurisdictions listed in Annex A will exchange, but not receive, the information specified in paragraph 2. Jurisdictions not listed in Annex A will always receive the information specified in paragraph 2 but will not exchange such information with the Jurisdictions listed in Annex A.

This mandates automatic exchange of information annually. Section 2, Article 2 continues to set out the information required to be exchanged. It provides:

2. The information to be exchanged is, with respect to each Reportable Account of another Jurisdiction:
   a) the name, address, TIN(s) and date and place of birth (in the case of an individual) of each Reportable Person that is an Account Holder of the account and, in the case of any Entity that is an Account Holder and that, after application of due diligence procedures consistent with the Common Reporting Standard, is identified as having one or more Controlling Persons that is a Reportable Person, the name, address, and TIN(s) of the Entity and the name, address, TIN(s) and date and place of birth of each Reportable Person;
   b) the account number (or functional equivalent in the absence of an account number);
   c) the name and identifying number (if any) of the Reporting Financial Institution;
   d) the account balance or value (including, in the case of a Cash Value Insurance Contract or Annuity Contract, the Cash Value or surrender value) as of the end of the relevant calendar year or other appropriate reporting period or, if the account was closed during such year or period, the closure of the account;
   e) in the case of any Custodial Account:
      (1) the total gross amount of interest, the total gross amount of dividends, and the total gross amount of other income generated with respect to the assets held in the account, in each case paid or credited to the account (or with respect to the account) during the calendar year or other appropriate reporting period; and

(2) the total gross proceeds from the sale or redemption of Financial Assets paid or credited to the account during the calendar year or other appropriate reporting period with respect to which the Reporting Financial Institution acted as a custodian, broker, nominee, or otherwise as an agent for the Account Holder;

in the case of any Depository Account, the total gross amount of interest paid or credited to the account during the calendar year or other appropriate reporting period;

...

It then continues with the general "catch all", saying:

> ... in the case of any account not described in subparagraph 2(e) or (f), the total gross amount paid or credited to the Account Holder with respect to the account during the calendar year or other appropriate reporting period with respect to which the Reporting Financial Institution is the obligor or debtor, including the aggregate amount of any redemption payments made to the Account Holder during the calendar year or other appropriate reporting period.

Section 3, Article 3 provides:

3. with respect to paragraph 2 of Section 2, information is to be exchanged with respect to [xxxx] and all subsequent years and will be exchanged within nine months after the end of the calendar year to which the information relates. Notwithstanding the foregoing sentence information is only required to be exchanged with respect to a calendar year if both Jurisdictions have in effect legislation that requires reporting with respect to such calendar year that is consistent with the scope of exchange provided for.

This drives the timetable for exchange, though it should of course be remembered that countries can avoid activating an exchange relationship by not notifying, so that the requirements under the MCAA (and CRS more broadly) will not apply as between that jurisdiction and jurisdictions with which there is no active relationship.

6.8 Where do you apply CRS?

CRS is essentially a global regime. It is enacted into the national law of any jurisdiction that applies it (which is most countries in the world), and thus there are many different regimes. This gives rise to several potential issues, the first of which (and the only one which we address here) is whether any particular regime applies.

This is an interesting question. One of the points about CRS is that it is broadly drawn; this serves its purpose, but also means that it can result in multiple applications of the regime in different jurisdictions. This can be for a variety of reasons, including because an entity might be classified in one of a number of ways and/or because the entity in question might reasonably be considered to be subject to the reporting requirements of more than one jurisdiction. So how do you determine the CRS legislation of which jurisdiction should be applied?

The answer is the residence of the entity in question (which at base goes to jurisdiction, i.e. the ability to enforce rules against the entity). The importance of the residence of entities in their classification for CRS purposes can be seen from the definitions in CRS. CRS, Section VIII(A)(1) defines a 'Reporting Financial Institution' as:

> any Participating Jurisdiction Financial Institution that is not a Non-Reporting Financial Institution

There are two requirements to be a Reporting FI[26], the first being that the entity must be a Participating Jurisdiction Financial Institution (the second, and not relevant for these purposes, being that it is 'not a Non-Reporting Financial Institution', which is not relevant for these purposes). This is defined in Section VIII(A)(2):

> The term 'Participating Jurisdiction Financial Institution' means (i) any Financial Institution that is resident in a Participating Jurisdiction, but excludes any branch of that Financial Institution that is located outside such Participating Jurisdiction, and (ii) any branch of a Financial Institution that is not resident in a Participating Jurisdiction, if that branch is located in such Participating Jurisdiction

Ultimately, therefore, the residence of the Financial Institution (in most cases, but see further below) will determine whether it is subject to a requirement to analyse those 'accounts' it holds and is determinant of which jurisdiction's regulations are applicable to it.

The matter of which jurisdiction's rules should apply is also addressed in the 'FAQs' issued by the OECD in relation to CRS. The relevant question and answer is 17 in the FAQs on Sections II to VII (page 109)[27], which says:

> Which jurisdiction's rules should apply to determine an Entity's status?
>
> The Commentary provides that an Entity's status as a Financial Institution or nonfinancial entity (NFE) should be resolved under the laws of the Participating Jurisdiction in which the Entity is resident. See Commentary on Section IX, paragraph 2. If an Entity is resident in a jurisdiction that has not implemented the CRS, the rules of the jurisdiction in which the account is maintained determine the

---

[26] The meaning of financial institution is discussed further below.

[27] Page 8 of the CRS FAQs

> Entity's status as a Financial Institution or NFE since there are no other rules available
>
> When determining an Entity's status as an active or passive NFE, the rules of the jurisdiction in which the account is maintained determine the Entity's status. However, a jurisdiction in which the account is maintained may permit (e.g. in its domestic implementation guidance) an Entity to determine its status as an active or passive NFE under the rules of the jurisdiction in which the Entity is resident provided that the jurisdiction in which the Entity is resident has implemented the CRS

It is important to note (and possibly this is more often the question in point for a practitioner) that the distinction between a Passive NFE or Active NFE is to be considered in accordance with the rules of the jurisdiction in which the account is held, and *not* the jurisdiction of residence of the entity in question. The jurisdiction of residence of the financial institution is the matter in point, and the treatment of NFEs in accordance with the location of the account is entirely consistent with this. By extension, therefore, the categorisation of an account holder as a Financial Institution for the purposes of assessing reportability of the account in question must also be made in accordance with the location of the account.

6.9 Double reporting

Inevitably, there is a risk of double reporting. The CRS Commentary on Section VIII expands on the FAQs quoted in the preceding paragraph, saying (at page 158):

> For this purpose, a Financial Institution is 'resident' in a Participating Jurisdiction if it is subject to the jurisdiction of such Participating Jurisdiction (i.e. the Participating Jurisdiction is able to enforce reporting by the Financial Institution). In general, where a Financial Institution is resident for tax purposes in a Participating Jurisdiction, it is subject to the jurisdiction of such Participating Jurisdiction and it is, thus, a Participating Jurisdiction Financial Institution

Where non-trust Financial Institutions are resident in two or more jurisdictions, the CRS Commentary (again at page 159) explains:

> Where a Financial Institution (other than a trust) is resident in two or more Participating Jurisdictions, such Financial Institution will be subject to the reporting and due diligence obligations of the Participating Jurisdiction in which it maintains the Financial Account(s)

While this is an attempt to ensure that there is a minimum of double reporting, it does not address the situation that could arise where Financial Accounts are maintained in two or more Participating Jurisdictions.

The position in relation to trusts is, however, different. The CRS Commentary explains (at page 159):

> In the case of a trust that is a Financial Institution (irrespective of whether it is resident for tax purposes in a Participating Jurisdiction), the trust is considered to be subject to the jurisdiction of a Participating Jurisdiction if one or more of its trustees are resident in such Participating Jurisdiction except if the trust reports all the information required to be reported pursuant to the CRS with respect to Reportable Accounts maintained by the trust to another Participating Jurisdiction because it is resident for tax purposes in such other Participating Jurisdiction ...

This is also addressed in the CRS Implementation Handbook, which explains[28]:

> 248. A trust that is a Financial Institution will be a Reporting Financial Institution if it is resident in a Participating Jurisdiction and does not qualify as a Non-Reporting Financial Institution. A trust may be a Non-Reporting Financial Institution such as a Broad Participation Retirement Fund or Narrow Participation Retirement Fund. A trust could also be a Non-Reporting Financial Institution where the trustee itself is a Reporting Financial Institution, and that trustee undertakes all information reporting in respect of all Reportable Accounts of the trust (and all such reports are exchanged with the relevant jurisdictions concerned)[29].
>
> 249. A trust will be considered to be resident where the trustee(s) is resident. If there is more than one trustee, the trust will be a Reporting Financial Institution in all Participating Jurisdictions in which a trustee is resident. In other words, if the trustees are each resident in different jurisdictions, the trust would be a Reporting Financial Institution in each of those Participating Jurisdictions, and would each separately report in respect of their Reportable Accounts
>
> 250. However, where the trust is considered to be resident for tax purposes in a particular Participating Jurisdiction, and the trust reports all the information required to be reported with respect to Reportable Accounts maintained by the trust that will relieve the trust from reporting in the jurisdictions of residence of the other co-trustees. To obtain such relief, each trustee should be able to demonstrate that all necessary reporting by the trust is actually taking place

---

[28] At pages 107 – 108

[29] This approach is a common one adopted by trust companies and is discussed further below. It can minimise the reporting for institutions

The Mauritian Guidance is different and more limited. Paragraph 4.3.3 provides:

> Where an entity, other than a trust, is resident in two or more Participating Jurisdictions, it is required to report the Financial Account it maintains to the tax authorities in each of the Jurisdictions in which it maintains them.[30]
>
> Thus if an FI is resident in Mauritius as well as in any other jurisdiction, it will still have to operate the CRS in respect of any Reportable Account maintained in Mauritius.

While this may result in double reporting, it has the merit of simplicity.

In the case of a trust, the Mauritian Guidance states:

> In the case of a trust, notwithstanding the provisions of the Income Tax Act, it is considered to be resident in Mauritius for reporting purposes if one or more of its trustees are resident in Mauritius, unless all the information required to be reported in relation to the trust is reported to another Participating Jurisdiction's tax authority because it is treated as resident for tax purposes there[31]

HMRC take a slightly different approach in their guidance, focussing not on the possibility of double reporting, but on whether something is a UK Financial Institution, saying[32]:

> The various UK regulations for automatic exchange of financial account information impose obligations on UK Financial Institutions.
>
> A UK Financial institution is any Financial Institution resident in the UK, as well as any branch of a non-resident Financial Institution located in the UK.
>
> In many cases [the issue of] whether or not a Financial Institution is resident in or located in the UK will be clear, but there may be situations where this is less obvious.
>
> In these cases HMRC will look to determine the entity's status for the various automatic exchange of information agreements from the tax residence of the entity. If the Financial Institution is resident for tax purposes in the UK, then HMRC will regard the Financial Institution as within the scope of the UK Agreement.

---

[30] Page 15

[31] Ibid

[32] IEIM400620

It goes on to set out the position in relation to companies, trusts and partnerships[33]:

For these purposes, resident for tax purposes in the UK means the following:

> **For a company**
> If the company is incorporated in the UK or centrally managed and controlled in the UK. For example, a UK incorporated subsidiary of a foreign banking group will be a UK tax resident entity.
>
> **For a company not resident in the UK under the above test**
> Where it is within the charge to corporation tax if, and only if, it carries on a trade in the UK through a permanent establishment in the UK. For example, a UK branch of a foreign bank that trades through a permanent establishment in the UK will be UK tax resident.
>
> **For trusts**
> For CDOT, CRS and DAC purposes, if one or more of the trustees are resident in the UK for tax purposes then the trust is UK resident unless the trust is resident for tax purposes in another jurisdiction with which the UK automatically exchanges financial account information and the trust reports details of Reportable Accounts to that jurisdiction.
>
> For FATCA purposes a trust will be regarded as resident in the UK for reporting purposes where most or all of the trustees are resident in the UK for tax purposes. Where some of the trustees, but not all are UK tax resident, then the Trust is also to be treated as UK resident if the settlor is both resident and domiciled in the UK for tax purposes.
>
> **For partnerships**
> If the control and management of the business of the partnership takes place in the UK, or the partnership registers with and submits Partnership Tax Returns to HMRC.
>
> If an entity (other than a trust) is dual resident in the UK and in another CRS Participating Jurisdiction, **the obligation to report under the CRS is only to the jurisdiction(s) where the accounts are maintained. Where the accounts are maintained is a question of fact**.
>
> Entity Classification Elections made to the IRS are irrelevant for determining whether an entity is in scope for the agreements.
>
> Subsidiaries and branches of UK tax resident Financial Institutions that are located outside of the UK are not UK Financial Institutions.

---

[33] IEIM400620

> However, where such subsidiaries and branches act as introducers of business to a UK Financial Institution resulting in the financial accounts being held and maintained by the UK Financial Institution then the UK Financial Institution will be required to undertake the appropriate due diligence procedures and report the details of the accounts to HMRC
>
> (Emphasis added).

There is a risk of entities having a 'dual' reporting requirement because they are considered to be resident in more than one jurisdiction or, in the case of trusts, because they have trustees resident in more than one jurisdiction. In relation to corporate entities, this is likely to be because they are incorporated/registered in one jurisdiction, but are managed and controlled in another. There are, therefore, a number of different reporting outcomes for dual resident entities, somewhat dependent on the jurisdiction and its independent approach in guidance. In particular, the Guernsey Guidance (in relation to foundations)[34] states that where an entity is dual resident (in Guernsey and elsewhere), the Guernsey legislation should be applied in relation to Reportable Accounts maintained in Guernsey; however, dual resident Entities are apparently able to rely on the tiebreaker rules contained in tax conventions, in order to determine a single tax residence[35].

The other risk is that there is no jurisdiction to which the entity 'belongs' (most likely because it is not tax resident anywhere – though this will occur relatively rarely).[36]

6.10 Terminology: introduction

This is set out in Section VIII of the CRS[37]. The CRS-defined terms are heavily based on FATCA, though as set out above, they are not identical[38]. They adopt a 'linked approach', making it necessary to review several consecutive

[34] The Guernsey Guidance, paragraph 4.1.5

[35] This is permitted more generally by page 158 of the CRS Commentary.

[36] Indeed it may be the case that this cannot occur. The Bermuda Guidance, page 11 explains: 'However, where a Financial Institution (other than a trust) does not have a residence for tax purposes (e.g. because it is treated as fiscally transparent, or it is located in a jurisdiction that does not have an income tax), it is considered to be subject to the jurisdiction of a Participating Jurisdiction and it is, thus, a Participating Jurisdiction Financial Institution if:

a) it is incorporated under the laws of the Participating Jurisdiction;

b) it has its place of management (including effective management) in the Participating Jurisdiction; or

c) it is subject to financial supervision in the Participating Jurisdiction'

[37] It is a particular bugbear of at least one of the authors that increasingly legislation relegates defined terms to the end, thereby compelling the reader to study the legislation without the benefit of having perused the defined terms. While the CRS is not strictly legislation, the same issue arises.

[38] The Implementation Handbook, Part III compares CRS with FATCA and thus provides a simple guide to key differences between the two regimes.

parts of Section VIII to understand the exact meaning of the term 'initially defined'. For this reason, we take the terms out of their given order in the CRS, so as to – hopefully – aid comprehension.

'Entity'[39] means a legal person or a legal arrangement, such as a corporation, partnership, trust, or foundation. Note that this is wider than the common law definition (used in the UK and several other jurisdictions, including Jersey, Guernsey, Gibraltar and the Isle of Man) of a 'person'[40] which extends only to those with legal personality such as corporations. It is also wider than the OECD Model Treaty on Income and Capital definition of 'person'[41] which, again, differs from that commonly used in domestic legislation.

The Implementation Handbook echoes this, explaining that[42]:

> The definition of Entity is broad and consists of legal persons and legal arrangements, such as corporations, partnerships, trusts, and foundations. Individuals, including sole proprietorships, are therefore excluded from the definition of Reporting Financial Institutions

6.11 Financial Institutions

The term 'NFE'[43] means any Entity that is not a Financial Institution[44]. Thus, to distinguish, we must understand what constitutes a Financial Institution (Financial Institutions are further subdivided, but this is discussed further below).

The term 'Financial Institution' means:
(i) a Custodial Institution,
(ii) a Depository Institution,
(iii) an Investment Entity, or
(iv) a Specified Insurance Company.

'Investment Entity' is the broadest, and arguably, therefore, the most important of these definitions, particularly for those involved in private client and/or trusts work. It is also the most commonly found in trust and private client work. Consequently, we deal with the other categories of Financial Institution first, and more briefly. Before doing so, however, it is helpful to consider the definition of 'Financial Asset'[45], an understanding of which is essential to understand and apply many of the following

[39] Section VIII, paragraph E3
[40] Both of which are themselves different from the definition of person in DAC6 and MDR.
[41] Article 3(1): the term 'person' includes an individual, a company and any other body of persons
[42] Paragraph 117
[43] Section VIII, paragraph D7
[44] This is a good example of the definitional approach common to the CRS and FATCA (increasingly – and some might say, unfortunately – common in domestic legislation)
[45] Section VIII A(7)

definitions, for example, determining whether something qualifies as an Investment Entity, is reliant upon a thorough understanding of what qualifies as a Financial Asset. The OECD Commentary also notes:

> The term 'Financial Asset' is used in the definition of the terms 'Custodial Institution', 'Investment Entity', 'Custodial Account' and 'Excluded Account'. While it does not refer to assets of every kind, it intends to encompass any assets that may be held in an account maintained by a Financial Institution with the exception of a non-debt, direct interest in real property.

It is an important definition, often under-accounted for in domestic guidance and legislation.

It is defined in the following way:

> The term 'Financial Asset' includes a security (for example, a share of stock in a corporation; partnership or beneficial ownership interest in a widely held or publicly traded partnership or trust; note, bond, debenture, or other evidence of indebtedness), partnership interest, commodity, swap (for example, interest rate swaps, currency swaps, basis swaps, interest rate caps, interest rate floors, commodity swaps, equity swaps, equity index swaps, and similar agreements), Insurance Contract or Annuity Contract, or any interest (including a futures or forward contract or option) in a security, partnership interest, commodity, swap, Insurance Contract, or Annuity Contract. The term 'Financial Asset' does not include a non-debt, direct interest in real property

The form of language used – 'includes' – shows that the definition is intended to be illustrative rather than exhaustive; while the things listed will be Financial Assets, there are other things that may also be within the definition. This method of definition by illustration is seemingly designed to allow scope for authorities to expand on what can be imagined today at a later date, without revising the base definitions. It is being seen increasingly and allows leeway for authorities in guidance and practice, creating uncertainty and leading to conservative approaches on the part of practitioners. It is another example of authorities leaving a certain 'creative ambiguity', to ensure taxpayers feel that anything other than the most conservative approach is a risk not worth taking.

In relation to Financial Assets, the Implementation Handbook says:

> The definition of Financial Asset in the Standard is consistent with the current US FATCA Regulations except that nondebt direct investments in real property have been specifically excluded from the Standard as a clarification. Jurisdictions could adopt the

> approach in the Standard and rely on it for purposes of both the Standard and the Model 1 FATCA IGA[46]

This could, of course, result in domestic rules requiring an excess of reporting in relation to FATCA. It will be necessary to consult the domestic rules where there is a concern of excess FATCA reporting (and indeed, the USA is unlikely to accept that OECD guidance on the CRS is in any way conclusive of what should be reported under FATCA).

The term 'Custodial Institution'[47] means any Entity that holds, as a substantial portion of its business, Financial Assets for the account of others. An Entity holds Financial Assets for the account of others as a substantial portion of its business if the Entity's gross income attributable to the holding of Financial Assets and related financial services equals or exceeds 20% of the Entity's gross income during the shorter of: (i) the three-year period that ends on 31 December (or the final day of a non-calendar year accounting period) prior to the year in which the determination is being made; or (ii) the period during which the Entity has been in existence.

The OECD Commentary says:[48]

> custodian banks, brokers and central securities depositories,[49] would generally be considered Custodial Institutions. Entities that do not hold Financial Assets for the account of others, such as insurance brokers, will not be Custodial Institutions.

HMRC give examples of when certain types of entities will be considered Custodial Institutions. In relation to Trusts, it says:[50]

> A trust can be either a financial institution or a Non-Financial Entity. Where a trust meets one of the definitions for being a Financial Institution [see IEIM400600] it is most likely to be an Investment Entity [see IEIM400760] but it may, alternatively, meet the requirements for being a Custodial Institution [see IEIM400640].
>
> For example, shares held in trust may be in a Custodial Account [see IEIM402200] and therefore subject to reporting by the trust as the Custodial Institution that holds the account. This may be the case where a trust such as an Employee Benefit Trust continues to hold financial assets, such as shares, for an employee after they have been granted.
>
> Where an Employee Benefit Trust holds shares for the future benefit of employees, but the shares are not allocated, then under most

---

[46] Page 129
[47] Section VII, paragraph A4
[48] Commentary, page 160, paragraph 11
[49] HMRC disagree with the OECD in relation to central securities depositories
[50] IEIM400070

> circumstances this right to a future allocation would not fall to be a custodial account. Similarly, when shares are allocated and the trustee is directed to transfer the assets as soon as reasonably possible to the beneficiary, a broker, a custodian, etc., then the trust will not be treated as maintaining a financial account for the duration of time it takes to complete the transfer

This – in our view – illustrates that entity classification under CRS is not always straightforward. It is not entirely clear why an employee benefit trust would be a Custodial Institution and not an Investment Entity; at the very least this would presumably depend on the circumstances of the individual EBT. It is also plausible that a trust could meet the criteria of a Custodial Institution and an Investment Entity. This may not make any difference to the classification of the entity in question as an NFE or Financial Institution but may have a 'knock on' effect when classifying accounts.

Of particular interest in this category is the central securities depository. In this respect HMRC say:[51]

> In the UK a Central Securities Depository (CSD) will not be treated as maintaining financial accounts. The participants of UK securities settlement systems that hold interests recorded in the CSD are either Financial Institutions in their own right, or they access the system through a Financial Institution (a sponsor), or are not subject to reporting obligations. It is these Financial Institutions that maintain the accounts and it is these participants and/or sponsors that are responsible for undertaking any reporting obligations.
>
> For example, members of the CREST securities settlement system (CREST system) operated by Euroclear UK & Ireland Limited (EUI), or the Financial Institution that accesses the CREST system on their behalf, are responsible for i) ensuring that the relevant member is compliant and ii) any reporting required by the agreement in respect of securities held by means of the CREST system. EUI acting as the CSD is not required to undertake any due diligence and reporting required by the agreement in respect of such securities

As mentioned above the OECD Commentary and the HMRC International Exchange of Information Manual disagree on this point. How to resolve this conflict? Guidance and commentary are not binding, however, it is not wise to ignore them. The options are the following:

(i) to develop one's own interpretation of the application of the provision in the context of the facts at hand;
(ii) to adopt the (tax-) cautious position of adopting the approach that requires the most reporting; or

[51] IEIM400680

(iii) to adopt the more generally cautious approach of reporting the least information possible, which may protect the Financial Institution from accusation of data protection breaches and protect the client from reporting.

Which is the correct approach? If you have doubts that the interpretation or approach in guidance is correct, you should not follow it merely because it is guidance. Guidance is not law. Thus the first approach is always the best (indeed we would say the only truly correct) approach. What about the position where each is equally arguable?

The term 'Depository Institution' means any Entity that accepts deposits in the ordinary course of a banking or similar business. Central banks are not Depository Institutions. The Implementation Handbook explains:

> 13. An Entity is considered to be engaged in a 'banking or similar business' if, in the ordinary course of its business with customers, the Entity accepts deposits or other similar investments of funds and regularly engages in one or more of the following activities:
>
> a) makes personal, mortgage, industrial, or other loans or provides other extensions of credit;
> b) purchases, sells, discounts, or negotiates accounts receivable, instalment obligations, notes, drafts, checks, bills of exchange, acceptances, or other evidences of indebtedness;
> c) issues letters of credit and negotiates drafts drawn thereunder;
> d) provides trust or fiduciary services;
> e) finances foreign exchange transactions; or
> f) enters into, purchases, or disposes of finance leases or leased assets.
>
> An Entity is not considered to be engaged in a banking or similar business if the Entity solely accepts deposits from persons as a collateral or security pursuant to a sale or lease of property or pursuant to a similar financing arrangement between such Entity and the person holding the deposit with the Entity.
>
> 14. Savings banks, commercial banks, savings and loan associations, and credit unions would generally be considered Depository Institutions. However, whether an Entity conducts a banking or similar business is determined based upon the character of the actual activities of such Entity

The term 'Investment Entity' is likely the broadest category, and covers (initially) two separate situations. It is preferable to set out the definition as given in the CRS:

> The term 'Investment Entity' means any Entity:

a) that primarily conducts as a business one or more of the following activities or operations for or on behalf of a customer:
   i) trading in money market instruments (cheques, bills, certificates of deposit, derivatives, etc.); foreign exchange; exchange, interest rate and index instruments; transferable securities; or commodity futures trading;
   ii) individual and collective portfolio management; or
   iii) otherwise investing, administering, or managing Financial Assets or money on behalf of other persons; or
b) the gross income of which is primarily attributable to investing, reinvesting, or trading in Financial Assets, if the Entity is managed by another Entity that is a Depository Institution, a Custodial Institution, a Specified Insurance Company, or an Investment Entity described in subparagraph A(6)(a).

This covers two separate matters:
i) Investment Entities in their own right (under (a)); and
ii) 'managed by' Investment Entities under (b).

An Entity is treated as primarily conducting as a business one or more of the activities described above, if the Entity's gross income attributable to the relevant activities equals or exceeds 50% of the Entity's gross income during the shorter of:
(i) the three-year period ending on 31 December of the year preceding the year in which the determination is made; or
(ii) the period during which the Entity has been in existence.

An Entity is '<u>managed by</u>' another Entity if the managing Entity performs, either directly or through another service provider, any of the requisite activities or operations on behalf of the managed Entity. However, an Entity does not manage another Entity if it does not have discretionary authority to manage the Entity's assets (in whole or part). Where an Entity is managed by a mix of entities and individuals, it is considered to be managed by a financial institution, if any of the managing Entities is such another Entity.

The Commentary explains:

> 15. The term 'Investment Entity' includes two types of Entities: Entities that primarily conduct as a business investment activities or operations on behalf of other persons, and Entities that are managed by those Entities or other Financial Institutions

In relation to 'managed by' Investment Entities the Commentary says:

> 17. Subparagraph A(6)(b) defines the second type of 'Investment Entity' as any Entity the gross income of which is primarily attributable to investing, reinvesting, or trading in Financial Assets, if the Entity is managed by another Entity that is a

> Depository Institution, a Custodial Institution, a Specified Insurance Company, or an Investment Entity described in subparagraph A(6)(a). An Entity is 'managed by' another Entity if the managing Entity performs, either directly or through another service provider, any of the activities or operations described in subparagraph A(6)(a) on behalf of the managed Entity. However, an Entity does not manage another Entity if it does not have discretionary authority to manage the Entity's assets (in whole or part). Where an Entity is managed by a mix of Financial Institutions, NFEs or individuals, the Entity is considered to be managed by another Entity that is a Depository Institution, a Custodial Institution, a Specified Insurance Company, or an Investment Entity described in subparagraph A(6)(a), if any of the managing Entities is such another Entity.

Thus this gives three useful points of clarification:

(i) The meaning of 'managed by' is restricted by reference to subparagraph A(6)(a);
(ii) 'Discretionary authority' is a requisite part of being 'managed by' another entity; and
(iii) Where there are a mix of Financial Institutions and NFEs or individuals that manage an entity, the simple fact that one of its 'managers' is a Financial Institution should be sufficient to render it a 'managed by' financial institution.

In relation to the second of these, the Isle of Man Guidance explains (at paragraph 4.2.2):

> For the purposes of the 'managed by' test, a distinction should be made between one Entity 'managing' another and one Entity 'administering' another.
>
> For instance, the following services provided by an Entity to another will not constitute the latter entity being 'managed by' the former:-
> - provision of co-secretary and/or company secretarial services;
> - provision of registered office;
> - preparation of final financial statements (from company books and records);
> - preparation of Tax and/or VAT returns;
> - provision of bookkeeping services including budgeting and cash-flow forecasts.

We consider that this is accurate. In relation to the third, the Isle of Man Guidance continues:

> Where an Isle of Man company's directors are employees of an Isle of Man TCSP, which itself is a Financial Institution, or where the director is a corporate director wholly owned by that Isle of Man TCSP, and the Isle of Man company is administered by that Isle of

Man TCSP Financial Institution, the Isle of Man company may be treated as being 'managed by' a Financial Institution, and so be an Investment Entity itself, so long as those directors have the discretionary authority to manage the Entity's Financial Assets.

Where an Entity is managed by a mix of Financial Institutions, NFEs or individuals, the Entity is considered to be managed by another Entity that is a Depository Institution, a Custodial Institution, a Specified Insurance Company or an Investment Entity described in subparagraph a), if any of the managing Entities is such another Entity.

Similarly, HMRC say[52]:

Trusts Managed by a Financial Institution
A trust is typically regarded as being managed by a Financial Institution where either one or more of the trustees is a Financial Institution [see IEIM400600] or the trustees have appointed a Financial Institution, such as a discretionary fund manager, to manage the trust's assets or to manage the trust.

Does a Financial Institution Manage the Trust?
A Financial Institution will manage the trust where it has been appointed by the trustees to carry out the day-to-day functions of the trust on behalf of the trustees. This goes beyond managing the investment of the trust's assets and includes other management functions that the trustees have to perform but which are contracted to the Financial Institution.

Does a Financial Institution Manage the Financial Assets of the Trust?
A Financial Institution manages the financial assets of the trust where it has discretion to manage the investments or investment strategy for the assets. This will usually be where the trust has appointed a discretionary fund manager to manage their portfolio or a part thereof. The appointment of a discretionary fund manager will be evidenced by an agreement between the parties that provides for discretionary management.

Where the trustees of a trust invest in retail investments and the trustees make the decision on what investments to make, the arrangement will not amount to discretionary management. The Glossary of Definitions in the Financial Services Handbook defines both retail investment and retail investment activity

We also consider it correct to say that a trust is managed by a trustee that has been instructed to carry out its day-to-day functions. While this is

---

[52] IEIM400820

undoubtedly correct, thought should be given to whether something less than this might be sufficient. For example, what about a trust where day-to-day administrative decisions are made elsewhere, but the fiduciary decisions are made by the trustee? It is considered at least arguable that such a trust would potentially qualify as a 'managed by' investment entity.

The OECD Commentary continues:

> The term 'Investment Entity', as defined in subparagraph A(6), does not include an Entity that is an Active NFE because it meets any of the criteria in subparagraphs D(9)(d) through (g) (i.e. holding NFEs and treasury centres that are members of a nonfinancial group; start-up NFEs; and NFEs that are liquidating or emerging from bankruptcy).
>
> An Entity would generally be considered an Investment Entity if it functions or holds itself out as a collective investment vehicle, mutual fund, exchange traded fund, private equity fund, hedge fund, venture capital fund, leveraged buy-out fund or any similar investment vehicle established with an investment strategy of investing, reinvesting, or trading in Financial Assets.
>
> An Entity that primarily conducts as a business investing, administering, or managing non-debt, direct interests in real property on behalf of other persons, such as a type of real estate investment trust, will not be an Investment Entity

Whilst lacking any guidance which deviates from the bare bones of the legislation, the language is certainly clear, although that very clarity forces some absurd outcomes upon those consulting it. For example, a business (Company A) is actively carrying out trade or some other activity, such as renting property, and has surplus funds that amount to a minority of its assets. If those funds are placed into a discretionary investment account, managed by a financial institution (such as an investment bank) then it is the logical conclusion (and one drawn by banks on a daily basis) that Company A will satisfy the 'Investment Entity' test because the investment bank is managing Company A's assets 'in whole or in part'. This will then impose a set of reporting obligations on a company which, depending on its status as an active or passive NFE, would otherwise simply have to take no action or complete a self-certification form and leave the investment bank to make any reports.

Another point arises: what determines whether an Entity's gross income is primarily attributable to `investing, reinvesting, or trading in Financial Assets? This requires consideration of the definition of Financial Assets but also of what is primarily attributable? This is not set out in the CRS. The Isle of Man Guidance[53] states:

> When using the CRS definition of an Investment Entity an Entity which meets the 'managed by' test must also consider whether its gross income is primarily attributable to Financial Assets.
>
> Income is only primarily attributable where the Entity holds a **direct** investment in the Financial Asset

It goes on to set out the following example. BB is a trust which holds a debenture, from which it receives interest, which is BB's only source of income. It is managed by a trust company service provider, and so meets both elements of a 'managed by' Investment Entity. This is straightforward.

The Isle of Man Guidance develops more complex examples, including that of the DD Trust holding shares in DEF Limited, which receives rental income from real property. While DEF Limited holds non-Financial Assets, the only asset of the DD Trust is shares (a Financial Asset) and its 'income' is dividends paid by DEF Limited. Thus, while the indirect source is non-Financial Assets, DD Trust's gross income is directly attributable to the Financial Asset – the shares in DEF Limited. Thus, we agree with the Isle of Man Guidance that DD Trust would be an Investment Entity.

The obligations of a Reporting Financial Institution – discussed in more detail below – essentially amount to the following:

(i) Identify its 'accounts';
(ii) Identify the account holders;
(iii) From individual account holders – seek self-certification of tax residence;
(iv) For corporates – classify corporates into their CRS classification;
(v) From corporate account holders – seek self-certification as to CRS classification;
(vi) Identify 'indicia' (indicators) in the pre-existing database of information held by the Reporting Financial Institution;
(vii) Test whether the information provided by the account holder on the self-certification form is reasonable by comparison to the information already held;
(viii) Notify those account holders on whom reports will be made; and
(ix) Make reports on the account holders.

These requirements are discussed in greater detail below.

6.12 Reporting status of financial institutions

This requires a little introduction. Essentially, Financial Institutions (and indeed Financial Accounts) that are at low risk of being used for tax evasion have different, or no reporting requirements (though they may still have

---

[53] At paragraph 4.2.3

obligations under the CRS – for example their categorisation for the purposes of CRS. This is – should be – axiomatic). These Financial Institutions are made 'Non-Reporting'. In relation to Non-Reporting Financial Institutions there are (really) two categories – (i) those that the CRS expressly identifies as being Non-Reporting Financial Institutions; and (ii) those which domestic law identifies as being Non-Reporting Financial Institutions (see Section VIII, B)(1)(c)). In relation to the latter the Implementation Handbook explains[54]:

> 37. Given the standardised approach taken in the CRS, there may be jurisdiction-specific Financial Institutions and Financial Accounts that present a low risk of being used for tax evasion but which the CRS does not specifically identify as such. The CRS therefore provides for jurisdictions to identify these as Non-Reporting Financial Institutions or Excluded Accounts (i.e. non-reportable accounts) in their domestic law. This is a key area for jurisdictions to consider during the legislative process.
>
> 38. Jurisdictions will then need to consider whether the institutions and accounts that have been identified as potentially low risk meet the terms of the Standard. The Standard requires that either the institution or account meets the conditions required by the categories of low-risk institutions or accounts contained in the CRS, or they must be similar to the specified categories and have equivalent conditions to any particular requirements they do not meet. Finally, their inclusion as low risk must not frustrate the purposes of the Standard

Thus again, this is an area where approach may differ between jurisdictions. Recourse to domestic law is therefore of particular importance in these circumstances.

CRS sets out a number of entities that are low risk, and therefore qualify as Non-Reporting Financial Institutions. Again, many of these will not arise frequently in practice, but we consider the following of particular importance:

(i) a Broad Participation Retirement Fund;
(ii) a Narrow Participation Retirement Fund;
(iii) an Exempt Collective Investment Vehicle; and
(iv) a trust to the extent that the trustee of the trust is a Reporting Financial Institution and reports all information required to be reported pursuant to Section I with respect to all Reportable Accounts of the trust (often referred to as a 'Trustee Documented Trust' (the FATCA name for a

---

[54] At page 28

similar concept thereunder) or 'TDT'[55]). We focus on these four categories.

Section VIII, B(1) defines Non-Reporting Financial Institution:

Non-Reporting Financial Institution

1. The term 'Non-Reporting Financial Institution' means any Financial Institution that is:
   a) a Governmental Entity, International Organisation or Central Bank, other than with respect to a payment that is derived from an obligation held in connection with a commercial financial activity of a type engaged in by a Specified Insurance Company, Custodial Institution, or Depository Institution;
   b) a Broad Participation Retirement Fund; a Narrow Participation Retirement Fund; a Pension Fund of a Governmental Entity, International Organisation or Central Bank; or a Qualified Credit Card Issuer;
   c) any other Entity that presents a low risk of being used to evade tax, has substantially similar characteristics to any of the Entities described in subparagraphs B(1)(a) and (b), and is defined in domestic law as a Non-Reporting Financial Institution, provided that the status of such Entity as a Non-Reporting Financial Institution does not frustrate the purposes of the Common Reporting Standard;
   d) an Exempt Collective Investment Vehicle; or
   e) a trust to the extent that the trustee of the trust is a Reporting Financial Institution and reports all information required to be reported pursuant to Section I with respect to all Reportable Accounts of the trust

Some of these terms are dealt with further in the CRS, in the definitions following that of a Non-Reporting Financial Institution. It is convenient to set them out. We do not go into detail on many of these specific forms of Non-Reporting Financial Institution, since they will rarely arise in practice. One such type of entity is the 'Governmental Entity'[56], which is defined in the following way:

The term 'Governmental Entity' means the government of a jurisdiction, any political subdivision of a jurisdiction (which, for the avoidance of doubt, includes a state, province, county, or municipality), or any wholly owned agency or instrumentality of a jurisdiction or of any one or more of the foregoing (each, a

[55] Indeed, the CRS Commentary calls such entities 'Trustee-Documented Trusts' It is a shame the term is not also imported into the CRS itself.

[56] Section VIII, B(2)

'Governmental Entity'). This category is comprised of the integral parts, controlled entities, and political subdivisions of a jurisdiction.

a) An 'integral part' of a jurisdiction means any person, organisation, agency, bureau, fund, instrumentality, or other body, however designated, that constitutes a governing authority of a jurisdiction. The net earnings of the governing authority must be credited to its own account or to other accounts of the jurisdiction, with no portion inuring to the benefit of any private person. An integral part does not include any individual who is a sovereign, official, or administrator acting in a private or personal capacity.
b) A controlled entity means an Entity that is separate in form from the jurisdiction or that otherwise constitutes a separate juridical entity, provided that:
    i) the Entity is wholly owned and controlled by one or more Governmental Entities directly or through one or more controlled entities;
    ii) the Entity's net earnings are credited to its own account or to the accounts of one or more Governmental Entities, with no portion of its income inuring to the benefit of any private person; and
    iii) the Entity's assets vest in one or more Governmental Entities upon dissolution.
c) Income does not inure to the benefit of private persons if such persons are the intended beneficiaries of a governmental programme, and the programme activities are performed for

the general public with respect to the common welfare or relate to the administration of some phase of government. Notwithstanding the foregoing, however, income is considered to inure to the benefit of private persons if the income is derived from the use of a governmental entity to conduct a commercial business, such as a commercial banking business, that provides financial services to private persons.

The CRS Guidance[57] goes on to say:

33. In order to promote international trade and development, many jurisdictions have established export or development financing programmes or agencies which may either provide loans directly or insure or guarantee loans granted by commercial lenders. Those agencies would generally be considered Governmental Entities and, thus, Non-Reporting Financial Institutions (see paragraph 31 above).

---

[57] At page 167

Similarly, 'International Organisation' is defined thus in Section VIII, B(3):

> The term 'International Organisation' means any international organisation or wholly owned agency or instrumentality thereof. This category includes any intergovernmental organisation (including a supranational organisation) (1) that is comprised primarily of governments; (2) that has in effect a headquarters or substantially similar agreement with the jurisdiction; and (3) the income of which does not inure to the benefit of private persons.

'Central Bank'[58] is defined in the following way:

> The term 'Central Bank' means an institution that is by law or government sanction the principal authority, other than the government of the jurisdiction itself, issuing instruments intended to circulate as currency. Such an institution may include an instrumentality that is separate from the government of the jurisdiction, whether or not owned in whole or in part by the jurisdiction

A 'Broad Participation Retirement Scheme' is (Section VIII, C(5)):

> The term 'Broad Participation Retirement Fund' means a fund established to provide retirement, disability, or death benefits, or any combination thereof, to beneficiaries that are current or former employees (or persons designated by such employees) of one or more employers in consideration for services rendered, provided that the fund:
>
> a) does not have a single beneficiary with a right to more than five per cent of the fund's assets;
>
> b) is subject to government regulation and provides information reporting to the tax authorities; and
>
> c) satisfies at least one of the following requirements:
>
>   i) the fund is generally exempt from tax on investment income, or taxation of such income is deferred or taxed at a reduced rate, due to its status as a retirement or pension plan;
>
>   ii) the fund receives at least 50% of its total contributions (other than transfers of assets from other plans described in subparagraphs B(5) through (7) or from retirement and pension accounts described in subparagraph C(17)(a)) from the sponsoring employers;
>
>   iii) distributions or withdrawals from the fund are allowed only upon the occurrence of specified events related to retirement, disability, or death (except rollover distributions to other retirement funds described in

[58] Section VIII, C(4)

subparagraphs B(5) through (7) or retirement and pension accounts described in subparagraph C(17)(a)), or penalties apply to distributions or withdrawals made before such specified events; or

iv) contributions (other than certain permitted make-up contributions) by employees to the fund are limited by reference to earned income of the employee or may not exceed USD 50 000 annually, applying the rules set forth in paragraph C of Section VII for account aggregation and currency translation

Further clarification is given by the CRS Commentary, which explains:

> 37. Information reporting required in subparagraph B(5)(b) may vary among jurisdictions. While one jurisdiction could require that the fund provides annual information about its beneficiaries, another jurisdiction could require that the fund provides monthly information about contributions and associated tax relief, and annual information about its beneficiaries and total contributions from sponsoring employers. However, whether a fund provides information reporting to the relevant tax authorities in the jurisdiction in which the fund is established or operates is determinative of whether a fund satisfies the requirement under that subparagraph

'Narrow Participation Retirement Fund' means:

> The term 'Narrow Participation Retirement Fund' means a fund established to provide retirement, disability, or death benefits to beneficiaries that are current or former employees (or persons designated by such employees) of one or more employers in consideration for services rendered, provided that:
>
> a) the fund has fewer than 50 participants;
> b) the fund is sponsored by one or more employers that are not Investment Entities or Passive NFEs;
> c) the employee and employer contributions to the fund (other than transfers of assets from retirement and pension accounts described in subparagraph C(17)(a)) are limited by reference to earned income and compensation of the employee, respectively;
> d) participants that are not residents of the jurisdiction in which the fund is established are not entitled to more than 20% of the fund's assets; and
> e) the fund is subject to government regulation and provides information reporting to the tax authorities

Again, the CRS Commentary offers the following clarification:

39. Subparagraph B(6)(c) requires that the employee and employee contributions to the fund are limited by reference to earned income and compensation of the employee, respectively. While that subparagraph excludes certain transfers of assets from the threshold (i.e. those from retirement and pension accounts described in subparagraph C(17)(a)), other transfers of assets could also be excluded, such as those from other plans described in subparagraphs B(5) through (7).

40. Information reporting required in subparagraph B(6)(e) may vary among jurisdictions. As mentioned in paragraph 37 above, whether a fund provides information reporting to the relevant tax authorities in the jurisdiction in which the fund is established or operates is determinative of whether a fund satisfies the requirement under that subparagraph

Thus the position, in relation to the impact of domestic law on qualification as both a Broad and Narrow Participation Retirement Fund, is similar.

Turning to 'Exempt Collective Investment Vehicles', these are:

> The term 'Exempt Collective Investment Vehicle' means an Investment Entity that is regulated as a collective investment vehicle, provided that all of the interests in the collective investment vehicles are held by or through individuals or Entities that are not Reportable Persons, except a Passive NFE with Controlling Persons who are Reportable Persons.
>
> An Investment Entity that is regulated as a collective investment vehicle does not fail to qualify under subparagraph B(9) as an Exempt Collective Investment Vehicle, solely because the collective investment vehicle has issued physical shares in bearer form, provided that:
>
> a) the collective investment vehicle has not issued, and does not issue, any physical shares in bearer form after [xx/xx/xxxx];
> b) the collective investment vehicle retires all such shares upon surrender;
> c) the collective investment vehicle performs the due diligence procedures set forth in Sections II through VII and reports any information required to be reported with respect to any such shares when such shares are presented for redemption or other payment; and
> d) the collective investment vehicle has in place policies and procedures to ensure that such shares are redeemed or immobilised as soon as possible, and in any event prior to [xx/xx/xxxx]

Finally, we come to what is probably for most practitioners in the private client and trusts world, the most important type of Non-Reporting Financial

Institution. This is the TDT, which is 'a trust to the extent that the trustee of the trust is a Reporting Financial Institution and reports all information required to be reported pursuant to Section I with respect to all Reportable Accounts of the trust'. This is a particularly important form of Non-Reporting Financial Institution, because it means that where you have trusts that are Financial Institutions, the reporting requirements in relation to them can be 'pooled' and dealt with by a single entity: the trustee. This is usually of great importance for trust companies, since they might otherwise have hundreds or thousands of 'managed by' trust Financial Institutions, all with their own reporting requirements.

The CRS Commentary is particularly instructive here. It says:

> 55. A trust that is a Financial Institution (e.g. because it is an Investment Entity) is a Non-Reporting Financial Institution, according to subparagraph B(1)(e), to the extent that the trustee of the trust is a Reporting Financial Institution and reports all information required to be reported pursuant to Section I with respect to all Reportable Accounts of the trust.
>
> 56. This category of Non-Reporting Financial Institution reaches a similar result as that under paragraph D of Section II, according to which Reporting Financial Institutions may be allowed to rely on service providers to fulfil their reporting and due diligence obligations.[59] The only difference between that paragraph and this category is that the reporting and due diligence obligations fulfilled by service providers remain the responsibility of the Reporting Financial Institution, while the responsibility of those fulfilled by the trustee of a Trustee-Documented Trust is transferred by the trust to its trustee. This category does not modify, however, the time and manner of the reporting and due diligence obligations which remain the same as if they still were the responsibility of the trust. For example, the trustee must not report the information with respect to a Reportable Account of the Trustee-Documented Trust as if it were a Reportable Account of the trustee. The trustee must report such information as the Trustee-Documented Trust would have reported (e.g. to the same jurisdiction) and identify the Trustee-Documented Trust with respect to which it fulfils the reporting and due diligence obligations. This category of Non-Reporting Financial Institution may also apply to a legal arrangement that is equivalent or similar to a trust, such as a fideicomiso

---

[59] This is the equivalent of FATCA's 'sponsored entity'. Again, it is a useful position which can reduce the number of Reporting Financial Institutions with which an organisation has to deal, in favour of one such Reporting Financial Institution dealing with reporting for all.

It is left to the person applying CRS to decide whether a legal arrangement is 'similar to' a trust. In such cases, we would suggest it would be a simpler and more certain result – at least from a practical perspective – for entities that are 'similar to' a trust to be dealt with under Section II, D. This eliminates the risk that the entity in question is not considered to be sufficiently similar to a trust and to have failed to comply with its obligations as a reporting Financial Institution.

6.13 Non financial entities

Another essential definition is that of 'NFE' – Non-Financial Entity (essentially something that is not a Financial Institution). These are further divided into active and passive NFEs. Status as an active or passive NFE determines the severity of the reporting[60]. The CRS Commentary explains[61]:

> 122. The term 'NFE' is an acronym for Non-Financial Entity and it means, according to subparagraph D(7), any Entity that is not a Financial Institution. An NFE can be either a Passive NFE or an Active NFE. Subparagraphs D(8) and (9) set forth the meaning of the terms 'Passive NFE' and 'Active NFE', respectively

The next three or four definitions go together. The CRS Commentary continues:

> 121. Subparagraphs D(6) through (9) define the terms 'NFE', 'Passive NFE', 'Active NFE' and 'Controlling Persons', which are relevant for purposes of determining whether an Entity is a Passive NFE with one or more Controlling Persons who are Reportable Persons. When that is the case, as described in subparagraphs D(2) of Section V and A(2) of Section VI, then the account must be treated as a Reportable Account[62]

Active NFEs and Passive NFEs compromise all sorts of entities that are not Financial Institutions (and indeed some entities can be classified either as a Financial Institution or an NFE). The distinction between active and passive is essentially one of risk; those entities that are low risk for evasion – for example, trading companies – are assigned to the 'Active NFE' category and are not subject to reporting in the same way as higher risk Passive NFEs. In practice, most NFEs involved in financial planning will be Passive NFEs, but it is important to be able to spot an active NFE.

'Passive NFE'[63] means any:

(i) NFE that is not an Active NFE; or

---

[60] Active NFEs are those that pose lower risk of being used for evasion purposes, such as trading entities.

[61] Page 195

[62] Ibid. This may be as close as possible as we can get to the 'essence' of CRS reporting, which is discussed in greater detail below.

[63] Section VIII A(8)

(ii) a 'managed by' Investment Entity that is not a Participating Jurisdiction Financial Institution.[64]

Thus, to understand what a passive NFE is (to which greater reporting requirements attach) it is necessary to understand what constitutes an Active NFE.

In relation to the latter type of passive NFE, the CRS Commentary[65] says:

> In principle, a 'Passive NFE' means an NFE that is not an Active NFE. However, subparagraph D(8) also includes an Investment Entity described in subparagraph A(6)(b) [managed by Investment Entity] that is not a Participating Jurisdiction Financial Institution. As a result, Reporting Financial Institutions are required to look-through that type of Investment Entity, as illustrated by the following example: Jurisdiction A has a reciprocal agreement on the automatic exchange of financial account information in place with Jurisdiction B, but has no agreement in place with Jurisdiction C. W, a Jurisdiction A Reporting Financial Institution, maintains Financial Accounts for Entities X and Y, both of which are Investment Entities as described in subparagraph A(6)(b). Entity X is resident in Jurisdiction B and Entity Y is resident in Jurisdiction C. From the perspective of W, Entity X is a Participating Jurisdiction Financial Institution and Entity Y is not a Participating Jurisdiction Financial Institution. As a result, W must treat Entity Y as a Passive NFE pursuant to subparagraph D(8)

'Active NFE'[66] means any NFE that meets any of the following criteria:

(i) less than 50% of the NFE's gross income for the preceding calendar year or other appropriate reporting period is passive income; and

(ii) less than 50% of the assets held by the NFE during the preceding calendar year or other appropriate reporting period are assets that produce or are held for the production of passive income.

---

[64] This is where the definitions can become somewhat obscure. A Participating Jurisdiction Financial Institution is defined at Section VIII A(2), which provides:

The term 'Participating Jurisdiction Financial Institution' means

(i) any Financial Institution that is resident in a Participating Jurisdiction, but excludes any branch of that Financial Institution that is located outside such Participating Jurisdiction, and

(ii) any branch of a Financial Institution that is not resident in a Participating Jurisdiction, if that branch is located in such Participating Jurisdiction.

A Participating Jurisdiction is 'means a jurisdiction (i) with which an agreement is in place pursuant to which it will

provide the information specified in Section I, and (ii) which is identified in a published list'. This doesn't add much but in practice we will usually know whether something is or is not a Participating Jurisdiction.

[65] Page 195

[66] Section VIII, A(9)

In relation to Active NFEs, the CRS Commentary[67] explains:

> Any NFE can be an Active NFE, provided that it meets any of the criteria listed in subparagraph D(9). In summary, those criteria refer to:
> a) active NFEs by reason of income and assets;
> b) publicly traded NFEs;
> c) Governmental Entities, International Organisations, Central Banks, or their wholly owned Entities;
> d) holding NFEs that are members of a nonfinancial group;
> e) start-up NFEs;
> f) NFEs that are liquidating or emerging from bankruptcy;
> g) treasury centres that are members of a nonfinancial group; or
> h) non-profit NFEs

The CRS Commentary on the eight separate categories is extensive. We take them in order, although the CRS Commentary does not encompass all categories.

The CRS Commentary starts by explaining[68]:

> 125. Subparagraph D(9)(a) describes the criterion to qualify for the Active NFE status for 'active NFEs by reason of income and assets' as follows: less than 50% of the NFE's gross income for the preceding calendar year or other appropriate reporting period is passive income and less than 50% of the assets held by the NFE during the preceding calendar year or other appropriate reporting period are assets that produce or are held for the production of passive income.
>
> 126. In determining what is meant by 'passive income', reference must be made to each jurisdiction's particular rules. Passive income would generally be considered to include the portion of gross income that consists of:
> a) dividends;
> b) interest;
> c) income equivalent to interest;
> d) rents and royalties, other than rents and royalties derived in the active conduct of a business conducted, at least in part, by employees of the NFE;
> e) annuities;
> f) the excess of gains over losses from the sale or exchange of Financial Assets that gives rise to the passive income described previously;

[67] Page 195
[68] Page 196

> g) the excess of gains over losses from transactions (including futures, forwards, options, and similar transactions) in any Financial Assets;
> h) the excess of foreign currency gains over foreign currency losses;
> i) net income from swaps; or
> j) amounts received under Cash Value Insurance Contracts.
>
> Notwithstanding the foregoing, passive income will not include, in the case of a NFE that regularly acts as a dealer in Financial Assets, any income from any transaction entered into in the ordinary course of such dealer's business as such a dealer
>
> 127. The value of a NFE's assets is determined based on the fair market value or book value of the assets that is reflected on the NFE's balance sheet.

Thus, there is some degree of control left to the domestic law. This is a clear reminder that we always need to consider the domestic legislation and, to a lesser extent, the domestic guidance, rather than simply relying on the model terms as set out by the OECD. However, in the case of the UK – for example – its own legislation does not appear to discuss the rules on passive income.

Turning to publicly traded Active NFEs, the CRS Commentary[69] says:

> Subparagraph D(9)(b) describes the criterion to qualify for the Active NFE status for 'publicly traded NFEs' as follows: the stock of the NFE is regularly traded on an established securities market or the NFE is a Related Entity of an Entity the stock of which is regularly traded on an established securities market. As mentioned in paragraph 112 above, stock is 'regularly traded' if there is a meaningful volume of trading with respect to the stock on an on-going basis, and an 'established securities market' means an exchange that is officially recognised and supervised by a governmental authority in which the market is located and that has a meaningful annual value of shares traded on the exchange.

A 'Related Entity' is defined in the CRS[70] as follows:

> An Entity is a 'Related Entity' of another Entity if either Entity controls the other Entity, or the two Entities are under common control. For this purpose control includes direct or indirect ownership of more than 50% of the vote and value in an Entity

While paragraph 112 of the CRS Commentary is largely repeated in relation to Active NFEs in the publicly traded category, paragraphs 113 *et seq* are also

---

[69] Page 196

[70] Section VIII, E(4)

instructive in relation to identifying when something will be 'regularly traded'. These paragraphs[71] say:

113. With respect to each class of stock of the corporation, there is a 'meaningful volume of trading on an on-going basis' if (i) trades in each such class are effected, other than in de minimis quantities, on one or more established securities markets on at least 60 business days during the prior calendar year; and (ii) the aggregate number of shares in each such class that are traded on such market or markets during the prior year are at least 10% of the average number of shares outstanding in that class during the prior calendar year.

114. A class of stock would generally be treated as meeting the 'regularly traded' requirement for a calendar year if the stock is traded during such year on an established securities market and is regularly quoted by dealers making a market in the stock. A dealer makes a market in a stock only if the dealer regularly and actively offers to, and in fact does, purchase the stock from, and sell the stock to, customers who are not related persons with respect to the dealer in the ordinary course of a business.

115. An exchange has a 'meaningful annual value of shares traded on the exchange' if it has an annual value of shares traded on the exchange (or a predecessor exchange) exceeding USD 1 000 000 000 during each of the three calendar years immediately preceding the calendar year in which the determination is being made. If an exchange has more than one tier of market level on which stock may be separately listed or traded, each such tier must be treated as a separate exchange

In relation to holding NFEs that are members of a non-financial group, there are many terms requiring clarification. This is done in the CRS Commentary, though given the difficulties and uncertainties around the utility of commentary in interpreting domestic provisions, it would have been better had these matters been included in CRS itself. They are not, however, and so this is perhaps, of necessity, an area where we are going to be more heavily reliant on guidance (the CRS Commentary) than we would wish. In this respect it provides[72]:

129. Subparagraph D(9)(d) describes the criterion to qualify for the Active NFE status for 'holding NFEs that are members of a nonfinancial group' as follows: substantially all of the activities of the NFE consist of holding (in whole or in part) the outstanding stock of, or providing financing and services to, one

---

[71] Page 193

[72] Page 197

or more subsidiaries that engage in trades or businesses other than the business of a Financial Institution, except that an Entity does not qualify for this status if the Entity functions (or holds itself out) as an investment fund, such as a private equity fund, venture capital fund, leveraged buyout fund, or any investment vehicle whose purpose is to acquire or fund companies and then hold interests in those companies as capital assets for investment purposes.

130. With respect to the activities mentioned in subparagraph D(9)(d), 'substantially all' means 80% or more. If, however, the NFE's holding or group finance activities constitute less than 80% of its activities but the NFE receives also active income (i.e. income that is not passive income) otherwise, it qualifies for the Active NFE status, provided that the total sum of activities meets the 'substantially all test'. For purposes of determining whether the activities other than holding and group finance activities of the NFE qualify it as an Active NFE, the test of subparagraph D(9)(a) can be applied to such other activities. For example, if a holding company has holding or finance and service activities to one or more subsidiaries for 60% and also functions for 40% as a distribution centre for the goods produced by the group it belongs to and the income of its distribution centre activities is active according to subparagraph D(9)(a), it is an Active NFE, irrespective of the fact that less than 80% of its activities consist of holding the outstanding stock of, or providing finance and services to, one or more subsidiaries. The term 'substantially all' covers also a combination of holding stock of and providing finance and services to one or more subsidiaries. The term 'subsidiary' means any entity whose outstanding stock is either directly or indirectly held (in whole or in part) by the NFE.

The only remaining guidance by the CRS Commentary in relation to Active NFEs is in relation to non-profit Active NFEs. It says:

131. One of the requirements listed in subparagraph D(9)(h) for 'non-profit NFE' to qualify for the Active NFE status is that the applicable laws of the NFE's jurisdiction of residence or the NFE's formation documents do not permit any income or assets of the NFE to be distributed to, or applied for the benefit of, a private person or non-charitable Entity other than pursuant to the conduct of the NFE's charitable activities, or as payment of reasonable compensation for services rendered, or as payment representing the fair market value of property which the NFE has purchased. In addition, the income or assets of the NFE could be distributed to, or applied for the benefit of, a private

person or noncharitable Entity as payment of reasonable compensation for the use of property

This is an important category, because it includes charities, which are not subject to FATCA reporting. While they are subject to the CRS regime, the risk of an excess of administrative burden is addressed by categorising them as relatively low risk Active NFEs.

6.14 Accounts

'Reportable Account' means a Financial Account that is maintained by a Reporting Financial Institution and that, pursuant to due diligence procedures consistent with the Common Reporting Standard, has been identified as an account that is held by one or more persons that are Reportable Persons with respect to another Jurisdiction or by a Passive NFE with one or more Controlling Persons that are Reportable Persons with respect to another Jurisdiction.

This definition requires consideration of these terms:
(i) Financial Account
(ii) Due diligence procedures
(iii) Reportable Persons
(iv) Passive NFE
(v) Controlling Persons.

'Financial Account' means an account maintained by a Financial Institution. Only accounts that fall within any of the five categories of financial account defined by the various automatic exchange of information agreements need to be reviewed. Where such an account is held by a Reportable Person, it becomes a Reportable Account. It is (perhaps, unfortunately) helpful to set out the definition given in CRS, Section VIII, C(1) in full. This provides:

1. The term 'Financial Account' means an account maintained by a Financial Institution, and includes a Depository Account, a Custodial Account and:
    a) in the case of an Investment Entity, any equity or debt interest in the Financial Institution. Notwithstanding the foregoing, the term 'Financial Account' does not include any equity or debt interest in an Entity that is an Investment Entity solely because it (i) renders investment advice to, and acts on behalf of, or (ii) manages portfolios for, and acts on behalf of, a customer for the purpose of investing, managing, or administering Financial Assets deposited in the name of the customer with a Financial Institution other than such Entity;
    b) in the case of a Financial Institution not described in subparagraph C(1)(a), any equity or debt interest in the Financial Institution, if the class of interests was established with a purpose of avoiding reporting in accordance with Section I; and

c) any Cash Value Insurance Contract and any Annuity Contract issued or maintained by a Financial Institution, other than a noninvestment-linked, non-transferable immediate life annuity that is issued to an individual and monetises a pension or disability benefit provided under an account that is an Excluded Account

The term 'Financial Account' does not include any account that is an Excluded Account

This looks worse than it is! We have the following categories of accounts:

(i) Depository Accounts;
(ii) Custodial Accounts;
(iii) Any equity or debt interest in the Financial Institution, where the Financial Institution is an Investment Entity;
(iv) For Financial Institutions that are not Investment Entities, any equity or debt interest in the Financial Institution, if the class of interests was established with a purpose of avoiding CRS reporting (so here, arguably, we have a mini-DAC/MDR contained already within the rules of CRS)[73]; and

---

[73] At the time of writing we are in the midst of the Covid-19 pandemic of 2020/21. There is – possibly – the same logical fallacy in the Covid-19 rules and regulations proliferating around (at least parts of) the world and the approach to avoidance, both global and domestic. In both cases, the answer is always more rules. If the rules aren't working, we need more rules because the existing rules do not work. If the rules are working, then we need more rules, because they have worked, so surely more rules will work better? Anyone familiar with the tax legislation of the UK will be aware that barely a Finance Act goes by without some new, targeted, anti-avoidance rule being introduced. Defunct rules are not expunged and little thought is given to whether or not some existing rule might cover the situation (for example, the capital gains tax onward gift rule in relation to TCGA, section 87 was introduced following much consultation. However, TCGA, section 97 already clarified that a capital payment is to be regarded as received by a beneficiary from the trustees of a settlement if (*a*) he receives it from them directly or indirectly, or (*b*) it is directly or indirectly applied by them in payment of any debt of his, or is otherwise paid or applied for his benefit, or (*c*) it is received by a third person at the beneficiary's direction. It is hard to envisage circumstances in which there is an intention to make an onward payment that would not already be within the definition of capital payment because of TCGA, section 97(5). So what was the benefit of the new legislation, rather than applying what was already there? We do not know the answer). The proliferation of such rules is bad for taxpayers, and bad for advisers. Particularly where such rules come with draconian penalties – and at least the penalties involved with CRS, DAC6 and MDR appear not (yet) to be draconian the fact that they are legion, and often opaquely drafted fails to meet the standards of certainty, convenience, efficiency and fairness espoused by Adam Smith in 1776. But this seems to be the preferred approach domestically, and increasingly – with measures like CRS and the DAC – internationally. As much as anything, it appears to be driven by the urge of politicians to be seen to be 'doing something', regardless of whether the 'something' is either required or beneficial. It is a patently true that no politician ever taken power by saying 'things are just fine, let's not bother changing them' and therefore a regulatory proposal arms race is entered into by

(v) any Cash Value Insurance Contract and any Annuity Contract issued or maintained by a Financial Institution, other than a non-investment-linked, non-transferable immediate life annuity that is issued to an individual and monetises a pension or disability benefit provided under an account that is an Excluded Account.

The CRS Commentary says (at page 176):

> 62. In general, an account would be considered to be maintained by a Financial Institution as follows:
>
> - in the case of a Custodial Account, by the Financial Institution that holds custody over the assets in the account (including a Financial Institution that holds assets in street name for an Account Holder in such institution).
> - in case of a Depository Account, by the Financial Institution that is obligated to make payments with respect to the account (excluding an agent of a Financial Institution regardless of whether such agent is a Financial Institution).
> - in the case of any equity or debt interest in a Financial Institution that constitutes a Financial Account, by such Financial Institution.
> - in the case of a Cash Value Insurance Contract or an Annuity Contract, by the Financial Institution that is obligated to make payments with respect to the contract.
>
> 63. However, jurisdictions have diverse legal, administrative and operational frameworks and different financial systems, and the meaning of 'maintaining an account' may vary among jurisdictions, depending on how a particular financial industry is structured. In some cases, a Reporting Financial Institution may not possess all the information to be reported with respect to an account, and domestic guidance may be needed in such regard. In adopting such guidance, care should be taken to address any inconsistencies that may arise in a cross-border context, in particular with respect to jurisdictions that are not Participating Jurisdictions, or to Financial Institutions that are not Participating Jurisdiction Financial Institutions, so that the guidance does not frustrate the purposes of the Common

---

the various governments and opposition parties, leading to furious activity and much heat and light, but seemingly little progress. As an example, there was a period during the Brown premiership in UK where the then-Chancellor Alistair Darling introduced new anti-avoidance provisions every year, repeatedly claiming they would raise '£4bn' in lost taxes, and yet still the situation seems to be the same. Unfortunately, we advisers, like the taxpayers, must do the best that we can with the hand we are dealt.

Reporting Standard (see paragraph 5 of the Commentary on Section IX).

The CRS Commentary also discusses at length the meaning of 'Equity Interest' saying (at page 178):

69. The definition of the term 'Equity Interest' specifically addresses interests in partnerships and trusts. In the case of a partnership that is a Financial Institution, the term 'Equity Interest' means a capital or profits interest in the partnership. In the case of a trust that is a Financial Institution, an 'Equity Interest' is considered to be held by any person treated as a settlor or beneficiary of all or a portion of the trust, or any other natural person exercising ultimate effective control over the trust. The same as for a trust that is a Financial Institution is applicable for a legal arrangement that is equivalent or similar to a trust, or foundation that is a Financial Institution.

70. Under subparagraph C(4), a Reportable Person will be treated as being a beneficiary of a trust if such Reportable Person has the right to receive, directly or indirectly (for example, through a nominee), a mandatory distribution or may receive, directly or indirectly, a discretionary distribution from the trust. For these purposes, a beneficiary who may receive a discretionary distribution from the trust only will be treated as a beneficiary of a trust if such person receives a distribution in the calendar year or other appropriate reporting period (i.e. either the distribution has been paid or made payable). The same is applicable with respect to the treatment of a Reportable Person as a beneficiary of a legal arrangement that is equivalent or similar to a trust, or foundation.

71. Where Equity Interests are held through a Custodial Institution, the Custodial Institution is responsible for reporting, not the Investment Entity. The following example illustrates how such reporting must be done:

Reportable Person A holds shares in investment fund L. A holds the shares in custody with custodian Y. Investment fund L is an Investment Entity and, from its perspective, its shares are Financial Accounts (i.e. Equity Interests in an Investment Entity). L must treat custodian Y as its Account Holder. As Y is a Financial Institution (i.e. a Custodial Institution) and Financial Institutions are not Reportable Persons, such shares are not the object of reporting by investment fund L. For custodian Y, the shares held for A are Financial Assets held in a Custodial Account. As a Custodial Institution, Y is responsible for reporting the shares it is holding on behalf of A.

Points of particular note are as follows:

(i) The rights of a discretionary beneficiary are to be treated as being an equity interest (which is a stretch in the common law sense of either term); and
(ii) A settlor is considered to have an equity interest in a trust (which is, frankly, just untrue to common law ears, but we must assume that the usage in an international lexicon has little correspondence with the meaning of the term 'settlor' as understood in the common law world; this is, at least theoretically, not problematic, since we are provided with the OECD's view of what a settlor's 'interest' is).

Certain Financial Accounts are seen to pose low risk of use for tax evasion and are therefore specifically excluded from needing to be reviewed as 'Excluded Accounts'. The definition is lengthy, and it is helpful to divide it into smaller section. CRS explains that there are the following categories (the numbering used below is that from CRS):

a) a retirement or pension account that satisfies the following requirements:
   i) the account is subject to regulation as a personal retirement account or is part of a registered or regulated retirement or pension plan for the provision of retirement or pension benefits (including disability or death benefits);
   ii) the account is tax-favoured (i.e. contributions to the account that would otherwise be subject to tax are deductible or excluded from the gross income of the account holder or taxed at a reduced rate, or taxation of investment income from the account is deferred or taxed at a reduced rate);
   iii) information reporting to the tax authorities is required with respect to the account;
   iv) withdrawals are conditioned on reaching a specified retirement age, disability, or death, or penalties apply to withdrawals made before such specified events; and
   v) either (i) annual contributions are limited to USD 50 000 or less, or (ii) there is a maximum lifetime contribution limit to the account of USD 1 000 000 or less, in each case applying the rules set forth in paragraph C of Section VII for account aggregation and currency translation. A Financial Account that otherwise satisfies the requirement of subparagraph C(17)(a)(v) will not fail to satisfy such requirement solely because such Financial Account may receive assets or funds transferred from one or more Financial Accounts that meet the requirements of subparagraph C(17)(a) or (b) or from one or more retirement or pension funds that meet the requirements of any of subparagraphs B(5) through (7).

The second category within CRS Excluded Accounts is certain investment vehicles:

b) an account that satisfies the following requirements:
   i) the account is subject to regulation as an investment vehicle for purposes other than for retirement and is regularly traded on an established securities market, or the account is subject to regulation as a savings vehicle for purposes other than for retirement;
   ii) the account is tax-favoured (i.e. contributions to the account that would otherwise be subject to tax are deductible or excluded from the gross income of the account holder or taxed at a reduced rate, or taxation of investment income from the account is deferred or taxed at a reduced rate);
   iii) withdrawals are conditioned on meeting specific criteria related to the purpose of the investment or savings account (for example, the provision of educational or medical benefits), or penalties apply to withdrawals made before such criteria are met; and
   iv) annual contributions are limited to USD 50 000 or less, applying the rules set forth in paragraph C of Section VII for account aggregation and currency translation.

A Financial Account that otherwise satisfies the requirement of subparagraph C(17)(b)(iv) will not fail to satisfy such requirement solely because such Financial Account may receive assets or funds transferred from one or more Financial Accounts that meet the requirements of subparagraph C(17)(a) or (b) or from one or more retirement or pension funds that meet the requirements of any of subparagraphs B(5) through (7).

Next is life insurance contracts:

c) a life insurance contract with a coverage period that will end before the insured individual attains age 90, provided that the contract satisfies the following requirements:
   i) periodic premiums, which do not decrease over time, are payable at least annually during the period the contract is in existence or until the insured attains age 90, whichever is shorter;
   ii) the contract has no contract value that any person can access (by withdrawal, loan, or otherwise) without terminating the contract;
   iii) the amount (other than a death benefit) payable upon cancellation or termination of the contract cannot exceed the aggregate premiums paid for the contract, less the sum of mortality, morbidity, and expense charges (whether or not actually imposed) for the period or periods of the contract's

existence and any amounts paid prior to the cancellation or termination of the contract; and

iv) the contract is not held by a transferee for value.

The accounts of deceased are also Excluded:

d) an account that is held solely by an estate if the documentation for such account includes a copy of the deceased's will or death certificate.

There then follows a number of miscellaneous Excluded Accounts:

e) an account established in connection with any of the following:
   i) a court order or judgment.
   ii) a sale, exchange, or lease of real or personal property, provided that the account satisfies the following requirements:
      i) the account is funded solely with a down payment, earnest money, deposit in an amount appropriate to secure an obligation directly related to the transaction, or a similar payment, or is funded with a Financial Asset that is deposited in the account in connection with the sale, exchange, or lease of the property;
      ii) the account is established and used solely to secure the obligation of the purchaser to pay the purchase price for the property, the seller to pay any contingent liability, or the lessor or lessee to pay for any damages relating to the leased property as agreed under the lease;
      iii) the assets of the account, including the income earned thereon, will be paid or otherwise distributed for the benefit of the purchaser, seller, lessor, or lessee (including to satisfy such person's obligation) when the property is sold, exchanged, or surrendered, or the lease terminates;
      iv) the account is not a margin or similar account established in connection with a sale or exchange of a Financial Asset; and
      v) the account is not associated with an account described in subparagraph C(17)(f).
   iii) an obligation of a Financial Institution servicing a loan secured by real property to set aside a portion of a payment solely to facilitate the payment of taxes or insurance related to the real property at a later time.
   iv) an obligation of a Financial Institution solely to facilitate the payment of taxes at a later time.

Certain depository accounts are also Exlcluded:

f) a Depository Account that satisfies the following requirements:
   i) the account exists solely because a customer makes a payment in excess of a balance due with respect to a credit card or other revolving credit facility and the overpayment is not immediately returned to the customer; and
   ii) beginning on or before [xx/xx/xxxx], the Financial Institution implements policies and procedures either to prevent a customer from making an overpayment in excess of USD 50 000, or to ensure that any customer overpayment in excess of USD 50 000 is refunded to the customer within 60 days, in each case applying the rules set forth in paragraph C of Section VII for currency translation. For this purpose, a customer overpayment does not refer to credit balances to the extent of disputed charges but does include credit balances resulting from merchandise returns.

The final "sweep up" provides:

g) any other account that presents a low risk of being used to evade tax, has substantially similar characteristics to any of the accounts described in subparagraphs C(17)(a) through (f), and is defined in domestic law as an Excluded Account, provided that the status of such account as an Excluded Account does not frustrate the purposes of the Common Reporting Standard.

It will be essential to consider whether domestic legislation makes any provision for additional categories of Excluded Accounts. It will also be necessary to consider whether the domestic legislation Excluded Account frustrates the purposes of CRS, since it appears to be the case that the domestic legislation is overridden by CRS where this is the case (i.e. so that such accounts are not Excluded).

To accommodate jurisdiction-specific Financial Accounts which also present a low risk of being used to evade tax, the CRS provides for Participating Jurisdictions to define in their domestic law other Financial Accounts as Excluded Accounts. This is subject to certain conditions, including that the categorisation as such does not frustrate the purposes of the Standard. The Excluded Account can be considered as posing a low risk for tax evasion and that it has substantially similar characteristics to the categories of Excluded Accounts contained in the CRS. The Global Forum is reviewing the lists jurisdictions have established in this respect, with a view to ascertaining that all Excluded Accounts listed meet the requirements of the CRS, as summarised above. In general, it is expected that each jurisdiction would have only one list of domestically-defined Excluded Accounts (as opposed to different lists for different Participating Jurisdictions) and that it would make such a list publicly available.

So, let us assume that we have a Financial Account, maintained by a Reporting Financial Institution. Is it a Reportable Account? Only if: pursuant to due diligence procedures consistent with the Common Reporting Standard, it has been identified as an account that is held by one or more persons that are Reportable Persons with respect to another Jurisdiction or by a Passive NFE with one or more Controlling Persons that are Reportable Persons with respect to another Jurisdiction. Yet more terminology! Let us start with the 'due diligence procedures consistent with the' CRS.

Once a Reporting Financial Institution has identified the Financial Accounts they maintain, they are required to review those accounts to identify whether any of them are Reportable Accounts as defined in the CRS. Where they are found to be Reportable Accounts, information in relation to those accounts must be reported to the tax authority. This is discussed in Section I, which contains the general reporting requirements applicable to Reporting Financial Institutions. The early Paragraphs (A and B) take the usual approach of setting out a broad basis of what is included before the remaining paragraphs provide for exceptions.[74]

In relation to whether clients should be informed of reporting under CRS, the CRS Commentary says:

> Reporting Financial Institutions would often inform Account Holders (e.g. through a change to terms and conditions) that information relating to their accounts, if their accounts are Reportable Accounts, will be reported and may be exchanged with other jurisdictions. In some jurisdictions, Reporting Financial Institutions may be required to do so under their jurisdiction's privacy and disclosure rules. Reporting Financial Institutions would need to comply with such rules in this regard (e.g. by providing Account Holders, upon request, with a copy of the information reported)

This can hardly be said to come to grips with the complex interaction of international exchange of tax information and domestic privacy regimes. However, such a subject is beyond the scope of this book.

Under paragraph A, the following are reportable in relation to each Reportable Account held by the Reporting Financial Institution in question:

(i) individual Account Holders that are Reportable Persons: name, address, jurisdiction(s) of residence, TIN(s) and date and place of birth;

(ii) in the case of any Entity that is an Account Holder and a Reportable Person: the name, address, jurisdiction(s) of residence and TIN(s);

(iii) in the case of any Entity that is an Account Holder and that is identified as having one or more Controlling Persons that is a Reportable Person: name, address, jurisdiction(s) of residence, TIN(s) and date and place of birth.

[74] Paragraphs C through F provide for a series of exceptions in connection with TIN, date of birth, place of birth and gross proceeds.

6.15 Particular sorts of 'Persons'

'Reportable Person' is defined as follows:

> The term 'Reportable Person' means a Reportable Jurisdiction Person other than: (i) a corporation the stock of which is regularly traded on one or more established securities markets; (ii) any corporation that is a Related Entity of a corporation described in clause (i); (iii) a Governmental Entity; (iv) an International Organisation; (v) a Central Bank; or (vi) a Financial Institution

'Reportable Jurisdiction Person' means:

> The term 'Reportable Jurisdiction Person' means an individual or Entity that is resident in a Reportable Jurisdiction under the tax laws of such jurisdiction, or an estate of a decedent that was a resident of a Reportable Jurisdiction. For this purpose, an Entity such as a partnership, limited liability partnership or similar legal arrangement that has no residence for tax purposes shall be treated as resident in the jurisdiction in which its place of effective management is situated

'Reportable Jurisdiction' means:

> The term 'Reportable Jurisdiction' means a jurisdiction (i) with which an agreement is in place pursuant to which there is an obligation in place to provide the information specified in Section I, and (ii) which is identified in a published list

'Participating Jurisdiction' is:

> The term 'Participating Jurisdiction' means a jurisdiction (i) with which an agreement is in place pursuant to which it will provide the information specified in Section I, and (ii) which is identified in a published list

Finally, in this respect, 'Controlling Persons' are:

> The term 'Controlling Persons' means the natural persons who exercise control over an Entity. In the case of a trust, such term means the settlor(s), the trustee(s), the protector(s) (if any), the beneficiary(ies) or class(es) of beneficiaries, and any other natural person(s) exercising ultimate effective control over the trust, and in the case of a legal arrangement other than a trust, such term means persons in equivalent or similar positions. The term 'Controlling Persons' must be interpreted in a manner consistent with the Financial Action Task Force Recommendations.

6.16 Entity classification

This is an essential part of determining whether an entity has reporting obligations, or whether other entities will need to make reports in relation to it. Guidance from several jurisdictions sets out examples of how entities should be classified (as does the CRS Commentary and Implementation Handbook). We consider some of those here, as well as examples we have come across in practice. Instead, we focus on the more unusual and complex examples, and the solutions that we have identified. We are always keen to hear from readers who have found different solutions, or indeed different problems of entity classification and their solutions for the next edition.

6.16.1 Private trust company structure

We start by considering some common situations that arise in relation to trusts. The first one is a private trust company ('**PTC**'). A common PTC structure is a purpose trust, which beneficially owns the entire issued share capital of a limited company, which is a PTC. The PTC then acts as trustee for one or more (usually) discretionary trusts, which in turn are usually beneficially entitled to the entire issued share capital in one or more companies. Those companies may have underlying assets.

Such PTC structures can exhibit a variety of tax residences and jurisdictions, both between and within the PTC Structures. In most circumstances, it is possible to classify such structures in the following way:

(i) It should first be considered whether the purpose trust which holds the shares in the PTC can be classified as Non-Reporting Financial Institution – and usually as a Trustee Documented Trust – or if it must be classified as an NFE (almost certainly Passive). In many cases, the purpose trust holding the shares will qualify as a Trustee Documented Trust.

(ii) It is then useful to adopt a reporting approach where the PTC is classified as a Reporting Financial Institution so that it is in a position to report on some – or hopefully all – of the other entities in the PTC Structure.

(iii) The underlying trusts of which the PTC is trustee could then be classified as Non-Reporting Financial Institutions, by way of being Trustee-Documented Trusts. The PTC will in such circumstances be responsible for reporting on them.

(iv) Any underlying companies – which are likely to be Non Reporting Financial Institutions, and could potentially be addressed by entering into (written) agreements with the PTC to fulfil any obligation on behalf of the underlying company.

7 The Directive on Administrative Cooperation 6 ('DAC6') and the Mandatory Disclosure Regime ('MDR')

7.1 Purpose and scope of DAC6

The establishment of a single European mechanism for the exchange of information related to the tax affairs of individuals and entities has long been striven for. The main document which provides a framework within which various regimes and mechanisms are established is the Directive on Administrative Cooperation in the field of taxation (Council Directive 2011/16/EU) (the 'DAC'). In paragraph 1 of the preamble to the DAC, the EU Commission states:

> the Member States' need for mutual assistance in the field of taxation is growing rapidly in a globalised era. There is a tremendous development of mobility of taxpayers of the number of cross border transactions and the internationalisation of financial instruments which makes it difficult for Member States to assess taxes due properly.[1]

This is an admission that national governments are not omniscient enough properly to police their own tax revenue and require EU intervention to Paragraph 2 goes on to say:

> a single Member State cannot manage its internal taxation system, especially as regard direct taxation, without receiving information from other Member States

This purpose underpins the entire DAC and all its amendments. In June 2018, the EU adopted an amending directive known as DAC6 (Council Directive (EU) 2018/822). The aim of DAC6 was to fulfil the requirements of OECD BEPS Action Point 12 which called for 'recommendations regarding the design of mandatory disclosure rules for aggressive or abusive transactions, arrangements or structures.' In other words, aggressive tax planning should be reported to the authorities.

To ensure that there is a common understanding of what 'aggressive tax planning' means, those drafting the directive used an approach which seeks to identify the matters with which they are concerned. DAC6 is designed in such a way as to identify first whether an arrangement is a 'cross border arrangement' and secondly whether that arrangement exhibits one of the predefined characteristics (or 'hallmarks') of aggressive tax avoidance. It is important to note that DAC6 is not designed generally to catch tax avoidance, but instead to catch mandate reporting of specific types of avoidance. Practitioners should avoid the desire to report based on a general uneasiness that the client is 'up to something'.

---

[1] Preamble Para 1 Council Directive 2011/16/EU

The German Guidance on DAC6 goes further in explaining the intention and purpose of DAC6:

> The aim of Directive (EU) 2018/822 and the national legislation related to it is, on the one hand, to enable national legislators to respond to undesirable tax arrangements earlier than before in the interests of fair taxation in the internal market (legal analysis). On the other hand, the financial administrations of the Member States should be able to use the information obtained from the reports in the assessment procedure of users of cross-border tax arrangements, whether through general administrative instructions or through individual user investigative measures (assessment-supporting evaluation).

Thus clearly, the aim of DAC6, from a German perspective at least, is twofold. First, to allow legislation to be introduced to eliminate 'loopholes' quicker than previously and secondly to assist in individual assessments and investigations.

The scope of DAC6 is entirely aligned with the scope of the wider DAC of which it forms part. That is to say, the scope of the DAC is contained in Article 2 of the DAC:

> The Directive shall apply to all taxes of any kind levied by or on behalf of, a Member State or the Member State's territorial or administrative subdivisions, including the local authorities[2]

As to who DAC6 places the obligations upon; that is a slightly more complex matter. Setting aside the obligations on tax authorities to exchange information in accordance with DAC6, there is a varying number of private individuals or enterprises who are obliged to report information within the framework of DAC6. The various definitions of 'intermediary' and 'relevant taxpayer' will be discussed in detail. However, here it will suffice for us to note the following.

To be an 'intermediary' for the purposes of DAC6 (and thus be subject to reporting obligations) one must either:

(a) Be resident for tax purposes in a Member State;
(b) Have a permanent establishment in a Member State;
(c) Be incorporated in or governed by the laws of a Member State;
(d) Be registered with a professional association related to legal, taxation or consultancy service in a Member State.

(a) – (c) are entirely sensible. However, one is driven to ask if (d) amounts to an overreach. What is the likelihood of effective enforcement against a Portuguese member of the *Ordem dos Solicitadores e dos Agentes de Execução* who remains on the roll of solicitors whilst practicing in Dubai, or Indonesia? Does (d) require that such associations write DAC6 into their rules and

---

[2] Article 2 (1) Council Directive 2011/16/EU

regulations, or does it create a special class of people who are bound by extra-territorial reporting obligations simply because of their profession? The German guidance on this is even more expansive:

> This includes both professional associations whose membership is mandatory (e.g., professional associations) and professional associations whose membership is voluntary (e.g. interest groups).[3]

One really does wonder if this breadth of drafting is so wide as to be left without true meaning. Would a membership of The City of London Solicitors' Company be sufficient to give one a nexus in the UK, even if the body is entirely voluntary and combines a social nature with some 'interest groups' element? What about a social association which decides it has to intervene in a matter of public importance on behalf of its members? Does the status of its members change along with it? Would retaining membership of the Gibraltar Society of Accountants (an entirely voluntary body) so that one can occasionally attend a dinner on one's occasional visits back from your new home in Japan be sufficient? As far as the German tax authorities are concerned —it would seem so.

These are questions unanswered by the Directive or any guidance known to the authors. Suffice to say, it seems unlikely on a practical basis that accountants registered in the Netherlands or France or Germany but working in Tunisia, South Africa or Sri Lanka will be as rigorous in their compliance procedures as their counterparts in Amsterdam, Paris or Berlin. If only because distance means that training and professional development related to DAC6 may not be their priority.

The approach taken by many states is that they impose no obligation on intermediaries if they do not satisfy the nexus criteria in the directive (as written on an EU-wide basis) but are instead chopped down to the national level. Therefore, as per the Maltese Guidance:

> Irrespective of the tax residency of the participants involved in a reportable cross-border arrangement, a person falling within the definition of an intermediary will have an obligation to file information with the Commissioner for Revenue only where such person has a nexus with Malta. For this purpose, the intermediary needs to satisfy at least one of the following conditions:
> i) it is resident for tax purposes in Malta;
> ii) it has a permanent establishment in Malta through which the services with respect to the arrangement are provided;
> iii) it is incorporated in Malta, or governed by the laws of Malta;

[3] The German Guidance para 69

iv) it is registered with a professional association related to legal, taxation or consultancy services in Malta.'[4]

Thus, for Maltese purposes we have a double-layered test for being an intermediary, first the EU wide test (as contained in Chapter 2.1 of the Maltese Guidance), as to whether a professional is an 'intermediary' on a conceptual level and secondly a Maltese test as to whether an intermediary has any obligations forced upon him.

'Relevant taxpayer' is defined simply as:

> any person to whom a reportable arrangement is made available for implementation or who is ready to implement a reportable cross border arrangement or has implemented the first step of such an arrangement.

The Directive is silent as to the geographic location of the relevant taxpayer, and as with intermediaries outside the EU it is entirely conceptually possible that a 'relevant taxpayer' may not have a tax residence, or even a direct tax liability in the EU area (such as a group parent).

As we will see in the section below, in DAC6 definitions a 'relevant taxpayer' may well not be a taxpayer, or even a person. The only criterion is that a reportable cross border arrangement has been made available to them.

Thus, the scope of the directive can be summarised as the following. It imposes an obligation to report arrangements which exhibit the predefined hallmarks of aggressive tax avoidance. That obligation is imposed on anyone with a sufficient nexus to the EU/single jurisdiction, and it is imposed in connection with those taxes imposed by the European Union.

7.2 Purpose and scope of MDR

The purpose of DAC6 is obvious and transparent. It is designed to catch the purveyors and implementors of aggressive tax planning. It does so in terms of the European Union and is the product of a development process which encompassed a robust and centralised framework in the EU. The EU has experience of developing a myriad of regulations and rules in a way which cover 27 member states. It has two great advantages over the OECD when developing regulations such as DAC6. Firstly, it need only deal with 27 Member States, a large but manageable number, the OECD Inclusive Framework which monitors and implements the BEPS project has more than 135 members, each with their own issues and demands. This is a much more unwieldy body. Secondly, it has a more robust legal framework within which to work. EU law has primacy over national law in a way that OECD agreements and frameworks cannot have.

---

[4] Chapter 2.5 'Nexus with Malta' Guidelines on the Mandatory Automatic Exchange of Information in relation to Cross-Border Arrangements (S.L. 123.127)

In their Bari Declaration on 13 May 2017, the leaders of the G7 requested that the OECD should:

> ... start discussing possible ways to address arrangements designed to circumvent reporting under the Common Reporting Standard or aimed at providing beneficial owners with the shelter of non-transparent structures, considering also model mandatory disclosure rules inspired by the approach taken for avoidance arrangements outlined within the BEPS Action 12 Report.

It is important to understand this. The MDR grew from the Bari Declaration and is the result of the discussions Bari required. It is, therefore, not a fulfilment of the BEPS Action Point 12 requirements like DAC6. It is, instead 'inspired' by and, for many, rather like the comparison between a 1950s original Arne Jacobsen Model 3107 chair and the thousands of chair designs 'inspired' by it, it will prove cheaper and rather less effective than its inspiration.

Unlike a chair which is 'inspired' by Jacobsen's masterpiece, but which is still fundamentally a chair, however, the OECD MDR is not designed to play the same role as BEPS Action Point 12 (and its only international implementation to date, DAC6). Instead, it applies the same mechanisms utilised by BEPS Action Point 12 (that is reporting of arrangements) to an entirely different problem. Those problems are the avoidance of Common Reporting Standard reporting and the use of Opaque Offshore Structures to conceal the ultimate beneficial ownership of an asset or entity, not aggressive tax planning in itself.

This means that the MDR does cover some ground which is the same as DAC6. In fact, in the now defunct Guidance issued by HMRC in preparation for the aborted implementation for DAC6 by the UK, it stated:

> Hallmarks under Category D share substantial common ground with the Mandatory Disclosure Rules (MDR) developed by the OECD... Accordingly, where Hallmark D and the MDR cover similar ground, HMRC interpret Hallmark D in line with the MDR.[5]

It is the opinion of the authors that the MDR, as it is drafted, at the date of writing, is not a finished product, but instead simply a step on the road that will lead to a more comprehensive reporting regime. We fully expect that the legal framework established by the MDR will be extended to cover as many types of arrangements as DAC6 does today. The OECD cannot fulfil Action Point 12 without such an extension. Those practitioners in MDR jurisdictions would do well to read and learn about DAC6, as it seems to be the international prototype for an Action Point 12 implementation.

---

[5] IEIM645000 Hallmarks: Category D HMRC as was in place prior to 31 December 2020

As the MDR implementation in individual jurisdictions remains nascent, it is most helpful to review the MDR Model Mandatory Disclosure Rules for CRS Avoidance Arrangements and Opaque Offshore Structures[6] and their contents.

In comparison to DAC6, terminology is slightly different, but the framework is essentially the same. Intermediaries are obliged to report on cross border arrangements which exhibit certain predefined hallmarks.

The definition of 'intermediary' is functionally identical to that in DAC6 and maintains the Promoter/Service Provider distinction.

> 'Intermediary' means: (a) any person responsible for the design or marketing of a CRS Avoidance Arrangement or Opaque Offshore Structure ('Promoter'); and (b) any person that provides Relevant Services in respect of a CRS Avoidance Arrangement or Opaque Offshore Structure in circumstances where the person providing such services could reasonably be expected to know that the Arrangement or Structure is a CRS Avoidance Arrangement or an Opaque Offshore Structure ('Service Provider'). The standard of 'reasonably be expected to know' must be determined by reference to the Service Provider's actual knowledge based on readily available information and the degree of expertise and understanding required to provide the Relevant Services.'[7]

In various other matters the scope of the MDR is, however, more limited than DAC6. The drafters of the MDR have avoided the expansive and seemingly unenforceable and potentially unreasonable approach around the membership of professional bodies, the equivalent to the 'nexus' provisions of Article 3 (21) of the DAC in the MDR Rules merely states at Rule 2.1:

> Any person that is an Intermediary with respect to a CRS Avoidance Arrangement or Opaque Offshore Structure must disclose that Arrangement or Structure to the tax authorities in [Jurisdiction Name] if that person:
>
> (a) makes that CRS Avoidance Arrangement or Opaque Offshore Structure available for implementation, or provides Relevant Services in respect of that CRS Avoidance Arrangement or Opaque Offshore Structure through a branch located in [Jurisdiction Name];
>
> (b) is resident or has its place of management in [Jurisdiction Name]; or

[6] Model Mandatory Disclosure Rules for CRS Avoidance Arrangements and Opaque Offshore Structures OECD 2018

[7] Rule 1.3 Intermediary Model Mandatory Disclosure Rules for CRS Avoidance Arrangements and Opaque Offshore Structures OECD 2018

(c) is incorporated in, or established under the laws of, [Jurisdiction Name]'[8]

This seems a much more sensible approach, an intermediary is within scope if s/he/it has a branch in a jurisdiction, is resident in a jurisdiction, or is incorporated in a jurisdiction. No searching through peoples' memberships to see if they are within scope. This betrays a different approach on behalf of the OECD. The EU seems to seek to eliminate all and every logically possible scenario in their entirety, and as a result, leaves itself legislating for absurd outcomes. The OECD seems to take a more reasonable approach, and as a result it is likely that their provisions will garner more intellectual respect.

As the scope of the MDR in terms of the hallmarks which are covered is much narrower than DAC6 the scoping definition of 'Relevant Taxpayer', or in the case of the MDR, 'Reportable Taxpayer' can be more specifically delineated:

> 'Reportable Taxpayer' means, in respect of a CRS Avoidance Arrangement, any actual or potential user of that Arrangement and, in respect of an Opaque Offshore Structure, a natural person whose identity as a Beneficial Owner cannot be accurately determined due to the Opaque Offshore Structure[9]

Thus, those taxpayers in scope of MDR are defined by reference to their utilisation (or potential utilisation) of an arrangement. This is the same form as DAC6, which states that a relevant taxpayer is a person to whom an arrangement is made available. It is important to note, however, that the Opaque Offshore Structure Hallmark (or Hallmark D2 in DAC6) is restricted by this definition. No 'person' who is not an individual can be a 'reportable taxpayer' for the purposes of the MDR for this hallmark. DAC6 (if it is interpreted widely) does not contain such a provision and one wonders whether a relevant taxpayer could include the entity itself which is 'opaque' for DAC6 purposes. This clarification in the MDR is useful to avoid multiple reporting on many jurisdictions from the perspective of many taxpayers.

7.3 Summary

It is clear that there are differences between DAC6 and MDR in their scope, both in terms of arrangements, intermediaries and taxpayers. However, they are fruit of the same tree, and there is a large amount of overlap, for a European centric commentator MDR is 'DAC6 lite', for a non-European commentator DAC6 is 'MDR plus'. What is clear, absolutely, is that MDR does not fulfil BEPS Action Point 12, and will not remain static, or may remain static and may be supplemented by an entirely new reporting regime

---

[8] Rule 2.1 Intermediary Model Mandatory Disclosure Rules for CRS Avoidance Arrangements and Opaque Offshore Structures OECD 2018

[9] Rule 1.4 Intermediary Model Mandatory Disclosure Rules for CRS Avoidance Arrangements and Opaque Offshore Structures OECD 2018

to cover similar ground to DAC6. The international community is taking steps on a road to an entirely free flow of information between authorities and intermediaries in which there is no safe harbour from scrutiny. That journey will be lengthy and may well involve wrong turns, but it is one they are committed to continue.

7.4 The UK's abandonment of DAC6

Even though the UK referendum held on the 23 June 2016 decided that the UK should leave the EU, the UK remained within the EU for quite some time, eventually leaving on 31 January 2020. This was not the end of the story, however, and the UK remained in a half-in, half-out position during what was known as the 'Transition Period' until 31 December 2020. Given the fact that the UK had been a member of the EU at the point when the translation of DAC6 into domestic law was mandated, and the fact that much of the work had already been carried out by the intermediaries in the UK, there was little public indication that the UK would do anything other than implement DAC6 in its totality. In fact, HMRC issued rigorous guidance and was continuing to issue exhortations to register to major financial institutions well into December.

However, the European Union/UK Free Trade Agreement did feature one puzzling clause, which in the general brouhaha of a deal after so much waiting, went mostly unremarked.

Article 5.2: Taxation standards

1. A Party shall not weaken or reduce the level of protection provided for in its legislation at the end of the transition period below the level provided for by the standards and rules which have been agreed in the OECD at the end of the transition period, in relation to:
   (a) the exchange of information, whether upon request, spontaneously or automatically, concerning financial accounts, cross-border tax rulings, country-by-country reports between tax administrations, and potential cross-border tax planning arrangements;
   (b) rules on interest limitation, controlled foreign companies and hybrid mismatches

The contents of Article 5.2 state that all parties will abide by the OECD standard and need not follow any EU provisions which go beyond that standard. Regarding the exchange of information on 'cross border tax planning arrangements' at the end of 2020 that standard was simply the OECD MDR and not the full gamut of DAC6. Consequently, on 31 December 2020 the UK announced that it would implementing DAC6 only in connection with Hallmark D (which aligns almost entirely with the OECD MDR). This announcement was made 30 days before first reporting was required under the Covid-19 delayed reporting requirements.

This came as somewhat of a relief to practitioners who had struggled in a Covid-19 environment to carry out the necessary reviews of files and documents to be able to report. It is also worth noting that this is a primary example of Brexit impacting on the daily lives of professionals and business. Literally millions of pounds had been spent in training and systems design, reviews, etc. Gallons of ink had been spilt in writing articles and papers about the minutiae of DAC6 and the HMRC guidance, only for the professionals in question to be told with 30 days to go that much of it was no longer required.

Only one other British jurisdiction had implemented DAC6; Gibraltar. Gibraltar's position with regard to DAC6 is entirely unique, as a British Overseas Territory which was within the EU, it has no parallel. Its relationship with Spain is also unique, in that Spain actively claims the territory of the jurisdiction and was handed an effective veto over any post-Brexit arrangements relating to it by the EU's negotiating guidelines. Similarly, Gibraltar had the added complication of the fact that the then-unratified 'International Agreement on Taxation and the Protection of the Financial Interests between the Kingdom of Spain and the United Kingdom of Great Britain and Northern Ireland concerning Gibraltar' contained provisions mandating the maintenance of EU Directives and the further implementation of information exchange between Gibraltar and Spain. It was against this backdrop that Gibraltar paused for two to three weeks until finally announcing that it, too, would be expecting reports simply on the reduced basis of Hallmark D.[10] As with UK practitioners, this was a cause for relief.

The implementation of DAC6 has been complicated by the pandemic and technological issues. Many countries did not have their IT portals ready for first reporting, and the entire affair has been mired in delay and confusion, guidance has been held back and many countries were still implementing legislation well into 2020 and 2021. The UK and Gibraltar's 'chopped down' version of DAC6 allowed reporting to occur smoothly in these difficult circumstances. In consequence, the authors do query what use reports made by intermediaries with little to no guidance, garbled law, bad computer systems and an inability to train their employees during the pandemic will be to those authorities suffering under the same circumstances.

---

[10] Gibraltar has since implemented a full DAC6 reporting regime solely in connection with those cross-border arrangements which 'concern' both Gibraltar and Spain.

8 DAC6 Definitions

8.1 Person

The DAC definition predates the amending directive which introduced DAC6 and is worded as follows:

> 'person' means:
> a. A natural person;
> b. A legal person;
> c. Where the legislation in force so provides, an association of persons recognised as having the capacity to perform legal acts but lacking the status of a legal person; or
> d. Any other legal arrangement of whatever nature and form, regardless of whether it has legal personality, owning or managing assets, which, including income derived therefrom are subject to any of the taxes covered by this Directive.[1]

At first glance, this appears to be a very widely drafted definition which can be summarised as 'a person is a person and anything which is not a person'; drafted in an expansive way to catch not only limited companies, or individuals but also trusts and partnerships, permanent establishments and other forms of business organization or relationships.

The impact of the definition of the term 'person' is manifold:

(a) in the analysis of whether an entity or relationship qualifies as an intermediary, in the definition of 'associated enterprise';
(b) in the definition of 'relevant taxpayer'; and
(c) in the scope of matters to be reported in that the relevant report must include details of a 'person' in a Member State 'likely to be affected by the arrangement'.

The Irish and German authorities seem to agree that the definition of 'Person' is relatively uncontroversial in that they dedicate almost nothing in their guidance to a discussion of it. Both the Bundesministerium der Finanzen ('BdF') and Irish Tax and Customs (ITC) dedicate little time to the actual definition. Both the ITC and the BdF clarify that the actions of employees and other 'vicarious agents' (as the German Guidance has it) are the actions of the principal and not the employee, therefore, no obligation falls on an employee personally. The Irish Guidance states:

> 'when assessing whether a person falls with the definition of intermediary, it should be noted that the term 'person' is given a broad meaning in the EU mandatory disclosure regime. As such an intermediary may be an individual (i.e. a natural person), a legal

[1] Article 3(11)

> entity such as a company or a non-legal entity such as a partnership.'[2]

The BdF state that a 'user' can be:

> 'any natural or legal person, partnership, community or asset'[3]

This is a simple approach to the definition, but it is not entirely satisfactory when compared to the text of the DAC. It is satisfactory as far as limbs (a), (b) and (c) of the definition are concerned. However, limb (d) is by necessity more complex, in that it attempts to delineate those things that are often referred to as if they were persons (certain partnerships or trusts) for shorthand purposes, but in legal reality are not persons in the usual English (or possibly, common law) sense.[4]

Breaking down limb (d) into its constituent parts allows us to see how the concept of expanding the meaning of 'person' is achieved for the purposes of the DAC. In order to qualify for limb (d), the situation must:

- Be a legal arrangement;
- That arrangement must involve the owning or managing of assets; and
- Those assets or income derived therefrom must be subject to a tax within the scope of the DAC.

The taxes within scope of the DAC are defined at Article 2 (1) of the DAC:

> 'This Directive shall apply to all taxes of any kind levied by, or on behalf of, a Member State or the Member State's territorial or administrative subdivisions, including the authorities.'[5]

This leads us to the conclusion that a legal arrangement without legal personality, such as a trust or (certain) partnerships, which is not itself subject to tax within the EU, and manages or owns assets which do not generate a tax liability within the EU levied on persons/entities either managing or benefitting from the assets cannot be a 'person' for the purposes of DAC6, and therefore falls outside the scope of the definition of 'intermediary', 'relevant taxpayer' and a person 'likely to be affected by the arrangement'.

It seems odd, and one must question the level of consistency here, that an individual or incorporated entity has no requirement for the assets in their control or the income generated by them to be subject to an EU tax to qualify

---

[2] The Irish Guidance Chapter 4.1

[3] The German Guidance Para 13

[4] CRS attempts to do a similar thing, though takes a slightly different approach – see Chapter 6 It is interesting that this different approach, which verges on the tautologous does not aim for consistency of approach with the CRS (however, it is considered probable that consistency of outcome is achieved).

[5] Article 2(1)

as a 'person' for the purposes of the DAC, and yet an unincorporated form does. But in practice it should not matter.

8.2 Cross-border arrangements

Rather unhelpfully the DAC does not include a definition of 'arrangement'.[6] This could be interpreted as a deliberate move on the part of the draftsmen to encourage a more conservative approach and to create uncertainty when professionals are designing schemes and arrangements with a tax effect. Even if that is not the intention, it has had a similar effect. It could be argued that the lack of a full definition results in a position where everything must be regarded as an 'arrangement' just to be sure.

The Dutch Guidance states:

> The concept of 'arrangement' is meant to be neutral. An arrangement can be multifaceted, for example a transaction, act, agreement, loan, appointment, or a combination thereof. An arrangement also means a series of arrangements and an arrangement can consist of several steps or parts. Where an arrangement begins and ends may depend on the type of arrangement and the appropriate characteristic[7]

The Irish Guidance takes a similar stance as to the expansive nature of the definition of 'arrangement':[8]

> The term 'arrangement' is broadly defined and includes of all types of arrangements, transactions, payments, schemes and structures, whether or not legally enforceable. For instance, a verbal agreement may constitute an arrangement.
>
> The term includes arrangements comprising more than one step or part and a series of arrangements. For instance, one arrangement could comprise: entering into a loan agreement; the advance of the loan, successive payments of interest on the loan and the repayment of the loan principal

This is reflected in the guidance issued by the LTA and included in the implementation legislation in Luxembourg, passed on the 20 March 2020.

Setting aside the innate circularity of an explanation (in the Irish Guidance) that effectively defines an arrangement as including 'all types of arrangements' this guidance is so wide that it almost amounts to a tautology. There is little help to be had from attempting to define a word which is

---

[6] Though it should be noted that English tax legislation has been using the terms since – at least – 1922 without definition, so perhaps, at least initially, it was thought that its ordinary meaning was sufficient explanation. Sadly, no more – see further below.

[7] 'Taxes. Reporting cross-border structures'. Directorate-General for Tax Administration/Corporate Department of Professional Technology, Decision of 24 June 2020, No 2020-11382

[8] The Irish Guidance Chapter 2.1

designed to encompass the widest possible circumstances. The answer to this difficult problem is, at least from a common law perspective (so in relation to those jurisdictions within the EU with a common law base to their legal systems) perhaps, to consider how 'arrangements' have been considered in other contexts and common law jurisdictions.

English tax legislation is rich in this respect, 'arrangements' being a mainstay of its targeted anti-avoidance rules and indeed of the general anti-abuse rule in FA 2013 (see ss 207 and 214). The term is usually given a wide ambit (as here). In FA 2013, section 214 it is defined to 'include'[9] any agreement, understanding, scheme, transaction or series of transactions (whether or not legally enforceable). It is not clear why the two regimes merit different definitions;[10] however, since both definitions use the 'includes' method of list drafting, they are likely to be similar in scope.

For detailed analysis on the interpretation of 'arrangements' in English legislation – see James Kessler, *Taxation of Non-UK Residents and Foreign Domiciliaries*. In short, it seems probable that arrangement should bear its usual meaning. This is the view the English courts have taken in a domestic context. In *Newton v Federal Commissioner of Taxation* [1958] AC 450 (page 465):

> ... the word 'arrangement' is apt to describe something less than a binding contract or agreement, something in the nature of an understanding between two or more persons - a plan arranged between them which may not be enforceable at law.

Similarly, in *Farnborough Airport v HMRC* [2019] 2 All ER 435 (paragraph 74) the English Court of Appeal said 'The concept of "arrangements"... involves an element of deliberate planning or co-ordination to bring about a particular state of affairs'. In TFD, James Kessler QC notes (at Appendix 2, paragraph 2.2):

> Basically, anything with an element of volition is an arrangement. I do not think there is a single case where a taxpayer has succeeded in arguing that an act, or transaction, or indeed anything at all, is not an arrangement. 'Arrangement' is a word of wide meaning.

---

[9] A note on legislative drafting: the modern form of drafting, in which a definition 'includes' a list of things, is deployed where the list is intended to be non-exhaustive, i.e. 'these things are definitely within the definition, but other things may also be'. To persons other than law draftsmen, this might be taken as hedging one's bets.

[10] Though this is not the only example in English law of 'arrangement' being defined differently in different places. There are two 'standard' definitions of arrangements used in English tax legislation. The first is commonly used in income and capital gains contexts (since around 2005) and defines arrangements to include 'any agreement, understanding, scheme, transaction or series of transactions (whether or not legally enforceable)'. The second, used for IHT purposes (since 2012) includes any 'scheme, transaction or series of transactions, agreement or understanding, whether or not legally enforceable, and any associated operations'.

The DAC, whilst omitting a definition of 'arrangement' – which considering the issues arising with the definitions used in English law, may be a more sensible approach than attempting to define an intangible concept – does define the term 'cross border arrangement' at Article 3(18) of the Directive, which provides:

> 18. "cross-border arrangement" means an arrangement concerning either more than one Member State or a Member State and a third country, where at least one of the following conditions is met:
>   (a) not all of the participants in the arrangement are resident for tax purposes in the same jurisdiction;
>   (b) one or more of the participants in the arrangement is simultaneously resident for tax purposes in more than one jurisdiction;
>   (c) one or more of the participants in the arrangement carries on a business in another jurisdiction through a permanent establishment situated in that jurisdiction and the arrangement forms part or the whole of the business of that permanent establishment;
>   (d) one or more of the participants in the arrangement carries on an activity in another jurisdiction without being resident for tax purposes or creating a permanent establishment situated in that jurisdiction;
>   (e) such arrangement has a possible impact on the automatic exchange of information or the identification of beneficial ownership. For the purposes of points 18 to 25 of this Article, Article 8ab and Annex IV, an arrangement shall also include a series of arrangements. An arrangement may comprise more than one step or part.[11]

It is tolerably clear that, while the legislation does not use the standard form wording (or one of the variants of the standard form wording) the conditions are cumulative, not alternative, i.e. both one of Conditions (a) – (d) ***and*** concern two different jurisdictions (at least one of which is a Member State).

Thus, to be a cross-border reportable arrangement, the arrangement in question must firstly 'concern' more than one member state, or an EU member state and a third country. For these purposes UK and Gibraltar (in terms of their limited implementation) will continue to be considered member states, and they should not be considered the same member state for these purposes.[12]

---

[11] Article 3 (18) Directive on Administrative Cooperation in the field of taxation 2011/16/EU

[12] The treatment of Gibraltar and UK as if they are the same Member State has been much debated within Gibraltar. Prior to exit from the EU, Gibraltar had a unique status as an EU

This, of course, begs the question 'what does "concern" mean?' HMRC explores this matter at some length in the HMRC Guidance, saying:

> Whether or not an arrangement 'concerns' multiple jurisdictions will be crucial in determining whether there is a reportable cross-border arrangement. HMRC is of the view that in order for the arrangement to 'concern' multiple jurisdictions, those jurisdictions must be of some material relevance to the arrangement. Whether any particular arrangement is of material relevance to, and therefore concerns, multiple jurisdictions will be a question of fact and degree...

The use of language is interesting, and in our view, significant. HMRC state that the interpretation of the word 'concerns' is crucial (and we agree!). However, they go on to say it is merely their view that the jurisdictions must be of material relevance to the arrangement. This is unusual in HMRC guidance, but perhaps not too much should be read into it. An alternative interpretation would be the reverse: test if the arrangement is relevant to the jurisdiction. This alternative approach could be applied in the following circumstances: completely arbitrarily a certain jurisdiction is chosen for a single step in a complex arrangement, which could trigger a tax liability or a reporting under domestic legislation (and thus would be materially relevant to the jurisdiction), but which does not constitute a 'material relevance' to the arrangement.

On balance, however, we consider that HMRC is probably correct; it is the arrangement that must be cross-border and it is reasonable to suppose that, if the jurisdiction is material to the arrangements, then it is 'concerned' in them[13]. The HMRC Guidance then continues:

---

territory 'for which a member state was responsible for its external relations' under Article 355(3) of the Treaty on the Functioning of the European Union. The effect of that status and whether Gibraltar should be treated as a separate Member State in relation to the UK has been subject to several pieces of litigation, the history of which is beyond the remit of this work. However, suffice to say the application of the principal is somewhat inconsistent, the UK sees Gibraltar as the same Member State for most purposes, including TFEU, Articles 49, 56 and 63 (see C192/16 *Fisher v HMRC* and C591/15 *Gibraltar Betting and Gaming Duties Association*) and the purposes of the parent subsidiary directive (see C458/18 *GVC Services (Bulgaria) EOOD v Direktor na Direktsia Obzhalvane I danachno-osiguritelna praktika*), but as a separate Member State for the purposes of DAC6 (as per HMRC Guidance IEIM630030 – Meaning of Cross Border). This approach of treating Gibraltar and the UK as separate jurisdictions for this purpose is similar to the approach taken by the Kingdom of the Netherlands in regard to those parts of the Netherlands which lie outside the EU (Aruba, the BES Islands, Curaçao and Sint Maarten)

[13] This does leave the broader question, however, of when a jurisdiction upon which the arrangements touch would *not* be material. For example, it cannot be the case that the jurisdiction is not material merely because any one of a number of jurisdictions could have been selected (this must be against the purpose of the rules), but is there a minimal extent to which a jurisdiction could be involved, without its involvement becoming material? For example, would

If there are tax consequences in a particular jurisdiction as a result of the arrangement in question, HMRC would normally consider that the arrangement will concern that jurisdiction. However, that may not be the case where the tax effect is more removed. For example, consider a company, resident in one jurisdiction, but carrying on a trade through a permanent establishment in another jurisdiction. **The company may enter into an arrangement through its permanent establishment, which only concerns the permanent establishment (and counterparties resident in the jurisdiction where the permanent establishment is) and has no implications for other jurisdictions**. In this example, the fact that the company is tax resident in a different jurisdiction to the counterparties does not mean that the arrangement itself 'concerns' multiple jurisdictions. The arrangement in this example would be between a permanent establishment in jurisdiction X and other parties also resident in jurisdiction X and the jurisdiction where the company is tax resident will not be of material relevance to the arrangement.

Equally, **there may be situations where there are no tax consequences directly as a result of an arrangement, but it nonetheless concerns multiple jurisdictions. For example, an arrangement involves funds belonging to a person resident in member State A being moved from an account in country B to an account in country C. There may be no immediate tax consequences following the movement of funds. However, if country C had not implemented the Common Reporting Standard (CRS), whereas country B had, and the effect of the arrangement was to undermine the CRS by ensuring that the funds would not be reported, then the jurisdictions involved would be of material relevance to the arrangement.** As a result, the arrangement would clearly concern multiple jurisdictions.

If an arrangement would otherwise only concern one jurisdiction, the fact that an intermediary involved in the arrangement is located in a different jurisdiction will not automatically mean that the arrangement is cross-border. For example, if two companies in member State A (not the UK) are involved in an arrangement, which only involves the transfer of assets within member State A, the arrangement is clearly not cross-border. The fact that a UK lawyer provides some of the paperwork for the arrangement, or that a bank resident in member State B only provides the account from which the funds are transferred, does not mean that the arrangement itself is cross-border. This would also apply if the arrangement only

---

it be immaterial if a bearer instrument were held in a jurisdiction? We consider it unlikely, but in all probability, this will turn on the specific facts of each individual arrangement.

> involved non-UK, non-EU member state jurisdictions, but where there was a UK intermediary
>
> (Emphasis added)

This sheds quite a lot of light on the two-stage nature of the test for a 'cross-border arrangement'. Here we can see, it is not relevant that Art 3(18)b would be satisfied (i.e. that one of the participants is resident in one jurisdiction and carries on a business through a permanent establishment in another jurisdiction, and the arrangement relates to that permanent establishment) if the company in question being resident in another jurisdiction is insufficient, on the facts as they are, to establish that that jurisdiction is materially relevant to the arrangement.

Once it has been established that the arrangement in question concerns either two member states or a member state and a third country, Article 18(3) goes on to establish a further four-part test to establish that the arrangement is in fact cross-border. The four stages are:

(a) not all of the participants in the arrangement are resident for tax purposes in the same jurisdiction;
(b) one or more of the participants in the arrangement is simultaneously resident for tax purposes in more than one jurisdiction;
(c) one or more of the participants in the arrangement carries on a business in another jurisdiction through a permanent establishment situated in that jurisdiction and the arrangement forms part or the whole of the business of that permanent establishment;
(d) one or more of the participants in the arrangement carries on an activity in another jurisdiction, without being resident for tax purposes or without creating a permanent establishment situated in that jurisdiction.

It will be noticed that each of these limbs rests on the status of the 'participants' to the arrangement. The definition of a participant is not entirely clear from the DAC as drafted, and yet is obviously of some importance, since without any arrangement meeting the 'cross-border' test, it is beyond the remit of the DAC entirely[14]. Irish Tax and Customs have included a discussion of 'participant' in their guidance:

> the participants in an arrangement will be those persons that play an active role in it. For instance, where an arrangement is a contract, the participants in the arrangement will be those persons who are party to the contract[15]

[14] Poland and Portugal have established that DAC6 reporting is applicable to arrangements which are entirely domestic. In the absence of some other regime similar to the UK's 'Disclosure of Tax Avoidance Schemes' provisions, it is likely that this application of DAC6 principles to domestic arrangements will be extended across the EU over time.

[15] The Irish Guidance Chapter 2.2

However, being central to an arrangement is not the only way in which one can participate in it. Irish Tax and Customs go on to say:

> a parent company would be regarded as a participant in an arrangement where a shareholders' resolution is required in order for an arrangement to proceed between its subsidiary and another party.[16]

This may seem a mere statement of the obvious, but it leads to some interesting complexities. If, instead of the shareholders' resolution being 'required', the directors of a company seek a shareholders' resolution, to confirm there has been no breach of fiduciary duty, or to ensure that a non-commercial decision is confirmed by the shareholders, without a necessity on the directors to do so, does that amount to the parent company being a participant? It is probable that the parent company remains a participant, because while it did not have to participate, it chose to do so. However, the alternative is probably arguable as well.

If the shareholders of the company requesting or requiring a shareholder's resolution are not companies, but individuals resident in a different jurisdiction, does the arrangement in question qualify as a cross-border arrangement because one of its participants (the shareholder) is resident elsewhere? It would seem a harsh outcome that a family company which seeks a shareholders' resolution to confirm a restructure of its affairs or other arrangement which concerns two member states but does not otherwise meet the criteria of Art 3(18) (a) to (d) simply because, for example, one minority shareholding cousin happens to have moved to Ireland from the UK a couple of years earlier. There is no clear answer to this apparent harshness – other than observing, perhaps, that sometimes legislation will have unfair outcomes – however, it is a problem with which advisers will have to grapple. One answer may be the extent to which the individual shareholder is able to influence the outcome. If the 'cross-border' shareholder has such a minority shareholding that he cannot make a difference either way, even if he does vote, could he be said not to be a 'participant' in the real, or purposive sense of the word?

If, however, it is not possible for an arrangement to concern more than one member state or a member state and a third country and simultaneously not meet the criteria in (a) to (d), then one is left asking 'what is the purpose of this two-part test?' The Irish Guidance on the test gives a possible basis:

> This interpretation [the example of a parent company granting a shareholders' resolution] is consistent with the broad meaning given to the word 'arrangement'[17]

[16] Ibid

[17] Ibid

The intention seems entirely to catch as many situations as possible, and logical inconsistencies or unexpected results are not relevant to the overarching intention and purpose of ensuring that facts should not be able to be manipulated to avoid reporting.

In interpreting the test, it is considered that other expressions should be interpreted in accordance with standard rules of interpretation, i.e. the meaning of 'tax residence' should be taken to mean the rules of tax residence in the jurisdiction in question, as should other terms such as 'permanent establishment' (this is of course, more readily appreciated when it is considered that the DAC is enacted in national legislation where it is primarily to be interpreted.

Once the meaning of 'participant' is understood, the four tests in Art 3(18)(a) – (d) become clearer. Test (a) is an entirely mechanical analysis of the facts of the tax residence of the participants. Test (b) is similarly a simple analysis of tax residence; and test (c) can be measured in accordance with the standard rules on permanent establishment contained in local legislation.

Test (d), however, is somewhat more complex. It hinges on the fact that the participant 'carries on an activity in another jurisdiction without being resident for tax purposes or creating a permanent establishment situated in that jurisdiction.' What it is to 'carry on' an activity is not clear. The Irish Guidance does give one example:

> A medical supplies company that is tax resident in the US appoints a dependant agent in Ireland. The US company is not tax resident in Ireland under Ireland's tax residence rules and, given its level of activity in Ireland, it has no PE in Ireland under the terms of the Ireland-US Double Tax Convention. However, the agent is carrying on activities in Ireland on behalf of the company. Therefore, if the US company participates in a transaction with, for example, a company that is tax resident in Ireland, the transaction will come within the definition of 'cross-border arrangement' because the condition under point (d) is met. If the medical supplies company had made supplies of goods to customers in Ireland, but had no presence on the ground there, then the condition would not be met.[18]

Thus, it seems that carrying on an activity which, save for its scale, would qualify as a permanent establishment would satisfy (d). However, does the holding of and renting out for value a property in a second jurisdiction from one's residence amount to 'carrying on an activity'? Under UK law, renting a property is not a 'trade' in certain circumstances, and it would not be considered so in jurisdictions which have English law as the basis of their own tax law (such as Gibraltar), but whether it amounts to an 'activity' for these purposes is a point for discussion.

---

[18] Ibid

The Irish Guidance makes clear that if a person makes a supply but has 'no presence on the ground' then the condition would not be met. If the conceptualisation of rental income as passive, more akin to bank interest than to the proceeds of trade is correct and holds across the entire EU, then we could continue to draw the analogy that earning interest from a bank deposit does not amount to carrying on an activity, and therefore neither does the mere renting out of a property. The passivity of the income requires that there be no activity. The language itself implies a lack of action. This treatment would arguably be consistent with English law principles (though not necessarily with the activity required in letting property in certain circumstances).

8.3 Reportable cross-border arrangements

Whilst not all cross-border arrangements are reportable, all reportable arrangements are cross-border[19]. The difference between a cross-border arrangement and a reportable cross-border arrangement is entirely based on the characteristics of the arrangement in question. It is always important for those considering DAC6 and applying its provisions, to remember that DAC6 is a targeted provision, aimed at specific activities deemed to be the tools of the tax avoider of particular concern. It is not a general avoidance reporting obligation, such as section 41 of the Income Tax Act 2010 of Gibraltar, which simply imposes a duty to disclose any arrangement which:

> (ii) enable[s], or might be expected to enable, any person to obtain an advantage in relation to any tax under this Act that is so prescribed in relation to arrangements of that description

Instead DAC6 is designed simply to trigger reporting around specific actions and scenarios. These are listed in Annex IV to the DAC and are described as 'hallmarks'. We discuss the hallmarks in great detail elsewhere in this book, but suffice to say for the purposes of this section, no cross-border arrangement can be reportable without exhibiting at least one of the hallmarks.

8.4 Marketable arrangement

One of the sub-categories of arrangement is that of a 'marketable arrangement'. Marketable arrangements are subject to a periodic bulk reporting requirement rather than an individual reporting requirement within 30 days of the initiation or readying of the arrangement for implementation.

A 'marketable arrangement' is defined as:

[19] Except in Portugal and Poland where domestic only arrangements are similarly be reportable.

> 'marketable arrangement' means a cross-border arrangement that is designed, marketed and ready for implementation or made available for implementation without a need to be substantially customised.[20]

As ever, it is important to remember that if an arrangement qualifies as a 'marketable arrangement', then that does not necessarily mean it is reportable. It will still be subject to the application of an analysis to see if the arrangement in question exhibits one or more of the hallmarks.

The Irish Tax and Customs guidance is clear as to the critical element qualifying an arrangement as a marketable arrangement:

> the key feature of a marketable arrangement is that it is available for use without a need for substantial customisation[21].

There is much overlap between Hallmark A3 and the definition of a marketable arrangement. One matter of prime concern for some professionals is the settlement of a trust using precedent trust documentation. It would be wrong merely to make the analysis of whether an arrangement is 'marketable' simply focus on the percentage of the document which has been amended. Trust Deeds can be lengthy and contain many identical provisions. However, almost all of those provisions can be stripped away and the trust continues to function in its material effects. The material clauses of the trust are:

- the act of settlement itself, that is the certainty of the intention to create a trust by the transfer of the subject matter of the trust to the trustees;
- the certainty of the subject matter itself (i.e. the assets); and
- the certainty of those who benefit

(these are the three certainties required to establish a trust, and each has been the subject of lengthy judicial discussion).

In the case of each trust created, these three areas are subject to much consideration and amendment relevant to the situation at hand. However, on a mere word count, the clauses relevant to these three certainties may amount to a few lines of a lengthy document made up of boilerplate clauses around trustees' powers. It would seem wrong entirely to amend the material clauses of an arrangement, only for that materiality to be overwhelmed by the quantity of the non-material clauses. Not taking this materiality-based line of interpretation would lead to a situation where, not only the creation of trusts, but also potentially the incorporation of a company using standard articles would automatically qualify as a 'marketable arrangement'. This cannot be the correct approach, in the context of the purpose of the provisions.

---

[20] Article 3(24) DAC

[21] The Irish Guidance Chapter 2.3

As stated above, Hallmark A3 and the definition of a 'marketable arrangement' have much in common and we shall return to these themes later in our discussion of Hallmark A3 below.

8.5 Bespoke arrangement

Article 3(25) defines 'Bespoke Arrangement' as 'any cross-border arrangement that is not a marketable arrangement'. This is an entirely simple 'sweeping-up' class of definition.

In practice, given the complexity of modern tax matters, it is probable that in most circumstances the arrangements encountered will fall within the definition of a bespoke arrangement rather than a marketable arrangement. Marketable arrangements outside the realms of those arrangements, similar in nature to insurance wrappers and savings product, are uncommon, but not unknown. Modern tax planning, however, tends to deal with clients as individuals, and the work carried out by the tax authorities on closing what the media describe as 'loopholes' through such innovations as General Anti-Avoidance Rules and DOTAS reporting, means that such bulk sales arrangements are now mostly closed down within a short period. One should, however, remain vigilant for marketable arrangements.

8.6 Hallmarks

The hallmarks are defined in Annex IV of the DAC and will be discussed in detail in Chapter 9.

8.7 Intermediary

The DAC itself defines an intermediary as follows: 'intermediary' means any person that designs, markets, organises or makes available for implementation or manages the implementation of a reportable cross-border arrangement.'

It also means any person that, having regard to the relevant facts and circumstances and based on available information and the relevant expertise and understanding required to provide such services, knows or could be reasonably expected to know that they have undertaken to provide, directly or by means of other persons, aid, assistance or advice with respect to designing, marketing, organising, making available for implementation or managing the implementation of a reportable cross-border arrangement. Any person shall have the right to provide evidence that such person did not know and could not reasonably be expected to know that that person was involved in a reportable cross-border arrangement. For this purpose, that person may refer to all relevant facts and circumstances as well as available information and their relevant expertise and understanding.

To be an intermediary, a person shall meet at least one of the following additional conditions:

(a) be resident for tax purposes in a Member State;
(b) have a permanent establishment in a Member State through which the services with respect to the arrangement are provided;

(c) be incorporated in, or governed by the laws of, a Member State;
(d) be registered with a professional association related to legal, taxation or consultancy services in a Member State.

From this it is clear that there are two types of intermediaries, firstly those who design, market, organise, make available for implementation or those who manage implementation of arrangements (in the first paragraph), and secondly, those who provide aid, assistance or advice to those performing such tasks (within the second paragraph).

These two types of intermediary — those who are deeply embedded and those who are peripheral — are called 'Promoters' and 'Service Providers' by HMRC, 'First Category' and 'Second Category' intermediaries by ITC while the Dutch Guidance defines them as 'Intermediaries' and 'Auxiliary Intermediaries'. For the sake of clarity and simplicity, we will use the HMRC designations (though to confuse matters, they also refer to the same things as 'First' and 'Second' category intermediaries).

8.8 Promoters

The role of a promoter is central to an arrangement, and promoters can be thought of as those whose role is intrinsic to the design, marketing and implementation of an arrangement. They are not merely incidental and will 'almost invariably have a full understanding of the material aspects of the arrangement'[22].

The definition of 'intermediary' promoter appears to be an objective one, i.e. it does not matter whether you consider yourself to be within it, there is an objective standard of what constitutes an intermediary promoter. Of course, it is not a particularly clear standard, focussed on a number of undefined terms. As with many of the definitions within the DAC, it appears to be drafted broadly, and designed to reduce or eliminate the risk of a person who should be within the definition falling outside it, at the expense of pulling in others who, perhaps, should not be within it.

An individual or entity will be expected to understand and have knowledge of events as is commensurate with their role. A director of a holding company who specifically closes his eyes to events and information to avoid becoming a promoter will still be considered a promoter due to the objective nature of the test.

What if an intermediary is simply incompetent? An incompetent director who administers the implementation of an arrangement and honestly believes himself not to be a promoter, or who does not understand the reportability of the arrangement, will nonetheless be a promoter. However, since the meaning of 'designs', 'markets', 'organises', 'makes available for implementation' or 'manages the implementation' are not defined, and the

---

[22] The HMRC Guidance - IEIM621030 Promoter

fact of having wide boundaries can hardly be considered equivalent to being unbounded, this will, undoubtedly, be fertile ground for litigation in the coming years.

Irish Guidance describes a promoter as:

> This category of intermediary will comprise those that actively design and advise on tax planning schemes for their clients, such as lawyers specialising in tax law and professional tax advisers. It will also include companies in corporate groups that design and advise on such schemes using in-house experts for implementation by other group members.[23]

This puts the role of the promoter onto the tax advisers. This leads us to believe that clients receiving tax advice in future should insist on a DAC6 analysis being included as standard in a tax paper of any kind. Given the prospects of their meeting the definition of 'promoter' in any given situation, tax advisers must already be analysing their proposals as part of their internal governance and compliance procedures, and they should share that analysis at a very early stage in a way which can be relied upon. It is no longer good enough for an adviser to propose changes without considering exchange of information consequences, and those advisers who do not do so are, arguably, failing in their professional duties. This marks a sea change in the approach which advisers are being forced to make, and it is both a direct consequence of DAC6 and an indirect one of BEPS.

HMRC go on to explain:

> it follows that a person involved in a cross-border arrangement but without knowledge of those material aspects is unlikely to be a promoter and will normally be a service provider instead.[24]

The Dutch Guidance contains a somewhat similar paragraph regarding Service Providers (which they call 'Auxiliary Intermediaries') stating:

> The auxiliary intermediary has no duty to investigate. That is, a person is not obliged to collect additional information in order to assess whether he qualifies as an auxiliary intermediary, if that additional information is not necessary in order to provide the relevant service – taking into account the expertise and understanding required for it.[25]

The German Guidance takes a similar line:

> All relevant facts (i.e. all factual information required for legal advice) and the relevant expertise and understanding required for

[23] The Irish Guidance Chapter 4.2

[24] The HMRC Guidance IEIM621030 Promoter

[25] The Dutch Guidance Chapter 3.2 Taxes.

> the provision of such services shall be taken into account. No further investigation is required.[26]

In terms of tax authority guidance, these sections are unusually clear. They boil down to this: if a person is performing their function properly, is not deliberately being blind, and they do not know the ins-and-outs of an arrangement, then they are highly unlikely to be a promoter.

8.9 Service providers

Service Providers are defined in the DAC as:

> any person that, having regard to the relevant facts and circumstances and based on available information and the relevant expertise and understanding required to provide such services, knows or could be reasonably expected to know that they have undertaken to provide, directly or by means of other persons, aid, assistance or advice with respect to designing, marketing, organising, making available for implementation or managing the implementation of a reportable cross-border arrangement. Any person shall have the right to provide evidence that such person did not know and could not reasonably be expected to know that that person was involved in a reportable cross-border arrangement. For this purpose, that person may refer to all relevant facts and circumstances as well as available information and their relevant expertise and understanding.

This is a secondary and less onerous category of intermediaries. It is helpful to breakdown the dense text to establish when an intermediary is a service provider:

(a) The intermediary must be a person (see discussion above at E1);
(b) The intermediary must know that they have provided directly or otherwise, aid, assistance or advice regarding designing, marketing, organising, making available for implementation or managing the implementation of a cross-border arrangement; and
(c) If they do not know that they satisfy (ii) then if it is reasonable, based on what is required, to deliver the relevant service and taking into account all the facts, to assume that they should know they have provided aid, and thus are deemed to know they have done so.

This provision is a double-edged sword. It imputes knowledge onto the incompetent who does not fully understand what he is doing or who has deliberately closed his eyes to what he is doing. Alternatively, it provides the competent and diligent individual with a defence that:

(a) He does not know;

[26] The German Guidance Para 61

(b) That a person providing that service cannot be reasonably expected to know.

This is of particular relevance to those who provide ancillary services and who are concerned that they will be brought into the scope of DAC6 as an intermediary.

The following are examples which explain the boundaries of the definition of service provider:

(a) A bank is instructed to make a payment to a BVI Company. The client presents a loan agreement to fulfil the bank's due diligence procedures. In this case, the bank does not know and neither does it need to know, that it has provided (if it has) aid, assistance or advice with respect to designing, marketing, organising, making available for implementation or managing the implementation of a reportable cross-border arrangement to provide the service of executing a bank instruction. By providing commercial justification, the client has allowed the bank to fulfil its regulatory requirements, and it is required to look no further;
(b) An auditor discovers a reportable arrangement in the preparation of his audit. The arrangement was entered into in the previous financial year and the auditor does not actively provide support. The auditor is not an intermediary because he simply knows of the existence of the arrangement. Additionally, and alternatively, he is not a service provider, as the service he is providing takes place after the event. In other words, he has not provided 'aid, assistance, or advice' as the arrangement has completed, he has merely chanced upon its existence; and
(c) A fiduciary is asked to reclassify the share capital of a company and redeem some preference shares. He is given a copy of a tax paper and asked to read it. The tax paper details the tax effect of the redemption upon the recipients. The fiduciary may well not need to know the effect of the arrangement to provide the service, but he has actual knowledge of its effect and therefore is knowingly providing aid to the implementation of an arrangement.

It is interesting to note that the Dutch Guidance goes further than most in defining the limitations of the situations in which a Service Provider is required to report. It specifically deals with a situation where a professional has actual knowledge of an arrangement but is not required to have such knowledge to provide the service in question.

> A potential auxiliary intermediary sometimes has more information than is necessary to provide the relevant service. Think, for example, of a lawyer who receives a complete file from a client, while he only advises on one aspect of that file. In such a case, for the assessment of whether there is a mandatory cross-border arrangement, the lawyer may in principle confine himself to the facts and

> circumstances and information contained in the file necessary to provide the relevant opinion. The lawyer is therefore not obliged to take note of the other available information in the file to determine whether there is a mandatory cross-border arrangement.[27]

It is also of note that the German Tax Code appears entirely to omit the definition of 'Service Provider'. The relevant section states:

> 's138(d)(1) Any person who markets a cross-border tax arrangement within the meaning of paragraph 2, designs, organises or provides for use for third parties or manages its implementation by third parties (intermediaries), must notify the Federal Central Tax Office'

However, this omission is somewhat mitigated by the inclusion of the 'do not know, do not need to know' defence in Part I Chapter 3.1.2 of the German Guidance. This seems to indicate that, regardless of the omission in the legislation, the German authorities will practically implement in a manner consistent with the existence of two differing categories and permit the Service Provider Defence.

8.10 Relevant taxpayer

The term 'relevant taxpayer' is used surprisingly little in DAC6, which demonstrates that the primary object of the DAC6 is to identify arrangements, not taxpayers. Relevant taxpayers are primarily featured in the text of DAC6 as passive recipients who receive or have 'made available' to them 'for implementation' arrangements. It is only in matters of reporting that they feature as active participants, and only then as a backstop for reporting, in matters where the intermediary is either hobbled by legal professional privilege or are not subject to the writ of EU law.

The term itself is defined thus:

> 'relevant taxpayer' means any person to whom a reportable cross-border arrangement is made available for implementation, or who is ready to implement a reportable cross-border arrangement or has implemented the first step of such an arrangement[28]

Firstly, of note concerning the definition of 'Relevant Taxpayer' is that the definition does not include a requirement for a relevant taxpayer to be a taxpayer. For example, an entirely tax-exempted charity can be a 'relevant taxpayer' or a partnership which qualifies as a 'person' under the definition of person at Article 3(11), yet is an entirely see-through entity which is not a taxpayer in its own right.

This is a classic example of misleading drafting. The words themselves are defined so widely that they entirely deviate from the normal meaning. How, exactly, can a 'Relevant Taxpayer' include those things and relationships

---

[262] The Dutch Guidance Chapter 3.2

[28] Article 18(22)

which do not pay tax? In any realm other than the legal, they cannot. What this does betray is the aim of the legislation. It is designed to cast its net as wide as possible, even if doing so means that the meanings of words become so stretched as to render them almost entirely meaningless. Language and logic can be no barrier to the aim, which is to ensure that information flows.

The German Guidance and legislation specifically avoids the words 'relevant taxpayer' and instead chooses the word 'User'. This is a much more helpful and efficient use of language, and it is defined in s138(d)(5) of the German Tax Code as:

> 5. The user of a cross-border tax arrangement shall be any natural or legal person, partnership, community or asset:
> which cross-border tax arrangements are made available for implementation;
> which is ready to implement cross-border tax arrangements, or
> which has taken the first step towards the implementation of cross-border tax design.'

Regardless of how we feel about the choice of language, we have the words as defined in our various jurisdictions, and it will always be the case that a 'person' who qualifies as a relevant taxpayer will:

- Be obliged to file a report where there is no intermediary, a non-EU intermediary or the intermediary has notified the relevant taxpayer of the requirement to file and that the intermediary is subject to legal professional privilege[29]; and
- Be identified in any report made under DAC6.

Other than this the relevance of a relevant taxpayer is a method of identifying the relevant member states (i.e. the member state of residence of the relevant taxpayer is relevant to reporting but also to the technical provisions around waiver of legal privilege, etc.).

[29] Article 8b(6) and (7)

9 The Hallmarks and Reporting

9.1 The Main Benefit Test

Several of the hallmarks require what is called the Main Benefit Test (MBT) to be satisfied before they can be engaged, understanding the MBT is 'required reading' before moving on to the hallmarks themselves. The MBT is contained at Annex IV Part I of the DAC and states:

> That test will be satisfied if it can be established that the main benefit or one of the main benefits which, having regard to all the relevant facts and circumstances, a person may reasonably expect to derive from an arrangement is the obtaining of a tax advantage.

In the context of DAC6, the MBT is designed both to temper and refine the hallmarks to which it is applicable. It is also the latest in a long line of tests designed to allow tax authorities to include the intention or effect of an arrangement in their consideration on whether to disallow that effect.

9.1.1 Objective or subjective

The MBT sits well in the tradition of anti-avoidance tools which have been at the disposal of tax authorities for many years. The need for some sort of test allowing the tax authority to disallow an arrangement on the grounds that it is tax-driven has motivated the UK's (amongst others) legal draftsmen since at least 1960, when the Finance Act 1960 s.28 referred to transactions which have 'as their main object, or one of their main objects to enable tax advantages to be obtained.' The difference in language between 'benefit' and 'object' marks the boundaries between the tests which delineate what can be disallowed by the authorities, which are to some extent subjective, and the more objective versions of this form of test as to whether a report should be made.

The motivation for this form has been regularly discussed and as Shiers and Miller put it:

> the Chancellor was keen to ensure that legitimate commercial transactions were not impacted and that the legislation should only be used to counter the 'fiddling and dodging' cases practiced by the minority (Hansard 7 April 1960 column 690)[1]

It would seem obvious that a draftsman should have a preference for objective rather than subjective tests. A subjective test requires the courts to look into the heart of the taxpayer and decipher intention, rather than a measure of factual outcomes. This is necessarily uncertain, and such subjective tests often fall down in the arena of tax because there are a multitude of reasons which can be appealed to as the 'main intention or intentions' underlying a transaction. There have been some lengthy

---

[1] R Shiers, P Miller *'The Whole or Main Purpose Test' Tax Journal*, 876, 8 12 March 2007

discussions in various pieces of case law in the UK and Ireland around the wording of subjective tests. Rimmer L.J. summed it up when he said:

> 'I should say that I do not regard [the section in question] as a cleverly drafted piece of legislation. To make the availability of a capital allowance dependent on what is ultimately the subjective intention of a party to a transaction is a recipe for dispute and litigation'[2].

However, subjective tests are still routinely added to the statute book. In UK legislation, the complex provision generally known as the GAAR (or 'General Anti Abuse Rule') has at its heart the following provision:

> **207 Meaning of 'tax arrangements' and 'abusive'**
>
> (1) Arrangements are 'tax arrangements' if, having regard to all the circumstances, it would be reasonable to conclude that the obtaining of a tax advantage was the main purpose, or one of the main purposes, of the arrangements.[3]

Which can be seen to be reaching again for a measure of purpose of intention.

In contrast to this, we can look at the tax arrangement reporting requirement included in s.41 of the Income Tax Act 2010 of Gibraltar, one of whose definitions of 'reportable arrangements' is:

> iii) are such that the main benefit, or one of the main benefits, that might be expected to arise from the arrangements is the obtaining of that advantage

This is an entirely accurate mirror of the third limb of section 306 of the Finance Act 2004 of the UK which similarly states:

> c) are such that the main benefit, or one of the main benefits, that might be expected to arise from the arrangements is the obtaining of that advantage

Considering the subjective GAAR and objective disclosure regime tests together, one can see an element of design to this difference of approach. The objective disclosure regimes (examples of which are the UK disclosure regime (known colloquially as the 'Disclosure of Tax Avoidance Schemes' or DOTAS regime) and its Gibraltarian sister section 41) are, in effect, a first filter. It is designed to be implemented by professionals to sift arrangements into those which are worthy of consideration and those not. They are designed to maximise reporting so as to allow the tax authorities and the courts to filter out those regimes which do not qualify as avoidance, but to also catch all those schemes and arrangements which are avoidance. A

---

[2] *Lloyds TSB Equipment Leasing (No1) Ltd v Revenue and Customs Commissioners* [2014] EWCA Civ 1062

[3] Section 207 Finance Act 2013

professional acting for his or her client must assess not intention (and is thus not to be tempted to err in favour of their client) but instead effect, a tax adviser must have sufficient knowledge to assess actual effect. It is left to the courts to assess intention.

The Irish regime bears out this analysis. In the Irish Guidance the only truly objective test given as an example is the DAC6 MBT. Section 811C of the Taxes Consolidation Act 1997 of the Republic of Ireland combines both forms as it defines a tax avoidance transaction as:

> (2)(a) Subject to paragraph (b), for the purposes of this section a transaction shall be a 'tax avoidance transaction' if .... it would be reasonable to consider that—
>
> (A) the transaction gives rise to, or but for this section would give rise to, a tax advantage, and
>
> (B) the transaction was not undertaken or arranged primarily for purposes other than to give rise to a tax advantage.

Here we can see the combined effect of an objective first filter and a subjective second filter. The transaction must first give rise to an advantage before we can analyse whether that advantage was intentional, or the arrangement had as its purpose that advantage.

It can be further seen in the combination of the DAC6 main benefit test and the EU mandated GAAR contained at Article 6 of the Anti-Tax Avoidance Directive.

> 1. For the purposes of calculating the corporate tax liability, a Member State shall ignore an arrangement or a series of arrangements which, having been put into place for the main purpose or one of the main purposes of obtaining a tax advantage that defeats the object or purpose of the applicable tax law, are not genuine having regard to all relevant facts and circumstances. An arrangement may comprise more than one step or part.[4]

DAC6 is seemingly designed to ensure that those arrangements which will fail the Article 6 GAAR and those which will not fail it are both reported. The designers of the regime clearly believed that the only way to ensure all the 'fiddling and dodging' cases are within the view of the authorities is to ensure that all cases which could be 'fiddling and dodging cases' are reported, so those which are not of that type can be discarded. This is achieved by taking an objective mechanical approach to sift those arrangements to be reported so that they can then be measured against the subjective GAAR by the tax authorities and ultimately the court.

---

[4] Article 6 COUNCIL DIRECTIVE (EU) 2016/1164

DAC6 should not and cannot be considered in isolation of the rest of the EU framework on tax avoidance. It is an integral part of that framework, and the reasons for its design should be considered within that framework.

9.1.2 The meaning of 'tax advantage'

For the MBT to be satisfied a taxpayer must obtain a 'tax advantage'. The phrase 'tax advantage' is not strictly defined in the DAC6 Directive.

> 10. That phrase is placed in context by the 2012/772/EU: Commission Recommendation of 6 December 2012 on aggressive tax planning which gives guidance to Member States on how to ascertain if an arrangement has led to a tax benefit:
>
> > 4.7. In determining whether an arrangement or series of arrangements has led to a tax benefit as referred to in point 4.2, national authorities are invited to compare the amount of tax due by a taxpayer, having regard to those arrangement(s), with the amount that the same taxpayer would owe under the same circumstances in the absence of the arrangement(s).
>
> In that context, it is useful to consider whether one or more of the following situations occur:
> (a) an amount is not included in the tax base;
> (b) the taxpayer benefits from a deduction;
> (c) a loss for tax purposes is incurred;
> (d) no withholding tax is due;
> (e) foreign tax is offset

This would seem to indicate that the Commission, at least, believes that a tax advantage amounts to either, a non-inclusion in taxable income or gains, a granting of a deduction, a loss occurring, a relief or exemption from withholding tax, or a double taxation relief.

The Luxembourg guidance takes a wider approach, which can be described as the 'Legislative Intent Approach' when it states:

> the main benefit test is not met when the tax advantage obtained as a result of the arrangement is consistent with the object or purpose of the applicable legislation and consistent with the intention of the legislator[5]

The German legislation at s138(d) states:

> (3) tax advantage within the meaning of paragraph 2 sentence 1 point 3 (a) exists if:
> 1. There is a refund of taxes grant or tax allowances increased, or tax is to be waived or reduced;

---

[5] The Luxembourg Guidance

2. Claims to tax are prevented from arising, or
3. Tax claims are shifted to other tax periods.

> A tax advantage also exists if it is to arise outside the scope of this Act. In agreement with the highest tax authorities of the Länder, the Federal Ministry of Finance may stipulate in a letter to be published in the Federal Tax Gazette for certain case groups that no tax advantage within the meaning of sentences 1 and 2 is to be assumed, in particular because the tax advantage of a cross-border tax arrangement has an exclusively effect within the scope of this Act and is provided for by law, taking into account all the circumstances of the tax structure.'

It is interesting that the German legislation permits a ruling by the authorities if the arrangement is within the scope of the Act. This goes some way to showing 'legislative intent' and can be seen almost as a halfway-house between a purely objective approach and a subjective legislative approach.

The Irish Tax and Customs choose to remain silent in their guidance as to whether a tax advantage must be at odds to the intention of the legislator to meet the MBT.

The Maltese Guidance sits squarely in the Legislative Intent Approach camp, stating:

> A tax advantage would be considered for the purposes of the main benefit test to the extent that it is not consistent with the legislator's intention for the particular provision in terms of which the tax advantage is being obtained[6]

It is also worthy of note that in the now-defunct UK implementation (defunct to the extent that the MBT is not relevant to those remnants of the DAC6 which the UK has retained post 31 December 2020) of DAC6 the Legislative Intent Approach was contained within the relevant legislative provisions.

The Belgian Guidance (whilst referring to the contents of the 06 December 2012 Recommendation as 'particularly useful') takes a slightly different approach from all the other guidance discussed here in that it states:

> In order to determine whether there is a tax advantage, the tax payable by the taxable person, taking into account the arrangement, must be compared with the amount that the same taxable person would be liable in identical circumstances in absence of the structure in question.[7]

---

[6] Chapter 5.2.1 The Maltese Guidance

[7] The Belgiam Guidance

This mandates a simple mathematical calculation, 'does the arrangement result in less tax being paid?' as opposed to seeking out certain outcomes which will lead to less tax being paid, as per the 06 December 2012 Recommendation

The French implementation of DAC6 is modified by a Legislative Intent Approach within certain boundaries:

> Where the main benefit obtained in France through the cross-border scheme results from the use of a tax incentive provided by the French legislator, it is not considered a primary tax benefit within the meaning of the CGI Article 1649 AH, subject to respect for the intention of the legislator[8]

The Italian Guidance contained in the Italian Revenue Agency Circular No 2 of 10 February 2021 does seem to stand out as a separate piece which takes a unique approach. The Italian MBT guidance divides the test into two pieces:

(i) A tax benefit must be achievable for one or more Italian taxpayers; and
(ii) The tax advantage must outweigh non-tax advantages.

The Circular in question articulates that a tax advantage unrelated to an Italian taxpayer cannot be reported by an Italian intermediary. This seems somewhat at odds to the loose definition of 'relevant taxpayer' and other terms which seek to cast the net as wide as possible.

The criterion of tax advantages outweighing those of non-tax relevant considerations is reduced to a mathematical calculation whereby the tax advantage must equate to more than 50% of the advantage of the arrangement as a whole. This seems to eliminate one of the main elements of the MBT that 'the or one of the main benefits of the arrangement is a tax advantage' (in other words the tax benefit need not be overriding). It is difficult to understand how the test can meaningfully include those benefits which are 'one of the main benefits' if in order to satisfy the test, the benefit must be, by definition, *the* main benefit of the arrangement.

Setting aside the Italian position, if the analysis above — that the DAC6 Main Benefit Test is deliberately objective to act as a 'first filter' which mandates reporting of matters in a mechanical way — is correct, then the Legislative Intent Approach on the terms 'tax advantage' and 'main benefit' are a deviation from that design of the Directive. If the aim is a mechanical approach with minimal interpretative requirements, and since DAC6 is part-implemented by professionals in their day-to-day practice, it would seem odd to force upon them an analysis of the legislature's intent as to the relevant provisions.

---

8 The French Guidance

In contrast the Commission's position seems to be consistent with the approach described in the 06 December 2012 Recommendation. The 06 December 2012 Recommendation simply lays out a factual test which can be measured by any high street accountant or lawyer. The two-step process is confirmed by the preamble to the DAC6 Directive which points out:

> Moreover, it is appropriate to recall that aggressive cross-border tax-planning arrangements, the main purpose or one of the main purposes of which is to obtain a tax advantage that defeats the object or purpose of the applicable tax law, are subject to the general anti-abuse rule as set out in Article 6 of Council Directive (EU) 2016/1164[9]

Again, we see, the DAC6 Directive is designed to flush out arrangements which give factual results to an objective test, so that they can have the subjective GAAR applied to them.

This aim, if it is in fact the aim of those drafting the directives, seems somewhat undermined by the Maltese Guidance, Luxembourg Guidance, French Guidance and other jurisdictions which take a Legislative Intent Approach on the part of the professional assessing whether he has an obligation to report. Who is to be the arbiter of the Parliament's intention? Is it the tax authorities? If it is, are they effectively making law through the power they have to interpret? That would be a novel approach, since previously only the courts have been those empowered to interpret the will of Parliament definitively, but as the urge to catch avoiders strengthens and the tools become ever more draconian, the power of the tax authorities to set the boundaries of discussion continues to grow.

Whilst not crippling to the objective of an entirely mechanical assessment and reporting exercise, the Legislative Intent Approach complicates matters for the professionals in question and puts an extra onus of high-level understanding and knowledge upon smaller practitioners.

It would be wrong to assume universal acceptance of the proposition that the DAC6 main benefit test and the GAAR main purpose test (and its domestic brethren) are an objective filter and a subjective final test respectively. Oliver Hoor in his book *The Mandatory Disclosure Regime in Luxembourg: A practical guide* states:

> The MBT [that is the DAC6 main benefit test] focusses on the 'main benefit or one of the main benefits' of an arrangement being a tax advantage, the GAAR and the PPT [principal purpose test as contained in various bilateral treaties] is a tax advantage. Accordingly, the GAAR and the PPT focus on the purpose of an arrangement, whereas the MBT focusses on the outcome of an arrangement.

---

[9] Para 14 Preamble Council Directive EU 2018/822

> As it can be assumed that the outcome of an arrangement is consistent with its intended purpose (or, in other words the intention of the parties), the analysis of the GAAR (and where applicable the PPT) can inform the analysis of the MBT[10]

It must first be noted that neither of the authors is qualified to advise on Luxembourg law, and as such cannot comment on the utility of the second paragraph quoted above in Luxembourg. However, in terms of the Directive and the laws of Jersey, England and Wales, Gibraltar and the underlying principles of common law jurisdictions around the world, we reject the analysis contained in the second paragraph. It is not true that an assumption can validly be drawn from effect to intention, neither in logic, case law nor life.

This is not, however, to say that a measure of the intention of the parties as relevant to the GAAR/PPT would be entirely unhelpful in analysing the applicability of the main benefit test. The GAAR/PPT is made up of a test of intention and the power which the authorities have to ignore an arrangement if that test of intention is applicable. By reference to 'the GAAR/PPT intention test', we mean solely this first element as to the intention of the parties. It is logically correct to say that the following combinations of the main benefit test and the GAAR/PPT intention test are possible:

(a) one of the main benefits is a tax advantage, but the benefit was accidental (MBT satisfied but GAAR/PPT intention test not applicable);
(b) there was no tax advantage as a main benefit because an intended tax advantage failed to materialise (MBT not satisfied, GAAR/PPT intention test applicable but no tax effect);
(c) one of the main benefits is a tax advantage and the benefit was intentional (both MBT and GAAR/PPT intention test are satisfied)
(d) there is no main benefit which is a tax advantage, and there was no intention to take one (both MBT and GAAR/PPT intention test not satisfied)

It will be clear that the only case in which the main benefit test can be left unsatisfied and the GAAR/PPT intention test can be triggered, outcome (b), results in no actual tax loss. The ATAD states its GAAR thus:

> 1. For the purposes of calculating the corporate tax liability, a Member State shall ignore an arrangement or a series of arrangements which, having been put into place for the main purpose or one of the main purposes of obtaining a tax advantage that defeats the object or purpose of the applicable tax law, are not genuine having regard to all relevant facts and

---

[10] p91 '*the Mandatory Disclosure Regime in Luxembourg: A practical guide*' Oliver R Hoor Legitech 2020

> circumstances. An arrangement may comprise more than one step or part.[11]

So it can be seen that the MBT's sister provision, the ATAD GAAR, will not have any effect in the outcome (b) above, as to ignore an arrangement which was intended to have a tax effect but did not in itself has no effect.

Therefore, by the simple application of logic, it is obvious that the only outcome in which the GAAR/PPT can be actioned by the authorities is also a case where the main benefit test is met. In other words, if the GAAR has been triggered and the authorities have applied it correctly, the arrangement is always reportable, though not all reportable arrangements will satisfy the GAAR. That will help, at least, where action has been taken by the authorities, but it falls some way short of Hoor's second paragraph:

> 'As it can be assumed that the outcome of an arrangement is consistent with its intended purpose (or, in other words the intention of the parties), the analysis of the GAAR (and where applicable the PPT) can inform the analysis of the MBT.' [12]

Which conflates two very different tests, incorrectly in our opinion.

9.1.3 The meaning of 'main'

The final element for consideration in the MBT is that the benefit which is accrued as a result of the arrangement in question must be the or one of the 'main benefits which a person may reasonably expect to derive from an arrangement'.

Given that a requirement for the tax advantage to be the main effect or purpose of an arrangement is present in both the objective and subjective tests which have been used in anti-avoidance regimes, there is some substantial case law guidance around such matters.

The fact that a tax advantage is acquired at all does not mean it is conclusive that the arrangement must be reported. Irish Tax and Customs' guidance attempts to explain:

> The main benefit test requires an objective comparison of the value or significance of an expected tax advantage vis-à-vis any other benefit likely to be obtained from an arrangement. Such a comparison is to be carried out in the context of the arrangement itself and the range of benefits expected to arise from it.
>
> … If, on the other hand, it is the case that a tax advantage is one of a number of benefits that are likely to be obtained from an

[11] Article 6 COUNCIL DIRECTIVE (EU) 2016/1164

[12] p91 *The Mandatory Disclosure Regime in Luxembourg: A Practical Guide*, Oliver R. Hoor, Legitech 2020

> arrangement, but not a main benefit, then the tax advantage will simply be the 'icing on the cake'[13] and the test will not be satisfied[14]

This reference in the Irish Guidance to *Sema* makes it clear that simply receiving a tax advantage is not conclusive proof that the MBT is met.

As a practical example of this test in action:

> A relevant taxpayer purchases units in an investment fund. The investment fund is what is known as an accumulation fund. That is, instead of distributing any income it receives, it rolls that income up into the investment of the relevant taxpayer. This increases the capital value of the units the relevant taxpayer receives. It also means that income which the fund receives is converted into capital in the hands of the relevant taxpayer if he/she redeems his/her units. Any profits or gains on the redemption of his/her units are taxed as capital gains, rather than as income.

In some very early interpretations of DAC6, this situation was contemplated as reportable. However, on reflection it is clear, the 'arrangement' (even if it amounts to an arrangement) fails the MBT (which would be relevant to the Category B Hallmark in point). The benefits of an accumulation fund are many. They provide capital growth, and aid in the provision of long term investments, there is no obligation to distribute income and thus administratively they are much simpler, no dividends means that the fund is much more liquid and can resist the effects of demands to redeem units, they are the industry standard approach to this kind of investment, and given the Europe-wide application of such a structure, it is even uncertain that a tax advantage would be gained, given that the citizens of 27 countries have access to it. The tax advantage to be gained is only one of many advantages to be gained by structuring the investment fund in such a way.

The acquiring of a limitation of tax remains as one of the standard activities of a commercial decision maker and is not in itself a signifier that the MBT is satisfied. As Lord Upjohn stated in an echo of the *Westminster* principle.

> 'No commercial man in his senses is going to carry out a commercial transaction except upon the footing of paying the smallest amount of tax that he can. The question whether in fact one of the main objects was to avoid tax is one for the Special Commissioners to decide upon a consideration of all the relevant evidence before them'[15]

Thus, we can see that, whether a tax advantage is one of the main benefits of an arrangement or not is a matter of fact, and may well change with each individual relevant taxpayer on a case-by-case basis. No simple principles

---

[13] *Commissioner of Inland Revenue v Sema Group Pension Scheme Trustees* 74 TC 593 at 637

[14] The Irish Guidance Chapter 2.5.3

[15] *Brebner v IRC* [1967] 1 AC 18 at p30E

can be drawn that this or that arrangement always provides a tax advantage which is a 'main benefit' for that taxpayer in question. Only a factual analysis of the facts as they are and an assessment of all the benefits accrued can adequately apply the MBT.

9.1.4 Conclusion

In the MBT we can observe that DAC6 is very much not a standalone provision. It interacts with, and is integral to the EU's entire approach to tax avoidance. Too often practitioners and commentators become bogged down in the minutiae of the provision, but to do so is to lose sight of its design and intention. Repeatedly in their commentary, tax authorities declare that reporting does not imply that an arrangement is necessarily going to be disallowed, that a reportable arrangement is not necessarily avoidance. This is the truth. The design of the DAC is that it gathers information. It does not judge the value of that information. It merely makes it available for analysis.

9.2 Category A: generic hallmarks linked to the main benefit test

9.2.1 Category A

When considering category, it is worth noting the title of the category, that is that it describes 'generic' hallmarks which are linked to the MBT. The aim of Category A is to identify those arrangements which are wholly generic. That is, schemes which are replicated on an industrial scale, and are designed, and wherein the same mechanism is repeated over and over again, regardless of the individual affairs of a taxpayer. These schemes may well be sold by agents which were not fully involved in their design; they may feature proprietary concepts and documents which give rise to a particular tax treatment; or they may have jealously-guarded intellectual property at their core.

In addition to this industrial nature, the arrangement must have a tax advantage as one of its main benefits. The text of the hallmark reads:

> A. Generic hallmarks linked to the main benefit test
>
> 1. An arrangement where the relevant taxpayer or a participant in the arrangement undertakes to comply with a condition of confidentiality which may require them not to disclose how the arrangement could secure a tax advantage vis-à-vis other intermediaries or the tax authorities.
> 2. An arrangement where the intermediary is entitled to receive a fee (or interest, remuneration for finance costs and other charges) for the arrangement and that fee is fixed by reference to:
>   (a) the amount of the tax advantage derived from the arrangement; or
>   (b) whether or not a tax advantage is actually derived from the arrangement. This would include an obligation on the

intermediary to partially or fully refund the fees where the intended tax advantage derived from the arrangement was not partially or fully achieved.

3. An arrangement that has substantially standardised documentation and/or structure and is available to more than one relevant taxpayer without a need to be substantially customised for implementation.[16]

9.2.2 Hallmark A1

Hallmark A1 specifies that those arrangements which are subject to a confidentiality requirement on the part of the relevant taxpayer or other participant which stops them revealing the mechanism by which the arrangement is able to secure a tax advantage to other intermediaries or the tax authorities be reported.

By breaking down the hallmark into its constituent parts we can see the test which is required to be satisfied, in order for the hallmark to be present in an arrangement.

(i) The relevant taxpayer or a participant (both of which must be 'persons' as per the definition discussed above at Chapter 8) must be bound to confidentiality whether formally or otherwise;
(ii) That confidentiality clause must relate to the nature of the expected tax effect of the arrangement in producing a tax advantage;
(iii) That confidentiality clause must bind or restrict the relevant taxpayer or participant in connection with disclosure to the tax authorities or other intermediaries; and
(iv) The main benefit test must be met.

It is important to note that a general confidentiality clause, such as is found in many commercial contracts, would not necessarily trigger Hallmark A1. The hallmark is aimed at situations which stop a taxpayer revealing mechanisms to the authorities or other intermediaries thereby enabling tax authorities to counter the design of an arrangement. If a confidentiality clause has the actual effect of such a restriction, it will trigger the hallmark, those drafting such clauses should be careful not to stray too far from what is necessary.

This approach is borne out by the guidance issued by the Irish Customs and Tax which states:

> it is not necessary that the confidentiality condition refer explicitly to the limitation on disclosure. It is only necessary that the confidentiality condition has the effect of limiting disclosure of the

[16] Directive on Administrative Cooperation Annex IV Part II A.

> expected tax advantage vis-à-vis other intermediaries or the tax authorities[17]

The Dutch Guidance makes clear that commercially standard confidentiality clauses will not be sufficient to trigger the hallmark:

> Hallmark A1, concerns an arrangement in which the relevant taxable person or a participant in the arrangement undertakes confidentiality and on this basis may not disclose to other intermediaries or the tax authorities how the arrangement provides a tax advantage. This hallmark does not envisage normal situations in which, for example, terms and conditions include a confidentiality clause under which a client may not disclose or share opinions and the like with third parties. Such clauses may, for example, be agreed from a commercial or business point of view and to avoid liability. They are not intended to specifically keep the tax advantage secret and, in the Dutch situation, they will not prevent the client or relevant taxable person from providing the Tax Office with information on the construction based on the investigatory powers.[18]

This seems a slight modification of the Irish position that, simply, outcome is all that is in point. Seemingly for the Dutch, a confidentiality condition could be applied between intermediaries (for example a legal opinion given to an ultimate client restricted as to its circulation if that restriction is in accordance with 'normal' behaviour) as long as the Dutch authorities can access such data under their investigatory powers.

It is worthy of noting the inclusion of conditions that restrict the disclosure of information to other intermediaries. At first sight, this may seem puzzling. However, in a situation where several intermediaries contribute to the implementation of an arrangement, if an unscrupulous intermediary were attempting to limit DAC6 reporting, and a second intermediary conducted their own analysis of the arrangement, concluding that it was reportable, then that would be a route for the authorities to discover the arrangement. If such an unscrupulous intermediary were to attempt to control reporting by limiting access to information by other intermediaries, then that would obviously be a matter for concern. Hence confidentiality in connection with intermediaries is a trigger for this hallmark.

9.2.3 Hallmark A2

Hallmark A2 is somewhat lengthier that A1. It states:

> 2. An arrangement where the intermediary is entitled to receive a fee (or interest, remuneration for finance costs and other charges) for the arrangement and that fee is fixed by reference to:

---

[17] The Irish Guidance Chapter 2.6

[18] The Dutch Guidance Chapter 6.1.1

(a) the amount of the tax advantage derived from the arrangement; or
(b) whether or not a tax advantage is actually derived from the arrangement. This would include an obligation on the intermediary to partially or fully refund the fees where the intended tax advantage derived from the arrangement was not partially or fully achieved.

It is worthy of note that Hallmark A2 requires the presence of an intermediary. Normally a hallmark can be triggered in the absence of an intermediary, in which circumstance the reporting obligation falls on the relevant taxpayer. This is so that a relevant taxpayer who designs his/her/its own arrangement is still obliged to report. However, for A2 as it is related to intermediary fees, an intermediary must exist for the arrangement to be reportable. When broken down, the hallmark requires a four-part test to be met before it is triggered:

(i) there must be an intermediary; and
(ii) the intermediary must be remunerated, whether by taking an interest, receiving a fee, finance charges etc; and
(iii) that remuneration must be fixed by reference to:
  (a) the amount of any tax advantage; or
  (b) whether or not a tax advantage is gained. This also includes a discount or refund if the arrangement fails to garner an advantage; and
  (c) the main benefit test must be met.

The language of the hallmark and the application of the MBT do not necessitate the triggering of the hallmark simply by a fee being linked to the amount of tax recovered, or if there is a recovery or other advantage related to tax at all. This was originally reflected in the first draft of the Irish Guidance which stated:

> A person may link their fee to the obtaining of a tax advantage without hallmark A 2 being met. This could apply, for example, where a service provider is engaged by a participant in a cross-border transaction to apply for a withholding tax repayment on their behalf. Unless it is reasonable to conclude that the withholding tax repayment is itself the main benefit or one of the main benefits expected to be obtained from the cross border transaction, then this hallmark will not be met.[19]

This paragraph from the earlier draft of the Irish Guidance drives home the importance of considering the arrangement holistically, and not as a series of steps to be analysed independently of each other. In this example of a

---

[19] Irish Tax and Customs EU Mandatory Disclosure of Reportable Cross Border Arrangements Part 33-03-03 Edition: 3rd November 2020

claim for a rebate of withholding tax, a simple analysis of that example claim would trigger Hallmark A2. However, when the withholding tax rebate claim is considered as part of a wider transaction, it becomes clear that the rebate is possibly not the main benefit or one of the main benefits of the arrangement, but a necessary consequence of a normal commercial transaction. Only by analysing cross-border transactions as a whole can we understand the benefits and whether it has been engineered deliberately to trigger a benefit, or whether the benefit is ancillary to a normal transaction, and can be considered as the 'icing on the cake'.

However, the Irish have now amended their guidance and the most up to date edition states:

> The key feature of the hallmark is that the intermediary's fee (or other form of compensation) for providing a service in relation to a cross-border arrangement is linked to the tax advantage being obtained.[20]

Which seems to be somewhat of a tightening of the guidance. Though one wonders if they are really saying that completing a tax rebate form and saying "pay me if you get a rebate" amounts to a reportable arrangement.

The original Irish position is broadly supported by the Belgian Guidance, which seems to take a view that, where there are multiple intermediaries acting on a complex arrangement, one need only review the position with regards to one's own fee and not those of those around you:

> When several intermediaries provide (or have committed to provide) advice or are involved in the design, marketing, organisation, provision or implementation of a cross-border scheme, the assessment of the existence of such a hallmark within the scheme must be carried out by each intermediary in relation to its own remuneration. There is, in principle, no need to take into account the remunerations received by other intermediaries in determining whether or not the A2 marker is met by the arrangement[21]

As to the question of what amounts to a fee, the Belgian Guidance is clear:

> The A2 hallmark refers to arrangements where the intermediary collects fees (or interest, payment of financing costs and other expenses), where these fees are determined either by reference to the amount of tax benefit derived from the scheme, or by reference to the fact that a tax benefit actually derives from the scheme. This includes an obligation for the intermediary to partially or fully reimburse the fees if the expected tax benefit resulting from the scheme has not been fully or partially realised.

---

[20] The Irish Guidance Chapter 2.6

[21] The Belgian Guidance Chapter 4.1.4

Therefore, any transfer of value including a rebate of fees, however it is affected, is sufficient to trigger the Hallmark.

9.2.4 Hallmark A3

Hallmark A3 is the shortest of the Category A Hallmarks, but is also the one which generates the most discussion amongst professionals:

> An arrangement that has substantially standardised documentation and/or structure and is available to more than one relevant taxpayer without a need to be substantially customised for implementation.

The immediate response from any person who works as a professional accountant, lawyer, or tax adviser is a series of questions which can be summed up as follows: do the following common occurrences, amongst others, trigger the hallmark:

(i) using a precedent when drafting a contract or other document?
(ii) incorporating a company with standard constitutional documents?
(iii) establishing a trust?
(iv) using an insurance wrapper or:
(v) filling in a tax return?

This is, of course, a non-exhaustive list of examples of the myriad operations which may have tax consequences, and which utilise standard documentation and previously considered solutions.

At this point, we should remember that the underlying principles of DAC6 remain in place, and that what may appear at first blush to be a series of actions triggering this hallmark (such as the simple creation of an entity), may well not be once considered in context. As we have seen the approach to be taken to an arrangement should be a holistic one. An intermediary should not simply consider the incorporation of a company as a separate arrangement if it is part of a series of transactions which make up a larger arrangement that should be considered as a whole. Simply utilising a standard document with minimal customisation is not itself reportable, it is one characteristic of a wider arrangement, which may trigger reporting based on its consequences and effects.

When broken down into its constituent parts, the A3 Hallmark amounts to the following test:

(i) there must be substantially standardised documentation or structure;
(ii) the arrangement must be made available to more than one relevant taxpayer;
(iii) there must be no requirement for substantial customisation; and
(iv) the main benefit test must be met.

In essence, limbs i) and iii) of the test are very close in their application. Limb i) envisages that the intermediary starts the process with standard documentation or a standard structure; iii) requires that that standard documentation shall not be substantially customised.

Limb ii) provides that the arrangement must be made available to more than one relevant taxpayer.

The Irish Guidance discusses limb ii) when it states:

> this hallmark is intended to capture what are referred to as 'mass marketed' or 'off the shelf' schemes. The fundamental characteristic of such schemes is their ease of replication. Essentially, the client purchases a finished tax product that requires little, if any, modification. To modify it would not require a client to receive significant additional professional advice or services. Such products are primarily tax driven and it is highly unlikely that the product would be sold without the expected tax benefits.[22]

This does seem to indicate that the consistent replication of the same product over and over to achieve the same tax result would satisfy limb (ii) of the hallmark. No general principles can be drawn from this, however, and a case-by-case analysis understanding the context within any wider arrangement is required.

Limb iii), though linked to limb i) discusses the treatment of the standardised documentation once an intermediary is engaged. The Irish Guidance examines limb iii) at some length, as you would expect from a jurisdiction which has positioned itself as a leader of the world's finance centres. It states:

> Many types of documentation and structures can be substantially standardised and made available for use by more than one person... However, for the hallmark to be met, there must be a link between the documentation and/or structure in question and the tax advantage that was obtained or expected to be obtained. As such, while a group may use standard documentation for all group loans, there is unikely to be a link between the fact the documentation is standardised and any tax benefit that may arise meaning the Hallmark is unlikely to be met.[23]

In a similar vein, the Belgian Guidance states:

> This hallmark focuses on mass-marketed schemes, namely standardised arrangements that are fiscally attractive, to which several persons can have access and which are accompanied by standardised documentation that does not need to be significantly adapted in order to take into account the specific circumstances specific to the taxable person. That is 'prefabricated' tax products that can be purchased and implemented as offered or after making

[22] The Irish Guidance Chapter 2.6

[23] Ibid

> limited adjustments. The taxpayer does not need significant support in the form of professional advice to set up the structure.[24]

The Belgian Guidance makes the point that, to trigger Hallmark A3, the arrangement should be 'off the shelf' and require no detailed, specific advice. By extension of this, it must be fair to assume that the detailed customisation of a small number of material clauses in a large and extensive document containing a large number of 'boilerplate' elements — if those amendments require considered and taxpayer specific advice — must similarly be considered sufficient to relieve the intermediary of a liability to report under the hallmark.

The point is driven home in an even more explicit manner in the Maltese Guidance which states:

> Taken on its own, the use of such documentation [precedent forms] will not normally constitute the hallmark to be met - for example, merely setting up a company in Malta using relatively standard articles of association or opening a bank account using standardised documentation[25]

As such it will prove to be of great relief for fiduciary providers across Europe.

The Dutch Guidance gives three examples of arrangements which would not trigger A3[26]. Firstly, an example of a collective investment scheme which allows investors to spread risk and garner various investment benefits and also has a tax benefit. In this case, the Dutch Guidance argues that the tax benefit is outweighed by the investment benefit, even though they would use standard documents and are available to more than one taxpayer. The second example is one of a hedging instrument, which begins as a standard document, but is adapted to the needs of the individual contracting party. Thirdly, the use of a standard loan document for loans made 'as if at arm's length' between members of the same group; the Dutch authorities note that this would fail the MBT.

All the guidance we have reviewed emphasise that mere standardisation of documentation (as with a precedent) is not sufficient for the hallmark to be triggered.

This matter was discussed in more detail at Chaptr 8 but in essence, there is a large amount of overlap between discussions of Hallmark A3 and the concept of 'marketable arrangement' both of which require a lack of 'substantial customisation'.

---

[24] The Belgian Guidance Chapter 4.1.5

[25] The Maltese Guidance Chapter 5.3.3

[26] The Dutch Guidance Chapter 6.1

Whether a document requires substantial customisation will be a matter of fact. As with the definition of marketable arrangement, it would seem erroneous for the measure of whether a document is substantially customised to be a mere mathematical assessment of the percentage of amended words within a document. Therefore, in the assessment of whether a document is 'substantially customised' it would seem that the assessment should consider a balance of the amount of customisation and the materiality of that customisation. It must be acknowledged that a detailed and well-considered amendment of the operative and material clauses in a trust document, for example, should be acknowledged as more substantial customisation than an arbitrary tinkering with boilerplate clauses simply to establish a degree of customisation without any amendments to the material clauses.

Limb iv) of the test is the application of the MBT. The MBT requires us to examine the effects of the arrangement as they are in fact. Without establishing that the main benefit, or one of the main benefits of the arrangement, is a tax advantage (as discussed at Chapter 9.1), then Hallmark A3 will not be satisfied.

9.3 Category B: specific hallmarks linked to the main benefit test

The Category B Hallmarks are unified by the idea that an artificial transaction which generates a tax advantage is something which should automatically be scrutinised by the authorities. Whilst it could be truly said that this is the overarching aim of the entirety of DAC6, it is most obvious within the Category B Hallmarks.

The hallmarks themselves identify a number of such artificial transactions which create an unfair tax advantage at odds to the intention of the legislation in question. Unlike Category A, there is no generality to them and a transaction which does not exhibit the specific features of the hallmarks would not trigger reporting under Category B.

The text of the hallmark reads:

> **B. Specific hallmarks linked to the main benefit test**
>
> 1) An arrangement whereby a participant in the arrangement takes contrived steps which consist in acquiring a loss-making company, discontinuing the main activity of such company and using its losses in order to reduce its tax liability, including through a transfer of those losses to another jurisdiction or by the acceleration of the use of those losses.
> 2) An arrangement that has the effect of converting income into capital, gifts or other categories of revenue which are taxed at a lower level or exempt from tax.
> 3) An arrangement which includes circular transactions resulting in the round-tripping of funds, namely through involving interposed entities without other primary commercial function

or transactions that offset or cancel each other or that have other similar features.'[27]

9.3.1 Hallmark B1

Understanding Hallmark B1 hinges on an understanding of group loss relief. Without understanding the mischief that it aims to expose, it cannot be truly grasped. Group loss relief is rather succinctly summed up by the Irish Tax and Customs in their online guidance section 'Group Relief':

> Group Relief allows members of a group of companies to transfer certain Corporation Tax (CT) losses to other members of the group. For example, Company A can surrender a loss to Company B of the same group. The transferred loss reduces the amount of CT that Company B must pay.[28]

This definition requires little-to-no elaboration, save to say that group relief is limited by a number of complex anti-avoidance measures in most sophisticated jurisdictions.

To understand how Hallmark B1 defines the characteristics of an arrangement to be reported, one should break down the hallmark into its constituent parts:

(i) A participant must take contrived steps;
(ii) Those steps must include the acquisition of a loss-making company;
(iii) Those steps must also include the discontinuation of the main activity of the loss-making company;
(iv) The losses of the loss-making company must be used by the participant to reduce its tax liability, whether by a transfer of losses to another jurisdiction, or by accelerating those losses; and
(v) The tax benefit must be the, or one of the main benefits of the arrangement.

A purely literal interpretation of this five-limbed test would seem to leave us with a highly specific fact pattern in need of fulfilment before the hallmark is satisfied. Several questions spring to mind immediately. What are the rules around continuing to trade? What does 'contrived' mean? What happens if the participant is a subsidiary, but it is the tax liability of the parent that is reduced?

The Irish Tax and Customs discuss the meaning of 'contrived' in their DAC6 Guidance:

> steps will be contrived where they are pre-planned and artificial. An arrangement will bear this hallmark where it can be established that the main benefit or one of the main benefits that the participant may

[27] Council Directive 2011/16/EU Annex IV Part II

[28] Group Relief (revenue.ie)

> reasonably expect to obtain from the arrangement is the reduction of its tax liability.[29]

This sentence bears some examination.

Hallmark B1 is subject to the MBT by virtue of Annex IV Part I of the DAC, which states:

> Generic hallmarks under category A and specific hallmarks under category B and under points (b)(i), (c) and (d) of paragraph 1 of category C may only be taken into account where they fulfil the 'main benefit test'[30]

The effect of this is to make Hallmark B1 subject to the MBT, and to eliminate any need for the MBT to be restated within the text of the hallmark itself. The Irish Guidance seems to wish to import a further version of the MBT amongst the meaning of the word 'contrived'. In fact, as formulated above, the Irish test deviates from the MBT by redefining what the 'advantage' has to be narrowing it in comparison with the expansive definition in 2012/772/EU: Commission Recommendation of 6 December 2012[31]. Instead, here the test is simply that a 'reduction of its tax liability' is the result which excludes several other forms of 'tax advantage' envisaged by the Commission Recommendation.

Further in deviation from the MBT in Annex IV, the Irish Guidance goes on to state that tax liability must be expected by the 'participant' of the arrangement, rather than the relevant taxpayer or, as in the MBT in Annex IV, simply, 'a person'.

It is not entirely clear whether the Irish Tax and Customs meant this confusing element of the above paragraph to be a simple restating of the MBT or whether it was an attempt simply to clarify the wording of the hallmark itself.

The Maltese Guidance is more succinct and states:

> For the purposes of hallmark B1, steps are considered to be 'contrived' where they are preplanned and, having regard to all facts, it is reasonable to conclude that they are artificial and have no evident commercial reason.[32]

This is a much more satisfactory formulation and removes any reference to benefit. It is simply a test of whether the steps are artificial.

The second element of the five-limbed test for Hallmark B1 is that the operation of the loss-making company must be discontinued. Both the

---

[29] The Irish Guidance Chapter 2.7

[30] Council Directive 2011/16/EU Annex IV Part I

[31] See above 'The Main Benefit Test'

[32] The Maltese Guidance Chapter 5.4.1

Maltese and Irish Tax and Customs are silent on this matter in their guidance. Could a loss-making company be operated for a period of time stripped of its losses and then discontinued after say, two years, or are we left with a simple 'reasonableness' test hinging on the fact that the discontinuation of the company is prearranged? It is not clear, but what is clear is that a reasonable approach will be taken and from other elements of the relevant guidance, we can see that the authorities generally believe that, where a step is designed or deliberately taken to manufacture a tax advantage, it will be considered to be part of the relevant arrangement when viewed holistically, and therefore will fall to be reported. It is the fact of pre-planning that is most relevant, not a mere period of years elapsing. For example, take these two scenarios:

(a) Company A buys loss-making Company B through a complex chain of steps to make the losses available. A uses B's losses to reduce the group liability. After six months, a defect in the design of B's main product is discovered and A decides to cut its losses and close B.
(b) Company C similarly buys Company D through a complex chain of steps to make the losses available. C uses the losses and closes D after 3 years, in order to avoid DAC6 reporting.

In (a) a commercial event has triggered the closure of Company B, in (b) Company D is closed simply as part of the wider loss-buying arrangement. If a pre-planned decision to close the acquired entity is part of the arrangement's design, then this limb of the test will be satisfied.

The German Guidance does shed some light on the meaning of 'discontinuation of the main activity' of the loss-making company.

> Termination of the principal activity before or after the acquisition of the loss-making undertaking is an overriding element. For example, there is an end to the main activity in the event of a change of industry. It does not therefore cover arrangements which, without the intention of terminating the main activity, are aimed solely at acquiring a loss-making undertaking to reduce the acquirers tax burden. The main activity is the activity with the highest gross income of the company on average over the previous three years.'[33]

Thus, for the German implementation of DAC6, it is explicitly stated that acquiring a loss-making company and utilising such losses is not reportable, as long as the principal activity remains.

As a final comment on the second limb of Hallmark B1, it is worthy of note that the internal logic and timeline of DAC6 is seemingly violated by the requirement to predict a future event. DAC6 reporting must occur:

> within 30 days beginning:

[33] The German Guidance Chapter

> (a) on the day after the reportable cross-border arrangement is made available for implementation; or
> (b) on the day after the reportable cross-border arrangement is ready for implementation; or
> (c) when the first step in the implementation of the reportable cross-border arrangement has been made,
>
> whichever occurs first.[34]

If the arrangement does not include a pre-ordained step of the closure of the company, then this 30-day deadline will necessarily not be met, since the intermediary cannot predict the future.

The third limb of the test is that the 'participant' must use the losses to reduce its tax liability. It is interesting that those drafting this hallmark chose the word 'participant' as opposed to 'relevant taxpayer' or even just a general word which would allow those not 'participating' in the arrangement to be caught.

The Irish Guidance elaborates on the definition of 'participant'

> The participants in an arrangement will be those persons that play an active role in it. For instance where an arrangement is a contract, the participants in the arrangement will be those persons who are party to the contract. However, a person does not need to play a major role in an arrangement in order to be a participant in it. For example, a parent company would be regarded as a participant in an arrangement where a shareholders' resolution or other consent is required for an arrangement to proceed between its subsidiary and another party[35]

The Belgian Guidance seems to indicate that to be a participant, a person (other than a relevant taxpayer, or some other specified roles) must be active in the arrangement.[36]

This then begs the question: 'if a subsidiary enters into an arrangement without consent or approval of its parent which then has the effect of reducing the parent's tax liability, is that sufficient to trigger Hallmark B1?' In other words, is a mere disassociation between benefit and participation sufficient to neutralise the hallmark in its entirety, and if so, does that dissociation need to be deliberate, or accidental? Obviously, an analysis of the facts as they subsist should be undertaken, but one can see that the language of the hallmark is not entirely clear, and the boundaries of what is and is not reportable are, at best, uncertain.

---

[34] Article 8ab Council Directive 2011/16/EU

[35] The Irish Guidance Chapter 2.2.2

[36] The Belgian Guidance Chapter 3.2.2

The fourth limb of the test requires little elaboration and the fifth is simply a restating of the MBT

Ultimately what such a close textual analysis exposes here is the impossibility of the job undertaken by those drafting the DAC. No short hallmark description can adequately cover all situations possible in 27 countries and several territories, with differing legal and taxation systems which have developed independently of each other (albeit that they are beginning to harmonise). A purposive approach is the only one which makes any sense, and those jurisdictions which have transposed DAC6 with minimal customisation (such as Malta, Cyprus and many others) will necessarily see the internal contradictions and inconsistencies of the DAC replicated in their own law.

Suffice to say, the aim of Hallmark B1 is to expose those artificial arrangements which make loss-buying possible in the face of anti-avoidance mechanisms, and such arrangements should be actively considered for reporting by intermediaries.

9.3.2 Hallmark B2

In keeping with the overarching theme of Category B, Hallmark B2 is again focussed on a specific circumstance or scheme which artificially captures a beneficial tax treatment. It states:

> An arrangement that has the effect of converting income into capital, gifts or other categories of revenue which are taxed at a lower level or exempt from tax.[37]

By breaking the hallmark down into its required elements, one can see a four-limbed test:

(i) There must be income;
(ii) The effect of the arrangement must be to convert income into other categories of designation of revenue, such as capital or gifts;
(iii) Those other categories of designation of revenue must be taxed at a lower level, or be exempt from tax;
(iv) The tax advantage gained by the arrangement must be the, or one of the main benefits of the arrangement.

In analysing whether there is income, one should apply normal accounting rules and any 'exotic' definition of income should be rejected.

Whether the effect of the arrangement is to convert income into capital, or 'other categories of revenue' will be a matter of fact and should, similarly, be analysed in line with normal accountancy rules. The language of the Directive is sufficiently clear for 'other categories of revenue' to be

[37] Council Directive 2011/16/EU Annex IV Part II

interpreted as wider than the mere conversion of income into capital. HMRC's now-defunct guidance was helpful when it pointed out:

> This could include, for example, a conversion from employment income into. Although dividends are still 'income', they are still taxed at a lower rate.[38]

This sentence in itself gives rise to some questions, with answers not entirely clear. Imagine Mr X owns Company B, and he is also an employee of Company B. Company B is a full-service printing company based in Belgium, with six employees other than Mr X. Mr X lives in Luxembourg and commutes to Belgium on a daily basis. Company B has a particularly good year in 2020. Company B pays Mr X's normal wage of €35,000 per year (which is low, but within acceptable commercial parameters) and pays its entire distributable reserves to him at year end by way of dividend.

Is this an arrangement which has converted employment income into dividend income? It really depends on your starting assumptions. If one assumes all income should be taxed at the maximum rate, and that any deviation is a form of avoidance, then one would probably take that position. However, when Company B sets Mr X's wage at the start of the financial year, it is unaware of what its profits will be at year end. That commercial uncertainty means that, at the point it decides to pay Mr X €35,000 and the remainder of any profits, if any, by dividend, it has sufficient commercial uncertainty to undermine whether the 'arrangement' is a coherent whole. It could also be argued that, at that point, there is no 'income' to convert into 'other categories of revenue', and thus there is no 'first step' to trigger the 30-day reporting period on the intermediary.

The Luxembourg position would, of course, be that this does not satisfy the objective version of the MBT contained in its guidance:

> the main benefit test is not met when the tax advantage obtained as a result of the arrangement is consistent with the object or purpose of the applicable legislation and consistent with the intention of the legislator[39]

In this case, it is true that a company has the commercial freedom to contract with its shareholders in any way which it sees fit, and that any transaction with a related party is allowable, as long as it is within the parameters of the general regime of anti-avoidance. The scenario as described would not seem to be in any way 'inconsistent with the intent of the legislator' when treating dividends issued to shareholders differently.

However, if the situation was reversed and Mr X lived on the Belgian side of the border, while his printing business was in Luxembourg, he would be

---

[38] The HMRC Guidance: IEIM643020 – Hallmark B2

[39] The Luxembourg Guidance

subject to the Belgian DAC6 regime. The subjective element of the definition of 'tax advantage' contained in Luxembourg Guidance would then apply, and it would seem that Mr X's perfectly normal, commercial arrangement would fall as reportable. This injustice would be compounded by the fact that, if Mr X and Company B were located in the same Member State, then no obligation would rest on him at all, other than to pay his taxes.

This is an example of DAC6's draconian side. As noted previously, and whilst the attitude of the authorities is still not yet clear, it is the case that many perfectly normal modes of operation will be caught by a strict interpretation of the reporting obligation. The only saving grace is that situations such as Mr X crossing borders between workplace and home are rare. However, it is likely that the authorities will eventually introduce an element of subjectivity equivalent to a 'legislative intent' test. It would seem not to be in the public interest to levy a fine on Mr X's accountant, or on Mr X himself simply for not reporting something that business owners have done since the concept of the limited liability company was invented, and which his cousin, who lives and works wholly in Belgium, could freely do without a reporting obligation.

The Irish Tax and Customs Guidance goes some way towards an attempt to resolve this issue in its discussion of the third limb of the B2 test, in stating:

> In assessing whether an arrangement bears this hallmark, the key test to apply will be whether, viewed objectively, an amount that would normally be taxed as income is instead taxed in another category of revenue that attracts a lower rate of tax or is tax exempt. As such, normal commercial transactions are unlikely to be caught by this hallmark.[40]

Those who drafted this paragraph have fallen into the trap of believing that placing the words 'viewed objectively' amidst the description of a subjective test somehow alters its nature to one of objectivity. It does not. Concepts such as 'normality' (without functioning definitions) have no place in an objective test. What constitutes 'normal'? Is it behaviour which is known and understood, but less common than it once was, or is it behaviour which is almost universal, or any other formulation? This is not answered by the Irish Guidance, but we must understand this paragraph to be an attempt, whether conscious or unconscious, to temper the draconian side of DAC6 and to set it within parameters of reasonableness This may be an echo of Ireland's Common Law past and the general principle that no obligation on an individual should be greater than is reasonably required.

It would seem just and appropriate to modify the blanket approach of the text of the directive with a recognition of commercial realities. Many commercial choices are taken with the primary intention of saving tax and

---

[40] The Irish Guidance Chapter 2.7

as a result, they have become normal commercial practice through constant repetition. For example, in Gibraltar, there is no capital gains tax, and thus a share buyback from distributable reserves has the effect of taking the revenue released by such a transaction entirely out of tax in the hands of the recipient when compared to dividends (which may or may not be taxable on the facts as they are). Therefore, share buybacks have long been a common event. They are entirely 'normal', and that normality is a consequence of their tax treatment. Similarly, the appointment of a lower rate taxpayer (such as a spouse or adult child) to a family business in a real but less necessary role such as company secretary alongside a higher rate tax payer so as to spread income is common practice amongst family businesses. One would hope that tax authorities take a pragmatic approach, acknowledging that commercial behaviour has historically been modified by the fact that conversion of income into capital gives a desirable tax effect, and seeking not to have all such occurrences reported, but only those deviating from the norm of modern commercial behaviour and containing 'contrived steps'.

This seems to be a deviation from the language of the directive, but it is one which will hopefully be driven by reasonableness and a recognition of some endemic activities which are known to, and accepted by the authorities. It is an approach borne of pragmatism and an urge to ensure that those most egregious examples are reported.

The question as to whether the income is now to be taxed at a lower level than previously appears to be simple. The Irish Guidance explains:

> To establish whether the other category of revenue is taxed at a lower level or is exempt from tax, it will be necessary to quantify the amount of tax that would have been payable had the conversion of income not taken place and then compare it with the amount of tax that is payable, if any.[41]

In other words, without understanding the treatment of 'income' prior to the arrangement, one cannot understand if an advantage has been gained. If one has correctly identified that a conversion has occurred, then it will be apparent what the base treatment of the revenue would be, and therefore it will be easily understood if any tax advantage has been gained.

The final step of an analysis regarding Hallmark B2 is the application of the MBT.

Hallmark B2 is not an entirely satisfactory piece of drafting. It attempts to mandate reporting of any arrangement which simply re-characterises revenue into less taxable categories via contrived steps. The Irish and UK guidance attempt to deal with the fact that such re-characterisation is widespread and endemic in commercial decision-making, and therefore not considered 'contrived' but 'normal' — if one applies the Irish Guidance

---

[41] Ibid

detailed above. Therefore, both sets of guidance attempt to go beyond the simple re-characterisation of revenue and make deviating from the commercial norm a secondary element of the test in the directive. This is not entirely supported by the language of the directive, but it is a practical and pragmatic compromise, one dictated by good sense and a wish to limit the taxpayer's obligations to those which are reasonable.

9.3.3 Hallmark B3

Hallmark B3 is aimed at exposing those arrangements which move value through a group creating claims, reliefs or deductions, without there being any commercial reasoning and which lead to the participants returning essentially to the same economic position as when they began.

A very simple example of a circular transaction would be as follows:

- Company A owns Company B.
- Company B is located in a zero-tax jurisdiction and dividends are tax-free in the location of Company A.
- Company A has taxable profit.
- To limit A's liability, B charges A an artificial fee which creates a deductible expense in A, thereby reducing its tax liability.
- Company B pays a dividend to A, returning all the fee.
- A & B remain in the same position as they were to begin with, except that A has a deductible expense to off-set against its profits.

This would be entirely consistent with the language of the hallmark, which states:

> An arrangement which includes circular transactions resulting in the round-tripping of funds, namely through involving interposed entities without other primary commercial function or transactions that offset or cancel each other or that have other similar features.[42]

When broken down into its constituent parts, the hallmark requires the following:

(i) The arrangement must be circular and 'round trip' funds; and, either
(ii) It may do so by interposing entities with no primary commercial function; or
(iii) The steps should cancel each other or do something similar; and
(iv) The main benefit or one of the main benefits of the arrangement should be a tax advantage.

As with many of the hallmarks, the underpinning commercial reality of the arrangement is the critical element in determining whether the hallmark is satisfied or not. All the B Hallmarks have at their core an unreality to the arrangement in question, a reportable arrangement under Category B is designed to create an unfair triggering of a tax treatment which is available

[42] Council Directive 2011/16/EU Annex IV Part II

in the correct circumstances. Those analysing arrangements should keep an eye to the commerciality of the arrangement under discussion.

This is reflected in the Irish Guidance:

> It will be clear from such an arrangement whether the round tripping of funds serves little or no purpose and has been done primarily in order to obtain beneficial tax treatment that would not otherwise be available.[43]

The Belgian Guidance makes a similar point:

> The circular transaction consists of the 'back and forth' movements of funds (round-tripping), using intermediate entities without a primary commercial motive or resulting in the netting off of the transactions or having similar characteristics.[44]

The truth of the matter is that commerciality will be evident on the facts as they are, and the inclusion of the MBT ensures that the outcomes of the arrangement will be taken into consideration.

Are limbs ii) and iii) merely characteristics of an arrangement which would indicate that the hallmark is satisfied, or descriptive of required characteristics for the hallmark to be satisfied? In this instance, all hinges on the meaning of the word 'namely'. The Irish Guidance summarises this element of Hallmark B3 thus:

> such round tripping will be facilitated by the use of –
> - Interposed entities that serve no primary commercial function (in the context of the relevant arrangement) other than facilitating the round tripping of funds; or
> - Transactions that offset or cancel each other (or have similar functions)'[45]

Arrangements which involve round trip funds can be as simple or as complex as required by the individual facts. The Irish Guidance uses the example of *Revenue Commissioners v O'Flynn Construction Limited*[46] a case in which over 40 steps were taken in order to return the funds to their place of origin. In contrast, the German Guidance specifies that an arrangement must have a minimum of two steps.

Hallmark B3 is aimed at many differing types of arrangements, not merely those creating deductible expenses; also potentially within its remit are arrangements which trigger tax treatments designed to encourage either foreign investment or to encourage the exporting of goods.

---

[43]The Irish Guidance Chapter 2.7

[44] The Belgian Guidance Chapter 4.2.5.1

[45]The Irish Guidance Chapter 2.7

[46] *Revenue Commissioners v O'Flynn Construction Ltd* [2011] IESC47

The Irish Guidance uses the *O'Flynn* case as an example of an arrangement designed to trigger the Irish Export Sales Relief scheme.

In light of this, we should reconsider our initial example of a simple fee being charged by subsidiary and returned as a dividend; in reality such an arrangement would be subject to a number of anti-avoidance regimes, such as transfer pricing rules, controlled foreign companies regimes and a relevant general anti-avoidance rule. This means that, in practical terms, the more sophisticated examples of round tripping of funds will be the most likely for an organisation to enter into.

It is clear from the various versions of guidance that a measure of the commerciality of the transaction in question is relevant to several different steps in the test for this hallmark and that, therefore, commerciality is vital to an arrangement ot being reportable or not.

We can restate the limbs above in light of this discussion, and say that, to be reportable, an arrangement must feature:

(i) Round tripping, which is either defined as likely to be a non-commercial transaction or evidence of non-commerciality; and
(ii) Feature interposing entities without commercial function; or
(iii) Transactions which have no commercial effect as a result of cancelling each other out; or
(iv) Transactions which perform similar non-commercial functions; and
(v) The main benefit test must be satisfied.

The relevance of commerciality at every step means that the MBT is almost entirely redundant. We must also conclude that a commercial transaction will most likely not satisfy Hallmark B3.

9.4 Category C

Hallmark C is aimed at capturing the least sophisticated forms of profit-shifting: the simple payment of deductible expenses to related entities. In addition, it deals with double claiming for reliefs and deductions. It does so in the following terms:

> C. Specific hallmarks related to cross-border transactions
>
> 1. An arrangement that involves deductible cross-border payments made between two or more associated enterprises where at least one of the following conditions occurs:
>   (a) the recipient is not resident for tax purposes in any tax jurisdiction;
>   (b) although the recipient is resident for tax purposes in a jurisdiction, that jurisdiction either:
>   (i) does not impose any corporate tax or imposes corporate tax at the rate of zero or almost zero; or
>   (ii) is included in a list of third-country jurisdictions which have been assessed by Member States collectively or

within the framework of the OECD as being non-cooperative;
   (c) the payment benefits from a full exemption from tax in the jurisdiction where the recipient is resident for tax purposes;
   (d) the payment benefits from a preferential tax regime in the jurisdiction where the recipient is resident for tax purposes;
2. Deductions for the same depreciation on the asset are claimed in more than one jurisdiction.
3. Relief from double taxation in respect of the same item of income or capital is claimed in more than one jurisdiction.
4. There is an arrangement that includes transfers of assets and where there is a material difference in the amount being treated as payable in consideration for the assets in those jurisdictions involved.[47]

By the standards of many of the other hallmarks, Category C is quite lengthy and has many layers to it. It can be divided into two sections: Paragraph 1 which deals with simple profit-shifting payments, and Paragraphs 2, 3 and 4 which deal with other more sophisticated methods of replicating the effect of profit-shifting, such as double deductions and double-dipping double taxation relief.

The initial draft of the Irish Guidance was almost entirely silent on the Category C as a whole, which is surprising given the complexity and importance of this hallmark. Category C covers those arrangements which meet the classic definition of 'profit shifting' and as such, the initial approach of the Irish Guidance was quite startling. One must ask if Ireland's position as a global finance centre has some influence on the willingness of the Irish Tax and Customs to take a strong position on this hallmark and its meaning. We cannot know the motivation for such an omission, but it is worthy of note. Also worthy of note is that the omission has now been rectified, and the Irish Guidance contains a much more comprehensive discussion than its initial version. However, it does still contain this puzzling statement:

> The hallmarks in category C are aimed primarily at hybrid mismatch arrangements. Broadly speaking, hybrid mismatch arrangements are arrangements that exploit differences between the tax systems of different jurisdictions resulting in a double deduction mismatch outcome (where an expense is deductible for tax purposes twice) or a deduction without inclusion mismatch outcome (where a payment is deductible but the person that receives the payment does not see it as taxable). In Irish law, rules to address hybrid mismatches are provided for in Part 35C TCA 1997.[48]

---

[47] Council Directive 2011/16/EU Annex IV Part II

[48] The Irish Guidance Chapter 2.8

The authors believe that this statement is somewhat misleading. We believe that Hallmark C is not primarily aimed at hybrid mismatches, which, as defined by the Anti-Tax Avoidance Directive, are:

> (9) 'hybrid mismatch' means a situation involving a taxpayer or, with respect to Article 9(3), an entity where:
>
> (a) a payment under a financial instrument gives rise to a deduction without inclusion outcome…
>
> (b) a payment to a hybrid entity gives rise to a deduction without inclusion and that mismatch outcome is the result of differences in the allocation of payments made to the hybrid entity under the laws of the jurisdiction where the hybrid entity is established or registered and the jurisdiction of any person with a participation in that hybrid entity;
>
> (c) a payment to an entity with one or more permanent establishments gives rise to a deduction without inclusion and that mismatch outcome is the result of differences in the allocation of payments between the head office and permanent establishment or between two or more permanent establishments of the same entity under the laws of the jurisdictions where the entity operates;
>
> (d) a payment gives rise to a deduction without inclusion as a result of a payment to a disregarded permanent establishment;
>
> (e) a payment by a hybrid entity gives rise to a deduction without inclusion and that mismatch is the result of the fact that the payment is disregarded under the laws of the payee jurisdiction;
>
> (f) a deemed payment between the head office and permanent establishment or between two or more permanent establishments gives rise to a deduction without inclusion and that mismatch is the result of the fact that the payment is disregarded under the laws of the payee jurisdiction; or
>
> (g) a double deduction outcome occurs.[49]

The implication of the language of the Irish Guidance is that this hallmark is aimed at hybrid mismatches, it makes reference to Part 35C of the Taxes Consolidation Act 1997 as providing for anti-hybrid rules, almost as if to say 'this is not allowed in Ireland and therefore we do not expect reporting under this hallmark'. To take this approach would be to narrow the point of Hallmark C1 and is misleading. It is, however, commendable that the Irish Guidance was expanded in March 2021, even if it continues to include this particular statement.

---

[49] Article 2(9) Directive (EU) 2016/1164

9.4.1 Hallmark C1

Hallmark C1 is both simple in principle and highly complex in delivery. It aims to do a very simple thing. To make reportable a situation where a group of companies shifts profits from a high tax jurisdiction to a jurisdiction which is classed as a 'tax haven'. It is not aimed solely at a hybrid mismatch, as the Irish Guidance implies, but instead at simple profit-shifting.

C1 can be divided roughly into two halves. First the requirement for a qualifying payment and secondly, the refining of that broad approach by clarifying those kinds of target jurisdictions that will trigger the hallmark.

The requirement of a qualifying payment is stated in the following way:

> An arrangement that involves deductible cross-border payments made between two or more associated enterprises[50]

This breaks down into various limbs:

(i) There must be a payment;
(ii) That payment must be cross border;
(iii) That payment must be deductible; and
(iv) That payment must be between associated enterprises.

Despite being expansive on Category C, as a whole guidance seems to be silent on the meaning of 'payment', though in the context of the language of Hallmark C1, it is reasonable to assume any transfer of value which can be treated as a 'deductible expense' would qualify as a payment. Given the purposive approach to interpretation preferred for European legislation — which is partly forced upon us by the nature of a directive being an instruction to Member States, rather than a finalised piece of legislative drafting — the authors would not like to become bogged down with a limited definition of 'payment' relying solely on cash movements or some other deliberately narrow approach.

As to the inclusion of the requirement for the payment to be 'cross border', this goes further than the early requirement for an arrangement to be 'cross border' to be reportable. In the requirement for an arrangement to be cross border, the arrangement must concern more than one Member State or a Member State and a third country, in addition to which, the following must be met:

(a) not all of the participants in the arrangement are resident for tax purposes in the same jurisdiction;
(b) one or more of the participants in the arrangement is simultaneously resident for tax purposes in more than one jurisdiction;
(c) one or more of the participants in the arrangement carries on a business in another jurisdiction through a permanent establishment situated in

---

[50] Ibid

that jurisdiction and the arrangement forms part or the whole of the business of that permanent establishment;

(d) one or more of the participants in the arrangement carries on an activity in another jurisdiction without being resident for tax purposes or creating a permanent establishment situated in that jurisdiction;

(e) such arrangement has a possible impact on the automatic exchange of information or the identification of beneficial ownership. For the purposes of points 18 to 25 of this Article, Article 8ab and Annex IV, an arrangement shall also include a series of arrangements. An arrangement may comprise more than one step or part.[51]

For the purposes of Hallmark C1, this technical definition of what it means to be cross border is discarded. Instead 'cross border' simply means that the payment leaves one jurisdiction and enters another. Again, the authors believe that a purposive approach should be taken to this. Let us imagine the following situation:

- Company A is registered in Cyprus;
- Company B is registered in Guernsey;
- They are both owned by Company C;
- Company B charges Company A a fee.
- Company A pays Company B

The authors are not of the opinion that in the above scenario, the sole condition for a payment to be considered as not 'cross border', would be Company B opening a bank account in Cyprus. Or Companies A and B both opening an account in Malta, thus restricting the physical movement to within one jurisdiction. That would be far too narrow an approach. Given the context of the hallmark, and its talk of deductions and tax residence, it is far more reasonable to presume that the 'cross border' nature of the payment is not one of physical cash moving across international boundaries, but instead the transfer of value from the country of residence of one entity to the country of residence of another. A very simplistic approach, such as the one rejected, would make the directive entirely avoidable with regard to Hallmark C1, and it is unconscionable that such a result was the intention of those drafting the Directive.

The Belgian Guidance seems to agree as it contains the following:

> For the purposes of Hallmark C1, the place of establishment of the parties and the relationship between the parties. The fact that the payment is carried out in practice through two banks established in the same Member State is not relevant for the application or non-application of Hallmark C1[52]

---

[51] Article 3 (18) Directive on Administrative Cooperation in the field of taxation 2011/16/EU

[52] The Belgian Guidance Chapter 4.3.3.7

As to whether a payment is 'deductible', matters are slightly more complex. The now-defunct HMRC Guidance does give some limited assistance:

> whether or not a payment is deductible will depend on the full facts of the situation, and the application of the relevant law in the payer's jurisdiction.

The authors can find little other guidance from the remnant member states.

Given that the member states are most likely to be the payer jurisdiction in reference to DAC6, it is a little puzzling that they do not take more time over this definition. One can only assume they felt that what is or is not deductible is so entirely obvious as to require little comment. However, where one deals with a less traditional tax regime such as the Resident Non-domiciled Regime in Malta, or Gibraltar's territorial regime, then what is or is not considered 'deductible' becomes more relevant. In both those jurisdictions (or similarly due to Gibraltar's lack of capital gains tax), not all income and payments are included in the tax computation, by virtue of the fact that the tax base is smaller than in the majority of member states. It is perfectly possible for a payment to be made to a zero-tax jurisdiction by a Malta resident non-domiciled entity, and that payment being wholly omitted from the tax computation and therefore being in no way 'deductible'. The payment has no effect on the tax due. It would seem odd to make a report over such a payment simply because the payment fell into some overarching understanding of 'deductible'. It is this to which HMRC allude when they say that the matter of a payment being deductible or not will depend on 'the full facts of the situation and the application of the relevant law in the payer's jurisdiction'. It is wholly reasonable, therefore, to say that a payment is only deductible if it has an actual, rather than a theoretical effect by being set off against income and reducing profits or gains available for taxation. This is consistent with the aim of DAC6, in exposing those matters which exhibit the predefined hallmarks of tax avoidance. If a payment is not taken into account in the tax computation, then it will not be a cause of tax avoidance. The fact that an undeducted payment is sent to a low tax jurisdiction has no tax effect in the paying jurisdiction. The funds will either not be taxed at home, or they will be sent abroad, where they will not be taxed.

The final limb of the first section of Hallmark C1 is that the payment must be made between 'associated enterprises'. The term is defined at Article 18(23):

> 23. for the purposes of Article 8ab, 'associated enterprise' means a person who is related to another person in at least one of the following ways:
>   (a) a person participates in the management of another person by being in a position to exercise a significant influence over the other person;
>   (b) a person participates in the control of another person through a holding that exceeds 25 % of the voting rights;

(c) a person participates in the capital of another person through a right of ownership that, directly or indirectly, exceeds 25% of the capital;

(d) a person is entitled to 25 % or more of the profits of another person.

If more than one person participates, as referred to in points (a) to (d), in the management, control, capital or profits of the same person, all persons concerned shall be regarded as associated enterprises.

If the same persons participate, as referred to in points (a) to (d), in the management, control, capital or profits of more than one person, all persons concerned shall be regarded as associated enterprises.

For the purposes of this point, a person who acts together with another person in respect of the voting rights or capital ownership of an entity shall be treated as holding a participation in all of the voting rights or capital ownership of that entity that are held by the other person.

In indirect participations, the fulfilment of requirements under point (c) shall be determined by multiplying the rates of holding through the successive tiers.

A person holding more than 50% of the voting rights shall be deemed to hold 100%.

An individual, his or her spouse and his or her lineal ascendants or descendants shall be treated as a single person.[53]

This rather lengthy definition boils down to a test consisting of the following:

A person is connected to another person if:
(i) Person A has significant influence over Person B through management of B;
(ii) Person A has 25% voting rights in Person B;
(iii) Person A has 25% ownership of Person B;
(iv) Person A receives 25% of the profits of Person B.

The following further rules apply:
(i) If more than one person fulfils (i), (ii) or (iii) then they are all associated;
(ii) If the same people fulfil (i), (ii) or (iii) then they are all associated;
(iii) Holdings should be aggregated if the persons involved are acting in concert;
(iv) Indirect participations should be treated as one regardless of the layers;
(v) Anyone with more than 50% shall be deemed to have 100%; and
(vi) Family holdings shall be aggregated.

---

[53] Article 18(23) Directive 2011/16/EU

Lengthy though this is, it is clear and requires little elaboration. Those who are literate in anti-avoidance measures will have seen similar provisions in their respective countries as they are not uncommon.

This then moves us to the second part of the Hallmrk C1, that is the characteristics of the recipient, as opposed to the characteristics of the payment. On satisfaction of the fact there is a cross-border deductible payment between associated enterprises, we must now look at the following conditions which state:

> where at least one of the following conditions occurs:
>
> (a) the recipient is not resident for tax purposes in any tax jurisdiction;
> (b) although the recipient is resident for tax purposes in a jurisdiction, that jurisdiction either:
>   (i) does not impose any corporate tax or imposes corporate tax at the rate of zero or almost zero; or
>   (ii) is included in a list of third-country jurisdictions which have been assessed by Member States collectively or within the framework of the OECD as being non-cooperative;
> (c) the payment benefits from a full exemption from tax in the jurisdiction where the recipient is resident for tax purposes;
> (d) the payment benefits from a preferential tax regime in the jurisdiction where the recipient is resident for tax purposes[54]

This four-limbed test is complicated further by the fact that conditions (b)(i), (c) and (d) are all subject to the MBT, but are not evidence of its satisfaction in their own right. This means that a commercial transaction will not trigger reporting if it does not have, as one of its main benefits, a tax advantage made up of a payment to an associated enterprise in a zero-tax jurisdiction. Further, when analysing the main benefits, one must not assume that simply because the recipient is located in such a jurisdiction, a tax advantage is automatically one of the main benefits.

To understand the location of the recipient, one must first understand who the recipient is. We agree with the now-defunct HMRC Guidance in that:

> the recipient will generally be the person (or people) who is taxable on the receipt.[55]

This language is not entirely consistent with the hallmark. For example, who is 'taxable on the receipt' if the recipient is in receipt of an exemption for the payment? Given the status of this language as guidance (and defunct guidance at that) one can read it as consistent with the hallmark simply by assuming the meaning to be: 'who would be taxable where it not for the

[54] Council Directive 2011/16/EU Annex IV Part II

[55] The HMRC Guidance: IEIM644030 – Hallmark C1

issues as (a) to (d)?' Ultimately this is another example of the difficulty of drafting such a wide-ranging provision; to create something sufficiently flexible to meet the requirements of almost 30 taxation systems, there will necessarily be inconsistencies and difficulties of language. These problems are a recurrent characteristic of all international exchange regimes and will be found just as frequently in the Common Reporting Standard as in DAC6. It can only be hoped that, as the authorities gain experience in such drafting, such flaws will become less frequent.

The newly expanded Irish Guidance spends some time talking about the status of 'see-through' vehicles:

> Where the recipient of a deductible cross-border payment is transparent for tax purposes, the entity may be 'looked through' for the purpose of determining whether this hallmark is met.[56]

The authors would go further than this and extend special treatment to a permanent establishment (PE) in that a PE cannot, by its nature, be tax resident in a jurisdiction. This would seem to mean that a payment from a headquarters to a PE in a qualifying jurisdiction can never trigger Hallmark C1, as the PE is effectively resident in its parent jurisdiction, regardless of the tax effects. This position is backed up by the now-defunct HMRC Guidance, but the authors have not identified a similar piece of guidance elsewhere.

Once it has been established who the recipient is and where they are located, the nature of the jurisdiction in which they are resident must be analysed:

The recipient is resident in no jurisdiction (Hallmark C(1)(a)).

It is not impossible for an entity or individual to fail all relevant tests of residence. For example, prior to 1999 the test for management and control in Ireland was simply concerned with the location of central management and control (and similarly in UK until 1988), entities would often ensure that their management and control was not located in any one place, making them fiscally nomadic. Similarly, individuals may move rapidly around the world and ensure they fail to meet any of the relevant tests (such as 183 days in any one jurisdiction, as per many EU-member states). In such a case, the recipient company or individual would escape from a tax on his/her/its worldwide income in any one place, and various other charges based on residence. This can be manipulated for the purposes of ensuring no or very low tax is paid. This test is not subject to the main benefit test.

(i) The recipient is resident in a jurisdiction which corporate tax at a rate of 0 or almost 0. (Hallmark C(1)(b)(i)).

It seems that there is no EU-wide standard for what 'almost zero' means.

---

[56]The Irish Guidance Chapter 2.8.1

The German guidance sets the threshold at 4%[57], whereas the Maltese guidance emphasises that it is the 'nominal' rate of tax that is important and states that the threshold is 1%, an approach supported by the now-defunct HMRC Guidance. It is further supported by the Belgian Guidance, which states that:

> A near zero corporate tax rate is a statutory tax rate that is between 0 % and 1 %[58]

It is important to understand that, for Malta it is the 'nominal' rate and for Belgium the 'statutory' rate that are relevant, not the effective rate charged. This means that regimes which reduce rates, or which do not include items in the tax base, are not 'jurisdictions which do not impose any corporate tax or imposes corporate tax at the rate of zero or almost zero'. The test is not 'is this particular item of income subject to corporate tax at zero or near zero?' but is instead, 'is the corporate tax rate 0 or near 0?' This hallmark is subject to, but not evidence of, the main benefit test.

(iii) Is the recipient resident in a jurisdiction included in a list of third-country jurisdictions which have been assessed by Member States collectively or within the framework of the OECD as being non-cooperative? (Hallmark C(1)(b)(ii)).

The draftsmen of the directive have ensured the EU's primacy in matters of tax compliance with the wording of this hallmark. The hallmark applies only to third countries, i.e. countries which are not part of the EU. Therefore, it is impossible for an EU jurisdiction to be subject to reporting under this hallmark, even if the OECD were to list it as non-cooperative. It is highly unlikely that such a state of affairs would occur, but it is worthy of note that the drafting makes it impossible. It is also interesting to consider how the UK will interact with this hallmark after Brexit. This is uncertain, as with so many things Brexit-related at the time of writing. However, if the member states simply deem the UK a member state for the purposes of DAC6 does the reference to 'third country' jurisdictions exclude the UK for DAC6 purposes (just as it excludes France or Belgium etc.).

Many of the pieces of guidance go on to elaborate that the date of the reporting obligation (i.e. 30 days after the first step of the arrangement, etc.) is the relevant date for measuring whether a jurisdiction is included in a list. This hallmark is not subject to the MBT.

(iv) the payment benefits from a full exemption from tax in the jurisdiction where the recipient is resident for tax purposes (Hallmark C(1)(c))

---

[57] The German Guidance para 150

[58] The Belgian Guidance Chapter 4.3.3.3

One should note that this hallmark is worded by reference to the nature of the payment, that is 'is the payment subject to an exemption', not the recipient itself. This means that an exempt body such as a pension fund will not automatically be 'caught'. This hallmark is subject to the MBT

(iv) the payment benefits from a preferential tax regime in the jurisdiction where the recipient is resident for tax purposes (Hallmark C(1)(d)).

The Maltese tax authorities avoid giving a definition of 'preferential' in their guidance by simply directing the reader to the EU Code of Conduct Group and Forum on Harmful Tax Practices websites[59]. They are however, somewhat caught by their interpretation of C(1)(c) above. The Maltese authorities state that, for C(1)(c) to be applicable, it is the nature of the payment that requires exemption. However, in their commentary on C(1)(d), which uses almost identical language to C(1)(c), they simply accept that inclusion on the lists of the Code of Conduct Group and the FHTP is sufficient for a payment to trigger reporting under this hallmark. A review of the FHTP lists reveals that they include not only regimes which exempt specific types of payments, but also those regimes which exempt certain types of companies from tax (such as the classic 'International Business Company' regime). Given the language of the hallmark and Malta's interpretation of C(1)(c), one is left with the feeling that tax authorities take whichever interpretation suits them. If it is the payment which is to be subject to a preferential regime to trigger the hallmark, but instead the recipient is subject to a preferential regime, then by a strict approach one would say the hallmark was not triggered. Such an interpretation would be wholly consistent with the language of the Directive.

The German Guidance is a little dismissive of the benchmark approach to the FHTP and EU lists taken by other jurisdictions. It states boldly:

> It does not matter whether or not they are classified as 'harmful' by the FHTP. Cross-border tax arrangements relating to preferential arrangements that comply with OECD BEPS Action Point 5 must therefore also be notified.[60]

The Irish take a third approach in their guidance and state:

> A 'preferential tax regime' means a regime that offers some form of tax preference in comparison with the general principles of taxation in the relevant country[61]

---

[59] Namely Harmful Tax Practices - Peer Review Results on Preferential Regimes (2018 Progress Report) - Update November 2020 (oecd.org) and Search in the register - Consilium (europa.eu) respecitively.

[60]The German Guidance Para 155

[61] The Irish Guidance Chapter 2.8.6

This would seem to indicate that an intellectually coherent tax regime which deviates from the EU standard does not amount ot a "preferential regime". Therefore, regimes such as territorial regimes which do not tax residents on their worldwide income and gain will not amount to preferential regimes under the Irish Guidance so long as they do not permit a special deviation from that system. In other words systems which remain true to their own principles should nto amount to 'preferential regimes'.

9.4.2 Hallmark C2

After the lengthy and inconsistent Hallmark C1, the brevity of Hallmark C2 comes as a blessed relief. It simply states:

> 2. Deductions for the same depreciation on the asset are claimed in more one jurisdiction[62]

C2 is clearly aimed at permanent establishment arrangements, where a company can depreciate its fixed assets in a permanent establishment in jurisdiction A as well as against its own tax liability in its home jurisdiction. This somewhat echoes the Irish Guidance in their statement that:

> The hallmarks in Category C are aimed at hybrid mismatch arrangements.[63]

The ability to claim a deduction in two different jurisdictions arises from a difference in treatment of the permanent establishment in the two different jurisdictions. If jurisdiction A regards the PE as a taxpayer in its own right and allows a deduction, while the home jurisdiction ignores the existence of the PE and allows a deduction for depreciation, then a double deduction will be allowed. This should be reported.

However, one should query whether a double deduction matched correctly by double taxation would amount to a reportable arrangement. If the arrangement has no tax effect should it be reportable? This hallmark is not subject to the main benefit test, however, one must query whether an arrangement with no discernible tax effect (or exchange of information effect) can really be seen to 'concern' a jurisdiction. As a result, on balance, the authors feel that a PE arrangement with a double deduction, which has corresponding double taxations and no discernible tax benefit at all, would most likely fall as non-reportable, since it would not properly meet the test of 'concerning two member states or a member state and a third country'.

9.4.3 Hallmark C3

Hallmark C3 is a similar hallmark to C2. It simply states:

---

[62] Council Directive 2011/16/EU Annex IV Part II

[63] The Irish Guidance Chapter 2.8

> Relief from double taxation in respect of the same item of income or capital is claimed in more than one jurisdiction[64]

The Dutch Guidance elaborates to a certain extent, in that it states:

> The fact that there is a claim for double taxation in more jurisdictions, for example because in more than one jurisdiction tax is charged on the worldwide income of the entity, does not mean that there is a reportable cross-border arrangement.

It seems, thus, that the Dutch are happy to acknowledge that where an entity is resident for tax purposes in two jurisdictions and has income in a third jurisdiction, then the correct position is that relief is claimed more than once, and that does not trigger the hallmark (despite the apparent clarity of the language). The Dutch Guidance seems to be suggesting that the aim of this hallmark is to report 'double non-taxation' rather than multiple double taxation relief claims. This would seem to be a wholly pragmatic approach and sensible on the part of the Dutch.

The Irish Guidance follows a similar tack in its example of C3, which is in relation to a withholding tax relief in a three-state scenario. This emphasises the aim of the hallmark is to identify not simply double claims but in fact non-taxation as a result of multiple claims.

9.4.4 Hallmark C4

Hallmark C4 states:

> There is an arrangement that includes transfers of assets and where there is a material difference in the amount being treated as payable in consideration for the assets in those jurisdictions involved[65]

When broken down to its constituent parts, this hallmark requires the following to be satisfied:

(i) there is a transfer of assets;
(ii) the value treated as consideration must be different in the jurisdictions involved.
(iii) the difference must be material.

The matters for discussion are: what is meant by 'value treated as consideration', and what is 'material'.

The German Guidance gives, as the test of materiality, a threshold of a 10% and is at least €100,000 or the difference exceeds €500,000 difference between values[66]. The Irish Guidance then goes into greater detail on the conceptual differences, rather than simply applying a bland mathematical formula. The Irish Guidance envisages a difference in the classification of a payment or

---

[64] Council Directive 2011/16/EU Annex IV Part II
[65] Council Directive 2011/16/EU Annex IV Part II
[66] The German Guidance Para 169

the point at which the income is recognised. For the Irish Tax and Customs, these differences would not amount to a definitive difference in materiality. In other words, they are willing to consider that a difference in systems may well lead to a mismatch in treatments, and that is not necessarily material for these purposes.

The 'value treated for consideration' must logically be that value which is considered for tax purposes. This is confirmed by the Irish Guidance which states:

> In applying this hallmark, 'the amount being treated as payable in consideration for the assets' is the amount treated as payable for tax purposes. For example, in a cross-border merger involving a transfer of assets between two companies, one jurisdiction may regard the consideration payable for tax as the original cost of the assets, while the other may regard the consideration payable as the current market value of the assets.[67]

9.4.5 Conclusion

In the opinion of the authors, Category C is the most complex of the categories. It is an attempt to identify any payment which qualifies as a shift of profits from a high tax jurisdiction to a low tax jurisdiction in addition to shifts to jurisdictions which are deemed non-cooperative. The breadth of the ambition for Category C is very wide, and the differences in the guidance to reflect that different jurisdictions are taking their own approach. The German Guidance appears to be the most aggressive of those reviewed in this respect, its threshold of 'near zero' is four times the threshold of most other jurisdictions and the German tax authorities seem to take a maximalist approach to reporting in general. It can only be hoped that the professionals of Europe have such matters clarified for them as soon as possible. Until this occurs, multiple reporting regimes will be legislated for through guidance, in the absence of a directive drafted sufficiently well as to be applied consistently across the Member States.

9.5 Category D

9.5.1 The UK and Gibraltar

On New Year's Eve 2020, the United Kingdom announced that it would withdraw from DAC6, save for those provisions required for it to satisfy the Free Trade Agreement which it had signed the previous week with the EU. That is:

> **Article 384**
> **Taxation Standards**
> 1. A Party shall not weaken or reduce the level of protection provided for in its legislation at the end of the transition period below the level provided for by the standards and rules which

[67] The Irish Guidance Chapter 2.8

have been agreed in the OECD at the end of the transition period, in relation to:

(a) the exchange of information, whether upon request, spontaneously or automatically, concerning financial accounts, cross-border tax rulings, country-by-country reports between tax administrations, and potential cross-border tax planning arrangements;

(b) rules on interest limitation, controlled foreign companies and hybrid mismatches[68]

The practical effect of this is that the UK repealed all the provisions of DAC6, save Category D Hallmark 1 and 2. These provisions will remain in force within their DAC6 superstructure until their repeal on the introduction of the OECD Mandatory Disclosure Regime in the coming years. Gibraltar followed suit some three weeks later and both countries entered the DAC6 regime operating a 'DAC6-lite'[69] unlike any other of their European neighbours.

Despite this difference, the text of Category D remains as it was prior to New Year's Eve 2020 in the UK and Gibraltar. This means that HMRC guidance is more relevant for Category D than any other hallmark (though it remains generally acknowledged as a strong piece of work which has served as the basis for at least one other, if not more sets of national guidance) and can be used as a resource for those working within the English common law tradition without attempting to shoehorn civil law guidance into a common law framework.

9.5.2 Category D

The aim of Category D is to serve as the EU's (and other nations that may later subscribe to DAC6) implementation of the OECD's Mandatory Disclosure Regime There is a general consensus that it should be interpreted as such, and that when the OECD MDR is fully implemented, it will be done through the framework of DAC6, and there will be no second parallel regime. If this is the case (and we are yet to see confirmation), then Category D must logically be interpreted in ways which are consistent with the OECD MDR. They must be synonymous. If not, there will be inconsistent reporting and Category D will generate results which make no sense within the OECD framework.

---

[68] Article 286 Trade and Cooperation Agreement between the United Kingdom and the European Union

[69] Gibraltar's regime is entirely unique given its relationship to Spain. Gibraltar, through its International Agreements on Taxation Matters (Spain) Regulations 2021 has implemented a Spanish-facing form of DAC6 which deals only with arrangements which 'concern' Spain and Gibraltar. The operation of this Iberian form of DAC6 is beyond the remit of his work, but its existence is worthy of note.

In the preamble to the DAC6 Directive, the Commission make clear that they see the two (MDR and Category D) as two peas in a pod.

> In implementing the parts of this Directive addressing CRS avoidance arrangements and arrangements involving legal persons or legal arrangements or any other similar structures, Member States could use the work of the OECD, and more specifically its Model Mandatory Disclosure Rules for Addressing CRS Avoidance Arrangements and Opaque Offshore Structures and its Commentary, as a source of illustration or interpretation, in order to ensure consistency of application across Member States, insofar those texts are aligned with the provisions of Union law.[70]

HMRC agree with this analysis in their guidance, which states:

> Where Hallmark D and MDR cover similar ground, HMRC will interpret Hallmark D in line with MDR.

This means that not only do we now have available to us the gamut of national guidance around Hallmark D but also, where Hallmark D and MDR intersect, any OECD guidance. Therefore, to avoid unnecessary duplication, this chapter will be limited to reviewing the Category D hallmarks as written in the directive, and the national guidance specific to DAC6, that will allow our chapter on the MDR to act as the main point of reference for the wider implementation of Category D.

Category D itself states:

1. An arrangement which may have the effect of undermining the reporting obligation under the laws implementing Union legislation or any equivalent agreements on the automatic exchange of Financial Account information, including agreements with third countries, or which takes advantage of the absence of such legislation or agreements. Such arrangements include at least the following:
   (a) the use of an account, product or investment that is not, or purports not to be, a Financial Account, but has features that are substantially similar to those of a Financial Account;
   (b) the transfer of Financial Accounts or assets to, or the use of jurisdictions that are not bound by the automatic exchange of Financial Account information with the State of residence of the relevant taxpayer;
   (c) the reclassification of income and capital into products or payments that are not subject to the automatic exchange of Financial Account information;
   (d) the transfer or conversion of a Financial Institution or a Financial Account or the assets therein into a Financial

[70] Preamble Para 13 Council Directive (EU) 2018/822

Institution or a Financial Account or assets not subject to reporting under the automatic exchange of Financial Account information;

(e) the use of legal entities, arrangements or structures that eliminate or purport to eliminate reporting of one or more Account Holders or Controlling Persons under the automatic exchange of Financial Account information;

(f) arrangements that undermine, or exploit weaknesses in, the due diligence procedures used by Financial Institutions to comply with their obligations to report Financial Account information, including the use of jurisdictions with inadequate or weak regimes of enforcement of anti-money-laundering legislation or with weak transparency requirements for legal persons or legal arrangements.

2. An arrangement involving a non-transparent legal or beneficial ownership chain with the use of persons, legal arrangements or structures:

(a) that do not carry on a substantive economic activity supported by adequate staff, equipment, assets and premises; and

(b) that are incorporated, managed, resident, controlled or established in any jurisdiction other than the jurisdiction of residence of one or more of the beneficial owners of the assets held by such persons, legal arrangements or structures; and

(c) where the beneficial owners of such persons, legal arrangements or structures, as defined in Directive (EU) 2015/849, are made unidentifiable.[71]

Thus, it can be seen that Category D mirrors the MDR and is divided into two hallmarks. D1 and D2. D1 seeks to deal with those arrangements which 'may have the effect of undermining' CRS or its equivalents[72], and D2 sets out to ensure reporting of those arrangements which use non-transparent chains of ownership to conceal the true beneficial ownership of assets.

9.5.3 Hallmark D1

Hallmark D1 is the anti-CRS avoidance arm of DAC6, and it sets out, in very broad terms, that any arrangement which undermines CRS (or equivalent) must be reported. It is important to understand this word 'undermines'. As the German Guidance makes clear in language echoed throughout the various pieces of national guidance:

---

[71] Annex IV Council Directive 2011/16/EU

[72] It is interesting to note that HMRC's guidance states that the UK's agreement with the United States to implement the Foreign Account Tax Compliance Act (FATCA) is not an equivalent agreement since it does not provide for the same reciprocal level of reporting as DAC2 and the CRS' IEIM645010

> The mere fact that, as a result of a design, a notification or exchange of information is not reported in accordance with the common reporting standard does not in itself permit the assumption that legislation implementing the common reporting standard would be circumvented.[73]

We see similar language in the HMRC Guidance:

> An arrangement does not have the effect of undermining or circumventing CRS, simply because, as a consequence of the arrangement, no report under CRS is made.[74]

Therefore, one must accept that there exist certain transactions which result in no report being made and which do not in themselves 'undermine or circumvent' CRS and its equivalents. The Directive itself is silent on this matter, however HMRC (applying their method of ensuring Category D is as close in interpretation as possible to the MDR) point us to the OECD MDR in that:

> The MDR describes a CRS avoidance arrangement as any arrangement for which it is reasonable to conclude that it is designed to circumvent or is marketed as, or has the effect of, circumventing CRS legislation or exploiting an absence thereof.[75]

Similarly, the German Guidance points out:

> In particular, the exploitation or avoidance of the corresponding set of rules does not take place if the focus of a design is on comprehensible economic considerations, which automatically result in the absence of a notification or exchange of information in accordance with the common reporting standard.'[76]

Therefore, the test as to whether Hallmark D1 (if interpreted in accordance with the MDR) must be that a reasonable intermediary concludes an intention to circumvent or undermine the CRS or its equivalents. This is not a mechanical test. This is a test of intention, not simply 'did X occur?' but instead 'was the intention of doing X to create effect Y?'. It is this kind of test which is so difficult for bank compliance departments to understand and implement with any reasoning. The authors fully expect a flurry of litigation around overzealous reports made because a perfectly legitimate bank transfer occurs to America from the UK (for example). Banks and other institutions should note this and rein in their reporting reflex. They must guard against defensive reporting and be aware of their obligations not only under DAC6, but also under the General Data Protection Regulations to not

[73] The German Guidance Para 174

[74] The HMRC Guidance IEIM645010 – Hallmark D

[75] Ibid

[76] The German Guidance Para 174

process confidential data in a manner beyond the demands of the law. Defensive reporting should be strongly discouraged.

The German authorities reinforce their position that there must be intention in the action for a report to be mandated, when stating in their guidance:

> 173. It must be assumed that the common reporting standard will be circumvented or undermined, in particular: if one or more of the uses, transfers, conversions, reclassifications, or similar constructs listed in Paragraph 138e (2) No. 2 AO are knowingly and wilfully used by persons in paragraph 138d (1) and 6 AO in order not to be subject to notification to the competent authorities on the basis of the due diligence obligations applied by financial institutions.[77]

In other words, for the list of examples to automatically trigger a report, it must be 'knowingly and wilfully' utilised to avoid reporting. Therefore, the intermediary must make a judgment as to whether they believe (on a reasonableness test) that the intent of the arrangement is to avoid reporting.

Therefore, the list of examples given in Hallmark D1 must be read with this in consideration. They are not a marker of an immediate need to report, they are instead warning signs that a report needs to be considered.

The list (with examples) is as follows:

(a) the use of an account, product or investment that is not, or purports not to be, a Financial Account, but has features that are substantially similar to those of a Financial Account. **Example:** an 'e-money' account which is not regulated by CRS.

(b) the transfer of Financial Accounts or assets to, or the use of jurisdictions that are not bound by the automatic exchange of Financial Account information with the State of residence of the relevant taxpayer. **Example:** a transfer from Italy (inside the CRS zone) to Puerto Rico (outside the CRS zone)

(c) the reclassification of income and capital into products or payments that are not subject to the automatic exchange of Financial Account information;

(d) the transfer or conversion of a Financial Institution or a Financial Account or the assets therein into a Financial Institution or a Financial Account or assets not subject to reporting under the automatic exchange of Financial Account information. **Example:** the deliberate conversion of an FI into a non-reporting FI such as a broad participation retirement fund

(e) the use of legal entities, arrangements or structures that eliminate or purport to eliminate reporting of one or more Account Holders or Controlling Persons under the automatic

[77] The German Guidance Para 173

exchange of Financial Account information. **Example:** manipulation of the ownership of entities to reduce holdings below the reporting threshold and remove individuals from the definition of 'Controlling person'

(f) arrangements that undermine, or exploit weaknesses in, the due diligence procedures used by Financial Institutions to comply with their obligations to report Financial Account information, including the use of jurisdictions with inadequate or weak regimes of enforcement of anti-money-laundering legislation or with weak transparency requirements for legal persons or legal arrangements. **Example:** In a jurisdiction where there are 'golden visa' or 'digital nomad' type schemes which do not require physical presence, knowingly using such status to conceal residence in another jurisdiction on the basis that the financial institution will accept local tax registration without question.

The drafting of the various pieces of guidance around this position may give us an insight into the minds of the draftsmen and the back and forth that has surely taken place in the relevant committees. The draftsmen of D1 clearly wanted to permit a situation whereby a normal economic transaction being undertaken for good reason is not reportable (for example, the purchase of a house converts cash into a house, and as a result there will be no CRS report post-completion, since this is clearly not a reportable transaction) but also did not want to paralyse the relevant compliance teams by obliging them to look into the hearts of those undertaking the arrangement.

This tension is written into the hallmark itself in its use of the word 'undermine'. It seems difficult to comprehend that one can undermine something without knowing or intending to do so.

As a result, the guidance reflects this tension:

> The test in hallmark D(1) is an objective one, but in determining whether an arrangement has the effect of undermining the CRS the intent of those involved will be relevant as it will offer a good indication as to whether the arrangement may have the relevant effect.

In other words, we are seeking to report things that actually have the result of undermining CRS and a good indicator is whether the person undertaking the arrangement meant to do so.

This of course now brings us to the ancillary question of 'what does "undermining CRS" mean?'. The Maltese tax authorities give us some assistance:

> The OECD MDR CRS Rules also clarify that '*an Arrangement is not considered to have the effect of circumventing CRS Legislation solely because it results in non-reporting under the relevant CRS Legislation,*

provided that it is reasonable to conclude that such non-reporting does not undermine the policy intent of such CRS Legislation.'[78]

Thus, 'undermining CRS' means 'undermining the policy intent of the CRS legislation'. While not entirely comprehensive or helpful, one could interpret it as referring us to the OECD's documentation on the CRS. For example, the OECD CRS Implementation Handbook states in its Introduction:

> 'The Standard intends to equip tax authorities with an effective tool to tackle offshore tax evasion by providing a greater level of information on their residents' wealth held abroad.'[79]

It seems, then, that the policy intent of CRS is to provide data on otherwise concealed overseas holdings to authorities in the jurisdiction of residence, such that tax evasion may be tackled.

This tension, between the requirement for intent, and the requirement to make reportable anything which utilises accounts or similar and puts things beyond reporting, is not, in the opinion of the authors, satisfactorily resolved and we hope that litigation will be undertaken to establish the boundaries of what is required. In our experience in practice, we have seen reports made under Hallmark D1 based on a simple transfer of funds to an investment desk based in New York, but we have also seen the opposite position taken. The equivocation in the literature issued by the relevant authorities means that both positions can be defended. However, on grounds of proportionality, we feel that reporting a transaction for which there are justifiable economic reasons goes beyond what is intended.

9.5.4 Hallmark D2

Hallmark D2 is aimed at those arrangements which have the effect of concealing the true ownership of assets and entities by the use of opaque ownership structures. In previous eras, the popular vision of the offshore world, so-called 'shell companies' and other means of concealing ownership entailed shady men in trilbies standing on the station platform or in the airport departure lounge in (depending on which decade we are talking about) Basel or some other Swiss canton, the Cayman Islands or some other dusty Caribbean island. Updated, the vision is now more likely to involve someone flying in or out of a small Gulf State jurisdiction, with the briefcase handcuffed to the wrist, still no doubt containing bearer bonds in the name of some deceased Count of the Imperial Russian nobility.

Of course, these days, men do not walk around with briefcases handcuffed to their wrists, quite to the extent that they ever did in reality, or in the popular imagination. Nor do they generally use bearer bonds or shares in an entirely unregulated space beyond the writ of civilised behaviour. However,

---

[78] The Maltese Guidance Chapter 5.6.1.

[79] p7 *Standard For Automatic Exchange of Information in Tax Matters Implementation Handbook*, Second Edition. OECD 2018

the OECD and the EU are quite rightly concerned that, given a set of reporting regulations and clients who would rather not be reported to their home jurisdictions, advisers will develop complex means to avoid reporting. These will have the aim of concealing ownership, using layers of entities characterised in different ways, to report on people other than the actual owners, or to conceal ownership altogether.

HMRC explain to us, in language almost identical to the Directive, that:

> Hallmark D(2) applies where arrangements involve non-transparent legal or beneficial ownership chains which use persons (whether legal or real), legal arrangements or structures:
> (a) that do not carry on a substantive economic activity supported by adequate staff, equipment, assets and premises; and
> (b) that are incorporated, managed, resident, controlled or established in any jurisdiction other than the jurisdiction of residence of one or more of the beneficial owners of the assets held by such persons, legal arrangements or structures; and
> (c) where the beneficial owners of such persons, legal arrangements or structures, as defined in Directive (EU) 2015/849, are made unidentifiable.[80]

Here we can see the test laid out clearly. In order for an arrangement to meet the test of Hallmark D2, there must be:

(i) A non-transparent legal and beneficial ownership chain using entities;
(ii) Those entities must carry out no substantive economic activity (and as a result have insufficient staff or assets, etc. to carry out the activity they purport to);
(iii) They are based in a different jurisdiction to the beneficial owner;
(iv) The beneficial owner must be rendered unidentifiable

The German guidance takes a slightly different approach, stating that the test for whether the ownership chain is non-transparent is made up of limbs (a), (b) and (c) in HMRC's articulation, stating:

> 179 In order to be able to affirm a non-transparent chain, the conditions set out in points (a) and (b) of Paragraph 138e(2)(3) of the AO must be met cumulatively and the identification of the beneficial owners of the persons, legal arrangements or structures involved must not be possible.[81]

We are of the opinion that this distinction is a false one, as the test at limb (c) simply states that it is satisfied if beneficial ownership is rendered

[80] The HMRC Guidance IEIM645020 – Hallmark D2
[81] The German Guidance Para 179

unidentifiable. Therefore, the test for whether or not something conceals beneficial ownership, is whether or not it conceals beneficial ownership.

However, the requirements of (a) and (b) in HMRC's description are highly relevant.

Firstly at (a) we have the requirement that the entities under analysis must carry out no substantive economic activity and must have insufficient staff and assets for the arrangement to be reportable.

This matter will be discussed in greater detail in the relevant chapter on the OECD MDR. However, it is worthy of note that this means that one can conceal the ownership of an asset perfectly well without reporting, provided that the relevant entities carry out substantive economic activity. Therefore, a foundation in a jurisdiction which is outside CRS, has no registration of beneficial ownership of foundations and no information exchange agreements, and which owns and operates a factory with sufficient staff and assets properly to undertake its business would seem to be outside the scope of Hallmark D2. The authors are sure that should such arrangements become commonplace, then D2 would be amended, but for now it is as it is.

Secondly at (b) we have the requirement that the relevant non-substantive entities are located in a jurisdiction other than that of the beneficial owner. Here, the draftsmen are bringing us back to the international nature of the provisions, and we are reminded of the policy intent of such arrangements; which is to stop concealment in foreign jurisdictions of assets which are otherwise taxable.

The final limb of the test which is applicable here for Hallmark D2 is that the beneficial owner of the assets must be rendered unidentifiable. The Maltese Guidance explains in clear terms what this means:

> The terms 'beneficial ownership' and 'beneficial owner' should be interpreted in accordance with the definitions outlined in S.L. 373.01 - Prevention of Money Laundering and Funding of Terrorism Regulations and any implementing procedures issued thereunder.
>
> Where the identity of the beneficial owners is available on public registers of beneficial ownership, hallmark D2 will not apply.
>
> Subject to the provisions in paragraphs (a) and (b) of hallmark D2, this hallmark is likely to be met where arrangements involve jurisdictions where there is no requirement to keep information on beneficial ownership or to disclose nominee shareholders.[82]

Therefore, we interpret the words 'beneficial owner' consistently with the money laundering regulations of the EU (in this case the reference is to the Maltese implementation), and it is automatically the case that a public

[82] The Maltese Guidance Chapter 5.6.2

beneficial ownership register would be sufficient to render an arrangement non-reportable.

The German Guidance at paragraph 181 adds a little more colour:

> 181 Identification [of beneficial ownership] is possible, in particular, where the persons, legal arrangements or structures involved in the design have complied with their obligations to register beneficial ownership and that such information can be reliably obtained by means of intergovernmental assistance through the exchange of information.[83]

Therefore, the German guidance makes clear to us the test is not: 'is a journalist from the local newspaper or an interested individual able to source beneficial ownership information?', but instead 'is such information available to properly constituted authorities utilising exchange of information regimes?' HMRC confirm this saying:

> The test in paragraph (c) is whether beneficial owners can reasonably be identified by relevant tax authorities, including HMRC. The identity of the beneficial owners does not have to be publicly available, although where such persons are listed on public registers of beneficial ownership, that will be sufficient for the hallmark not to be met.[84]

The German authorities, as ever, do not blanche at articulating exactly what HMRC mean when they use the words 'can reasonably be identified by the tax authorities' or what they themselves mean by 'can be reliably obtained'. The test is not some tick-box exercise querying whether there is this or that kind of register, or this or that information exchange agreement. The German tax authorities are clear: the jurisdiction in which the entities with no substantive economic substance are located must not only have infrastructure, they must also be 'reliable'.

> 173 In any event, reliable administrative assistance can no longer be assumed in that context if the State or territory in which the ownership information is available has been assessed as less than 'Largely Compliant' in the context of the recent review of the standard for the exchange of information at the request of the Global Forum, with an overall assessment.[85]

This shows us that the actual, correct delivery of information is more important than a lip-service compliance to simply 'doing enough'.

Of much interest to the fiduciary industry will be Malta's position on the position of discretionary trusts. Discretionary trusts, of course, have no fixed

---

[83] The German Guidance Para 181

[84] The HMRC Guidance IEIM645020 – Hallmark D2

[85] The German Guidance Para 182

beneficiaries and are therefore somewhat unusual when one is attempting to pin down beneficial ownership. Are the class of potential beneficiaries in any true sense 'owners' (beneficial or otherwise), in that a series of events and discretions must occur or be exercised before they can receive any benefit? Surely it is not fair to report a person as owning something when they cannot receive any benefit at present, exercise any rights, and may never do? They are nonetheless, not unconnected to the assets under the trust and should be considered more than disinterested bystanders. Malta tackles such an issue when it states:

> Where a beneficial owner is not identified because, for example, the ownership interest falls below the required ownership threshold or the arrangement involves a discretionary trust, this would not in itself mean that the hallmark is triggered. However, if there is an indication that an owner is deliberately keeping the interest just below the threshold or is being deliberately excluded from the trust temporarily to avoid being identified, the hallmark could then be met.[86]

Again, we are left with discretion on the part of the intermediary. The intermediary is being asked to analyse intention, or to attempt to 'feel' what is going on. The Maltese articulation is not perfect, but it does at least guard against reflexive reporting of all discretionary trusts by those who have no knowledge or understanding of their workings.

9.5.5 Conclusion

As detailed above, a full understanding of Category D can only be gathered by reading, not only this chapter but the relevant chapter on the Mandatory Disclosure Regimes. However, it is apparent that Category D is not entirely satisfactory: it is obvious that the authorities want reporting of things which remove assets from CRS reporting, but they also understand that doing things for good reason should not be reportable. There is a tension present therein and that much is clear from the guidance, which makes various statements seemingly at odds wonith each other.

Ultimately, when applying Category D the practitioner will be left to exercise common sense. Is the client doing what he is doing (for example, moving money to Puerto Rico) because he is trying to secrete it from sight, or because he operates a business in that jurisdiction? One is for good reason, and one is not. One thing is sure: simply taking a mechanical approach is wrong. Large institutions need to understand that, whether motivated by an unwillingness to consider the position properly, or an overly conservative attitude to the risk to which they expose themselves, reporting 'just in case' without proper thought would be wrong, and an abuse of their position which could have negative consequences for their clients.

---

[86] The Maltese Guidance Chapter 5.6.2.

9.6 Category E: specific hallmarks on transfer pricing

9.6.1 Transfer pricing

Transfer pricing or 'TP' is an area upon which much energy has been expended: in some jurisdictions, law and accountancy firms have huge departments dedicated to calculating the 'Transfer Price' of a service or good. Entire courses are dedicated to nothing else in the accountancy profession. In a mirror to this, swathes of office space in tax authority buildings are filled with people measuring and assessing the figures calculated by the law firms and accountants.

Given that Category E is a hallmark which concerns itself with transfer pricing, it is probably best to outline what it is, and why it is important. Firstly, as with so much legal jargon, the phrase 'transfer pricing' contains very little clue to the concept it is used to identify. In its own transfer pricing guidance, HMRC defines the term thus:

> A transfer price is the price charged in a transaction between two parties.[87]

This is, similarly, almost entirely lacking in content and unhelpful to those seeking to understand what transfer pricing is and how it functions. However, the advice goes on to say:

> The transfer pricing legislation concerns itself with the prices charged in transactions between connected parties as, in such circumstances, the price charged may not necessarily be that which would have been charged if the parties had not been connected.[88]

Here we can see the issue from the tax authority's perspective. It is trite law to state that consideration should be sufficient, but need not necessarily be adequate; translated into normal language, this amounts to saying that you are free to do a deal even if it is a bad deal. The problem arises if a business in a high-tax jurisdiction has a related entity in a low-tax jurisdiction. Company A (in Germany, for example) could engage its sister company, Company B in Jersey (for example); Company B could engage as a consultant with attendance at one meeting a year for a fee of £1,000,000, which would be far in excess of the market value of the services. This would be perfectly legal, because consideration need only 'be sufficient not adequate'.

As a result of the inflated price, Company A in Germany has a deductible expense in its accounts of £1,000,000. This will reduce profits in Germany, and consequently reduce the tax due by Company A. Company B, meanwhile, sitting in a zero-tax jurisdiction, will have an unfairly inflated

---

[87] HMRC International Manual INTM410520 – Transfer pricing: introduction: what is transfer pricing: an explanation

[88] Ibid

profit. In other words, profit will have been shifted from Company A to Company B.

This problem has been apparent for much longer than the existence of DAC6 and one solution has been almost universally accepted.

The United States permitted its Inland Revenue Service or IRS to allocate income and deductions amongst affiliated enterprises in 1917. By 1928, the IRS was authorised to make adjustments to combat tax avoidance and by 1935 the measure of those adjustments had been articulated in the 'arm's length principle', or ALP.

The standard definition of the ALP is contained in Paragraph 1 of Article 9 of the OECD Model Convention on Income and Capital, and it states:

> [Where] conditions are made or imposed between the two [associated] enterprises in their commercial or financial relations which differ from those which would be made between independent enterprises, then any profits which would, but for those conditions, have accrued to one of the enterprises, but, by reason of those conditions, have not so accrued, may be included in the profits of that enterprise and taxed accordingly.

What this means in practical terms, returning to our example, is that the German authorities will disallow the deduction granted to Company A for the inflated price of the consultancy services (insofar as it is inflated), and Company A will be taxed on the £1,000,000 (or the surplus above the ALP price) as if it were profit.

This arm's length principle is now enshrined in the law of the majority of the sophisticated jurisdictions of the world, including all the major global economies. The arm's length principle is a very simple one to articulate; however, it is a very difficult principle to carry out in practice. Hence such vast quantities of time and energy being dedicated to working out, first of all, the correct price to be charged and, secondly, to challenging the findings of such studies. Transfer pricing studies (as the processes for calculating the correct arm's length price for services are called) are very costly and complex, and often give uninspiring results.

A detailed analysis of the rules for ascertaining the correct price of a service or good in accordance with the arm's length principle is far beyond the remit of this work and the interested reader can find many excellent technical works. Suffice to say that the Category E hallmarks are aimed at revealing those transactions which may have an impact on transfer pricing issues.

It is important to note that a general transfer pricing gain is not a matter for reporting. Only those specific activities detailed in the hallmarks are to be reported, and it is further interesting to note that the main benefit test is not applicable to any of the Category E hallmarks. Instead, we have a simple mechanical reporting based on the satisfaction of simple (or more accurately somewhat complicated) factual scenarios.

9.6.2 The Hallmarks in general

Category E states the following:

> E. Specific hallmarks concerning transfer pricing
>
> i) An arrangement which involves the use of a unilateral safe harbour rule.
>
> ii) An arrangement involving the transfer of hard to value intangibles. The term 'hard to value intangibles' covers intangibles or rights or intangibles for which, at the time of their transfer between associated enterprises;
>
> (a) no reliable comparable exists;
>
> (b) at the time the transaction was entered into, the projections of future cash flows or income expected to be derived from the transferred intangible, or the assumptions used in valuing the intangible are highly uncertain, making it difficult to predict the level of ultimate success of the intangible at the time of the transfer
>
> iii) An arrangement involving an intragroup cross-border transfer of functions and/or risks and/or assets, if the projected annual earnings before interest and taxes (EBIT), during the three-year period after the transfer, of the transferor or transferors, are less than 50 % of the projected annual EBIT of such transferor or transferors if the transfer had not been made.[89]

The category thus highlights three specific issues which are required to be reported. Firstly, the utilisation of a tax system which, by virtue of a standardised approach to transfer pricing, may be used to undermine the transfer pricing regimes of other jurisdictions. Secondly, the transfer of intangible assets which cannot be valued. Thirdly, the transfer of businesses within groups.

9.6.3 Hallmark E1 – safe harbour rules

Hallmark E1 simply states:

> An arrangement which involves the use of a unilateral safe harbour rule

Understanding Hallmark E1 requires us to understand what is meant by 'unilateral safe harbour rules'. These are defined in the OECD Transfer Pricing Guidelines as:

> a safe harbour in a transfer pricing regime is a provision that applies to a defined category of taxpayers or transactions and that relieves eligible taxpayers from certain obligations otherwise imposed by a country's general transfer pricing rules. A safe harbour substitutes

---

[89] Directive 2011/16/EU – Annex IV Part 2 E

> simpler obligations for those of the general transfer pricing regime. Such a provision could for example allow taxpayers to establish transfer prices in a specific way, e.g. by applying a simplified transfer pricing approach provided by the administration.[90]

It must be understood at this point that safe harbour rules may be instituted for many reasons, not least of all simplification of the transfer pricing analysis. Smaller jurisdictions with fewer tax gathering resources may well impose a simplified regime to save time and money. For example, Gibraltar's transfer pricing regime (which can best be described as a hybrid, exhibiting some characteristics of a unilateral safe harbour in some cases) was introduced in response to this urge for simplification of administration. It has now been modified by the inclusion of the OECD Transfer Pricing Guidelines as the guide to what is or is not artificial, at section 41 of the Income Tax Act 2010 of Gibraltar.

Thus, we can see that a unilateral safe harbour rule takes the following form:
(i) The arm's length principle applies; unless
(ii) Predefined conditions apply; in which case
(iii) A simplified version of the arm's length principle will be deemed to be acceptable under the arm's length principle regardless of the outcome.

Essentially, a taxpayer will be excused the rigorous application of the arm's length principle and less rigorous rules will be deemed to be acceptable, even if they are a violation of the arm's length principle.

The Irish Guidance explains:

> Only arrangements involving the use of unilateral safe harbour rules come within the scope of this hallmark. Therefore, bilateral or multilateral Advanced Pricing Arrangements concluded between tax authorities are not unilateral safe harbours and do not fall within the scope of this hallmark.[91]

The Irish Guidance goes on to offer numerous examples of things which will <u>not</u> qualify as unilateral safe harbour arrangements:

> Arrangements involving the use of administrative simplification measures that do not directly involve the determination of arm's length prices, for example, simplified documentation requirements in the absence of a pricing determination.
>
> Arrangements that adopt the simplified approach to low value intra-group services. Revenue has issued guidance regarding its simplified approach to low value intra-group services. Revenue's practice of accepting a mark-up of 5% of the cost-base without

[90] Paragraph 4.102 OECD Transfer Pricing Guidelines for Multinational Enterprises and Tax Administrations (July 2017), OECD Publishing.
[91] The Irish Guidance Chapter 2.10

> requiring a taxpayer to provide a benchmarking analysis is consistent with international guidance in this area.
>
> Arrangements involving the use of provisions that exclude certain categories of taxpayers or transactions from the scope of transfer pricing rules. For instance, Small and Medium Enterprises are currently outside the scope of Ireland's transfer pricing rules
>
> Where a particular category of taxpayer or transaction falls within the scope of a unilateral safe harbour rule, but the arrangement does not rely on or involve the use of that rule.[92]

Providing a list of things which do not fall into the hallmark is less helpful than a further elucidation of the principles in play, but one may doubt whether the DAC supports the claim that an exemption for small and medium companies is not a safe harbour rule, nor that a *de minimis* rule for low value intragroup services is similarly exempt.

Regardless of whether the DAC supports those claims, the Irish Tax and Customs are clearly taking a sensible approach to reporting. Acknowledging that these exemptions are unilateral safe harbour rules would achieve nothing but a flood of unnecessary reports, which will not be actioned, but will need to be reviewed. From an administrative respect, if not a legal one, such an approach is entirely justified.

9.6.4 Hallmark E2 – hard to value intangibles

Hallmark E2 states:

> An arrangement involving the transfer of hard to value intangibles. The term 'hard to value intangibles' covers intangibles or rights or intangibles for which, at the time of their transfer between associated enterprises:
>
> (a) no reliable comparable exists;
>
> (b) at the time the transaction was entered into, the projections of future cash flows or income expected to be derived from the transferred intangible, or the assumptions used in valuing the intangible are highly uncertain, making it difficult to predict the level of ultimate success of the intangible at the time of the transfer[93]

This is a lengthy explanation and a hallmark which includes its own internal definition of 'hard to value intangibles'. The hallmark has a four-limbed test:

(i) There must be a transfer;

(ii) That transfer must occur between associated enterprises

(iii) The asset in question must be an intangible

(iv) The asset must be hard to value (as defined).

---

[92] Ibid

[93] Directive 2011/16/EU – Annex IV Part 2 E

The question of whether there is a transfer is a matter of fact, but it must be the case that the participant performing the transfer must have ownership, or other rights of exploitation, over the asset in question and that, after the arrangement has completed, it must cease to have such rights or ownership, at least in part. Secondly another party must take the ownership or right, or some sub-division of such right or ownership. Therefore, sub-licence amounts to a transfer for the purpose of the hallmark as an element of the master licence has been transferred to the sub-licensor. For example, where a geographic right is granted to exploit an asset (such as a licence to operate software within the EU) that is a transfer of the right to exercise that right in that geographic area, by the grantor of the licence.

When assessing if the transfer has occurred between associated enterprises, one should consider the same definition of 'associated enterprises' as contained in Article 18(23):

> 23. for the purposes of Article 8ab, 'associated enterprise' means a person who is related to another person in at least one of the following ways:
>
> (a) a person participates in the management of another person by being in a position to exercise a significant influence over the other person;
> (b) a person participates in the control of another person through a holding that exceeds 25% of the voting rights;
> (c) a person participates in the capital of another person through a right of ownership that, directly or indirectly, exceeds 25% of the capital;
> (d) a person is entitled to 25% or more of the profits of another person.

If more than one person participates, as referred to in points (a) to (d), in the management, control, capital or profits of the same person, all persons concerned shall be regarded as associated enterprises.

(i) If the same persons participate, as referred to in points (a) to (d), in the management, control, capital or profits of more than one person, all persons concerned shall be regarded as associated enterprises.
(ii) For the purposes of this point, a person who acts together with another person in respect of the voting rights or capital ownership of an entity, shall be treated as holding a participation in all of the voting rights or capital ownership of that entity that are held by the other person.
(iii) In indirect participations, the fulfilment of requirements under point (c) shall be determined by multiplying the rates of holding through the successive tiers.
(iv) A person holding more than 50% of the voting rights shall be deemed to hold 100%.

(v) An individual, his or her spouse and his or her lineal ascendants or descendants shall be treated as a single person.'[94]

This definition is comprehensive, for a wider discussion see Chapter 9.4 Category C above.

As to whether the asset is intangible: 'intangible asset' is a concept defined in common professional parlance as 'everything which isn't anything else', but more helpfully by International Accounting Standard 38 as:

> an identifiable non-monetary asset without physical substance. An asset is a resource that is controlled by an entity as a result of past events (for example purchase or self-creation) and from which future economic benefits (inflows or other assets) are expected. Thus the three critical attributes of an intangible asset are:
> (i) Identifiability
> (ii) Control (power to obtain benefits from the asset)
> (iii) Future economic benefits (such as revenues or reduced future costs)[95]

At first blush this appears to cover many assets which exist in the financial world, but should be distinguished from 'financial instruments', which are more closely defined in IAS32, and from interests in subsidiaries and joint ventures, which are dealt with in IAS27. In their IASPlus platform, Deloitte kindly give a list of examples of intangible assets:

- 'Patented technology, computer software, databases and trade secrets;
- Video and audiovisual material (e.g. motion pictures, television programmes)
- Customer lists
- Mortgage servicing rights;
- Licensing, royalty and standstill agreements;
- Import quotas;
- Customer and supplier relationships;
- Marketing rights[96]

Whilst the examples cover a diverse range of items, it is fair to say that they all exhibit the following characteristics: they are non-physical, and they do not fall easily into the category of 'equity', but they do give rights to future income if exploited. It is probably best summed up by the OECD in the Transfer Pricing Guidelines, where it states:

[94] Article 18(23) Directive 2011/16/EU

[95] IAS 38

[96] IAS 38 — Intangible Assets (iasplus.com)

> the word 'intangible' is intended to address something which is not a physical asset or a financial asset, which is capable of being owned or controlled for use in commercial activities[97]

Hallmark E2 is aimed at such assets, and whilst there is little to be gained for our purposes in further exhausting the definition of 'intangible', one can see the class of assets under discussion.

None of the various guidance notes we have reviewed provide adequate discussion of these matters, but from the above one can see that the concepts are well established and understood by the relevant professions, since they are commonly used terms with no special definitions.

Similarly, the final limb of the test — that the intangible to be transferred must be 'hard to value' — is equally defined both by reference to the hallmark itself and, in the Irish and HMRC guidance, by reference to the OECD transfer pricing guidelines[98].

The hallmark itself defines 'hard to value' as:

> intangibles for which, at the time of their transfer between associated enterprises;
> (a) no reliable comparable exists;
> (b) at the time the transaction was entered into, the projections of future cash flows or income expected to be derived from the transferred intangible, or the assumptions used in valuing the intangible are highly uncertain, making it difficult to predict the level of ultimate success of the intangible at the time of the transfer'[99]

This definition is entirely clear. If, at the time of the transaction, one cannot draw a comparison with another similar asset from which to base a valuation, or future cashflow projections are highly uncertain and thus the value and success of the intangible are equally uncertain, then the intangible is hard to value. In other words, if a professional valuer cannot adequately value the intangible with any certainty, it is hard to value. If it is hard to value, it is hard to value.

Never ones to allow clarity to go unpunished, the Irish Tax and Customs specifically refer us to Paragraph D4 of Chapter 6 of the OECD Transfer Pricing Guidelines for Multinational Enterprises and Tax Administrations 2017. The German Guidance makes a similar reference to Chapter 6 without any greater elaboration.

---

[97] Chapter 6 Part A Para 6.6 OECD Transfer Pricing Guidelines for Multinational Enterprises and Tax Administrations 2017, OECD Publishing

[98] The Irish Guidance Chapter 2.10

[99] Directive 2011/16/EU – Annex IV Part 2 E

D4 is a lengthy paragraph which goes into some detail as to the treatment and calculation of the arm's length nature of a transfer. Thankfully, from the perspective of those analysing an arrangement for DAC6 purposes, the arm's length nature of a transfer is not relevant to their analysis. Instead, all that is required is to identify whether an intangible is transferred, and if it is hard to value.

D4 does give us some insight into which features may well be present in a transfer of hard-to-value intangibles:

- The intangible is only partially developed at the time of the transfer;
- The intangible is not expected to be exploited commercially for several years following the transaction;
- The intangible itself does not fall within the definition of Hard to value intangibles in paragraph 6.189 [of the OECD Transfer Pricing Guidelines] but is integral to the development or enhancement of other intangibles which fall within that definition of hard to value intangible;
- The intangible is expected to be exploited in a manner that is novel at the time of the transfer and the absence of a track record of development or exploitation of similar intangibles makes projections highly uncertain;
- The intangible, meeting the definition of 'hard to value intangible' under paragraph 6.189 [of the OECD Transfer Pricing Guidelines], has been transferred to an associated enterprise for a lump sum payment; and
- The intangible is either used in connection with or developed under a Cost Contribution Agreement or similar arrangements'[100]

All of this boils down to saying — in highly complex terminology — that if something is hard to value, then you can identify it as such by the fact it is hard to value. One must have some sympathy with those in compliance departments and other teams tasked with implementing DAC6. The OECD Transfer Pricing Guidelines is an arcane and deeply technical document which people spend their entire working lives reading and trying to understand. It is beyond unreasonable to ask a team of compliance officers from a retail bank or a small fiduciary to understand the deeply technical elements of this and we hope some clarity can be given to those concerned about their lack of knowledge of this hallmark's underpinning principles.

In practical terms, if one is analysing whether an arrangement meets the test for this hallmark, one should ask:

---

[100] Chapter 6 Part D4 Para 6.186 OECD Transfer Pricing Guidelines for Multinational Enterprises and Tax Administrations 2017, OECD Publishing

> Is there a transfer of an intangible asset (most likely a form of intellectual property, but noting the other forms above)?
>
> Would a valuer find it hard to value because it either isn't complete, is part of something else, or is very new (i.e. there are no comparables, or one cannot accurately predict cashflows)?

For an ordinary individual without technical expertise or access to training, the above provides a helpful rule of thumb, but given the sometimes draconian penalties levied in some jurisdictions,[101] one has cause to wonder what cooling effect this might have on the development of intellectual property or intangible assets amongst the small-to-medium enterprises and individuals which often drive innovation.

It is in this hallmark, to which the relevant authorities dedicate so little guidance, that the authors see a potential for major issues in implementation and for overzealous action by the authorities against those failing to comply in error.

9.6.5 Hallmark E3 – intragroup transfers of risk, functions and assets

The Hallmark E3 states:

> An arrangement involving an intragroup cross-border transfer of functions and/or risks and/or assets, if the projected annual earnings before interest and taxes (EBIT), during the three-year period after the transfer, of the transferor or transferors, are less than 50 % of the projected annual EBIT of such transferor or transferors if the transfer had not been made.[102]

When broken down to its constituent elements, Hallmark E3 can be seen to be a three-limbed test:

(i) There must be a transfer of functions, risks, and/or assets;
(ii) That transfer must be intra-group; and
(iii) As a result of the transfer, the earnings before interest and tax of the transferor must fall by more than 50% for a three-year period.

The authors believe that many transfers of assets or risks will be immediately apparent to the relevant professionals. Such transfer need not be for consideration, whether arm's length or otherwise. All transfers which shift assets/risks/functions within groups are within the language of the hallmark, however funded, and whether innocent or not. No MBT applies and thus no measure of commerciality is allowed.

Some commentators, such as Oliver Hoor in his book *The Mandatory Disclosure Regime in Luxembourg: a practical guide,* seek to take a pragmatic

---

[101] In Poland, for example, the maximum fine sits at PLN 25million or approximately €5.5m.

[102] Directive 2011/16/EU – Annex IV Part 2 E

approach, delineating only those transfers which occur as part of a special type of transaction defined as a 'business restructuring':

> this hallmark targets business restructuring which falls within the scope of Chapter IX of the OECD Transfer Pricing Guidelines. Business restructurings undertaken by multinational enterprises ('MNEs') generally involve the cross-border redeployment (or termination) of functions, assets and risks. Such changes to the supply chain are typically accompanied by a reallocation of profits among the members of a restructured multinational group. In this context, the application of the arm's length principle to the restructurings as such and to the post restructuring intra-group transaction is an important issue.[103]
>
> and further:
>
> the mere transfer of assets (for example, participations or loan receivables) or the liquidation of a company are not a business restructuring that comes within the scope of this hallmark even if, in the case of a liquidation, the activities of the liquidated company are subsequently performed by another company[104]

The authors appreciate this pragmatic approach, but believe it to be unsupported by the directive or the legislation. It is clear from the text of the directive that the mere act of transfer is sufficient to meet the first limb of the test, and there is no special class of transactions (that is 'business restructures', words which are not used in the directive) into which the transfer needs to fall, in order for it to be under consideration. The guidance notes we have reviewed appear to be silent as to 'business restructures' as a separate class of transactions. The net which DAC6 casts is wide, and professionals should not seek to narrow it simply because they find it difficult; its aim is to gather as much information as possible.

However obvious the nature of a transfer may be, the authors are aware of several complex cases where a company is to be redomiciled from one jurisdiction to another, and such a scenario warrants some extra thought.

Redomiciliation is a process whereby a company transfers its seat of incorporation formally from one jurisdiction to another. It is related to, but more legalistic than, a change of tax residence (which can be achieved simply by relocating the management and control, or place of effective management).

---

[103] p75 *The Mandatory Disclosure Regime in Luxembourg: A Practical Guide,* Oliver R Hoor. Legitech 2020

[104] p76 *The Mandatory Disclosure Regime in Luxembourg: A Practical Guide,* Oliver R Hoor. Legitech 2020

For example, if a company redomiciles from Isle of Man to Jersey, it will cease to be an Isle of Man company, it will re-register with the Jersey authorities, and will no longer be governed by Manx law. It will be issued a Jersey certificate and be struck from the register in the Isle of Man. If changing a company's tax residence is akin to an individual moving his home from one country to another, then redomiciliation is more akin to surrendering one's current nationality and taking up the passport of another nation.

The process of redomiciliation is conceptually complex, and many jurisdictions do not recognise it or allow it (the UK for example); some jurisdictions treat a redomiciliation as a liquidation of an old company (with all the attendant tax consequences) and a new incorporation; others see it as a simple continuation of the same entity with no disposal or acquisition (hence a different tax treatment). The authors believe the most reasonable approach to be that the treatment of a redomiciliation for DAC6 purposes should be dictated by the treatment in the relevant jurisdiction. If the company to be redomiciled is incorporated in a jurisdiction which regards a redomiciliation as a disposal and reacquisition, then such would amount to a transfer between group entities. If it is located in a jurisdiction which regards a redomiciliation as a continuation of the same entity, then no disposal has occurred or is deemed to have occurred, and therefore there has been no 'transfer'. The authors appreciate this may lead to some unsatisfactory conclusions and inconsistencies, but until there is some multilateral agreement as to what constitutes a redomiciliation, this is unavoidable. To not take into account local law as applicable to the entity, and impose an external understanding by applying a unified approach would be to subvert the rights of jurisdictions to make law as they see fit, and multiply the number of unnecessary reports.

The only guidance we have reviewed specifically to address this issue is the Maltese Guidance, which states:

> Re-domiciliation or the transfer of tax residence to another jurisdiction are not targeted by this hallmark[105]

The second limb of the test for reportability under Hallmark E3 is that the transfer in question must be 'intra-group'. It is interesting to note that those drafting the directive have avoided the already-defined term, 'associated enterprises'. Instead they have chosen the phrase 'intra-group', which is left undefined. This difference would seem to indicate that the domestic test in question should be applied. This would be consistent with the aim of the directive in reporting those transactions which may have a tax effect.

In their guidance, the Maltese authorities take a more aggressive view, in stating that:

---

[105] The Maltese GuidanceChapter 5.7.3

> An intra-group cross-border transfer for the purposes of hallmark E3 refers to a cross-border transfer between associated enterprises. The term 'associated enterprise' is defined in Regulation 13(9) of the Cooperation Regulations

This is a very close echo of the now-defunct HMRC Guidance, which similarly added the requirement for the entities between which the transfer occurred to meet the test of 'associated enterprises' in the Directive.

By applying domestic tests as to the nature of 'groups', the Directive would ensure that reports are relevant to tax laws to which those entities are subject. If the Maltese Guidance is correct and the Directive applies an arbitrary test of 25% connectivity (as the associated enterprise test), divorced from actual tax relevant tests, that would produce reports which are irrelevant in some jurisdictions, but relevant in others. Given the difference in language between 'associated enterprises' and 'intragroup', it is not clear that this position is supported by the Directive.

The authors believe that until EU rules are harmonised as to group membership, there is no other practical approach than by reference to the domestic understanding of 'intragroup', and it is most likely that those drafting the Directive have avoided the use of the freely-available term 'associated enterprises' deliberately.

The final limb of the test is that the earnings before interest and tax (or 'EBIT') of the transferor must be less than 50% than they would have been had the transfer not occurred in the three-year period. Various pieces of guidance take some time discussing how to evaluate whether or not the EBIT of a company can be said to have fallen by more than 50% over three years. The practical difficulty they seek to resolve is best illuminated with an example:

(i) Ms Johnson is an intermediary who is carrying out an arrangement which involves Company A (a UK company) transferring part of its business to its sister company in Belgium (Company B).
(ii) Ms Johnson has the obligation to report within 30 days of the first step of the arrangement being taken.
(iii) On the day she must report, she cannot know if the actual effect of the transfer will be the reduction of the EBIT of Company A by more than 50% over three years.

Irish Tax and Customs solve this problem by projecting future outcomes from today's standpoint. They state:

> to establish whether this hallmark is met, it will be necessary to produce two sets of projections for the three-year period following the transfer – one based on what the position of the transferor would be without the transfer taking place and one based on the position of the transferor with the transfer taking place. This testing should be carried out having regard to all the relevant facts and circumstances

at the time the reporting obligation arises under the disclosure regime.[106]

The expectations on the relevant taxpayer to prepare projections embodied in this guidance seem to lose sight of the fact that the relevant taxpayer has, under the directive (though local legal implementation may vary), no obligation to report in most cases, and no obligation to co-operate in the gathering of information by those who do have an obligation to report. In practical terms what will happen is that an intermediary will identify a potential E3 relevant transfer, they will then ask for projections which the relevant taxpayer will either provide or not provide. If they do not provide them, the intermediary will be left, either unable to report, or with a much-reduced report of little utility to the tax office. This will be an unsatisfactory outcome for both intermediary and tax authority.

As a result, the authors believe that some of the less than obvious cases will go unreported as a result of this reliance on the relevant taxpayer to co-operate. This is a practical outcome of the design of the hallmark and may well be an outcome considered and accepted by those who drafted the hallmark. Large multinationals with big budgets and large teams of professionals will most likely comply by supplying projections, even though they have no outright obligation to do so. One can only wait and see how smaller entities behave.

In a position echoed by, amongst others, the Maltese, Irish Tax and Customs point out that:

> if the transferor would be projected to make a loss were the transfer to not go ahead and if the projected position of the transferor post transfer is still loss making but with reduced losses, nil earnings or a positive EBIT, this hallmark should not apply as these outcomes cannot be said to represent a 50% reduction in EBIT[107]

9.6.6 Conclusion

Category E seeks to shine a light on those transactions which are relevant to one of the most complex areas of tax law. It expects intermediaries of all levels to be alert to the transfer pricing consequences of the arrangements they enter into and it demands a level of knowledge of international regimes which is currently beyond that of many.

To a certain extent, one can see the level at which the designers of the DAC are thinking. They seem to perceive the world economy as made up mostly of large organisations, with big teams of highly qualified professionals at their disposal. However, this is not the case, it is mostly made up of small-to-medium sized enterprises with limited resources. Not every online business is Amazon, but many own intangible assets and trade cross-border.

---

[106] The Irish Guidance Chapter 2.10

[107] Ibid

Considering Category E will be a burden those SME businesses have not carried before, but one they must now carry all the same.

9.7 Reporting issues

9.7.1 Is the arrangement reportable?

For DAC6, the key matter for intermediaries is whether one should report or not report. All the other words and analysis around the interpretation of hallmarks and tests and definitions are irrelevant, if they do not assist in the real world assessment of whether or not an intermediary should report.

Therefore, in this chapter we will bring together all the foregoing concepts and analysis and show, step-by-step, the decision-making process as to reporting. This will, of necessity, be a much more practical chapter than those discussions which have preceded it. The following, much-simplified decision tree may be of assistance.

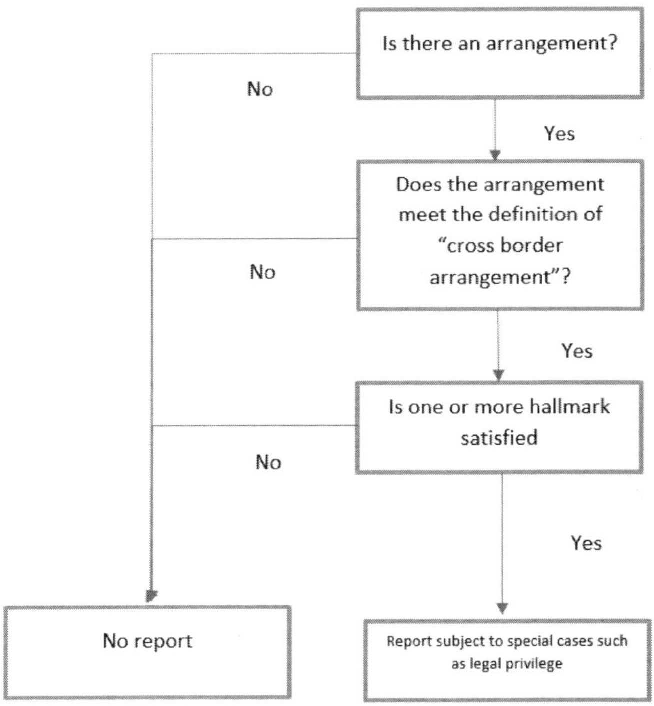

This is a vastly oversimplified flow chart, but useful in that it clarifies the nature of DAC6 as essentially no more than a complex flowchart or decision tree. A series of 'yes' or 'no' answers leads to a result of 'report' or 'no report'.

9.7.2 Intermediary Questions

Intermediaries are often exercised by a number of specific questions. We have discussed these issues above in the chapter on definitions, but some further issues remain.

9.7.3 Nexus

To be subject to the DAC6 reporting obligation, an intermediary must have an EU Nexus. In transposition into local law, this EU-wide nexus rule has often been converted into a domestic test. For example, the nexus test under the Luxembourg Law of 25 March 2020 regarding Reportable Cross-border Arrangements implementing EU Directive 2018/822/EU specifies that, to be subject to the obligation to report, one must have a Luxembourg nexus. However, Gibraltar's implementation at s10ZH(3) of the Income Tax Act 2010 remains an EU-wide nexus test. Intermediaries should confirm their obligation in terms of the relevant legislation.

An 'EU nexus' is defined as:

The intermediary is tax resident in an EU Member State;
The intermediary has a permanent establishment in a Member State through which the services relating to the arrangement are delivered;
It is incorporated in an EU Member State, or governed by the laws of an EU Member State;
It is registered with a professional association relating to the legal, taxation or consultancy services in an EU Member State.

Limbs 1 – 3 of the nexus test are entirely clear. However, limb 4 could be read to imply that arrangements which do not concern the EU are to be reported. The intermediary must remember that within scope are only those arrangements which concern either more than one Member State, or a Member State and a third country or countries. The Portuguese Advogado (for example) working in Dubai and dealing with companies in Malaysia (for example) need not worry, unless confronted with other matters that relate to the EU.

9.7.4 What periods are in scope?

In scope for consideration and reporting in the first 'lookback' reporting batch (originally due on 31 August 2020 and now delayed until 28 February 2021) are all arrangements, the first step of which is taken after 25 June 2018, but before 30 June 2020. First steps taken between 01 July 2020 and 01 January 2020 are reportable in January 2021[108]. All other arrangements are reportable, either: 30 days after they are made available for implementation; after the arrangement is ready for implementation; or the first step of implementation is taken, whichever is earlier.

---

[108] This delay in reporting is the maximum available to Member States, not all Member States have taken advantage of the options agreed by the Council of Europe on 4th June 2020. Local advice should be taken wherever possible.

The date of 25 June 2018 is not arbitrary. It is one month after the adoption of the DAC6 Directive on 25 May 2018.

All arrangements, the first step of which is taken after 25 June 2018, are in scope for consideration. HMRC's Guidance discusses what 'the first step' amounts to:

> when the first step of an arrangement is implemented is a question of fact

HMRC goes on to offer two examples:

> A company has designed an arrangement in-house which will involve the transfer of assets to an overseas subsidiary, The transfer is such that Hallmark E3 will be met. It is still finalising the precise details of certain later steps in the transaction but it does not want to risk delays so it incorporates a new company in the overseas jurisdiction ready for the transfer as soon as the details are finalised[109]

> a company is considering transferring some assets to an overseas subsidiary but has not yet worked out the details. It does not yet know whether the transaction will go ahead as the design is at too early a stage. However, in order to avoid delays at a later date, it decides to incorporate an overseas subsidiary now in case it does decide to go ahead[110]

In these two similar examples, HMRC tells us that in the first example incorporation of the subsidiary amounts to the first step, the second example incorporation is not the first step as the arrangement is insufficiently formed.

This shows that a reasonable approach must be taken and an application of common sense is required. This is not an answer generally welcomed by those designing systems and triggers, but there is no other. The infinite number of imaginable permutations means that we must ultimately question whether a material step of a meaningful arrangement, which can be understood holistically, is either taken or not. If it is, then the first step has been taken; if on the other hand, the action being considered is merely preparatory (preparing the ground, so to speak, without taking an active step) then no 'first step' is taken.

9.7.5 What do service providers need to know?

Service providers, or those who believe themselves to be service providers, are often concerned by the level of knowledge required of them. Specifically, compliance teams can become deeply concerned by gaps in their knowledge and an urge to answer questions which might well not, in fact, be asked of

---

[109] The HMRC Guidance IEIM651030 – Meaning of First Step

[110] Ibid

them. The level of knowledge demanded of service providers is discussed in the HMRC Guidance:

> a service provider will not always have full knowledge of the arrangements in respect of which they are providing aid, assistance or advice. A service provider can argue they are not an intermediary because they did not know and could not reasonably be expected to know that they were involved in a reportable arrangement.[111]

HMRC provides in-depth guidance as to the requirements on service providers. Particularly heartening for the internal compliance teams will be this sentence:

> HMRC does not expect service providers to do additional external due diligence to establish whether there is a reportable arrangement. A service provider should do the normal due diligence it would for the type of transaction and client(s) in question.[112]

This sets the standard of what an organisation is required to know of the purposes of DAC6 and it can be reduced to the single statement: DAC6 alters nothing in this regard. It is a standard which is echoed in almost all the guidance we have reviewed and should be a cornerstone of the approach taken. Compliance procedures need no alteration when it comes to gathering information, the simple fulfilment of pre-existing requirements is all that is required. However, as always, a wilful blindness will be no defence.

Similarly, HMRC deal with the issue of whether all information in an organisation can be deemed to be known and understood:

> if an intermediary receives an email which contained information suggesting that an arrangement was reportable, but they did not need to read the email in the normal course of business and had not done so, it would not be the case that they should be assumed to have knowledge of the arrangement just because the information was in the email.[113]

Irish Tax and Customs seem to shy away from such a conclusion, however, when stating:

> as regards a person's actual knowledge, such person must consider anything that they actually know about the arrangement and any information that is readily available to them when delivering a particular service[114]

[111] The HMRC Guidance IEIM621050 – Knowledge Test

[112] The HMRC Guidance IEIM621060 – Reasonably Expected to know

[113] Ibid

[114] The Irish Guidance Chapter 4.3

This difference in interpretation seems a little odd. A UK intermediary need not review the files in detail when considering whether an arrangement is reportable or not, but an Irish intermediary must pick through all his files to find what information is 'readily available'. Which of course leads to the question 'what is "readily available"?', and whether what is 'readily available' might differ in a large organisation with many depositories of information from what is 'readily available' to a sole practitioner. The Irish Tax and Customs do explain that:

> 'Readily available information will include information that is acquired during the course of providing the service, such as that acquired when carrying out the standard checks and due diligence procedures, subject to data protection rules.[115]

Which is swiftly followed by the more reassuring:

> There is, however, no onus on service providers to seek out any additional information or to carry out any additional checking or due diligence[116]

As with so much of DAC6, this appears to be a compromise and an attempt to make a widely drafted set of principles work as a unified piece of legislation. HMRC give us some indication of what procedural reviews they expect of intermediaries:

> to be reportable by an intermediary, information must be in its knowledge, possession or control. Any person fulfilling their reporting obligations, should take account of the information they know, and information that is available to them. They should review documents and information in relation to the arrangement to identify the information that is reportable.
>
> An intermediary would not have to trawl through all of an organisation's computer systems to try and find all information held in relation to a relevant taxpayer just to see if it is relevant. However, where relevant information is known to be held, the intermediary should report it.[117]

As ever, any attempt deliberately to fragment knowledge would not be acceptable to HMRC or, for that matter, to any other tax authority.

Once again, a simply reasonable approach is being taken. The boundaries of reasonableness in this case are not entirely clear, but the lack of a requirement for a fine-tooth approach is clear. Only that which is known is required to be reported, and there is no requirement to use best endeavours to acquire knowledge beyond what is already known, and no requirement

---

[115] Ibid

[116] Ibid

[117] The HMRC Guidance IEIM657010 – Knowledge, possession, or control

to pick over systems and files in detail to sift knowledge from the furthest corners of an organisation.

The conclusion to be drawn from this sensible approach seems to be that large organisations will necessarily have greater leeway than small ones, as mentioned above. An intermediary providing a personal level of service will not be able to hide behind large computer systems and disparate teams holding information in many different places.

9.7.6 More than one intermediary?

There will often occur a set of facts requiring several intermediaries to report, and they may well be in differing jurisdictions. This situation is considered in Article 8ab (4)[118] of the DAC, which states:

> 4. Where, pursuant to paragraph 3, there is a multiple reporting obligation, the intermediary shall be exempt from filing the information if it has proof, in accordance with national law, that the same information has been filed in another Member State.

We should note the requirement that evidence be in accordance with national law and take that as a reminder that local advice should be taken where possible, even in the case of European legislation like this. The Irish Tax and Customs makes the position in Ireland clear:

> For the exemption to apply, the relevant taxpayer should retain the following documentation:
>
> - a copy of the information that was provided to the competent authority of the other Member State, and
> - written confirmation of the Arrangement ID that was assigned to the arrangement by the other Member State.[119]

Where such guidance is missing or the legislation is silent on such matters, the authors believe a reasonable approach to evidencing should be taken. What is certain is that a mere undertaking from a fellow solicitor or barrister is insufficient to permit the exemption. The reporting by a fellow intermediary must actually occur, and be evidenced, not merely promised, however reliable that promise may be.

This matter of relying on fellow intermediaries will undoubtedly lead to practical issues. Should an intermediary be proposing to rely on a fellow intermediary, and that intermediary not provide such evidence as is required, then they should make a report of their own as soon as is practicably possible.

---

[118] Directive 2011/16/EU

[119] The Irish Guidance Chapter 5.2

9.7.7 More than one member state to report in?

It may be the case that an intermediary is due to file in more than one Member State. If so, the provisions of Article 8ab (3) are relevant:

> Where the intermediary is liable to file information on reportable cross border arrangements with the competent authorities of more than one Member State, such information shall be filed only in the Member State that features first on the list below:
> a. the Member State where the intermediary is resident for tax purposes;
> b. the Member State where the intermediary has a permanent establishment through which the services with respect to the arrangement are provided;
> c. the Member State where the intermediary is incorporated or governed by the laws of;
> d. the Member State where the intermediary is registered with a professional association related to legal, taxation or consultancy services.[120]

9.7.8 Am I covered by legal privilege?

Article 8ab(4) states:

> Each Member State may take the necessary measures to give intermediaries the right to a waiver from filing information on a reportable cross-border arrangement where the reporting obligation would breach the legal professional privilege under the national law of Member State. In such circumstances, each Member State shall take the necessary measures to require intermediaries to notify, without delay, any other intermediary or, if there is no such intermediary, the relevant taxpayer of their reporting obligation under paragraph 6. Intermediaries may only be entitled to a waiver under the first subparagraph to the extent that they operate within the limits of the relevant national laws that define their professions.[121]

The question of what is, and what is not protected by legal professional privilege poses too wide a discussion for a work of this nature, and many excellent pieces of writing exist to help the interested reader. However, one note must be struck. The boundaries of legal privilege are not infinite. For example, an English solicitor acting as a director of a client company will not be protected by legal privilege when he/she is acting on commercial matters for the client company. Such non-legal work is not 'within the limits… that define their professions' as defined by English law. Therefore, legal advisers should be highly conscious of their position on a daily basis and should

[120] Article 8ab(3) Council Directive 2011/16/EU
[121] Article 8ab(5) Council Directive 2011/16/EU

consult with their regulatory and professional bodies in their local jurisdiction.

If an adviser is required by his legal professional privilege to not report, he is not entirely free of obligations. Article 8ab(4) is entirely clear on this. The intermediary is obliged to notify either other intermediaries or the relevant taxpayer of the fact that there is an obligation to report. Failure to do so is as much a breach of DAC6 as a failure to report at all. The obligation to notify reportability is immediate and must be fulfilled 'without delay'. Professionals should be wary of this double-edged sword and conscious of their obligations.

9.7.9 No intermediary or an intermediary with legal privilege?

The fact that an arrangement is designed by a relevant taxpayer (and therefore there are no relevant intermediaries), or that the relevant intermediary is outside the EU or that the only intermediary involved is protected by legal privilege is no protection from reporting.

The Irish Guidance explains:

> A person coming within the definition of a relevant taxpayer in relation to a reportable cross border arrangement will be required to file a return with Revenue of all specified information that is within their knowledge possession or control in relation to that arrangement where –
>
> > There is an intermediary, the relevant taxpayer has not waived their rights to legal privilege to the extent necessary to allow the intermediary to disclose the information to Revenue… or there is no intermediary (within the meaning of the legislation), and
> >
> > The relevant taxpayer has a nexus to an EU Member State[122]

This guidance adequately explains the requirement under the Directive at Article 8ab(5) – (8). However, there is the addition of the requirement for the relevant taxpayer in this situation to have an EU Nexus. It is not entirely clear where this requirement comes from. The HMRC Guidance is silent at IEIM654000, and no reference to this requirement appears to be made in section 817RD of the Consolidated Taxes Act 1997 to which we are referred by the Irish Guidance.

Similarly to the Irish Guidance, Oliver Hoor's *The Mandatory Disclosure Regime in Luxembourg: A Practical Guide* states:

> in order for a taxpayer to have a reporting obligation under Article 4(1) of the MDR Law, it must be a Luxembourg taxpayer[123]

---

[122] The Irish Guidance Chapter 5.1

[123] p34 *The Mandatory Disclosure Regime in Luxembourg: A Practical Guide*, Oliver R. Hoor, Legitech 2020

As with the Irish Guidance, this does not seem to be supported by the text of the Luxembourg law. It would, however, make perfect sense that a relevant taxpayer must have an EU Nexus to make a report (as he is stepping into the shoes of an intermediary, who must also have an EU nexus to be subject to the reporting requirement), though it may well transpire this sensible approach is not supported by the legislation or the Directive.

In the case of an intermediary with legal professional privilege, other intermediaries should be notified as above. In the absence of other intermediaries, the obligation to report then falls onto the shoulders of the relevant taxpayer who has been so notified. Article 8ab(7) states:

> 7. The relevant taxpayer with whom the reporting obligation lies shall file the information within 30 days, beginning on the day after the reportable cross-border arrangement is made available for implementation to that relevant taxpayer, or is ready for implementation by the relevant taxpayer, or when the first step in its implementation has been made in relation to the relevant taxpayer, whichever occurs first.
>
> Where the relevant taxpayer has an obligation to file information on the reportable cross-border arrangement with the competent authorities of more than one Member State, such information shall be filed only with the competent authorities of the Member State that features first in the list below:
>
> (a) the Member State where the relevant taxpayer is resident for tax purposes;
> (b) the Member State where the relevant taxpayer has a permanent establishment benefiting from the arrangement;
> (c) the Member State where the relevant taxpayer receives income or generates profits, although the relevant taxpayer is not resident for tax purposes and has no permanent establishment in any Member State;
> (d) the Member State where the relevant taxpayer carries on an activity, although the relevant taxpayer is not resident for tax purposes and has no permanent establishment in any Member State.[124]

This is essentially a replication of the overlapping reporting requirements on intermediaries at Article 8ab(3) and requires no further discussion at this point.

9.7.10 Finally... make the report

Any intermediary who has come this far through the maze of DAC6 should be congratulated. Like a hero in a fantasy novel, your quest is complete. You

[124] Article 8ab(7) Council Directive 2011/16/EU

should now know whether you need to report or not. The question remains, however: what to report.

Firstly, the intermediary can only report information which it has in its 'knowledge, possession or control'. HMRC Guidance gives an element of procedural guidance as to how to ensure that all information in the knowledge, possession or control is caught:

> Any person, in fulfilling their reporting obligations, should take account of the information they know and information that is available to them. They should review documents and information in relation to the arrangement to identify the information that is reportable

The differences in approach between the authorities is discussed above, but all seem to be reaching for a reasonableness test and understand that organisations were not established with DAC6 in mind. However, as time progresses, and systems mature, one might imagine that the authorities would become less tolerant of errors and gaps in knowledge. Their attitudes are yet to be seen; the authors' understanding is that a reasonable approach will be taken, but that the authorities will not tolerate deliberate efforts to put information beyond knowledge, possession or control, or deliberately to confuse and disperse systems to make such reviews more difficult.

The information that must be reported is set out in the DAC at Article 8ab(14):

(a) the identification of intermediaries and relevant taxpayers, including their name, date and place of birth (in the case of an individual), residence for tax purposes, TIN and, where appropriate, the persons that are associated enterprises to the relevant taxpayer;
(b) details of the hallmarks set out in Annex IV that make the cross-border arrangement reportable;
(c) a summary of the content of the reportable cross-border arrangement, including a reference to the name by which it is commonly known, if any, and a description in abstract terms of the relevant business activities or arrangements, without leading to the disclosure of a commercial, industrial or professional secret or of a commercial process, or of information the disclosure of which would be contrary to public policy;
(d) the date on which the first step in implementing the reportable cross-border arrangement has been made or will be made;
(e) details of the national provisions that form the basis of the reportable cross-border arrangement;
(f) the value of the reportable cross-border arrangement;
(g) the identification of the Member State of the relevant taxpayer(s) and any other Member States which are likely to be concerned by the reportable cross-border arrangement;

(h) the identification of any other person in a Member State likely to be affected by the reportable cross-border arrangement, indicating to which Member States such person is linked.[125]

Those who have filed reports under either FATCA or CRS will notice a substantial difference in what is expected. There are elements of free text at Article 8ab(14)(c) and (e) amongst others. This is no mere mechanical reporting mechanism as with CRS. The intermediary is not simply transposing data, and this will require a level of understanding not previously demanded in processing reports. It is for this reason that the authors believe DAC6 reporting should not simply be left to compliance teams who do not have expertise in all levels of the relevant business.

Information should be gathered by those with understanding and collated by those with understanding. It is vital that professionals and advisers should review arrangements as they are being designed, not refer for sign-off just prior to implementation. An active approach will minimise the disruption DAC6 will cause to intermediaries.

9.7.11 Duty to file reference number

Under Irish, Luxembourg and UK law there is a requirement on the relevant taxpayer that has participated in a reportable cross-border arrangement to report such cross-border arrangement on the relevant tax return. This is an implementation of the option Article 8ab(11), which states:

> Each Member State may take the necessary measures to require that each relevant taxpayer file information about their use of the arrangement to the tax administration in each of the years for which they use it.

For this obligation to be fulfilled, the relevant intermediaries need to share any 'arrangement reference number' issued by a tax authority with the relevant taxpayers.

This obligation to share reference numbers is found in section 817RC(5) of the Consolidated Taxes Act 1997 in Ireland, though it seems to be merely implicit in Luxembourg and UK.

9.7.12 Marketable Arrangements

Filing of information on marketable arrangements by intermediaries is slightly different from the filing requirements on the intermediary or relevant taxpayer in the case of a bespoke arrangement.

The intermediary who provides a marketable arrangement, instead of making a report every time he/she sells his marketable arrangement, must instead make a return every quarter which includes the following:

---

[125] Article 8ab(14) Council Directive 2011/16/EU

- the identity of each intermediary and relevant taxpayer involved in the arrangement;
- the date on which the first step was taken or will be taken in implementing the arrangement;
- the identification of the Member State of each relevant taxpayer involved in the arrangement and any other Member State likely to be concerned by the arrangement;
- the identification of any other person in a Member State likely to be affected by the arrangement, indicating to which Member State(s) such person is linked.[126]

9.7.13 Electronic filing

Reports should be filed utilising each Member State's electronic filing system. It is not within the remit of this work to review the electronic systems implemented; save to say that these are related to the pre-exiting mechanisms designed for the CRS and FATCA filing systems and are based on file formats and schemas published by the various authorities. Intermediaries should refer to their local tax authorities, but they should rest assured that they will be familiar with the mechanisms, and many providers have produced software solutions to automate the filing requirements.

9.7.14 Penalties

The DAC does not, itself, mandate specific penalties to be levied on those who do not abide by the national implementation of the DAC. However, Article 25a states:

> Member States shall lay down the rules on penalties applicable to infringements of national provisions adopted pursuant to this Directive and concerning Articles 8aa and 8ab, and shall take all measures necessary to ensure that they are implemented. The penalties provided for shall be effective, proportionate and dissuasive.[127]

As implemented at the date of writing, the penalties imposed by the Member States are very wide-ranging. For example, in Luxembourg the maximum penalty for non-compliance is $250,000. Malta takes a different approach with a patchwork of penalties for a possible four offences, none of which has a maximum penalty in excess of €30,000. The UK has a penalty regime, which imposes a fee of £5,000 for those failing to comply with reporting obligations and a further £600 per day, with an option for HMRC to seek further penalties if these are found to be insufficient in fulfilling the intention to be 'effective, proportionate and dissuasive'. Poland seem to be the most draconian, with a maximum penalty of approximately €5.7m.

---

[126] The Irish Guidance Chapter 4.8

[127] Article 25a Council Directive 2011/16/EU

It is always difficult to understand why a jurisdiction chooses to take a given position on penalties. Where a jurisdiction seeks to impose a very heavy penalty, this behaviour could be explained in two possible ways. Either, the jurisdiction believes that this is a very serious offence in itself and wishes performatively to show that to its peers. Or, alternatively, the jurisdiction believes that the offence will be widespread and seeks to act as a deterrent. Neither of the authors is sufficiently knowledgeable in any of the jurisdictions around the EU to be able to comment as to which motivation is in play. However, it is worth noting that tax compliance is often linked very closely to whether or not a jurisdiction is a low-trust/low-efficiency tax environment or a high-trust/high-efficiency tax environment. In a low-trust/low-efficiency environment, tax evasion/avoidance and high levels of non-compliance in relation to provisions such as DAC6 are common, and draconian penalties are often highly unsuccessful in their aim[128].

9.7.15 Review of the Hallmarks and the effect of the DAC

The DAC does contain mechanisms for understanding the effect of the provisions and measures will be taken to review the impact periodically, in addition Article 27(1) requires the Commission to report on the application of the DAC as a whole every five years.

As to the ongoing reviews of implementation required for such a report to be effective, there is sometimes a tendency for authorities (and the Commission is included in this) to assume that, if reporting numbers are lower than their expectation, then something must be amiss. This should not be an automatic assumption.

The provisions of DAC6 are often highly complex and targeted, and many professionals are observing that reportable arrangements are less common than they expected. This is partially because the effect of anti-avoidance measures introduced in recent years has meant that the hallmarks (especially those in Category B and C) are much less likely to be exhibited by arrangements begun after 25th June 2018. It is also, in part, down to the provisions of the DAC itself being unclear, or the guidance issued being contradictory, absent or equally unclear.

The DAC itself contains a mechanism at Article 27(2) for the hallmarks to be reviewed every two years after 01 July 2020. The authors believe this may be the lever which the Commission pulls, should reporting be at a lower level than expected. However, it is to be hoped that they do not fall into the trap of demanding ever more stringent reporting; in effect, chasing an elusive goal.

---

[128] A very interesting review of this matter can be found in 'Explaining Italian Tax Compliance' by John D'Attoma in *The Leap of Faith: The Fiscal Foundations of Successful Government in Europe and America*, ed. S. Steinmo, Oxford Scholarship Online 2018

10 MDR

10.1 Introduction

'Mandatory disclosure rules' is becoming, internationally, an imprecise term. We use it – and its acronym MDR – to discuss the OECD Model Mandatory Disclosure Rules for CRS Avoidance Arrangements and Opaque Offshore Structures, and the domestic regimes of jurisdictions that have chosen to (or are in the process of choosing to) adopt rules based on these rules. However, many jurisdictions are implementing rules that – while bearing some resemblance to these rules – are also altering them. For example, all of Mexico, Argentina and Norway have either implemented, or are considering implementing rules dealing with both the international position and the domestic position. The domestic position – particularly, but not exclusively, in these jurisdictions – is beyond the scope of this book. We focus on the MDR and the regimes which include the types of tax-offending behaviour identified therein, or the definitions of which are based on it.

DAC6 is one such regime; while it goes far beyond the current MDR,[1] it does include the two key hallmarks for MDR in its Hallmark D. Consequently, the two regimes do have a great deal in common. However, there is also some significant divergence, both in the administrative operation of the regimes and in the key principles behind them.

10.2 Divergence between DAC6 and MDR

DAC6 and MDR could be said to have similar purposes. The purpose of DAC6 is said to be:

> The main aim of the Directive is to provide tax authorities with an early warning mechanism on new risks of tax avoidance and thereby enable them to carry our audits more effectively. Prior to the Directive, such cross-border arrangements did not need be reported under EU legislation[2].

The purpose of MDR is said to be:

> The purpose of the new rules is to provide tax administrations with information on arrangements that (purport to) circumvent the Common Reporting Standard (CRS Avoidance Arrangements) and on structures that disguise the beneficial owners of assets held offshore (Opaque Offshore Structures). The information required to be disclosed includes the taxpayers using such structures or arrangements and those involved with their design and set-up. This information will provide tax administrations both with additional intelligence for their tax compliance activities as well as for designing future tax policy. It is also expected that the rules will have a deterrent effect against the design, marketing and use of these

---

[1] Which is likely to change to better address the issues raised in BEPS Action 12

[2]ec.europa.eu/taxation_customs/sites/taxation/files/dac-6-council-directive-2018_en.pdf

> arrangements and schemes and bolster the overall integrity of the Common Reporting Standard

Thus, the key difference between the two should be clear. DAC6 is broader than MDR; MDR targets only 'avoidance' of reporting requirements. While this is an element of DAC6, DAC6 looks more widely at providing an 'early warning mechanism on new risks of tax avoidance'. So, it might be said that MDR remains more focussed on evasion – in particular preventing the avoidance of detection of such evasion, through the existing international reporting regimes, while DAC6 is an international reporting regime in relation to tax avoidance, which includes an element of identifying avoidance of CRS.

DAC6 has been more widely adopted, to date, because it is mandatory within the EU. However, a number of jurisdictions have, or are in the process of, adopting rules based on the OECD MDR and over the coming years, it will be interesting to see how widely adopted MDR ultimately is (and the extent to which, if at all, MDR is expanded into a tax avoidance regime).

10.3 The UK abandonment of DAC6

The UK initially adopted DAC6 in full. This was despite the fact that Brexit was due to be completed – once the commencement of DAC6 had been extended due to Covid-19 – before DAC6 came into effect. Until 31 December 2020, the UK had decided that it was implementing DAC6, even introducing extensive HMRC guidance. Consequently, it was considered probable that the UK would continue to participate in DAC6. On 31 December 2020, however, it was announced that the UK would not be fully participating in DAC6. Indeed, it would only be participating to the extent of the MDR.

Essentially the announcement was twofold:

(i) Reporting under DAC6 will still be required for a limited time, but only for arrangements which meet hallmarks under category D, in line with the UK's obligations under the FTA.
(ii) In 2021, the UK intended to consult on and implement the OECD's MDR to replace DAC6 and transition from European to international rules

The obligations under the FTA were the following:

> A Party shall not weaken or reduce the level of protection provided for in its legislation at the end of the transition period below the level provided for by the standards and rules which have been agreed in the OECD at the end of the transition period, in relation to (a) the exchange of information… concerning… potential cross-border tax planning arrangements'.

The phrase 'OECD rules on exchange of information on cross-border arrangements' is referring to the MDR. Thus, the UK must not reduce the level of protection in its legislation below that of the MDR. So, it seems probable that the UK's MDR/DAC6 provision is likely to change in the near future.

Thus, the UK regime is addressed here – with other regimes based on the OECD MDR, however, it should be noted that at present, it retains elements of DAC6.

10.4 Structure of MDR (and this Chapter)

The MDR is – compared to DAC6 – relatively short and lacking in complexity. DAC6 carries the difficulty of being an amendment to earlier legislation, and so it is necessary to consult other instruments etc, in addition to the national enacting legislation. However, MDR is not legislation and has no legal effect. It is – like the OECD Model Convention on Double Taxation – a model upon which actual agreements and domestic legislation are based.

Thus, while we consider the provisions of MDR in this Chapter, and indeed the Chapter's structure is based on that of the MDR, we also consider provisions from individual jurisdictions, including the UK.

The structure of the MDR Model Rules is also, thankfully, relatively straightforward. It is divided into two sections:

(i) Definitions/terminology; and
(ii) Requirement to disclose.

This is significantly more straightforward than the structure of DAC6, which reflects the simpler and more focussed purpose of the MDR. There is no reference to Hallmarks, simply two types of Arrangements, in relation to which there are reporting requirements. Confusingly, these two categories of Arrangements are included in the 'defintions' section. However, they are of significant substantive relevance. Consequently, we will deal first with the other definitions, which inform the interpretation of the two key definitions of 'CRS Avoidance Arrangement' and 'Opaque Offshore Structure'.

10.5 Terminology

An 'Arrangement' is defined in Rule 1.4 (Other Definitions), providing:

> 'Arrangement' includes an agreement, scheme, plan or understanding, whether or not legally enforceable, and includes all the steps and transactions that bring it into effect.

The Commentary explains:

> The term 'Arrangement' is used as part of the definition of CRS Avoidance Arrangement. As set out in the BEPS Action 12 Report, this definition is intended to be sufficiently broad and robust to capture any agreement, scheme, plan or understanding (whether enforceable or not) and all the steps and transactions that form part of or give effect to that Arrangement

'CRS Legislation' is also defined in Rule 1.4, which provides:

> 'CRS Legislation' means the Standard for Automatic Exchange of Financial Account Information in Tax Matters as implemented in the domestic laws of the jurisdiction where the relevant account, product, investment, or Arrangement is maintained and includes any international legal instrument that is in force and effect for that jurisdiction and which provides for the exchange of information collected pursuant to the Common Reporting Standard

Here the Commentary explains:

> The definition of CRS Legislation refers to the Standard for Automatic Exchange of Financial Account Information in Tax Matters, as implemented in the domestic laws of the jurisdiction where the relevant account, product or investment is maintained. It includes agreements in effect to exchange the information collected pursuant to such laws, in particular the Multilateral Convention on Mutual Administrative Assistance in Tax Matters and the Multilateral Competent Authority Agreement on Automatic Exchange of Financial Account Information. Thus an Arrangement will be treated as circumventing the CRS not only where it results in a Financial Institution failing to report (or reporting inaccurate) information to a tax authority but also where it avoids the information being exchanged with the tax authority in the Reportable Taxpayer's jurisdictions of tax residence

Thus, the MDR – as drafted in model form – is restricted to identifying CRS avoidance and not the avoidance of any other exchange of information regime, such as FATCA.

Rule 1.4 provides:

> 'Basic Information' on a Legal Person includes, at a minimum, information about the legal ownership and control structure of the Legal Person. This would include information about the status and powers of the Legal Person, its shareholders or members and its directors

It also defines 'Beneficial Ownership', providing:

> 'Beneficial Ownership' or 'Beneficial Owner' shall be interpreted in a manner consistent with the latest Financial Action Task Force Recommendations and shall include any natural person who exercises control over a Legal Person or Legal Arrangement. In the case of a trust, such term means any settlor, trustee, protector (if any), beneficiary or class of beneficiaries and any other natural person exercising ultimate effective control over the trust, and in the case of a Legal Arrangement other than a trust, such term means persons in equivalent or similar positions

The FATF Recommendations are important in interpretation and understanding of CRS and, therefore, MDR.[3] The current FATF Recommendations on beneficial ownership of legal persons and legal arrangements are as follows:

> **24. Transparency and beneficial ownership of legal persons**
>
> Countries should take measures to prevent the misuse of legal persons for money laundering or terrorist financing. Countries should ensure that there is adequate, accurate and timely information on the beneficial ownership and control of legal persons that can be obtained or accessed in a timely fashion by competent authorities. In particular, countries that have legal persons that are able to issue bearer shares or bearer share warrants, or which allow nominee shareholders or nominee directors, should take effective measures to ensure that they are not misused for money laundering or terrorist financing. Countries should consider measures to facilitate access to beneficial ownership and control information by financial institutions and DNFBPs[4] undertaking the requirements set out in Recommendations 10 and 22.
>
> **25. Transparency and beneficial ownership of legal arrangements**
>
> Countries should take measures to prevent the misuse of legal arrangements for money laundering or terrorist financing. In particular, countries should ensure that there is adequate, accurate and timely information on express trusts, including information on the settlor, trustee and beneficiaries, that can be obtained or accessed in a timely fashion by competent authorities. Countries should consider measures to facilitate access to beneficial ownership and control information by financial institutions and DNFBPs undertaking the requirements set out in Recommendations 10 and 22.

Recommendations 10 and 22 address customer due diligence procedures. It is the interpretive notes to Recommnedation 10 that – perhaps – provide the clearest indication as to what is meant by 'beneficial ownership' within the FATF Recommnedations. In this respect, the interpretive notes say:

> In this context, financial institutions should be required to:

[3] They can be found here: www.fatf-gafi.org/publications/fatfrecommendations/documents/fatf-recommendations.html.

[4] This stands for 'Designated Non-Financial Business or Profession'.

...

(b) Identify the beneficial owners of the customer and take reasonable measures[33] to verify the identity of such persons, through the following information:

(i) For legal persons

(i.i)[34] The identity of the natural persons (if any – as ownership interests can be so diversified that there are no natural persons (whether acting alone or together) exercising control of the legal person or arrangement through ownership) who ultimately have a controlling ownership interest[35] in a legal person; and

(i.ii) to the extent that there is doubt under (i.i) as to whether the person(s) with the controlling ownership interest are the beneficial owner(s) or where no natural person exerts control through ownership interests, the identity of the natural persons (if any) exercising control of the legal person or arrangement through other means.

(i.iii) Where no natural person is identified under (i.i) or (i.ii) above, financial institutions should identify and take reasonable measures to verify the identity of the relevant natural person who holds the position of senior managing official.

(ii) For legal arrangements:

(ii.i) Trusts – the identity of the settlor, the trustee(s), the protector (if any), the beneficiaries or class of beneficiaries[36], and any other natural person exercising ultimate effective control over the trust (including through a chain of control/ownership);

(ii.ii) Other types of legal arrangements – the identity of persons in equivalent or similar positions.

Footnotes

[33] Where the customer or the owner of the controlling interest is a company listed on a stock exchange and subject to disclosure requirements (either by stock exchange rules or throughlaw or enforceable means) which impose requirements to ensure adequate transparency of beneficial ownership, or is a majority-owned subsidiary of such a company, it is not necessary to identify and verify the identity of any shareholder or beneficial owner of such companies.

The relevant identification data may be obtained from a public register, from the customer or from other reliable sources.

[34] Measures (i.i) to (i.iii) are not alternative options, but are cascading measures, with each to be used where the previous measure has been applied without identifying a beneficial owner.

[35] A controlling ownership interest depends on the ownership structure of the company. It may be based on a threshold, e.g. any person owning more than a certain percentage of the company (e.g. 25%).

[36] For beneficiary(ies) of trusts that are designated by characteristics or by class, financial institutions should obtain sufficient information concerning the beneficiary to satisfy the financial institution that it will be able to establish the identity of the beneficiary at the time of the payout or when the beneficiary intends to exercise vested rights

In the context of the MDR, this is not as helpful as it might be. As can be seen from footnote 36, there is no need – within the FATF Recommendation – to be able to identify every beneficiary of a trust, provided there is confidence that there will be sufficient information to verify an identity when the trustee transfers assets to the beneficiary in question, or there is an exercise of vested rights. On this basis, therefore, it can clearly be argued that a discretionary trust does not constitute – simply by means of all the beneficiaries not being identifiable at the time of the exercise – a Passive Offshore Vehicle.

MDR does not include a definition of 'person', instead adopting a definition of 'Legal Persons' in Rule 1.4, which provides:

> 'Legal Person' means any entity and can include a company, body corporate, foundation, anstalt, partnership, association and other relevantly similar entity, but does not include a natural person

The lack of a definition of 'person' puts the MDR regime in contradistinction to DAC6. While the former is, perhaps, frustrating, of potentially greater difficulty is the lack of consistency across two regimes designed to be aligned. This is, perhaps, a concern that is more theoretical than realistic, since 'legal person' is largely only used in the definition of an Opaque Offshore Structure and many CRS definitions are in fact incorporated by reference. It is, however, worth being aware of this mismatch and the potential it may have to generate further uncertainty.

'Legal Arrangements' are also defined in Rule 1.4, which provides:

> 'Legal Arrangement' means an express trust or other similar legal arrangement, such as fiducie, treuhand and fideicomiso

Again, the approach of defining trusts as distinct from other entities such as companies, marks a departure from the definition used in the Model DTA (where a 'person' includes a 'body of persons'). While both the terms 'legal person' and 'legal arrangement' are used in the CRS, they are not defined. MDR is therefore, in this respect, likely to be an improvement in general terms.

Rule 1.4 defines 'Structure', providing:

> 'Structure' means an Arrangement concerning the direct or indirect ownership or control of a person or asset

'Partner Jurisdiction' is defined (again in Rule 1.4) as:

> 'Partner Jurisdiction' means a jurisdiction:
>
> (i) that has introduced rules that are substantially similar to those set out in this legislation; and
> (ii) that, with respect to the particular CRS Avoidance Arrangement or Opaque Offshore Structure, has international exchange of information instruments in effect with all jurisdictions of residence of the Reportable Taxpayer

This raises the question of what is meant by rules that are 'substantially similar', particularly where jurisdictions have significantly departed from the OECD MDR format (for example, Argentina and Norway. Canada also has mandatory disclosure rules, but which bear little or no resemblance to the MDR). This is likely to be a matter of fact (the 'facts' of the scope of the regimes in question) in each case.

Finally, Rule 1.4 defines 'Reportable Taxpayer', providing:

> 'Reportable Taxpayer' means, in respect of a CRS Avoidance Arrangement, actual or potential user of that Arrangement and, in respect of an Opaque Offshore Structure, a natural person whose identity as a Beneficial Owner cannot be accurately determined due to the Opaque Offshore Structure

In common with DAC6, the definition of Reportable Taxpayer makes no reference to a specific definition of 'taxpayer'. From the context, it is clear that one need not in fact pay, or be required or potentially required to pay tax to be a 'Reportable Taxpayer'. While this is, we suggest, tolerably clear from the terms of Rule 1.4, we also argue it is unhelpful to use the expression 'Taxpayer' when the MDR regime is, in fact, wholly divorced from whether any tax is paid or properly payable.[5]

10.6 CRS avoidance arrangement

The first relevant piece of terminology is 'CRS Avoidance Arrangement'[6]. This is one of the two elements which are reportable under MDR. The MDR, Rule 1.1 provides:

---

[5] It is possible that this is an attempt to future proof the Model rules in the event that they are extended in line with BEPS 12 in the future.

[6] It is to some extent misleading to refer to the definition of CRS Avoidance Arrangement as being part of the relevant 'terminology'. This is because it – together with the definition of 'Opaque Offshore Structure' – contains most of the substantive 'law' in the MDR. The things that are offensive to, and ultimately reportable under, the MDR are contained in these two definitions. Much of the remainder of MDR is merely procedural 'window dressing'. While this

A 'CRS Avoidance Arrangement' is any Arrangement for which it is reasonable to conclude that it is designed to circumvent or is marketed as, or has the effect of, circumventing CRS Legislation or exploiting an absence thereof, including through:

(a) the use of an account, product or investment that is not, or purports not to be, a Financial Account, but has features that are substantially similar to those of a Financial Account;
(b) the transfer of a Financial Account, or the monies and/or Financial Assets held in a Financial Account to a Financial Institution that is not a Reporting Financial Institution or to a jurisdiction that does not exchange CRS information with all jurisdictions of tax residence of a Reportable Taxpayer;
(c) the conversion or transfer of a Financial Account, or the monies and/or Financial Assets held in a Financial Account, to a Financial Account that is not a Reportable Account;
(d) the conversion of a Financial Institution into a Financial Institution that is not a Reporting Financial Institution or into a Financial Institution that is resident in a jurisdiction that does not exchange CRS information with all jurisdictions of tax residence of a Reportable Taxpayer;
(e) undermining or exploiting weaknesses in the due diligence procedures used by Financial Institutions to correctly identify:
    (i) an Account Holder and/or Controlling Person; or
    (ii) all the jurisdictions of tax residence of an Account Holder and/or Controlling Person;
(f) allowing, or purporting to allow:
    (i) an Entity to qualify as an Active NFE;
    (ii) an investment to be made through an Entity without triggering a reporting obligation under the CRS Legislation; or
    (iii) a person to avoid being treated as a Controlling Person; or
(g) classifying a payment made for the benefit of an Account Holder or Controlling Person as a payment that is not reportable under CRS Legislation;

where it is reasonable to conclude that such Arrangement is designed to circumvent or is marketed as, or has the effect of, circumventing CRS Legislation or exploiting an absence thereof.

For the purposes of this Rule 1.1, an Arrangement is not considered to have the effect of circumventing CRS Legislation solely because it results in non-reporting under the relevant CRS Legislation,

---

is, of course, important, it does not go to the heart of what the MDR is about. However, provided that it is understood that the MDR is about these two 'terms', the choice of structure, while perhaps unusual, is not problematic.

> provided that it is reasonable to conclude that such non-reporting does not undermine the policy intent of such CRS Legislation

Thus does simplicity of MDR come to an abrupt end! To understand the term 'CRS Avoidance Arrangement', it is necessary to understand a multitude of other definitions.

Many of the other terms used in the definition of CRS Avoidance Arrangement are terms from CRS itself. Analysis of these can be found in the Chapter on CRS (Rule 1.4 provides 'Capitalised terms that are not otherwise defined shall have the meanings given to them under the relevant CRS Legislation').

With that in mind, it is necessary to consider the Commentary and the legislation that has been enacted into the domestic law of some jurisdictions. In relation to the Commentary, while 'hallmark' is not used in the actual rules, it is used in the Commentary. The Commentary on Rule 1.1 starts by stating:

> Rule 1.1 provides a general description of the core features of CRS Avoidance Arrangements (the generic hallmark) and then provides examples of specific Arrangements that fall within this general description (specific hallmarks). This approach is designed to ensure that the hallmarks capture known CRS Avoidance Arrangements while retaining the flexibility to cover as yet unidentified Arrangements that may pose risks to the integrity of the CRS

While it is understandably desirable to include '… the flexibility to cover as yet unidentified Arrangements that may pose risks to the integrity of the CRS …' this does carry all the difficulties inherent in attempting to define something that is not known. This therefore leaves such a definition open to an overly broad interpretation – in the hope of identifying those 'unidentified Arrangements', which could not be identified at the time of drafting. The exercise becomes hopelessly circular. Unfortunately, the Commentary does not give any indication of how to deal with this dilemma; thus, one must do the best one can, by applying the relevant domestic principles of interpretation to the domestic legislation in question.

The Commentary continues by saying:

> The generic test covers Arrangements with features that take the Arrangement outside the scope of CRS reporting (de jure avoidance Arrangements) as well as Arrangements that while not legally removing a CRS disclosure obligation as a practical matter may avoid CRS reporting or result in the reporting of inaccurate or incomplete CRS information to the jurisdiction of residence of the user of that Arrangement

Again, this does nothing to help one define the scope of a CRS Avoidance Arrangement and indeed potentially it broadens it further (which, as is often the case, makes the definition more difficult to apply): extending from those things which 'legally' avoid CRS, to include those that 'as a practical matter **may'** avoid CRS reporting. Is it thus a requirement also to report things that may avoid CRS reporting? This is hopelessly muddled for the practitioner hoping to apply the domestic CRS regime. There is – as far as the authors are concerned – no satisfactory answer to this. It will be necessary to consider each arrangement in turn and 'feel out' whether or not the Arrangement comes within the meaning of the domestic legislation. That is not satisfactory, but until there is better guidance and case law, it is the best that we can do.

The Commentary continues by considering the meaning of '…designed to, marketed as or has the effect of …', saying:

> An Arrangement will fall within the scope of the generic hallmark if that Arrangement actually has the effect of circumventing CRS Legislation or if it is designed to have, or is marketed as having, that effect. This means that the generic hallmark covers both schemes that are or can be used to avoid or frustrate the legal requirements of the applicable CRS Legislation, as well as those based on a misinterpretation or misapplication of that legislation. An Arrangement should be treated as 'designed to' circumvent CRS Legislation if it is reasonable to conclude that it has been put in place deliberately to facilitate a non-reporting outcome. An Arrangement should be treated as 'marketed' as a CRS Avoidance Arrangement if the benefit of non-reporting under the CRS is used to promote or sell the Arrangement to a potential Client or customer. The term 'marketed' does not include providing a legal opinion to a Client on whether an existing or proposed Arrangement is subject to CRS reporting (or on the way in which an Arrangement should be reported under the CRS). It would, however, include any subsequent use of that opinion to sell an investment or investment structure based on its CRS treatment.

Thus it is clear that there are three different bases on which the Arrangement may fall within scope:

(i) Actually circumvents reporting;
(ii) Is designed to circumvent reporting; or
(iii) Is marketed as circumventing reporting.

Thus, it is important to emphasise to clients that – if they are in a relevant jurisdiction – and they are being sold something to avoid reporting, then the very fact that they are having it sold to them on that basis, may in itself be sufficient to bring them within an MDR regime. The Commentary then goes on to discuss what will not constitute a CRS Avoidance Arrangement:

> The simple fact that an Arrangement has the effect of non-reporting is not sufficient for it to be considered to have the effect of

> circumventing CRS Legislation. This will only be the case where it is reasonable to conclude that the Arrangement undermines the intended policy of the CRS Legislation. The mandatory disclosure rules are not intended to second guess clear policy choices that were made in the design of the CRS. For instance, real estate is an asset class that is not within the intended scope of the CRS. As a result, an Arrangement to withdraw funds from a reportable Depository Account to purchase an apartment will not constitute a CRS Avoidance Arrangement despite the fact that the Arrangement results in non-reporting of the funds that are used for the purchase. Similarly, the CRS expressly provides for categories of Excluded Accounts and Non-Reporting Financial Institutions that are excluded from reporting to minimise compliance burdens and because, on balance, they do not pose a substantial risk of non-compliance. Accordingly, a transfer of funds from a reportable Depository Account into a pension product that qualifies as an Excluded Account, will, in normal circumstances, not be considered to have the effect of circumventing CRS Legislation. However, the marketing of a scheme that makes use of such an exclusion in ways that undermine the policy rationale for providing that exclusion would be considered a CRS Avoidance Arrangement. An Arrangement does not have the effect of circumventing CRS Legislation if the Financial Account(s) information is exchanged under a FATCA Model 1A Intergovernmental Agreement with the jurisdiction(s) of tax residence of the Reportable Taxpayer. For example, if a Reportable Taxpayer that is tax resident in jurisdiction X transfers a Financial Account to the United States, that transfer would not have the effect of circumventing CRS Legislation, provided the account information is exchanged by the Competent Authority of the United States with jurisdiction X

This is an important indication of the boundaries of a CRS Avoidance Arrangement. The key points appear to be that:

(i) The effect of non-reporting is not sufficient in and of itself in order to render an Arrangement a CRS Avoidance Arrangement, because the regime is not intended to second-guess clear policy choices that were made in the design of the CRS;

(ii) This means that an Arrangement to withdraw funds from a reportable Depository Account to purchase real estate does not constitute a CRS Avoidance Arrangement, despite the fact that the Arrangement results in non-reporting of the funds used for the purchase;

(iii) Similarly, a transfer of funds from a reportable Depository Account into a pension product that qualifies as an Excluded Account, will not usually be a CRS Avoidance Arrangement; and

(iv) An Arrangement does not have the effect of circumventing CRS Legislation if the Financial Account information is exchanged under a

FATCA Model 1A Intergovernmental Agreement with the jurisdiction of tax residence of the Reportable Taxpayer.

(v) The last point is, perhaps, the most controversial, whilst also being of significance. When will this part of the Commentary apply? This is not necessarily straightforward. There must be a FATCA Model 1A agreement in place under which information is exchanged. A FATCA Model 1A Agreement is a Model 1 Agreement under which there is reciprocal exchange of information, i.e. the USA [US?]. is required to provide information to the other party as well as the flow of information from the other party to the USA. The UK, as well as many other jurisdictions, has a Model 1A Agreement. So to use the UK for illustration, the Commentary example should be the following: a Reportable Taxpayer that is tax resident in the UK transfers a Financial Account to the United States, that transfer would not have the effect of circumventing CRS Legislation, provided the account information is exchanged by the Competent Authority of the United States with the UK (which it should be under the Model 1A Agreement).

However, this is not so straightforward in relation to the UK. HMRC say[7]:

> Arrangements will be caught by hallmark D(1) if they have the effect of undermining or circumventing reporting obligations under DAC2 or equivalent agreements on the automatic exchange of financial account information, or which take advantage of the absence of AEOI. This includes reporting obligations under the Common Reporting Standard (CRS). **The UK's agreement with the United States to implement the Foreign Account Tax Compliance Act (FATCA is not an equivalent agreement since it does not provide for the same reciprocal level of reporting as DAC2 and the CRS**. Therefore, an arrangement which seeks to avoid reporting under FATCA would not be reportable under these regulations
>
> (Emphasis added).

However, this appears to be at odds with what is stated earlier[8]:

> Hallmarks under category D share substantial common ground with the Mandatory Disclosure Rules (MDR) developed by the OECD. Whilst DAC 6 and the MDR are separate instruments and there are some different rules, for example around the period for which reports are required prior to the rules entering into force, the preamble to DAC 6 makes clear that the MDR, and the guidance and commentary which accompany those rules, are a source of illustration and interpretation for hallmarks under Category D of DAC 6. **Accordingly, where Hallmark D and the MDR cover**

---

[7] See IEIM645010

[8] See IEIM645000

> **similar ground, HMRC will interpret Hallmark D in line with the MDR**
>
> (Emphasis added).

To interpret a FATCA Model 1A Agreement as not being equivalent to CRS is not in accordance with the MDR Commentary, which is in turn, potentially inconsistent with HMRC's own Guidance. HMRC gives no further explanation and it appears unlikely – if the UK abandons Hallmark D of DAC6 in favour of more MDR-focussed rules – that this will be clarified. However, there is a clear argument for a FATCA Model 1A Agreement being considered equivalent.

The Commentary then turns to consider the 'reasonable to conclude' test, saying:

> 6. The test of 'reasonable to conclude' is to be determined from an objective standpoint by reference to all the facts and circumstances and without reference to the subjective intention of the persons involved. Thus the test will be satisfied where a reasonable person in the position of a professional adviser with a full understanding of the terms and consequences of the Arrangement and the circumstances in which it is designed, marketed and used, would come to this conclusion.

The aim of this is to give the test an objective standpoint. Since the test is, in part, one of the purposes of the design of the Arrangements, this is to provide an objective take on a subjective position; however, this is a concept familiar to anyone with experience of the UK GAAR. Thus the test should be applied by standing in the shoes of the reasonable professional observer with a full understanding of the Arrangement, and determining what such a professional adviser would conclude.

The definition of CRS Avoidance Arrangement then goes on to set out several categories of Arrangements that will be 'included' within the definition of a CRS Avoidance Arrangement. The use of 'included' indicates that this list is not exclusive: other things will also be within the definition; this is in accordance with the intention to conclude as-yet unidentified arrangements within the CRS Avoidance Arrangement. These are the following.

(i) First, the use of an account, product or investment that is not, or purports not to be, a Financial Account, but has features that are substantially similar to those of a Financial Account. In this respect, the Commentary says:

> The first specific hallmark covers the use of a financial product that provides the investor with the core functionality of a Financial Account, but which includes features that take it outside the definition of a 'Financial Account' for CRS purposes.

> This specific hallmark could cover, for instance, the use of certain types of e-money[9] as a substitute for a Depository Account, or the issuance of certain types of derivative contracts by Financial Institutions that are out of scope of CRS Legislation, but replicate underlying financial assets covered by such legislation. The hallmark refers to the 'use' of such a product and would therefore cover the offering of such products, as well as Arrangements to transfer funds into such an investment

No mention is made of which derivative contracts are likely to meet this description. The CRS Commentary also appears to contain no information on this particular aspect of the scope of CRS. Presumably such derivative contracts (given derivatives are included in 'money market instruments' of Depository Account and Investment Entity in the CRS).

(ii) Second, the transfer of a Financial Account, or the monies and/or Financial Assets held in a Financial Account to a Financial Institution that is not a Reporting Financial Institution or to a jurisdiction that does not exchange CRS information with all jurisdictions of tax residence of a Reportable Taxpayer.

(iii) Third, the conversion or transfer of a Financial Account, or the monies and/or Financial Assets held in a Financial Account, to a Financial Account that is not a Reportable Account.

(iv) Fourth, the conversion of a Financial Institution into a Financial Institution that is not a Reporting Financial Institution or into a Financial Institution that is resident in a jurisdiction that does not exchange CRS information with all jurisdictions of tax residence of a Reportable Taxpayer

(v) In this respect, the Commentary deals with these hallmarks together. It says:

> The second to fourth specific hallmarks in the model rules cover Arrangements that shift money or Financial Assets to Financial Institutions, or accounts that are not subject to CRS reporting.
>
> Unlike the first hallmark which focuses on the specific features of the product that take it outside the legal scope of the CRS Legislation, **these hallmarks look to the jurisdiction where the financial product is offered and the domestic exemptions from reporting within that jurisdiction to identify Arrangements that give rise to CRS avoidance risks**. These hallmarks would include **moving**

---

[9] The European Central Bank describes 'e-money' as 'an electronic store of monetary value on a technical device that may be widely used for making payments to entities other than the e-money issuer. The device acts as a prepaid bearer instrument which does not necessarily involve bank accounts in transactions'

money to a Financial Institution in a jurisdiction that has not implemented the CRS or that is **not exchanging CRS information with the taxpayer's jurisdiction of residence for tax purposes**; as well as **certain transfers of funds to a non-reportable account of a Financial Institution in a Participating Jurisdiction or strategies such as dividing the amounts held in a Financial Account to remain under the USD 250,000 threshold for CRS reporting** (Emphasis added).

(vi) Again, the Commentary clearly favours a broad approach to the interpretation of these factors. In doing so, it raises several important points. To apply these elements of the definition, it is necessary to have a reasonably detailed background understanding of CRS, not only provisions in the CRS itself but also the domestic provisions of the jurisdictions in question. In addition it is necessary to have knowledge of, or access to the activated exchange relationships. This can be found on the OECD website[10] but it will be necessary to check this when determining whether there is a CRS Avoidance Arrangement.

(vii) The Commentary goes on to state:

> These specific hallmarks apply to transfers of money or Financial Assets and include those cases where there is a change in the investment structure that has the effect of taking the Financial Account outside the framework of CRS reporting. The hallmarks set a bright-line test that focuses on known risks which can be tested at a single point in time (i.e. the time of transfer or conversion), making it easier for Intermediaries such as investment managers to develop appropriate compliance procedures.

(viii) This is acurate, to the extent that there is more for a bright-line test here than in relation to the general, introductory part of the definition and the Arrangements described in Rule 1.1(a).

(ix) Fifthly, undermining or exploiting weaknesses in the due diligence procedures used by Financial Institutions to correctly identify: an Account Holder and/or Controlling Person; or all the jurisdictions of tax residence of an Account Holder and/or Controlling Person.

The Commentary describes the purpose behind this 'hallmark' as follows:

> The fifth specific hallmark targets Arrangements that **undermine or exploit weaknesses in the due diligence procedures used by Financial Institutions to collect CRS information on an Account Holder and the Controlling Persons of a Passive NFE.**

---

[10] www.oecd.org/tax/automatic-exchange/international-framework-for-the-crs/exchange-relationships/

> Arrangements undermining the effectiveness of due diligence procedures are those that **frustrate the intended outcomes of those procedures (such as the misuse of residence certificates** as described in the Commentary to Rule 1.1(e)(ii) below). Arrangements exploiting weakness in due diligence procedures include those **Arrangements that rely on the absence or inadequate implementation of such due diligence procedures, for example by taking advantage of weak implementation of the latest FATF Recommendations**[11], which are currently those of February 2012. This hallmark would cover the use of **Structures that do not allow the accurate determination of the identity of Account Holder and the Controlling Persons and that rely on the creation of indicia or documentary evidence to mislead a financial institution about the actual jurisdiction(s) of residence of an Account Holder in order to facilitate inaccurate or incomplete reporting under the CRS**
>
> (Emphasis added).

In relation to the last of these, presumably this would also – in many jurisdictions – constitute fraud. But that is not the point; it appears to be the case that anti-avoidance (and evasion) regimes work as much by deterrent (i.e. that by stating what is undesirable, many people will simply not do it) as providing a suitable regime of penalties and accountability for general categories of undesirable behaviour.

The Commentary then goes on to give guidance as to the types of Arrangements that might fall within each of the two sub-categories. In relation to Arrangements preventing accurate identification of Account Holders or Controlling Persons, it says:

> This sub-paragraph covers those cases where it is reasonable to conclude an Arrangement, such as an asset holding Structure, does not allow the accurate identification of the underlying Beneficial Owners in a way that it has the effect of frustrating the application of the due diligence procedures under the CRS. It should be noted that, in the simplest and commonly used Structures, the due diligence procedures applied by Financial Institutions will generally be sufficient to identify the Account Holders and Controlling Persons. For example:
>
> - a bank that opens an account for a trust with foreign beneficiaries could be expected to request a copy of the trust deed which should identify the beneficiaries (and other beneficial owners of the trust) named in the deed; and

[11] The FATF Recommendations are important in interpretation and understanding of CRS and, therefore, MDR. They can be found here: www.fatf-gafi.org/publications/fatfrecommendations/documents/fatf-recommendations.html

- a share broker that maintains a share trading account for an offshore entity can be expected to require that entity to provide information on its shareholders or other evidence that the entity is a Financial Institution or Active NFE.

These types of simple Structures will, on their own, not fall within the specific hallmark in Rule 1.1(e)(i) unless they contained features that would lead a reasonable person to conclude that the Arrangement, as a whole, would have the effect of undermining the due diligence procedures applied by Financial Institutions under the applicable CRS Legislation. For example, this could include an Arrangement designed to mislead a Financial Institution at account opening about the real discretionary beneficiaries of a trust, by appointing a charity as sole discretionary beneficiary at account opening and replacing the charity by the real intended discretionary beneficiaries after account opening without informing the Financial Institution

This seems uncontroversial, if not particularly illuminating of the 'hallmark' generally. In relation to Arrangements preventing accurate determination of the residency of Account Holders and Controlling Persons, the Commentary says:

> Sub-paragraph (ii) of this hallmark applies to Arrangements that can be used to avoid accurate and comprehensive reporting of CRS information to the jurisdiction of tax residence of the Account Holder or Controlling Person. This hallmark would, for instance, **apply to a person promoting the use of a tax residence certificate as a method of facilitating the avoidance of the CRS**.
>
> A number of jurisdictions offer tax incentives to individuals to encourage them to take up tax residence in that jurisdiction. **These incentives may involve temporary or permanent exemptions from tax on foreign source income and obtaining such tax residency may only require the resident to have a minimal presence in that jurisdiction. A person who is tax resident in more than one jurisdiction may use such a certificate to not declare the fact that he or she is a tax resident in another jurisdiction. Presenting such a certificate to a Financial Institution as proof of residence in order to undermine the Financial Institution's due diligence procedures would fall within the specific hallmark in Rule 1.1(e)(ii) as an Arrangement for which it is reasonable to conclude that it has the effect of undermining or exploiting weaknesses in, the due diligence procedures used by Financial Institutions** to correctly identify all the jurisdictions of tax residence of an Account Holder and/or Controlling Person.
>
> (Emphasis ours).

Again, it seems unlikely that that the additional punishment potentially available under enactments of the MDR would be the most effective deterrent against someone declaring that they have a single tax residence, in the full knowledge that they have two. However, it may serve as an effective reminder to Financial Institutions to ensure that they have sufficient procedures in place to ensure that they cannot be easily fooled by such an approach.

(x) Sixthly, allowing, or purporting to allow: an Entity to qualify as an Active NFE; an investment to be made through an Entity without triggering a reporting obligation under the CRS Legislation; or a person to avoid being treated as a Controlling Person. In this respect, the Commentary says:

> The sixth specific hallmark addresses Arrangements that take advantage of the fact that an Active NFE is not subject to disclosure or reporting obligations with respect to its Controlling Persons under the CRS and targets Arrangements involving the use of a Passive NFE that are designed to circumvent the requirement to disclose Controlling Persons. The model rules in Rule 1.1(f) focus on three areas of known risk:
>
> - the marketing of a company that purports to qualify automatically for Active NFE status in its jurisdiction of incorporation;
> - back-to-back investment Arrangements made through an NFE that are intended to prevent an investor from having to reveal their identity under the CRS; and
> - investments in a passive NFE that are structured in such a way as to prevent the investor falling within the definition of a Controlling Person under the CRS.

The final element of the hallmark would also cover a plan to switch from a trust to a company as an investment vehicle in order to avoid reporting of the trust's discretionary beneficiaries as Controlling Persons.

> 20. The hallmark uses the relevant definitions in the CRS Legislation to accurately target these risks without specifying the particular technique used to achieve them. The mere fact, however, that an Entity qualified as an 'Active NFE' under the CRS or that a person had a financial investment in an Active or Passive NFE would not bring the Arrangement within the scope of this hallmark **unless the transactions contain an element that is designed to qualify the Entity as an Active NFE for CRS purposes or the way the investment in the NFE was structured would lead a reasonable person to believe that the Arrangement had been expected to have the effect of undermining the CRS due diligence procedures**

(Emphasis ours).

Thus there are – according to the Commentary – four separate key risks targeted here: companies marketed as automatically being Active NFEs[12]: back-to-back investment arrangements that obscure the real identity of the investor; passive NFE investments that prevent the disclosure of the identity of the real owner by preventing them from falling within the definition of Controlling Person; and Arrangements involving a switch from a trust to a company as an investment vehicle, in order to avoid reporting on discretionary beneficiaries as the Controlling Persons. In relation to the latter, it is not clear how such Arrangements would be intended to work – again – unless there is some element of unreality. If all discretionary beneficiaries are potentially able to benefit from the investment, they would need to be shareholders.

Thus, where such beneficiaries could benefit without being shareholders, it seems probable that several breaches of duty would need to occur in order to benefit them. Such Arrangements are likely to be fraught with issues beyond those of the MDR.

(xi) Finally, classifying a payment made for the benefit of an Account Holder or Controlling Person as a payment that is not reportable under CRS Legislation. The Commentary on this point is mercifully brief, saying:

The final specific hallmark relates to Arrangements that classify a payment to an Account Holder or Controlling Person into one that is not reportable under the CRS. The model rules cover Arrangements that purport to 'classify' a payment as non-reportable even where that Arrangement has no legal effect, and include the additional precision that the payment must be to or 'for the benefit of' an Account Holder or Controlling Person. This hallmark could for instance pick up a trust that pays the bills on behalf of a beneficiary or crediting amounts to a pre-paid debit or credit card

10.7 CRS avoidance arrangements: individual jurisdiction approaches

While several jurisdictions have – or are in the process – of adopting MDR, unfortunately there remains little in the way of domestic legislation and guidance to address. The uptake of MDR to date – outside of the EU – has not been extensive (likely and largely due to their current optional nature). One such jurisdiction is Guernsey. Its rules are the Income Tax (Approved International Agreements) (Implementation) (Mandatory Disclosure Rules)

---

[12] Is it possible automatically to qualify as an Active NFE, which surely requires a consideration of the factual situation of the company in question? It could be said that this targets bad or unrealistic advice, which is a valid – and perhaps more understanding approach to preventing this type of avoidance by the average taxpayer. However, if this is the intention of the legislation, why not state it explicitly?

Regulations 2020 (the 'Guernsey MDR'). Regulation 2 gives the definition of CRS Avoidance Arrangement, providing:

> (1) A 'CRS avoidance arrangement' is any arrangement which, it is reasonable to conclude, is designed to circumvent or is marketed as, or has the effect of, circumventing the CRS Regulations or exploiting an absence of or any omission or deficiency within an enactment implementing the CRS, mcluding through or by means of –
>
> (a) the use of an account, product or mvestanent that is not, or purports not to be, a financial account, but has features that are substantially similar to those of a financial account,
>
> (b) the transfer of a financial account, or the monies or financial assets held in a financial account –
>
> (i) to a financial institution that is not a reporting financial institution, or
>
> (ii) to a jurisdiction that does not exchange CRS information with all jurisdictions of tax residence of a reportable taxpayer,
>
> (c) the conversion or transfer of a financial account, or the monies and/or financial assets held in a financial account, to a financial account that is not a reportable account,
>
> (d) the conversion of a financial institution into –
>
> (i) a financial instihition that is not a reporting financial institution, or
>
> (ii) a financial institution that is resident in a jurisdiction that does not exchange CRS information with all jurisdictions of tax residence of a reportable taxpayer,
>
> (e) undermining or exploiting weaknesses in the due diligence procedures used by financial institutions correctly to identify –
>
> an account holder and/or controlling person,
>
> (ii) all the jurisdictions of tax residence of an account holder and/or controlling person,
>
> (f) allowing or purporting to allow –
>
> (i) an entity to qualify as an Active NFE,
>
> (ii) an investment to be made through an entity without triggering a reporting obligation under the CRS Regulations, or
>
> (iii) a person to avoid being treated as a controlling person, or
>
> (g) classifying a payment made for the benefit of an acconnt holder or controlling person as a payment that is not reportable under the CRS Regulations.
>
> (2) For the purposes of this regulation, an arrangement is not considered to have the effect of circumventing the CRS Regulations solely because it results in non-reporting under those Regulations, provided that it is reasonable to conclude

> that such non-reporting does not undermine the policy intent of the CRS Regulations

This is almost identical to the provision in the Model MDR. This is discussed in the Mandatory Disclosure Rules on CRS Avoidance and Offshore Structures Briefing Note (the 'Briefing Note') produced by the States of Guernsey Revenue Service[13]. This is, unfortunately, not particularly fulsome. In explaining why this is so, the Briefing Note acknowledges:

> Whilst the model rules also contain commentary which seeks to elaborate further on the defined terms, it is acknowledged that the Revenue Service will need to provide some Guidance Notes. It is intended that such guidance will, where possible, be aligned across the Crown Dependencies on a principles basis

The particular concern in Guernsey relates to the 'reasonable to conclude' test. In this respect, the Briefing Note says:

> One area in particular is the potential to provide further clarity for a Service Provider concerning the principles behind the 'Reasonable to Conclude' test within the MDR framework (to assist in the decision making process as to whether an arrangement or structure is disclosable). This would not be relevant for promoters (they would have actual knowledge that the arrangement or structure had been designed and marketed for these purposes). It is, therefore, intended to work with the other Crown Dependencies to determine whether joint guidance can be issued for Service Providers which may include the following examples...

There follow a number of examples of what will and will not constitute a CRS Avoidance Arrangement. It is instructive to consider these examples (even though they have not as yet been formally adopted by any jurisdiction). The first example is:

> **Scenario 1** – Exchange of CRS data between Guernsey and other jurisdictions:
>
> Where assets are being moved to or from Guernsey to a jurisdiction with which Guernsey has a relationship to exchange CRS data, then it is reasonable to conclude that this transfer of assets is not being made to circumvent CRS reporting

We agree that this analysis should be correct, though it is hardly surprising. The second example given is:

> **Scenario 2** - the cumulative value of funds in the arrangement is less than £10,000:

---

[13] This can be found at www.gov.gg/mdr

> The legal and administrative costs suggest it would be highly unlikely that this isolated arrangement was being undertaken to circumvent CRS reporting requirements. If, however, a client enters into multiple instances (of creating arrangements with a value of less than £10,000 then the Service Provider would need to treat that as one arrangement and disclose such arrangement.

In this scenario, we are less convinced that the Briefing Note's analysis will always be correct. The Commentary tells us that when we are applying the 'reasonable to conclude' test we need to ask what a reasonable person in the position of a professional adviser would conclude, with a full understanding of the terms and consequences of the Arrangement and the circumstances in which it is designed, marketed and used. Whilst there may well be circumstances where setting up a large number of Arrangements below the CRS threshold would draw the relevant reasonable professional to conclude that they – in their entirety – form part of a CRS Avoidance Arrangement, it is not clear that this would always be the case.

For example, while pilot trusts are no longer common, they may still occur; we are not aware that one of their common uses is to avoid CRS reporting requirements (though they may also have this effect). According to the Commentary, though, simply having the effect of avoiding CRS reporting is not sufficient to engage the definition of CRS Avoidance Arrangement.

Scenario 3 is as follows:

> **Scenario 3** - Certain asset types which are excluded from CRS reporting (for example, the holding of real estate):
>
> Certain asset types are not reported under the CRS (such as the holding of real estate). As such a client simply investing funds in these assets does not circumvent the policy intentions behind the CRS and therefore the 'reasonable to conclude' test would not be met. It is intended that the list of the type of assets not included in CRS reporting would be provided in further Guidance

Such a list would be immensely helpful! Otherwise this scenario is uncontroversial and appears to be in line with the Commentary (and indeed with a common sense application of the principles in question).

Jersey and the Isle of Man have also produced legislation for their own MDR regimes. The definition of 'CRS Avoidance Arrangement' in the Income Tax (Mandatory Disclosure Rules) Regulations 2019 ('IoM MDR') is largely similar to that in the MDR itself. Despite IoM MDR being approved by the Tynwald, the Isle of Man does not appear to have produced any guidance[14].

---

[14] We may be incorrect about this, but at time of going to print, we have been unable to find any such guidance. We are happy to learn of any official guidance which this edition fails to mention; please contact the authors via the email addresses provided in the front of the book.

The Jersey iteration of the MDR is the Taxation (Implementation) (International Tax Compliance) (Mandatory Disclosure Rules For CRS Avoidance Arrangements And Opaque Offshore Structures) (Jersey) Regulations 2020 ('Jersey MDR'). Again, its implementation of 'CRS Avoidance Arrangements' is both substantially and substantively similar to the MDR. This is unsurprising. Indeed, the Assembly Proposition in relation to Jersey MDR[15] explains:

> P.129/2019 explains that the intention is that the draft Regulations will be supplemented by further guidance to be published by the Comptroller of Revenue, which will provide guidance on the important 'reasonable to conclude' decision that industry will need to make when deciding whether or not to report specific Arrangements or Structures.
>
> In developing the draft Regulations, the Government of Jersey has worked closely with the Governments of other Crown Dependencies (Guernsey and the Isle of Man) with the aim of providing consistency across the Islands to benefit those operating across jurisdictions…

This also draws attention to Jersey MDR, Regulation 4, which provides:

> **Power to issue guidance on determining 'reasonable to conclude'**
>
> (1) For the purposes of Regulations 2 and 3, the Comptroller may issue guidance on how to determine the expression 'reasonable to conclude'.
> (2) Regard must be had to any guidance issued under this Regulation.
> (3) The Comptroller may issue revised guidance, from time to time, and a reference to guidance in this Regulation includes a reference to revised guidance.
> (4) Guidance issued under this Regulation must be published by the Comptroller in a manner which the Comptroller considers will bring it to the attention of those most likely to be affected by it.

This is an interesting provision. Since Regulation 4(2) provides that regard ***must*** be had to the guidance from the Comptroller,[16] this is arguably akin to giving the tax authority power to legislate. This is a concerning devolution of power. No such guidance appears to have been published yet so it remains, at present, moot. Binding guidance may be an area that is ripe for judicial review in the future.

Turning to the Isle of Man, the Income Tax (Mandatory Disclosure) Regulations 2019 ('IoM MDR') also defines 'CRS Avoidance Arrangement'

---

[15] This can be found here: statesassembly.gov.je/assemblypropositions/2019/p.129-2019com.pdf

[16] 'Comptroller' means the Comptroller of Revenue within the meaning of the Revenue Administration (Jersey) Law 2019 – this is, effectively, the head of Revenue Jersey, Jersey's tax authority.

in a substantively similar way to the MDR itself. There appears – as of yet – to be no guidance from the Isle of Man. Consequently, as with the other jurisdictions mentioned, the Commentary is likely to be of significant note when interpreting the IoM MDR.

10.8 Opaque offshore structure

The second key description in the 'definitions' section is that of 'Opaque Offshore Structure'. This is found in MDR, Rule 1.2. This provides:

> An Opaque Offshore Structure means a Passive Offshore Vehicle that is held through an Opaque Structure

The introduction to the Commentary on Opaque Offshore Structures is particularly helpful in relation to the purpose of this 'hallmark'. It says:

> 25. Rule 1.2 sets out a hallmark for an Opaque Offshore Structure. This hallmark includes specific examples of Opaque Ownership Structures such as the use of nominee shareholders, indirect control Arrangements or Arrangements that provide a person with access to assets held by, or income derived from, the offshore vehicle, without being identified as the Beneficial Owner.
>
> 26. The hallmark **supplements the specific hallmark for CRS Avoidance Arrangements by specifically identifying those features of offshore Structures that do not allow the accurate determination of the identity of the Beneficial Owner**. As this hallmark **does not build on the notion of CRS avoidance, it also covers Structures that hold assets other than Financial Accounts, i.e. those not reportable under the CRS (e.g. real estate)**. In general terms, a Passive Offshore Vehicle will fall within the scope of this hallmark **where the ownership of that vehicle has been structured so as to not allow the accurate determination of the identity of natural person(s) with ultimate effective control over that vehicle**.
>
> (Emphasis ours)

The authors' view is that several clear policy intentions are shown in these paragraphs:

(i) The Opaque Offshore Structure 'hallmark' is designed as being supplementary to the CRS Avoidance Structure 'hallmark' and as such could be considered as a 'sweep-up' (though it does go beyond this) of matters which should be, but may not be, caught by the wide meaning given to CRS Avoidance Structure;

(ii) Its primary purpose is to identify structures that obscure ultimate beneficial ownership; and

(iii) This extends beyond structures that would merely constitute CRS Avoidance Arrangements, to include any Structure that is obscuring beneficial ownership. This means one must be careful, because such

> Structures will be caught even where the underlying property is exempt or outside the scope of CRS. It is not clear why it is considered necessary to do so (other than on general policy grounds), however, it is important to remember that, because of this 'hallmark', the MDR extends beyond those things simply preventing the proper application of CRS.

Other terms are used in the opening part of Rule 1.2, which are also necessary to understand. Rule 1.2 also provides the definition of a 'Passive Offshore Vehicle' and 'Opaque Structure'. In relation to the former, it provides:

> Subject to paragraph (c) below, a 'Passive Offshore Vehicle' means a Legal Person or Legal Arrangement that does not carry on a substantive economic activity supported by adequate staff, equipment, assets and premises in the jurisdiction where it is established or is tax resident.
>
> (c) A Passive Offshore Vehicle does not include a Legal Person or Legal Arrangement
> (i) that is an Institutional Investor or that is wholly-owned by one or more Institutional Investors or
> (ii) where all Beneficial Owners of that Legal Person or Legal Arrangement are only resident for tax purposes in the jurisdiction of incorporation, residence, management, control and establishment (as applicable) of the Legal Person or Legal Arrangement.

In this respect, the Commentary says:

> ... A combination of these four elements *[staff, equipment, assets and premises]* must be directly connected to the activities of the entity itself and not another party in order for an offshore vehicle to be treated as active (and therefore outside the scope of hallmark) under this test. An offshore entity established in Jurisdiction A that invoices a related company for services supplied by a contractor in Jurisdiction B would be considered 'passive' under the definition in Rule 1.2(b). Such an entity would not employ any staff or own any equipment, assets or premises from which the substantive economic activity is carried on. The recruitment of staff, purchase of assets or equipment or the leasing of premises should not be treated as giving rise to a substantive economic activity if this has been done solely for the purposes of avoiding the definition of a Passive Offshore Vehicle

Thus, the Commentary deals with the fairly obvious avoidance route of simply outsourcing activities to another company. This would not, in our view, be sufficient in most circumstances to avoid being caught. There must be reality to the substantive economic activity, and it must really be the substantive economic activity of the entity in question.

Finally in this respect, the Commentary notes, somewhat tortuously, that if there is substantive economic activity, but that substantive economic activity is engaged in only for the purposes of falling outside the definition of being a Passive Offshore Vehicle, then this should not be counted as substantive economic activity. This is not borne out by the words of the MDR itself (or any of the domestic legislation based on the MDR that we have considered to date) consequently, to come to this conclusion in relation to domestic law, a very broad purposive interpretation must be applied (though this is likely to be the correct approach in relation to domestic law based on international provisions) and some considerable weight placed on the Commentary (again this may well be permissible in domestic law, though commentaries are not generally considered to be binding, at least in English law).

The Commentary continues, in relation to the meaning of Passive Offshore Vehicle:

> 29. A vehicle is 'offshore' if it is incorporated, resident, managed, controlled or established outside the jurisdiction of residence of its Beneficial Owners. The types of entities and arrangements that will be treated as wholly-domestic (and therefore outside the intended scope of this hallmark) would generally include a locally incorporated company held only by resident shareholders and the domestic family trust with resident beneficiaries, where the trustees and others with control over the trust are all resident in the same jurisdiction as the beneficiaries.
>
> 30. The definition of 'offshore' is drafted in such a way that if any Beneficial Owner is resident in a jurisdiction other than the jurisdiction where the vehicle is incorporated, resident, managed, controlled or established then that vehicle will be treated as offshore with respect to all its beneficial owners. This is to prevent tax planners setting up an offshore entity with one or more local Beneficial Owners, simply in order to circumvent the reporting requirements of the model rules. It also means, however, that an otherwise plain vanilla domestic family trust with a single non-resident beneficiary will fall within the offshore definition. Note however, that the definition of Service Provider in Rule 1.3 applies where the person can reasonably be expected to know that the Structure is an Offshore Structure. This means that **a trust that was not a Passive Offshore Vehicle at the time the trust was established would not become reportable simply because the person who set up the trust subsequently learns that one of the beneficiaries of the trust has moved to another country. If that person was, however required to provide further services in respect of the same trust, then that person would then need to include that change**

> **of facts in any assessment of whether the trust was required to be disclosed under these rules**

(Emphasis added)

Again, this part of the Commentary appears to go far beyond the wording of the MDR itself.

There are two 'carve-outs' in the definition of Passive Offshore Vehicle: for Institutional Investors, and where all of the Beneficial Owners are in fact resident in the same jurisdiction as the jurisdiction to which the Structure 'belongs'. In relation to the former, Institutional Investor is defined in rule 1.4(f), which provides:

> 'Institutional Investor' means a Legal Person or Legal Arrangement:
>
> (i) that is regulated as a bank (including a depositary or custodial institution), insurance company, collective investment vehicle or pension fund;
> (ii) the shares or interests of which are regularly traded on an established securities market;
> (iii) that is a government entity, central bank, international or supranational organisation; or
> (iv) a Legal Person or Legal Arrangement wholly-owned by one or more of the foregoing

This carve-out does, therefore, appear to be in line with the general purposes of CRS and the general risk profile of Institutional Investors. The Commentary explains:

> The Opaque Offshore Structure definition only applies to private investment vehicles that are closely-held. Rule 1.2(c) therefore excludes from the definition of 'Passive Offshore Vehicle' any Legal Person or Arrangement that is an 'Institutional Investor', as defined in Rule 1.4(f), or wholly-owned by one or more 'Institutional Investors' as it is unlikely that such Legal Persons or Arrangements would be used to not allow the accurate identification of natural person(s) with ultimate effective control and there is a low-risk of non-compliance. More generally, shareholders of a widely-held vehicle will typically not be captured by this rule, since the definition makes use of the Beneficial Owner definition provided for in the FATF Recommendations and, therefore, they would not be Beneficial Owners, unless they owned more than a specific amount of shares or exercised actual control of that vehicle

In this respect, the FATF Recommendations make it clear that beneficial owners are those who exercise control, and that a controlling ownership interest depends on the ownership structure of the company. It may be based on a threshold, e.g. any person owning more than a certain percentage of the company (e.g. 25%).

In relation to the latter, Rule 1.2 provides:

(d) An Opaque Structure is a Structure for which it is reasonable to conclude that it is designed to have, marketed as having, or has the effect of allowing, a natural person to be a Beneficial Owner of a Passive Offshore Vehicle while not allowing the accurate determination of such person's Beneficial Ownership or creating the appearance that such person is not a Beneficial Owner, including through:

(i) the use of nominee shareholders with undisclosed nominators;
(ii) the use of means of indirect control beyond formal ownership;
(iii) the use of Arrangements that provide a Reportable Taxpayer with access to assets held by, or income derived from, the Structure without being identified as a Beneficial Owner of such Structure;
(iv) the use of Legal Persons in a jurisdiction where there is:
no requirement to keep, or mechanism to obtain, Basic Information and Beneficial Owner information, as defined in the latest Financial Action Task Force Recommendations, on such Legal Persons that is accurate and up to date;
no obligation on shareholders or members to disclose the names of persons on whose behalf shares are held; or
no obligation on, or mechanism for, shareholders or members of such Legal Persons to notify the Legal Person of any changes in ownership or control;
(v) the use of Legal Arrangements organised under the laws of a jurisdiction that do not require the trustees (or in case of a Legal Arrangement other than a trust, the persons in equivalent or similar positions as the trustee of a trust) to hold, or be able to obtain, adequate, accurate and current Beneficial Ownership information regarding the Legal Arrangement;
where it is reasonable to conclude that the Structure is designed to have, marketed as having, or has the effect of allowing a natural person to be a Beneficial Owner of a Passive Offshore Vehicle while not allowing the accurate determination of such person's Beneficial Ownership or creating the appearance that such person is not a Beneficial Owner

In this respect, the Commentary starts by explaining:

32. A Passive Offshore Vehicle will be treated as held through an 'Opaque Structure' (and therefore form part of an Opaque Offshore Structure) where the ownership of the vehicle is structured in such a way as to not allow the accurate

> determination of a person's Beneficial Ownership in that vehicle or to create the appearance that such person is not the Beneficial Owner. This description of an Opaque Offshore Structure, which is the generic element of the hallmark, covers those situations, for instance, where the Structure uses an entity established in a jurisdiction where the lack of transparency regarding ownership with respect to that entity makes it difficult to identify the Beneficial Owner of the Passive Offshore Vehicle. The term also includes Arrangements that provide a person outside the ownership chain with indirect control over the Passive Offshore Vehicle or its assets such as an undisclosed nominee Structure. The paragraphs below provide specific instances of the kinds of Arrangements that can trigger disclosure of the Structure under these rules

It is the Commentary on these 'specific instances' which is particularly interesting. In relation to nominee shareholders of undisclosed nominators, the Commentary says:

> 33. The FATF Guidance on Transparency and Beneficial Ownership (October 2014) identified (at paragraph 9(e)) that one of the important ways in which offshore Structures can be used to not allow the accurate determination of Beneficial Ownership is through the use of nominee shareholders where the identity of the nominator is undisclosed.
>
> 34. A nominee shareholder is any person that holds those shares on behalf of another person (the nominator). A precise legal nature of the nominee relationship will depend on the Arrangements between the nominee and nominator and the circumstances in which the nominee relationship arose. For example, a nominee could be operating as an agent or a bare trustee or could hold the shares on behalf of the purchaser under an uncompleted sale transaction. **A nominee Arrangement will only fall within the specific hallmark in Rule 1.2(d)(i), where the Arrangement or the identity of the underlying nominator is undisclosed. While actively traded shares of widely held entities are often held in nominee name by brokers and custodians, such nominee arrangements would typically not be targeted by this hallmark as widely held entities are not within the scope of the Opaque Offshore Structures**
>
> (Emphasis added)

Arguably, many nominee arrangements will not fall within this hallmark. While there appears to have been great concern that all, or almost all nominee relationships would be caught, this appears not to be the intention from the Commentary.

In relation to indirect control that does not amount to formal ownership, the Commentary says:

> 35. Another common feature of Opaque Offshore Structures is the ability of natural persons to indirectly control the offshore vehicle under informal Arrangements with persons with direct control over that vehicle. These types of informal control Arrangements do not allow the accurate identification of the Beneficial Owner, either by making it difficult to identify the natural persons with direct or icontrol over the Passive Offshore Vehicle or creating the appearance that the person with such control is the Beneficial Owner when, in reality, the effective control rests with a third party or parties.
>
> 36. For example, this hallmark would capture a trustee of a trust (including a lawyer) who habitually acts under the instructions of another person even though the person is not recognised as a trustee or protector under the trust deed.
>
> 37. This hallmark targets those legal or formal Arrangements that have the effect of depriving a legal owner of the economic benefit of the asset or income in favour of a third party such that the third party has the benefit of the asset without being recognised as the Beneficial Owner. This hallmark would apply to an Arrangement whereby a person provided funding to a non-affiliated company in exchange for an option to acquire all or substantially all of the assets of that company for a nominal sum. Such an Arrangement would have the effect of providing the option holder with ultimate effective control over the company or those assets held by that company without being identifiable as their legal owner.

Identifying such 'ownership' is a perennial problem for tax authorities[17] and has been addressed by way of judicial decisions on control by 'shadow directors'. Other examples of such non-formal control may, in domestic law, be arrangements that ultimately as a matter of law are shams[18]. Indeed, the example of the trustee acting on instructions from a third party may well, dependent on the facts, amount to a sham. Consequently, the types of 'ownership' and control being targeted will often, in any event, fall outside the boundaries of acceptable tax planning.

---

[17] For an early attempt to deal with taxing the person who had the economic benefit of assets over which they did not have formal ownership or control – necessarily – see the English Income Tax Act 2007, Part 13 (transfer of assets abroad regime)

[18] Very broadly speaking, in English law, a sham is an arrangement whereby documents governing a situation say one thing on their face, however, the parties to them know and are agreed that they will act on a different basis. Thus the document is used to mislead a third party (often a revenue authority).

This is not dissimilar to the situation in Rule 1.2(d)(iii) – arrangements that provide a person with access to assets or income without being identified as the Beneficial Owner. In this respect, the Commentary says:

> 38. This specific hallmark targets techniques used to take money or value out of an Opaque Offshore Structure without such payments coming to the attention of the tax administration in the jurisdiction of tax residence as well as Arrangements used to not allow the determination of the source of those funds. This would include the use of prepaid debit and credit cards and interest free loans

Finally, the Commentary turns to consider the use of jurisdictions with weak anti-money laundering rules. It says:

> 39. These specific hallmarks target the use of Legal Persons or Legal Arrangements in jurisdictions that have not adequately implemented the FATF transparency requirements set out in the hallmarks, but only if one or more of the obligations set out in these hallmarks do not apply with respect to the specific Legal Person or Legal Arrangement that is used in the Structure. The language of the Model Rules refers to the latest version of the FATF Recommendations, which are currently those of February 2012. Jurisdictions may wish to specifically refer to this version in their domestic legislation. That reference would then need to be updated when new or revised FATF Recommendations are issued

This poses a practical difficulty. It requires a knowledge of the state of implementation of the FATF Recommendations in the jurisdictions in question. There is, as yet, no straightforward way to do this, without a detailed understanding of the legislation and jurisdiction in question.

Since there is a suggestion that, upon implementation of legislation based on the MDR, jurisdictions may wish to use more up-to-date versions of the FATF Recommendations in their domestic legislation, this is a good point at which to consider the regimes currently in force, or due to come into force soon.

This addresses the 'substantive' elements of the Model MDR, i.e. what is offensive to the regime and, therefore, reportable. However, it fails to address the matter of upon whom the duty to report falls.

10.9 Duty to report

In short, this obligation falls on an 'Intermediary'. This is defined in MDR, Rule 1.3, which provides:

> 'Intermediary' means:

(a) any person responsible for the design or marketing of a CRS Avoidance Arrangement or Opaque Offshore Structure ('Promoter'); and
(b) any person that provides Relevant Services in respect of a CRS Avoidance Arrangement or Opaque Offshore Structure in circumstances where the person providing such services could reasonably be expected to know that the Arrangement or Structure is a CRS Avoidance Arrangement or an Opaque Offshore Structure ('Service Provider'). The standard of 'reasonably be expected to know' must be determined by reference to the Service Provider's actual knowledge based on readily available information and the degree of expertise and understanding required to provide the Relevant Services.

Thus there are two categories of intermediaries:

(i) Promoters; and
(ii) Service Providers.

There is an important distinction here, between the definition of Intermediary for MDR and that in BEPS 12, in that in the former, there is no requirement for an MDR Intermediary to be involved in the tax aspects, so the definition is consequently broader than that provided in BEPS 12. In this respect, the Commentary says:

> 44. ... While restricting the scope of the disclosure rules to tax advisers can be considered a sensible limitation in the context of rules targeting the Promoters of tax avoidance Arrangements it would be too restrictive for Arrangements that are designed to avoid reporting under the CRS, where the defining feature of the Arrangement is unlikely to be its tax consequences per se but rather the way the Arrangement can be used to circumvent CRS reporting obligations and undermine a Financial Institution's due diligence procedures. Restricting the definition of Intermediaries to tax advisers would have the effect of excluding a wide range of potential intermediaries (such as investment advisers and lawyers) who do not (and may not be authorised to) provide taxation services

While the sense of this can be seen, it does bring into scope many professionals who may have no knowledge of the CRS regime, nor the tax policy basis underlying it, and who are ill-equipped to grapple with MDR as a result.

In relation to Promoters, the Commentary explains:

> 45. A person is 'responsible' for the design of a CRS Avoidance Arrangement when that person introduces features into the Arrangement which have or are likely to have the effect of

circumventing the CRS. Similarly, a person will be treated as responsible for the design of an Opaque Offshore Structure, where that person includes features in the Structure that result in it being treated as opaque under the test set out in Rule 1.2(d).

> 46. The **'marketing' of an Arrangement or Structure means encouraging others to enter into that Arrangement based on its CRS treatment or the possibility that the Structure will not allow the identification of the Beneficial Owner**. A person can be considered to be marketing a CRS Avoidance Arrangement even if such Arrangement was not originally designed as such. For example, **a financial adviser that identifies an investment product and markets that product to a customer as a way of avoiding reporting under the CRS would be treated as an Intermediary in respect of CRS Avoidance Arrangement notwithstanding that the issuer may not have designed, marketed or intended the investment product to be used as a way of circumventing the CRS**

(Emphasis added)

The Commentary looks at Service Providers separately in relation to CRS Avoidance Arrangements and Opaque Offshore Structures. In relation to the former, it starts by saying:

> 48. The term 'Relevant Services' covers any assistance or advice provided by a Services Provider in respect of the design, marketing, implementation or organisation of an Opaque Offshore Structure or CRS Avoidance Arrangement. The term would apply, for instance, to the advice provided by a lawyer, accountant or financial adviser as part of a professional services business as well as management or compliance services provided by a corporate services provider to an offshore entity that is used in an Opaque Offshore Structure or CRS Avoidance Arrangement.

This appears to be directed at those Service Providers falling clearly within the definition of Intermediary, and is unremarkable. The Commentary continues:

> 49. The intention behind extending the reporting obligations to Service Providers is to ensure that the rules capture de facto promoters (i.e. **persons who play a key role in developing, implementing or organising a CRS Avoidance Arrangement without being the person responsible for its marketing or design**) and that they cover **advisers and service providers that have sufficient knowledge of and involvement in the Arrangement that it is appropriate to impose a disclosure obligation upon them.**

…

(Emphasis added)

There is no further guidance given as to what constitutes 'appropriate'. The Commentary continues:

> 50. However a person will not be treated as a Service Provider unless that person can 'reasonably be expected to know' that the Arrangement falls within the definition of CRS Avoidance Arrangement. This test requires that the Service Provider both has a sufficient knowledge of the facts of the Arrangement and understanding of its legal treatment to be in a position to determine whether the Arrangement has the effect of circumventing the CRS. As regards the facts of the Arrangement, Service Providers must take into account anything that they actually know about the Arrangement as well as any information that is readily available (including, for instance, in the case of Financial Institutions, information on the customer file or collected in connection with AML/KYC or CRS obligations). **These model rules do not impose any additional due diligence or enquiry obligations. As regards the legal treatment of the Arrangement (including under the relevant CRS Legislation) the Service Provider is only required to have the level of expertise that would ordinarily be expected of someone providing the Relevant Services.**

(Emphasis added)

This is an important restriction on the scope of the MDR, because it excludes from a reporting obligation those who – in the scope of their role – reasonably lack the knowledge, experience or information to know that there is a CRS Avoidance Arrangement. In practice, this is likely to exclude many of the non-tax related professionals potentially brought into scope by the extension of the definition beyond that given in BEPS 12.

The Commentary then goes on to discuss some examples of what is said to come within the Service Provider definition, in relation to a CRS Avoidance Arrangement, saying:

> 51. … The definition of Service Provider would, for example, capture a Service Provider that works closely with the Promoter in designing or marketing the Arrangement. It would also capture a person that does not assist the Promoter, but assists a Reportable Taxpayer to enter into an Arrangement knowing that it is a CRS Avoidance Arrangement. It would also capture a person that provides administration and compliance services in respect of a CRS Avoidance Arrangement where their familiarity with the Arrangement and the degree of expertise required to provide those services means that they can be

reasonably expected to know that the Arrangement is a CRS Avoidance Arrangement

52. … For example, the definition would generally not capture Financial Institutions when carrying out routine banking transactions (e.g. money transfer, custody etc.), because the nature of their involvement and the information readily available to them would typically not meet the 'reasonably be expected to know' standard.

53. The definition would also not, for example, capture a lawyer or corporate services provider who completed the necessary filing formalities for transferring shares in a foreign company unless that person had other information that would lead a reasonable person in the same position to conclude that the transfer was a one of the steps in the implementation of a broader Arrangement that fell within the scope of the hallmarks set out under the model rules

Again, this element of the Commentary is uncontroversial. However, it does show that it is difficult to capture the circumstances of the reporting obligation straightforwardly, and that there will be a large fact-based element in determining whether or not a Structure/Arrangements amount(s) to CRS Avoidance Arrangements, and whether or not a professional involved is likely to be a Service Provider in the context of those arrangements. Thus care should be taken when applying a software-based, or formulaic approach to identify reporting obligations; while these will suffice in many cases they are, inevitably, prone to failure where there are facts not captured, or where there are unusual features.

In relation to Service Providers in the context of Opaque Offshore Structures, the Commentary says:

54. As for CRS Avoidance Arrangements, the definition of Service Provider in respect of an Opaque Offshore Structure also covers persons that provide advice or assistance in respect of the design, marketing, implementation or organisation of the Structure, to the extent that such a person can be reasonably expected to know that the Structure has the features which bring it within the definition of an Opaque Offshore Structure in Rule 1.2.

55. Whether a person providing advice or assistance in respect of the design, marketing, implementation or organisation of the Structure can reasonably be expected to know that such Structure is an Opaque Offshore Structure, will depend on the nature of the services provided in respect of the Structure and whether:

(a) the person has actual knowledge of, or readily available information on, the relevant features of the Structure that bring it within the definition of an Opaque Offshore Structure; and

(b) given the type of the services provided, the person can reasonably be expected to have the expertise to understand that this is an Opaque Offshore Structure.

56. This should generally not affect Financial Institutions in their ordinary banking activities. For instance, a Financial Institution that, as part of its ordinary banking activities, opens an account for a nonresident entity, may hold sufficient information to determine whether it is offshore, but would, in ordinary circumstances, be unlikely have access to information that would allow the Financial Institution to determine whether the entity is passive or held through an Opaque Structure. On the other hand, for example, if a company service provider in a jurisdiction which has not adequately implemented the FATF transparency standards sets up companies in its own jurisdiction, which are clearly passive in nature (e.g. they all have the same postal box address), on behalf of a person whom he knows is marketing the use of such entities as Opaque Offshore Structures, the company service provider will be considered a Service Provider in respect of such Structures

Again, we consider this aspect of the Commentary uncontroversial.

Guernsey MDR defines an Intermediary in a similar, though not identical, way. It provides:

'Intermediary' means

(a) a person responsible for the design or marketing of a CRS avoidance arrangement or opaque offshore structure (a 'promoter'), and

(b) a person who provides relevant services in respect of a CRS avoidance arrangement or opaque offshore structure in circumstances where the person providing the services could reasonably be expected to know that the arrangement or structure is a CRS avoidance arrangeinent or an opaque offshore structure (a 'service provider'); and for the purposes of this definition the question of whether a service provider could 'reasonably be expected to know' shall be determined by reference to the service provider's actual knowledge based on readily available information and the degree of expertise and understanding required to provide the relevant services

The key difference is the wording in relation to actual knowledge, though this is unlikely to result in a different outcome in practice. The Guernsey Briefing Note does not add much, other than where it says:

> Intermediaries will be expected to be alert, during the course of their activities, to the possibility of involvement with either an Arrangement or Structure and therefore having an obligation to determine whether a disclosure is required

This is probably accurate, but may give the impression of a disclosure obligation that does not perhaps exist, because Service Providers are not required to look beyond the information they reasonably require to do their job.

10.10 Reporting

The majority of reporting obligations fall on Intermediaries. There is, however, an additional 'backstop' obligation on Relevant Taxpayers to disclose. Rule 2.1 provides the obligation on Intermediaries:

> Any person that is an Intermediary with respect to a CRS Avoidance Arrangement or Opaque Offshore Structure must disclose that Arrangement or Structure to the tax authorities in [Jurisdiction Name] if that person:
>
> (a) makes that CRS Avoidance Arrangement or Opaque Offshore Structure available for implementation, or provides Relevant Services in respect of that CRS Avoidance Arrangement or Opaque Offshore Structure through a branch located in [Jurisdiction Name];
>
> (b) is resident or has its place of management in [Jurisdiction Name]; or
>
> (c) is incorporated in, or established under the laws of, [Jurisdiction Name].

Thus, the obligation to disclose is controlled through a nexus between the Intermediary and the Jurisdiction in which the reporting requirement arises. While there are some operational MDR regimes, such regimes remain restricted to comparatively few jurisdictions, and therefore this 'nexus' test may be of important in decision-making by taxpayers as to the jurisdictions with which they engage. However, if – as intended by the OECD – such regimes become more common, such consideration is likely to fall away.

In relation to the Intermediary's obligation to disclose, the Commentary does not expand much on the wording of the MDR. It states:

> 57. Rule 2.1 sets out the basic disclosure obligations imposed on Intermediaries to disclose CRS Avoidance Arrangements and Opaque Offshore Structures. The Intermediary must have a nexus with the reporting jurisdiction for the disclosure obligation to be effective…
>
> 58. The nexus test is designed to capture any Intermediary with a sufficient connection with the reporting jurisdiction for the tax authorities to be able to require compliance with the disclosure rules. The three criteria for nexus would often also capture those cases where an Intermediary is subject to regulation or required

> to register as a professional services provider in the reporting jurisdiction, because such regulation and registration requirements typically apply to Intermediaries operating within that jurisdiction. Because the nexus criteria are separate and independent, the model rules contemplate that an Intermediary might be subject to reporting obligations in different jurisdictions in respect of the same scheme. Rule 2.5 includes rules designed to eliminate any unnecessary duplicative reporting

The timing of the disclosure is set out in Rule 2.2, which provides:

> The disclosure required under Rule 2.1 shall be made thirty days after the Intermediary:
>
> (a) makes the CRS Avoidance Arrangement or Opaque Offshore Structure available for implementation; or
> (b) supplies Relevant Services in respect of the CRS Avoidance Arrangement or Opaque Offshore Structure.

This is a relatively short timescale. When considering the existing regimes in Jersey, Guernsey and Isle of Man, all have adopted the 30-day requirement. Consequently, businesses that are expecting to be Intermediaries on a regular basis should have procedures in place to address this, since penalties may be applied where information is submitted outside of that time frame.

Rule 2.3 provides for the information to be disclosed. It provides:

> The information that an Intermediary is required to disclose under Rule 2.1 in respect of a CRS Avoidance Arrangement or Opaque Offshore Structure shall include:
>
> (a) the name, address, jurisdiction(s) and TIN(s) of tax residence of the following persons:
> (i) the person making the disclosure;
> (ii) any Client of that person in respect of that Arrangement or Structure (separately identifying any Client that is a Reportable Taxpayer, including the date of birth of such persons);
> (iii) any actual user of a CRS Avoidance Arrangement or Beneficial Owner of an Opaque Offshore Structure;
> (iv) any person that is an Intermediary with respect to that Arrangement or Structure (other than the person making the disclosure).
>
> (b) the details of that CRS Avoidance Arrangement or Opaque Offshore Structure including;
> (i) in respect of a CRS Avoidance Arrangement, a factual description of those features of the Arrangement that are designed to have, marketed as having, or have the effect of, circumventing the CRS Legislation; and

(ii) in respect of an Opaque Offshore Structure, a factual description of those features that have the effect of not allowing the accurate determination of the Reportable Taxpayer's Beneficial Ownership or creating the appearance that the Reportable Taxpayer is not a Beneficial Owner of the Passive Offshore Vehicle; and

(c) the jurisdiction or jurisdictions where the CRS Avoidance Arrangement or Opaque Offshore Structure has been made available for implementation; to the extent such information is within the knowledge, possession or control of the person providing the disclosure.

The restriction in relation to what is within the knowledge, possession or control of the disclosing Intermediary is important. Again, it limits the information to be disclosed to that which is already known to the Intermediary; no further investigation should need to be carried out. The Commentary adds the following:

63. A CRS Avoidance Arrangement or Opaque Offshore Structure will be treated as having been 'made available' for implementation at the time the material design elements of the Arrangement or Structure had been completed and communicated to a Client or Reportable Taxpayer. It is not necessary for all the material elements of the scheme to be in place before disclosure is required, rather it will be sufficient that the Intermediary has taken initial steps to market the Arrangement.

64. The model text sets a time limit for disclosure that is thirty (30) days after the scheme has been made available or the Relevant Services are provided. The filing date should be as soon as is practicable after the obligation to disclose has been triggered and, for those jurisdictions that already have mandatory disclosure regimes for other types of Arrangements should be consistent with the policy set by the filing requirements under those regimes.

There is also a requirement to report, and a deadline to report, pre-existing arrangements. Rule 2.7 provides:

Rule 2.7: Disclosure of Arrangements entered into after 29 October 2014 and before the effective date of these rules

A Promoter shall disclose a CRS Avoidance Arrangement within 180 days of the effective date of these rules where:

(i) that Arrangement was implemented on or after 29 October 2014 but before the effective date of these rules; and
(ii) that person was a Promoter in respect of that Arrangement;

irrespective of whether that person provides Relevant Services in respect of that Arrangement after the effective date.

No disclosure shall be required under paragraph (a) where the Promoter has documentation to demonstrate that the aggregate balance or value of the Financial Account subject to the CRS Avoidance Arrangement immediately prior to its implementation was less than USD 1,000,000.

(c) Notwithstanding Rule 1.4(e), for the purpose of interpreting defined terms with respect to this Rule 2.7, CRS Legislation means the Standard for Automatic Exchange of Financial Account Information in Tax Matters as published by the OECD on 15 July 2014.

The scope of the obligation in relation to pre-existing arrangements is more limited, being restricted by a minimum value. However if the 29 October 2014 date is adopted — as Guernsey has – Intermediaries may face the difficulty that they no longer have the retained files to be able to report pre-existing Arrangements.

Turning to the obligation on the Relevant Taxpayer, Rule 2.6 provides:

(a) Any Reportable Taxpayer that is resident in [Jurisdiction Name] and that is a user of a CRS Avoidance Arrangement or a Beneficial Owner under an Opaque Offshore Structure must disclose to the [Jurisdiction Name] tax authority any information on the Arrangement or Structure that is not disclosed by an Intermediary because the Intermediary is not subject to any disclosure requirements under Rule 2.1 or is not required to disclose the information pursuant to Rule 2.4.

(b) The Reportable Taxpayer is not required to disclose any information under Rule 2.6(a) to the extent that the Reportable Taxpayer has received documentation from the Intermediary demonstrating that the information has been disclosed by that Intermediary to the tax authority of a Partner Jurisdiction under mandatory disclosure rules that are substantially similar to those set out in this legislation.

The disclosure pursuant to Rule 2.6(a) above shall include all the information required to be disclosed under Rule 2.3 and be made within thirty days after the first step of the CRS Avoidance Arrangement or Opaque Offshore Structure has been implemented.

The Commentary explains:

83. The primary intention of these mandatory disclosure rules is to target Intermediaries that are responsible for the design, promotion or implementation of CRS Avoidance Arrangements and Opaque Offshore Structures. However, consistent with the framework for mandatory disclosure rules set out in the BEPS Action 12 Report, it is also necessary to consider the implications

> for the user of a CRS Avoidance Arrangement or Opaque Offshore Structure if the Intermediary is not subject to disclosure obligations as well as those cases where the Intermediary is unable to comply with its disclosure obligations under these rules

The Commentary subsequently continues:

> 86. The reason for imposing a secondary disclosure obligation on the taxpayer in these cases is to support the integrity of the disclosure rules. The disclosure obligation is imposed on the resident taxpayer in order to prevent that taxpayer from insulating itself from the effect of these rules by claiming legal privilege over information or by using the services of an offshore Intermediary that is not subject to equivalent disclosure obligations under foreign law. Disclosure by a taxpayer is not required where disclosure would be limited by domestic protections against self-incrimination. In addition, the adoption of these specific rules to combat CRS avoidance would be without prejudice to a jurisdiction's domestic rules (if any) requiring taxpayers to disclose their offshore assets

10.11 Exclusions and exemptions from reporting obligation

Certain circumstances will result in otherwise reportable Arrangements, or Intermediaries otherwise having reporting obligations, either not being reportable, or being obliged to report.

The first is found in Rule 2.4, which provides:

> (a) An Intermediary shall not be required to disclose any information set out under Rule 2.3 where that information is protected from disclosure under professional secrecy rules stipulated in domestic law, but only to the extent the disclosure would reveal confidential information held by an attorney, solicitor or other admitted legal representative with respect to a Client, as defined in the Commentary to Article 26 of the OECD Model Tax Convention.
>
> (b) An Intermediary that is not required to disclose information under this Rule 2.4 shall provide written notice to the Client of the Client's disclosure obligations under these rules by the time specified in Rule 2.2.

The Commentary explains:

> 80. Mandatory disclosure rules do not require an attorney, solicitor or other admitted legal representative to disclose any information that is protected by legal professional privilege or equivalent professional secrecy obligations. The same approach is reflected in Article 26 of the OECD Model Tax Convention and Article 21 of the Multilateral Convention on Mutual Administrative Assistance in Tax Matters. As noted in the BEPS

> Action 12 Report, however, the type of confidentiality obligations that exist between legal representatives and their Clients are generally designed to protect a Reportable Taxpayer's or Client's ability to obtain confidential advice. As such, domestic law in the jurisdiction of the Intermediary may have the effect that some or all of the information required to be disclosed under the model rules will be covered by the relevant domestic rules on legal professional privilege. Such information would be excluded from the disclosure requirements, but only to the extent that an information request for the same information could be denied under Article 26 of the OECD Model Tax Convention and Article 21 of the Multilateral Convention on Mutual Administrative Assistance in Tax Matters

It is instructive to consider the various regimes already in effect and/or under contemplation. Guernsey MDR, Regulation 7 provides:

> 7. (1) An intermediary is not required to disclose any information set out in regulation 6 where the information is contained in a cominiinication or item **subject to legal professional privilege and is in the possession of a person who is entitled to possession of it, but only to the extent that the disclosure would reveal confidential information held by an attorney, solicitor or other admitted legal representative with respect to a client**, as defined in the Commentary to Article 26 of the OECD Model Tax Convention (as published on the OECD website and as from time to time revised, updated or replaced, with or without modification).
>
> (2) Notwithstanding the provisions of paragraph (1), an advocate or other legal adviser niay be required to give the name and address (including an electronic address) of a client.
>
> (3) An intermediary who is not required to disclose information under this regulation shall provide written notice to the client of the client's disclosure obligations under these Regulations within the time limit specified in regulation 5
>
> (Emphasis added).

This is an interesting approach. It requires a number of separate elements, namely:

(i) The item is subject to legal privilege (such concept should be determined by reference to Guernsey's domestic law principles);

(ii) The item is not in the possession of someone who is not entitled to possess it (i.e. if you do not have the right to the document, you are not protected from disclosure); and

(iii) The exclusion from disclosure is limited to the extent that the item, etc. would reveal confidential information held by an attorney, solicitor or other admitted legal representative with respect to a client.

Thus in one respect, it is broader than it might otherwise be, given that it is not only applicable to legal professionals but – apparently – to legally privileged documents in the hands of third parties, where they are entitled to have possession of that item, etc. However, it is also narrower than a simple legal privilege might be. This is because the exclusion does not extend to information that would not reveal confidential information held by a legal professional, even if such items, etc. would ordinarily be within legal privilege. It is possible that this is more complex than it needs to be. The Guernsey Briefing Note, sadly, sheds no light on the form adopted.

Additionally, it is comment-worthy that the OECD Model DTA is, effectively, in part enshrined in domestic law, including to the extent that it changes. It may be that this is a phenomenon that will become more common, however, this is not without risks. Nonetheless it results in a degree of certainty for the taxpayer, since what the Model DTA says at any given time can be known.

Jersey MDR, Regulation 9 provides:

> (1) An intermediary is not subject to the requirement to disclose the information set out in Regulation 8 if that information is in respect of any information or document which a person would, in any court proceedings, be entitled to refuse to disclose or produce on the grounds of legal professional privilege –
>
> (a) except if that intermediary is a lawyer, the name and address of his or her client; and
>
> (b) only to the extent the disclosure would reveal confidential information held by an advocate, solicitor or other admitted legal representative with respect to a client, as defined in the commentary to Article 26 of the OECD Model Tax Convention (as published on the OECD website).
>
> (2) An intermediary that is exempted by paragraph (1) from the disclosure requirements set out in Regulation 8, must provide written notice to the client to fulfil the obligations set out in Regulations 6, 7 and 8.

Similarly, IoM MDR, Regulation 8 provides:

> (1) An intermediary shall not be required to disclose any information set out under regulation 7 where that information is protected from disclosure under professional secrecy rules stipulated in domestic law, but only to the extent the disclosure would reveal confidential information held by an attorney, solicitor or other admitted legal representative with respect to a client, as defined in the Commentary to Article 26 of the OECD Model Tax Convention.
>
> (2) An intermediary that is not required to disclose information under this regulation shall provide written notice to the client of

the client's disclosure obligations under these rules by the time specified in Regulation 6.

Both Jersey and the Isle of Man adopt wording more similar to that of the MDR in relation to the definition in Article 6 of the Model DTA. It is not clear if this will result in a different outcome than would be the case under Guernsey MDR. It is probable that it will not.

The second exclusion is found in Rule 2.5, which provides:

> An Intermediary is not required to disclose any information set out in Rule 2.3, to the extent that the Intermediary holds documentation demonstrating that:
> (a) such information was previously disclosed to the [Jurisdiction Name] tax authority;
> (b) the information relates to Relevant Services supplied, or a CRS Avoidance Arrangement or Opaque Offshore Structure made available for implementation, through a branch maintained by that Intermediary in a Partner Jurisdiction and such information has been disclosed to the tax authority of that Partner Jurisdiction; or
> (c) the Intermediary is required to disclose such information under Rule 2.1(c) and such information has been disclosed to the tax authority of a Partner Jurisdiction where that Intermediary is resident or has its place of management

Thus, this aims to prevent double reporting.

10.12 Reporting framework

As noted, MDR is not legislation, or international agreement, it is merely a model. Thus, for it to have any effect in addition to the actual MDR rules – or similar – being enacted into domestic legislation, it is also necessary for there to be a potential mechanism for the exchange of information. This is provided in a draft MCAA modelled on the CRS MCAA. The Introduction to the MDR MCAA explains:

> 4. In drafting the MCAA, an automatic exchange approach has been adopted, following the approach used for the CRS and CbC exchanges. This has been done in order to ensure that exchanges will be operationalised on the clear and unambiguous legal basis of Article 6 of the Convention and to provide clarity about the scope and periodicity of the exchanged information. The approach in the draft MCAA with respect to the information flows is that exchanges in principle are on a reciprocal basis between two jurisdictions that have implemented MDRs. This has the advantage that only jurisdictions that are familiar with the MDR and thus have a better understanding of the information will be receiving the information. It also provides

> an incentive for jurisdictions to adopt MDR to benefit from the automatic exchange network

The introduction continues:

> 5. The basic premise for the automatic exchange flows under the draft MCAA is that a jurisdiction that received information about a CRS Avoidance Arrangement or Opaque Offshore Structure under the MDRs would exchange such information with all jurisdictions of tax residence of the Reportable Taxpayer(s), which are other MDR implementing jurisdictions and are signatories to the MCAA. This will allow tax authorities of such jurisdictions to use such information to carry out compliance activities permitted under the Convention with respect to such Reportable Taxpayers

It appears to be the case that there are [no] activated exchange relationships using the MDR MCAA at present.

10.13 Penalties

The MDR itself contains no provisions as to penalties. The Commentary explains:

> 89. Mandatory disclosure regimes will not be effective unless both Intermediaries and taxpayers have incentives to ensure compliance with the rules. As noted in the BEPS Action 12 Report, mandatory disclosure regimes should include clear sanctions to encourage disclosure and to penalise those who do not fulfil their obligations while, at the same time, providing the flexibility to ensure that the Structure and amount of the penalty can be varied depending on the nature of the CRS Avoidance Arrangement or Opaque Offshore Structure and the Intermediary's role in that Arrangement or Structure.
>
> 90. The consequences that attach to non-disclosure will generally be determined by each jurisdiction in light of its particular circumstances. However this commentary includes an illustration of a possible approach to penalties that is designed to balance the need to ensure fairness while incentivising compliant behaviour

The Commentary suggests three categories of penalties: monetary and non-monetary penalties for Intermediaries and Reportable Taxpayers. and monetary penalties for Reportable Taxpayers. In relation to monetary penalties for Intermediaries, it says:

> 91. In considering an appropriate penalty to be imposed on Intermediaries for a failure to comply with its disclosure obligations, jurisdictions may consider setting the penalty at a fixed rate or (if greater) at a percentage of the fees paid to the

Intermediary for the services provided in respect of the CRS Avoidance Arrangement or Opaque Offshore Structure, with the percentage set at rate that removes any economic incentive for the Intermediary to avoid disclosure.

92. Jurisdictions could also consider the use of a daily penalty similar to the one used in the United Kingdom and Ireland under their mandatory disclosure rules. As described in the BEPS Action 12 Report, daily penalties put an emphasis on timely disclosure and they can be used in conjunction with minimum penalties

In relation to non-monetary penalties, it says:

94. Jurisdictions may also consider non-monetary penalties for Intermediaries and Reportable Taxpayers. Options include taking action to prohibit an Intermediary from providing regulated or professional services in the jurisdiction, publication of names and extension of time limits.

Publication of Names

95. While name publication may not be an appropriate tool in the context of tax avoidance schemes, it is frequently used by tax administrations in the area of tax evasion and fraud. Publication of names of non-compliant Reportable Taxpayers and Intermediaries has the additional benefit of allowing tax administrations to disrupt the promotion of such schemes by high-risk Intermediaries and warn taxpayers of Promoter behaviour that raises a systemic risk for the tax system. Publication may only be appropriate where it was proven in an applicable court or administrative tribunal or where it was admitted that the Reportable Taxpayer or Intermediary used the Arrangement or Structure to intentionally evade taxation and may not be appropriate where the failure to comply was inadvertent, or reasonable steps had been taken by the Reportable Taxpayer or Intermediary to ensure that disclosure was made.

Extension of time limits

96. Another consequence that can attach to a failure to disclose is to extend the time of assessment where any tax is collected in connection with an undisclosed Opaque Offshore Structure or CRS Avoidance Arrangement. The rationale for extending the time limits for assessment is that where the Arrangement is not disclosed the tax authority will need, and should have, more time to identify any noncompliance and correct it.

Again, it is helpful to consider the regimes adopted in jurisdictions already committed to MDR. In Guernsey, the penalty regime is extensive, including both civil and criminal penalties.[19] The civil penalties are found in Guernsey MDR, Regulations 13 and 14. To a limited extent, they adopt income tax penalties and appear to be confined to monetary penalties. Such penalties can be appealed using the procedure in Guernsey MDR, Regulation 15.

The criminal penalties again adopt income tax penalties and appear to relate primarily to fraud and to false statements.

Jersey MDR has adopted solely financial and non-criminal penalties. This is the same for the Isle of Man. So far, there are no regimes that adopt the suggestion of non-financial penalties.

---

[19] Criminal penalties in this respect are extreme. The consideration of any such penalty should be made in the context of human rights legislation.

11 TIEAs and Exchange Under Double Tax Treaties

11.1 Introduction: Why do we still need TIEAs?

In the writing of this text we – the authors – have noted a few areas of disagreement between us. This is another[1]. One of us considers TIEAs to be more relevant now than ever for the following reasons:

(i) First, the wide scale adoption of CRS has resulted in tax authorities holding a significantly greater amount of relatively basic information about many people. The use of TIEAs (or where appropriate, DTAs) to obtain on-request exchange seems like a natural next step to build on the basic information received under CRS. For this reason, again, one of us considers that we are likely to see an increase of on-request exchanges under TIEAs (and, where appropriate, DTAs). The other believes we will see a reduction because of the CRS mechanisms. At present, the anecdotal evidence from the jurisdictions with which we are most familiar (UK, Jersey and Gibraltar) confusingly points in both directions.

(ii) Second, while the requirement to have a network of TIEAs is less relevant now than prior to CRS and MDR, it remains the case that jurisdictions with a wider range of TIEAs are likely to be considered more transparent[2].

(iii) Thirdly in this respect, TIEAs – and information exchange provisions in some double tax agreements – are part of the basis on which CRS (and FATCA[3]) is founded. By this we mean that TIEAs and information exchange provisions in DTAs can be the basis on which CRS exchange is based. The Commentary to the preamble to CRS and CAA states:

> 5. The third clause sets out the legal basis that authorises the automatic exchange of financial account information and allows the Competent Authorities to agree the scope and modalities of such automatic exchanges. The scope agreed to must be consistent with the scope of exchange contemplated by Section 2 of this Agreement. Other legal instruments (i.e. instruments other than income tax conventions or the Convention on Mutual Administrative Assistance in Tax Matters) that permit the automatic exchange of information for tax purposes include certain tax information exchange agreements, or regional tax co-operation agreements. On a regional basis the automatic exchange of information could also be implemented on the basis

---

[1] In a text of this length, on topics as broad as those covered, we consider only two or three 'internal' disagreements to be a healthy amount of professional dischord.

[2] The TIEA network of a jurisdiction has for some time been considered an indicator of the degree of transparency. Since the inception of CRS, this is now less heavily relied on.

[3] You will recall from the FATCA chapter, that the FATCA model agreement on which a country will base its agreement is dependent on whether or not it has an existing TIEA with the USA.

> of e.g. EU law or Andean community legislation that covered the elements of the Model CAA and the CRS

Similarly, Annex 4 to the CRS and CAA states:

> A legal framework must ensure the confidentiality of exchanged tax information and limit its use to appropriate purposes. The two basic components of such a framework are the terms of the applicable treaty, TIEA or other bilateral agreement for the exchange of information, and a jurisdiction's domestic legislation

(iv) Finally, the OECD continues to provide a Model Protocol which '... may be used by jurisdictions, in case they want to extend the scope of their existing TIEAs to also cover the automatic and/or spontaneous exchange of information'.[4]

Thus, it is suggested (by at least one of us) that TIEAs are still of importance. The alternative position is that TIEAs are no longer required in most circumstances because of the availability of CRS information.

11.2 Interpretation of TIEAs and DTAs in light of the OECD model

The Model TIEA provides suggested terms that countries might use in their own TIEAs and provides a commentary explaining what each term is intended to do. In its introduction to the Model TIEA, the OECD explains:

> 1. The purpose of this Agreement is to promote international co-operation in tax matters through exchange of information.
> 2. It was developed by the OECD Global Forum Working Group on Effective Exchange of Information ("the Working Group"). The Working Group consisted of representatives from OECD Member countries as well as delegates from Aruba, Bermuda, Bahrain, Cayman Islands, Cyprus, Isle of Man, Malta, Mauritius, the Netherlands Antilles, the Seychelles and San Marino.
> 3. The Agreement grew out of the work undertaken by the OECD to address harmful tax practices5. The lack of effective exchange of information is one of the key criteria in determining harmful tax practices. The mandate of the Working Group was to develop a legal instrument that could be used to establish effective exchange of information. The Agreement represents the standard of effective exchange of information for the purposes of the OECD's initiative on harmful tax practices.
> 4. This Agreement is not a binding instrument but contains two models for bilateral agreements drawn up in the light of the

[4] www.oecd.org/ctp/exchange-of-tax-information/taxinformationexchangeagreementstieas.htm

[5] More information about harmful practices can be found at www.oecd.org/ctp/harmful/

> commitments undertaken by the OECD and the committed jurisdictions. In this context, it is important that financial centres throughout the world meet the standards of tax information exchange set out in this document. As many economies as possible should be encouraged to co-operate in this important endeavour. It is not in the interest of participating economies that the implementation of the standard contained in the Agreement should lead to the migration of business to economies that do not co-operate in the exchange of information. To avoid this result requires measures to defend the integrity of tax systems against the impact of a lack of co-operation in tax information exchange matters. The OECD members and committed jurisdictions have to engage in an ongoing dialogue to work towards implementation of the standard. An adequate framework will be jointly established by the OECD and the committed jurisdictions for this purpose particularly since such a framework would help to achieve a level playing field where no party is unfairly disadvantaged.

The introduction continues:

> 6. As mentioned above, the Agreement is intended to establish the standard of what constitutes effective exchange of information for the purposes of the OECD's initiative on harmful tax practices. However, the purpose of the Agreement is not to prescribe a specific format for how this standard should be achieved. Thus, the Agreement in either of its forms is only one of several ways in which the standard can be implemented. Other instruments, including double taxation agreements, may also be used provided both parties agree to do so, given that other instruments are usually wider in scope

While the Model TIEA seeks to establish a standard of effective information exchange, it does not prescribe how this is to be achieved. Practically, in interpreting a particular agreement, it will be important to consider which form has been used, and whether words have been changed.

The English courts have been required to interpret international agreements relating to tax on several occasions, and adopt the following approach. In *UBS AG v Revenue and Customs Commissioners* [2007] STC 588, the English Court of Appeal had to consider the interpretation of the DTA between the UK and Switzerland, which was based on the Model DTA (on income and capital). Arden LJ explained (at paragraph 61):

> …On questions of interpretation of the OECD convention, the commentary published with it is of persuasive value: see per Mummery J in IRC v Commerzbank AG …

> Article 23 forms part of an international treaty between the United Kingdom and Switzerland. Accordingly, **it must be interpreted in the manner applicable to such treaties and this means, among other things, that it should be interpreted in the light of its object and purpose**: see generally per Mummery J in IRC v Commerzbank AG, approved by this court in Memec plc v IRC ... the court must **seek out the meaning of the general provisions in art 23(2), giving each phrase its proper effect and consider whether art 23(2) has effect in relation to the particular provision of domestic law in issue**...
>
> (Emphasis added).

The dicta in *IRC v Commerzbank* has been quoted with approval in a number of other cases on DTAs, including by the Court of Appeal in *HMRC v Smallwood* [2010] STC 2045 and the High Court in *Revenue and Customs Commissioners v Ben Nevis (Holdings) Limited* [2012] STC 2157. The New Zealand Court of Appeal has also stated that the commentary should be considered[6]. In *Commissioner of Inland Revenue v JFP Energy Inc* [1990] 3 NZLR 536 it was held[7]:

> The OECD Convention rules have an international currency used as they are by and in countries throughout the world and accordingly the language of the rules should be construed on broad principles of general acceptance and have an appropriate regard to the Commentary.

While Arden LJ gives general principles of interpretation, she subsequently sounds a note of caution (at paragraph 63):

> When interpreting a double tax convention, it is important to recall that **double tax treaties are generally the subject of hard bargaining between contracting states** (as to this, see the comments of Lord Walker of Gestingthorpe in the Pirelli case …), and that contracting states have their own reasons for entering into such treaties. **For instance, a contracting state may take into account considerations of its own fiscal policy**. In so doing, it would be open to it to take the view (for example) that it should confer generous tax benefits on non-residents with a view to encouraging investment in its own state. But, likewise, it might take the contrary view that it did not wish to encourage investment (for example) by an enterprise resident in the other contracting state which carried on business within its own jurisdiction, but made losses, and thus paid no tax.

---

[6] While this was in relation to earlier versions of the Commentary, it established the general principle that the Commentary is likely to be relevant.

[7] A number of these cases were also quoted with approval by the Royal Court and Jersey Court of Appeal in the recent case of *Larsen v Comptroller of Income Tax* [2013] JRC 095, [2013] JCA 239.

These are not questions for the court interpreting the treaty, but underscore the **need for the court to interpret the treaty and any implementing legislation with attention to its precise terms.**

(Emphasis added).

These cases relate to double tax agreements, however, we consider that the same general principles are likely to apply to TIEAs. In relation to TIEAs themselves, the Jersey courts have considered their interpretation on a number of occasions. In deciding *APEF Management Company 5 Limited v The Comptroller of Income Taxes* [2013] JRC 205A the Royal Court did not refer to the OECD commentaries, and consequently it is not clear to what extent the courts may regard them in the future. Both the Court of Appeal and the Royal Court did, however, refer to *IRC v Commerzbank* in *Larsen v Comptroller of Taxes and Others* [2013] JCA 239, the Court of Appeal saying:

> In an attempt by the Appellants to dislodge this literal reading of Article 6(5), we were reminded of the well-known rules as to the interpretation of instruments of the character of the J/N TIEA based on the summary by Mummery J (as he then was) in IRC-v-Commerzbank Attorney General [1990] STC 285 of the approach of the House of Lords in Fothergill-v-Monarch Airlines Ltd [1981] AC 351 and of the Vienna Convention on the Law of Treaties ("the Geneva Convention") which, in broad and unnuanced terms, requires a court to search first for what appears to be the clear meaning of the words used without being overly literal, secondly to bear in mind the purpose of the instrument, thirdly to bear in mind that its wording will have been the product of negotiation between states; fourthly if the result of the exercise so far leaves the meaning unclear or ambiguous or produces a manifestly absurd or unreasonable result, to have recourse to supplementary materials.
>
> Albeit Jersey is not a party to the Vienna Convention, we proceed on the basis that the approach canvassed in the previous paragraph is appropriate to construction of the J/N TIEA…

Consequently, it seems relatively clear that international agreements ought not to be subject to the same principles of statutory interpretation as might ordinarily be applied to national legislation. Thus, we suggest the following 'rough guide' to the interpretation of TIEAs:

(i) The commentary on the OECD Model TIEA should be persuasive;
(ii) TIEAs should be interpreted in the light of their object and purpose (as set out, for example, in the introduction to the OECD model); and
(iii) They should be interpreted by seeking out the general meaning of provisions.

It can be seen, therefore, that a more purposive interpretation should be given to TIEAs, which should be considered in the light of the Model commentary.

11.3 The Model TIEA: key provisions

The Model TIEA contains 16 Articles and an extensive commentary. The key provisions are:

(i) Article 1: object and scope of the agreement;
(ii) Article 2: jurisdiction;
(iii) Article 5: exchange of information on request; and
(iv) Article 7: possibility of declining a request.

Of particular importance to practitioners are those provisions that limit the exchange of information under a TIEA; these provisions impose limits on what can be properly exchanged and while there are difficulties with enforcing such limits (see further below), it is important for practitioners to know when a TIEA request should be resisted. These provisions limit exchange of certain types of information, and circumstances in which the TIEA cannot force a jurisdiction to provide information (and consequently the requested jurisdiction should not force a taxpayer or third party to provide information pursuant to the request).

It is helpful to summarise these limits by reference to the Articles of the OECD Model:

(i) Article 1: foreseeable relevance - competent authorities of the Contracting Parties shall provide assistance through exchange of information that is foreseeably relevant to the administration and enforcement of the domestic laws of the Contracting Parties concerning taxes covered by this Agreement
(ii) Article 2: (territorial) jurisdiction - not obligated to provide information which is neither held by its authorities nor in the possession or control of persons who are within its territorial jurisdiction
(iii) Article 7(1): applicant Party law restriction - not required to obtain or provide information that the applicant Party would not be able to obtain under its own laws for purposes of the administration or enforcement of its own tax laws
(iv) Article 7(1): non-conformity of request - request is not made in conformity with the Agreement
(v) Article 7(2): trade secrets - obligation to supply information which would disclose any trade, business, industrial, commercial or professional secret or trade process
(vi) Article 7(3): legal professional privilege
(vii) Article 7(4): public policy
(viii) Article 7(6): discrimination - decline a request for information if the information is requested by the applicant Party to administer or enforce a provision of the tax law of the applicant Party, or any requirement connected therewith, which discriminates against a national of the requested Party as compared with a national of the applicant Party in the same circumstances

11.4 Article 1

Article 1 provides:

> The competent authorities of the Contracting Parties shall provide assistance through exchange of information that is foreseeably relevant to the administration and enforcement of the domestic laws of the Contracting Parties concerning taxes covered by this Agreement. Such information shall include information that is foreseeably relevant to the determination, assessment and collection of such taxes, the recovery and enforcement of tax claims, or the investigation or prosecution of tax matters. Information shall be exchanged in accordance with the provisions of this Agreement and shall be treated as confidential in the manner provided in Article 8. The rights and safeguards secured to persons by the laws or administrative practice of the requested Party remain applicable to the extent that they do not unduly prevent or delay effective exchange of information

The Commentary also provides:

3. The Agreement is limited to exchange of information that is foreseeably relevant to the administration and enforcement of the laws of the applicant Party concerning the taxes covered by the Agreement. The standard of foreseeable relevance is intended to provide for exchange of information in tax matters to the widest possible extent and, at the same time, to clarify that Contracting Parties are not at liberty to engage in fishing expeditions or to request information that is unlikely to be relevant to the tax affairs of a given taxpayer. Parties that choose to enter into bilateral agreements based on the Agreement may agree to an alternative formulation of this standard, provided that such alternative formulation is consistent with the scope of the Agreement.

4. The Agreement uses the standard of foreseeable relevance in order to ensure that information requests may not be declined in cases where a definite assessment of the pertinence of the information to an on-going investigation can only be made following the receipt of the information. The standard of foreseeable relevance is also used in the Joint Council of Europe/OECD Convention on Mutual Administrative Assistance in Tax Matters.

5. The last sentence of Article 1 ensures that procedural rights existing in the requested Party will continue to apply to the extent they do not unduly prevent or delay effective exchange of information. Such rights may include, depending on the circumstances, a right of notification, a right to challenge the exchange of information following notification or rights to challenge information gathering measures taken by the

> requested Party. Such procedural rights and safeguards also include any rights secured to persons that may flow from relevant international agreements on human rights and the expression "unduly prevent or delay" indicates that such rights may take precedence over the Agreement

According to the Commentary, the purpose of having a standard of 'foreseeable relevance' is to provide for collection of information in the widest possible sense, without allowing 'fishing expeditions'. On its face, this gives contracting parties very wide powers to gather tax information and indeed, this has been the approach taken by courts in a number of jurisdictions, including – possibly, in some cases – without much thought as to whether or not the TIEA request infringes on an internationally agreed human right.

In our view, there is a legitimate concern that the scope of the Model TIEA may be too wide, extending as it does to information which may not in the common sense be 'foreseeably relevant' because it cannot of course be known whether the information is relevant until the information has been received. However, this is in line with the development of international information exchange over the last two decades and, therefore, we consider that it will likely continue to be interpreted widely and in favour of the requester, rather than the taxpayer.

There is considerable international case law on foreseeable relevance. The standard is interpreted broadly. Some points picked up in the Model itself and the Commentary are that:

(i) It need not be certain that additional tax will be due when the information is provided, or that the information will be significant in calculating a customer's liabilities (for example, information from overseas may establish that no additional tax liabilities exist).
(ii) Information does not need to be certain to provide a 'smoking gun', it simply has to be capable of having an impact on a tax liability.
(iii) Requests for information on a speculative basis are not permitted. There must be foreseeable relevance to a particular taxpayer or group of taxpayers.

The case law comes not only from cases on TIEAs based on the model, but also on similar agreements with a similar standard. Much of the case law relates to Article 26 of the OECD Model double tax agreement (strictly speaking, to articles of actual treaties based on it) or the provision of the EU Directive 2011/16/EU — Administrative co-operation in the field of taxation – which is itself based on the wording of that Article 26 (see the Opinion of AG Wathelet in Case C-682/15 *Berlioz Investment Fund SA v Directeur de l'administration des Contributions directes*, at paragraph 102).

Berlioz is an important case because, following *Sabou*, it decided that a third party from whom a requested party requires information must be in a position to challenge the foreseeable relevance of the information requested. In *Berlioz* AG Wathelet described the concept of foreseeable relevance as being that '… the authority of the requested State must be in a position to answer the question whether the requested information can foreseeably be connected to the assessment of the tax which the requesting authority seeks to make'

The AG drew support for this from the Commentary on the OECD Model DTA, which explains that there must be 'a reasonable possibility that the requested information will be relevant'. Thus, for AG Wathelet the concept of 'foreseeable relevance' is intended to prevent a State from making requests for information 'that have no apparent nexus to an open inquiry or investigation'. He does, however, go on to say that that the concept of foreseeable relevance requires '[only] a brief and formal verification, of a factual nature'.

In its judgment, the CJEU seems to consider this as going too far, stating that 'the requested authority must nevertheless verify whether the information sought is not devoid of any foreseeable relevance to the investigation being carried out by the requesting authority', before going on to say:

> The review to be carried out by the requested authority is not limited, therefore, to a brief and formal verification of the regularity of the request for information in the light of those matters, but must also enable that authority to satisfy itself that the information sought is not devoid of any foreseeable relevance having regard to the identity of the taxpayer concerned and that of any third party asked to provide the information, and to the requirements of the tax investigation concerned

Thus, one point of challenge is whether the requested party has in fact carried out an adequate review. AG Kokott, in C-245/19 and C246/19 *Luxembourg v B* addressed how a requested party might approach such a question, saying (at paragraph 132):

> In order to enable the requested authority to proceed with such an — albeit limited — assessment, the requesting authority must provide an adequate statement of reasons explaining its request for information. It must explain the purpose of the information sought in the context of the tax procedure under way in respect of the taxpayer identified in the request. The reasons given must put the national court in a position in which it may carry out the review of the legality of the request for information. A purely formal statement of reasons that does not explain why the information requested is relevant under national law to the tax procedure in the requesting Member State does not satisfy these requirements. It is, however, for the referring court to review the statement of reasons for the request for information

AG Kokott goes on to state that:

> … [the] requesting authority must state the reasons for the request for information in order to enable the requested authority to assess whether the information is not manifestly lacking in foreseeable relevance to the tax assessment conducted by the requesting authority. The request must provide concrete evidence of the facts or transactions that are relevant for tax purposes, so as to rule out an impermissible 'fishing expedition'.

In its judgment in the same case, the CJEU held:

> 119. The referring court's doubts stem, however, from the fact that that decision, taken together with that request, concerns contracts, invoices and payments which are not specifically identified.
>
> 120. It must be observed, first, that that decision, taken together with that request, indisputably concerns information which is not manifestly devoid of any foreseeable relevance inasmuch as it concerns contracts, invoices and payments that were concluded or carried out, during the period covered by the investigation, by the person holding the information concerning those contracts, invoices and payments, and that are connected with the taxpayer concerned by that investigation.
>
> 121. Secondly, it should be borne in mind that both the decision and the request were made, as can be seen from paragraph 81 above, during the preliminary stage of the investigation, the purpose of which is to gather information of which the requesting authority does not, by definition, have full and precise knowledge.
>
> 122. In those circumstances, it is foreseeable that some of the information referred to in the decision ordering that information be provided giving rise to the dispute in the main proceedings in Case C-245/19, taken together with the request for exchange of information on which it is based, will ultimately prove, at the end of the investigation conducted by the requesting authority, to be irrelevant in the light of the results of that investigation.

This does not, however, mean that a challenge cannot be made[8]. This is because, in short, there remains a bar. As highlighted by the EU cases considering the concept, the request will need to demonstrate foreseeable relevance. If it does not, the requested party should refuse the request. If they do not, this clearly has potential for forming the basis of a claim. (Though

[8] Several other decisions also indicate a relatively low bar for 'foreseeable relevance', including: *Chartfield*, *Haskell* and *Volaw*

there remains the practical difficulty of obtaining the request to check whether it demonstrates foreseeable relevance within a suitable time frame).

11.5 Article 2

Article 2 provides that:

> A Requested Party is not obligated to provide information which is neither held by its authorities nor in the possession or control of persons who are within its territorial jurisdiction

In relation to Article 2, the commentary provides:

> Article 2 addresses the jurisdictional scope of the Agreement. It clarifies that a requested Party is not obligated to provide information which is neither held by its authorities nor is in the possession or control of persons within its territorial jurisdiction. The requested Party's obligation to provide information is not, however, restricted by the residence or the nationality of the person to whom the information relates or by the residence or the nationality of the person in control or possession of the information requested. The term "possession or control" should be construed broadly and the term "authorities" should be interpreted to include all government agencies. Of course, a requested Party would nevertheless be under no obligation to provide information held by an "authority" if the circumstances described in Article 7 (Possibility of Declining a Request) were met

In relation to the territorial restriction – i.e. that a party is not obligated to provide information which is neither held by its authorities nor in the possession or control of persons who are within its territorial jurisdiction – this does not restrict the requested Party's obligation by reference to the residence or the nationality of the person to whom the information relates, or to the residence or the nationality of the person in control or possession of the information requested. The Commentary on the Model opines that the term 'possession or control' should be construed broadly and the term 'authorities' should be interpreted to include all government agencies.

This probably asks more questions than it answers. In particular, it leaves questions about possession or control, and when a person will be within its territorial jurisdiction. It must necessarily also raise questions about digital information stored outside of the jurisdiction. While it seems probable that, where there was a person with power to control the information within the jurisdiction, such information would consequently be within scope, but in such circumstances certain conflict of laws issues might arise. They are beyond the scope of this book.

11.6 Article 5

Article 5 provides:

1. The competent authority of the requested Party shall provide upon request information for the purposes referred to in Article 1. Such information shall be exchanged without regard to whether the conduct being investigated would constitute a crime under the laws of the requested Party if such conduct occurred in the requested Party.
2. If the information in the possession of the competent authority of the requested Party is not sufficient to enable it to comply with the request for information, that Party shall use all relevant information gathering measures to provide the applicant Party with the information requested, notwithstanding that the requested Party may not need such information for its own tax purposes.
3. If specifically requested by the competent authority of an applicant Party, the competent authority of the requested Party shall provide information under this Article, to the extent allowable under its domestic laws, in the form of depositions of witnesses and authenticated copies of original records.
4. Each Contracting Party shall ensure that its competent authorities for the purposes specified in Article 1 of the Agreement, have the authority to obtain and provide upon request:
   a) information held by banks, other financial institutions, and any person acting in an agency or fiduciary capacity including nominees and trustees;
   b) information regarding the ownership of companies, partnerships, trusts, foundations, "Anstalten" and other persons, including, within the constraints of Article 2, ownership information on all such persons in an ownership chain; in the case of trusts, information on settlors, trustees and beneficiaries; and in the case of foundations, information on founders, members of the foundation council and beneficiaries. Further, this Agreement does not create an obligation on the Contracting Parties to obtain or provide ownership information with respect to publicly traded companies or public collective investment funds or schemes unless such information can be obtained without giving rise to disproportionate difficulties.
5. The competent authority of the applicant Party shall provide the following information to the competent authority of the requested Party when making a request for information under the Agreement to demonstrate the foreseeable relevance of the information to the request:
   (a) the identity of the person under examination or investigation;
   (b) a statement of the information sought including its nature and the form in which the applicant Party wishes to receive the information from the requested Party;

(c) the tax purpose for which the information is sought;
(d) grounds for believing that the information requested is held in the requested Party or is in the possession or control of a person within the jurisdiction of the requested Party;
(e) to the extent known, the name and address of any person believed to be in possession of the requested information;
(f) a statement that the request is in conformity with the law and administrative practices of the applicant Party, that if the requested information was within the jurisdiction of the applicant Party then the competent authority of the applicant Party would be able to obtain the information under the laws of the applicant Party or in the normal course of administrative practice and that it is in conformity with this Agreement;
(g) a statement that the applicant Party has pursued all means available in its own territory to obtain the information, except those that would give rise to disproportionate difficulties.

6. The competent authority of the requested Party shall forward the requested information as promptly as possible to the applicant Party. To ensure a prompt response, the competent authority of the requested Party shall:
   a) Confirm receipt of a request in writing to the competent authority of the applicant Party and shall notify the competent authority of the applicant Party of deficiencies in the request, if any, within 60 days of the receipt of the request.
   b) If the competent authority of the requested Party has been unable to obtain and provide the information within 90 days of receipt of the request, including if it encounters obstacles in furnishing the information or it refuses to furnish the information, it shall immediately inform the applicant Party, explaining the reason for its inability, the nature of the obstacles or the reasons for its refusal

Information under an OECD model-type TIEA can only be exchanged upon a request from the other contracting party. In addition, a government cannot give the excuse that it does not itself need the information requested, to avoid having to gather it.

In relation to Article 5(1), the commentary explains:

> 39. Paragraph 1 provides the general rule that the competent authority of the requested Party must provide information upon request for the purposes referred to in Article 1. The paragraph makes clear that the Agreement only covers exchange of information upon request (i.e., when the information requested relates to a particular examination, inquiry or investigation) and does not cover automatic or spontaneous exchange of information. However, Contracting Parties may wish to consider expanding their co-operation in matters of information

exchange for tax purposes by covering automatic and spontaneous exchanges and simultaneous tax examinations.

40. The reference in the first sentence to Article 1 of the Agreement confirms that information must be exchanged for both civil and criminal tax matters. The second sentence of paragraph 1 makes clear that information in connection with criminal tax matters must be exchanged irrespective of whether or not the conduct being investigated would also constitute a crime under the laws of the requested Party

The commentary emphasises the wide scope of the TIEA. It does provide some restriction on Article 5(1), in that the information requested must relate to a particular examination, inquiry or investigation. This is – in practice – not always seen in the TIEA paperwork that makes its way to taxpayers, third parties and their advisers. It is notoriously difficult – if not impossible – to check the form of any request made, so is equally difficult to consider whether these requirements have been complied with.

The Commentary continues in relation to Article 5(2):

42. Upon receipt of an information request the competent authority of the requested Party must first review whether it has all the information necessary to respond to a request. If the information in its own possession proves inadequate, it must take "all relevant information gathering measures" to provide the applicant Party with the information requested. The term "information gathering measures" is defined in Article 4, paragraph 1, sub-paragraph l). An information gathering measure is "relevant" if it is capable of obtaining the information requested by the applicant Party. The requested Party determines which information gathering measures are relevant in a particular case.

43. Paragraph 2 further provides that information must be exchanged without regard to whether the requested Party needs the information for its own tax purposes. This rule is needed because a tax interest requirement might defeat effective exchange of information, for instance, in cases where the requested Party does not impose an income tax or the request relates to an entity not subject to taxation within the requested Party

The commentary on Article 5(4) states:

46. Paragraph 4, sub-paragraph a), by referring explicitly to persons that may enjoy certain privilege rights under domestic law, makes clear that such rights can not form the basis for declining a request unless otherwise provided in Article 7. For instance, the inclusion of a reference to bank information in paragraph 4,

sub-paragraph a) rules out that bank secrecy could be considered a part of public policy (ordre public). Similarly, paragraph 4, sub-paragraph a) together with Article 7, paragraph 2 makes clear that information that does not otherwise constitute a trade, business, industrial, commercial or professional secret or trade process does not become such a secret simply because it is held by one of the persons mentioned.

...

48. Sub-paragraph a) mentions information held by banks and other financial institutions. In accordance with the Report "Improving Access to Bank Information for Tax Purposes" (OECD 2000), access to information held by banks or other financial institutions may be by direct means or indirectly through a judicial or administrative process. **As stated in the report, the procedure for indirect access should not be so burdensome and time-consuming as to act as an impediment to access to bank information**. Typically, requested bank information includes account, financial, and transactional information as well as information on the identity or legal structure of account holders and parties to financial transactions.

The requirement for the process by which to obtain information to not be time-consuming and burdensome has been problematic, in that it has led to political pressure for a quicker resolution of appeals in certain jurisdictions (Jersey being one of them). A balance must be maintained between the requirements of the treaties in force, the persuasive guidance of the Commentary and the rights of taxpayers and others guaranteed by domestic and international law.

The Commentary continues:

49. Paragraph 4, sub-paragraph a) further mentions information held by persons acting in an agency or fiduciary capacity, including nominees and trustees. A person is generally said to act in a "fiduciary capacity" when the business which he transacts, or the money or property, which he handles, is not his own or for his own benefit, but for the benefit of another person, as to whom he stands in a relation implying and necessitating confidence and trust on the one part and good faith on the other part. The term "agency" is very broad and includes all forms of corporate service providers (e.g., company formation agents, trust companies, registered agents, lawyers).

Again, the natural meaning of the words – particularly agency – is stretched by the Commentary, though perhaps it is intended to have an autonomous international law meaning. Whether or not a domestic court would be in a position to enforce such a meaning is by no means certain, particularly as the Commentary cannot be binding.

The Commentary continues to explain what it considers constitutes 'ownership' for the purposes of the Model TIEA:

> 50. Sub-paragraph b) requires that the competent authorities of the Contracting Parties must have the authority to obtain and provide ownership information. The purpose of the sub-paragraph is not to develop a common "all purpose" definition of ownership among Contracting Parties, but to specify the types of information that a Contracting Party may legitimately expect to receive in response to a request for ownership information so that it may apply its own tax laws, including its domestic definition of beneficial ownership.
>
> 51. In connection with companies and partnerships, the legal and beneficial owner of the shares or partnership assets will usually be the same person. However, in some cases the legal ownership position may be subject to a nominee or similar arrangement. Where the legal owner acts on behalf of another person as a nominee or under a similar arrangement, such other person, rather than the legal owner, may be the beneficial owner. Thus the starting point for the ownership analysis is legal ownership of shares or partnership interests and all Contracting Parties must be able to obtain and provide information on legal ownership. Partnership interests include all forms of partnership interests: general or limited or capital or profits. However, in certain cases, legal ownership may be no more than a starting point. For example, in any case where the legal owner acts on behalf of any other person as a nominee or under a similar arrangement, the Contracting Parties should have the authority to obtain and provide information about that other person who may be the beneficial owner in addition to information about the legal owner. An example of a nominee is a nominee shareholding arrangement where the legal title-holder that also appears as the shareholder of record acts as an agent for another person. Within the constraints of Article 2 of the Agreement, the requested Party must have the authority to provide information about the persons in an ownership chain.

It moves on to consider trusts and foundations, saying:

> 52. In connection with trusts and foundations, sub-paragraph b) provides specifically the type of identity information the Contracting Parties should have the authority to obtain and provide. This is not limited to ownership information. The same rules should also be applied to persons that are substantially similar to trusts or foundations such as the "Anstalt." Therefore,

a Contracting Party should have, for example, the authority to obtain and provide information on the identity of the settlor and the beneficiaries and persons who are in a position to direct how assets of the trust or foundation are to be dealt with.

53. Certain trusts, foundations, "Anstalten" or similar arrangements, may not have any identified group of persons as beneficiaries but rather may support a general cause. Therefore, ownership information should be read to include only identifiable persons. The term "foundation council" should be interpreted very broadly to include any person or body of persons managing the foundation as well as persons who are in a position to direct how assets of the trust or foundation are to be dealt with.

It then returns to general principles, stating:

54. Most organisational structures will be classified as a company, a partnership, a trust, a foundation or a person similar to a trust or foundation. However, there might be entities or structures for which ownership information might be legitimately requested but that do not fall into any of these categories. For instance, a structure might, as a matter of law, be of a purely contractual nature. In these cases, the Contracting Parties should have the authority to obtain and provide information about any person with a right to share in the income or gain of the structure or in the proceeds from any sale or liquidation.

The Commentary continues to discuss the importance of "ownership chains":

55. Sub-paragraph b) also provides that a requested Party must have the authority to obtain and provide ownership information for all persons in an ownership chain provided, as is set out in Article 2, the information is held by the authorities of the requested State or is in the possession or control of persons who are within the territorial jurisdiction of the requested Party. This language ensures that the applicant Party need not submit separate information requests for each level of a chain of companies or other persons. For instance, assume company A is a wholly-owned subsidiary of company B and both companies are incorporated under the laws of Party C, a Contracting Party of the Agreement. If Party D, also a Contracting Party, requests ownership information on company A and specifies in the request that it also seeks ownership information on any person in A's chain of ownership, Party C in its response to the request must provide ownership information for both company A and B.

56. The second sentence of sub-paragraph b) provides that in the case of publicly traded companies and public collective investment funds or schemes, the competent authorities need only provide ownership information that the requested Party can obtain without disproportionate difficulties. Information can be obtained only with "disproportionate difficulties" if the identification of owners, while theoretically possible, would involve excessive costs or resources. Because such difficulties might easily arise in connection with publicly traded companies and public collective investment funds or schemes where a true public market for ownership interests exists, it was felt that such a clarification was particularly warranted. At the same time it is recognised that where a true public market for ownership interests exists there is less of a risk that such vehicles will be used for tax evasion or other non-compliance with the tax law. The definitions of publicly traded companies and public collective investment funds or schemes are contained in Article 4, paragraph 1, sub-paragraphs e) through h).

This gives a very broad interpretation to the meaning of 'ownership'. This is – perhaps – broader even than that found in CRS. It potentially gives access to information about a wide range of people who arguably should not be in scope. The limits of 'ownership' appear not to have been extensively tested by the Courts; however, this may well be a fertile area for future litigation.

In relation to Article 5(5), the Commentary says:

57. Paragraph 5 lists the information that the applicant Party must provide to the requested Party in order to demonstrate the foreseeable relevance of the information requested to the administration or enforcement of the applicant Party's tax laws. While paragraph 5 contains important procedural requirements that are intended to ensure that fishing expeditions do not occur, subparagraphs a) through g) nevertheless need to be interpreted liberally in order not to frustrate effective exchange of information. The following paragraphs give some examples to illustrate the application of the requirements in certain situations.'

Finally, in relation to the Model TIEA, Article 7 provides:

1. The requested Party shall not be required to obtain or provide information that the applicant Party would not be able to obtain under its own laws for purposes of the administration or enforcement of its own tax laws. The competent authority of the requested Party may decline to assist where the request is not made in conformity with this Agreement.

2. The provisions of this Agreement shall not impose on a Contracting Party the obligation to supply information which would disclose any trade, business, industrial, commercial or professional secret or trade process. Notwithstanding the foregoing, information of the type referred to in Article 5, paragraph 4 shall not be treated as such a secret or trade process merely because it meets the criteria in that paragraph.

3. The provisions of this Agreement shall not impose on a Contracting Party the obligation to obtain or provide information, which would reveal confidential communications between a client and an attorney, solicitor or other admitted legal representative where such communications are:

   (a) produced for the purposes of seeking or providing legal advice or
   (b) produced for the purposes of use in existing or contemplated legal proceedings.

4. The requested Party may decline a request for information if the disclosure of the information would be contrary to public policy (ordre public).

5. A request for information shall not be refused on the ground that the tax claim giving rise to the request is disputed.

6. The requested Party may decline a request for information if the information is requested by the applicant Party to administer or enforce a provision of the tax law of the applicant Party, or any requirement connected therewith, which discriminates against a national of the requested Party as compared with a national of the applicant Party in the same circumstances.

Article 7 is of particular importance because it provides the only comprehensive and cogent restriction on the scope of such agreements. The Commentary explains:

> 71. The purpose of this Article is to identify the situations in which a requested Party is not required to supply information in response to a request. If the conditions for any of the grounds for declining a request under Article 7 are met, the requested Party is given discretion to refuse to provide the information but it should carefully weigh the interests of the applicant Party with the pertinent reasons for declining the request. However, if the requested Party does provide the information the person concerned cannot allege an infraction of the rules on secrecy. In the event that the requested Party declines a request for information it shall inform the applicant Party of the grounds for its decision at the earliest opportunity'

The Commentary continues, advocating for limiting the scope of Article 7, saying:

> 72. The first sentence of paragraph 1 makes clear that a requested Party is not required to obtain and provide information that the applicant Party would not be able to obtain under similar circumstances under its own laws for purposes of the administration or enforcement of its own tax laws.
>
> 73. This rule is intended to prevent the applicant Party from circumventing its domestic law limitations by requesting information from the other Contracting Party thus making use of greater powers than it possesses under its own laws. For instance, most countries recognise under their domestic laws that information cannot be obtained from a person to the extent such person can claim the privilege against self-incrimination. A requested Party may, therefore, decline a request if the applicant Party would have been precluded by its own self-incrimination rules from obtaining the information under similar circumstances.
>
> 74. In practice, however, the privilege against self-incrimination should have little, if any, application in connection with most information requests. The privilege against self-incrimination is personal and cannot be claimed by an individual who himself is not at risk of criminal prosecution. The overwhelming majority of information requests seek to obtain information from third parties such as banks, intermediaries or the other party to a contract and not from the individual under investigation. Furthermore, the privilege against self-incrimination generally does not attach to persons other than natural persons.
>
> 75. The second sentence of paragraph 1 provides that a requested Party may decline a request for information in cases where the request is not made in conformity with the Agreement.
>
> 76. Both the first and the second sentence of paragraph 1 raise the question of how the statements provided by the applicant Party under Article 5, paragraph 5, sub-paragraph f) relate to the grounds for declining a request under Article 7, paragraph 1. The provision of the respective statements should generally be sufficient to establish that no reasons for declining a request under Article 7, paragraph 1 exist. However, a requested Party that has received statements to this effect may still decline the request if it has grounds for believing that the statements are clearly inaccurate.
>
> 77. Where a requested Party, in reliance on such statements, provides information to the applicant Party it remains within the

framework of this Agreement. A requested Party is under no obligation to research or verify the statements provided by the applicant Party. The responsibility for the accuracy of the statement lies with the applicant Party

The Commentary considers that Article 7(2) will rarely be in point, and we agree. Consequently we do not consider it here.

In relation to Article 7(3) – legally privileged information – the Commentary explains:

84. A Contracting Party may decline a request if the information requested is protected by the attorney-client privilege as defined in paragraph 3. However, where the equivalent privilege under the domestic law of the requested Party is narrower than the definition contained in paragraph 3 (e.g., the law of the requested Party does not recognise a privilege in tax matters, or it does not recognise a privilege in criminal tax matters) a requested Party may not decline a request unless it can base its refusal to provide the information on Article 7, paragraph 1.

85. Under paragraph 3 the attorney-client privilege attaches to any information that constitutes (1) "confidential communication" between (2) "a client and an attorney, solicitor or other admitted legal representative," if such communication (3) "is produced for the purposes of seeking or providing legal advice" or (4) is "produced for the purposes of use in existing or contemplated legal proceedings."

86. Communication is "confidential" if the client can reasonably have expected the communication to be kept secret. For instance, communications made in the presence of third parties that are neither staff nor otherwise agents of the attorney are not confidential communications. Similarly, communications made to the attorney by the client with the instruction to share them with such third parties are not confidential communications.

87. The communications must be between a client and an attorney, solicitor or other admitted legal representative. Thus, the attorney-client privilege applies only if the attorney, solicitor or other legal representative is admitted to practice law. Communications with persons of legal training but not admitted to practice law are not protected under the attorney-client privilege rules.

88. Communications between a client and an attorney, solicitor or other admitted legal representative are only privileged if, and to the extent that, the attorney, solicitor or other legal representative acts in his or her capacity as an attorney, solicitor or other legal representative. For instance, to the extent that an

attorney acts as a nominee shareholder, a trustee, a settlor, a company director or under a power of attorney to represent the company in its business affairs, he can not claim the attorney-client privilege with respect to any information resulting from and relating to any such activity.

89. Sub-paragraph a) requires that the communications be "produced for the purposes of seeking or providing legal advice." The attorney-client privilege covers communications by both client and attorney provided the communications are produced for purposes of either seeking or providing legal advice. Because the communication must be produced for the purposes of seeking or providing legal advice, the privilege does not attach to documents or records delivered to an attorney in an attempt to protect such documents or records from disclosure. Also, information on the identity of a person, such as a director or beneficial owner of a company, is typically not covered by the privilege

The discussion on 'legal privilege' in relation to DAC6 and MDR may also be relevant here.

11.7 Human Rights

The application of the European Convention on Human Rights was considered in the context of TIEAs by the English Privy Council in *Volaw Trust and Corporate Services Limited and Others v Comptroller of Taxes (Jersey) and Others* [2019] UKPC 29. Before considering the views of the Privy Council, it is first necessary to give the point some context. The Court of Appeal summarised the issue as follows:

> ... the fact that the Royal Court exercises an appellate jurisdiction does not of itself identify what kind of appeal has been provided for and, accordingly, the extent of the material to which it can have regard. At the end of the spectrum are appeals stricto sensu in which the question for consideration is whether the decision subject to appeal was right on the material which the decision-making body had before it. In such an appeal fresh evidence cannot be called. At the other end are appeals de novo in which there is a fresh hearing with the parties being able to call fresh evidence. Quilter v Mapleson 1882 9 QBD 672 at p676.
>
> We approach the issue of classification from this point of departure. The Comptroller will necessarily have before him a request from the Requesting state. He will need to consider whether it provides the reasonable grounds for a belief or opinion that the 2008 Regulation require. Whether or not he had reasonable grounds for such a belief could be construed to restrict an appeal to the Royal Court to an assessment of whether the material that he had before him provided, objectively, reasonable grounds for his belief. If for example he was

unduly tolerant of an inadequately composed Request, on this footing, the Royal Court could set aside the notice.

An appeal on this limited basis supplemented by any further appeal to this Court, would involve a procedure without undue complexity.

There is nothing in the actual language of the 2008 Regulations inconsistent with such a construction: nor does the J/N TIEA insofar as relevant require its rejection since it does not oblige the Requested party to provide any safeguards: indeed the last sentence in Article 1 of the J/N TIEA suggests that the safeguards should not unduly hamper the exchange process.

...

Our presumptive conclusion is fortified by an appreciation of the legal context in which the 2008 Regulations were composed. There are in this jurisdiction rules of court governing the proceedings of the Royal Court, Royal Court Rules 2004, which must be taken to have been known to the maker of the Regulations. Within the general corpus there is a discrete category of rules for administrative appeals, which, while the phrase is not defined, would appear apt to embrace an appeal against the decision of an administrative officer such as the Comptroller...

This highlights both the problems apparent from treating something other than a judicial review as an 'administrative appeal' and the unusual nature of an appeal from the Comptroller's decision to the Royal Court. The issue of human rights was raised in the following way:

The Appellant's most substantial argument for applying Rules 14-15[9] to the 2008 Regulation so as to allow for a full re-hearing with fresh evidence was based on the ECHR incorporated into the Bailiwick since December 2006 via the Human Rights (Jersey Law) 2000.

48. Article 6 of the ECHR provides, so far as material:-

"In the determination of his civil rights and obligations, everyone is entitled to a fair and public hearing within a reasonable time by an independent and impartial tribunal established by law."

In response to this, the Court of Appeal held:

Article 6 does not, however, inevitably require an unrestricted appeal from the decisions of an administrative body based on findings of fact and the exercise of judgment. Indeed judicial review can in appropriate circumstances suffice. [Lester, Pannick and

[9] These rules, broadly, set out the limits of an administrative appeal with regards to evidence and other associated matters, and when such limits will be extended.

> Herberg: *Human Rights Law and Practice*: 4.6.24. [p299]] Fordham 59.5.7, p.600.
>
> Article 8.1. provides for the right to respect for, inter alia, private and family life subject to the well-known limitations in Article 8.2 (materially "There shall be no interference by a public authority with the exercise of this right except such as is in accordance with the law and is necessary in a democratic society in the interests of... the economic well-being of the country, for the prevention of... crime..."
>
> In B. Larsen Holdings v Norway [2013] ECHR 24117/08 a challenge to the acquisition by Norwegian tax authorities by seizure of a "back up" tape of information and documents pertaining to the tax payer was based on Article 8. The challenge failed. Materially for present purposes the ECtHR said the relevant provisions of domestic law were subject to "important limitations" and contained "adequate and effective safeguards" [paragraph 172].
>
> In our view the 2008 Regulations do contain "important limitations" by defining, and so restricting, circumstances in which the Comptroller can respond to a request from a competent authority (requiring notably not merely suspicion but reasonable belief) accompanied by "adequate and effective safeguards" i.e. (quite apart from the obliged provision of fairness before the Comptroller) a two stage appeal to judicial bodies. Moreover if Article 6 does not directly require that an appeal should be by way of unrestricted oral hearing, Article 8 cannot be construed indirectly to do so.
>
> We note too the distinction drawn by the ECtHR in B.L. Holdings Ltd between a "search and seizure" case and a demand by a public authority for information [paragraph 173], and its appreciation of "the public interest ensuring efficiency in the inspection of information provided by the Applicant company for tax assessment purposes"

The issue in the appeal to the Privy Council was whether the TIEA notice (and relevant associated legislation) was compatible with ECHR, Article 6. Lord Reed summarised the parties' positions as follows (at paragraph 37):

> 37. As has been explained, the TIEA Notices required Volaw to produce pre-existing documents for the purposes of an investigation in Norway into suspected criminal offences under Norwegian law. The same was true of the 1991 Law Notice when it was served. The situation has changed since then, so far as the latter notice is concerned, in that the investigation is now being conducted in Jersey and concerns suspected offences under Jersey law. In these circumstances, the question arises whether the notices violate article 6. The appellants argue that they do, on the basis that the compulsory production of

incriminating documents in the course of pre-trial investigations is in itself a violation of article 6, even in advance of, or in the absence of, any trial, whether in the jurisdiction in question or elsewhere. The respondents dispute this, arguing that the privilege has no application to pre-existing documents, and is in any event not violated in the absence of trial proceedings, or where such proceedings would take place in another jurisdiction.

38. The Commissioner observed that there were conflicting English authorities bearing on the application of the privilege under article 6 to pre-existing documents. In some cases the Court of Appeal had rejected (obiter, in some instances) the proposition that the compulsory production of pre-existing documents violated the privilege against self-incrimination either at common law or under the ECHR: see, for example, Attorney General's Reference (No 7 of 2000) [2001] EWCA Crim 888; [2001] 1 WLR 1879, paras 59-62, R v Kearns [2002] EWCA Crim 748; [2002] 1 WLR 2815, para 53, and C plc v P (Attorney General intervening) [2007] EWCA Civ 493; [2008] Ch 1, paras 28-34. In those cases, the court had focused on Saunders v United Kingdom (1996) 23 EHRR 313, where the European Court of Human Rights, stated at para 69:

> "The right not to incriminate oneself is primarily concerned, however, with respecting the will of an accused person to remain silent. As commonly understood in the legal systems of the Contracting Parties to the Convention and elsewhere, it does not extend to the use in criminal proceedings of material which may be obtained from the accused through the use of compulsory powers but which has an existence independent of the will of the suspect such as, inter alia, documents acquired pursuant to a warrant, breath, blood and urine samples and bodily tissue for the purpose of DNA testing."

Having set out this proposition, Lord Reed continued to explain:

> Since documents obtained by the use of compulsory powers had "an existence independent of the will of the suspect", they were considered by the Court of Appeal in those cases to fall outside the scope of the privilege protected by article 6. Judgments of the European court which could not readily be reconciled with that approach, such as Funke v France (1993) 16 EHRR 297 and JB v Switzerland (Application No 31827/96) given 3 May 2001, were put to one side as being inconsistent with Saunders. As the Commissioner noted, however, there were other decisions of the Divisional Court and the Court of Appeal which supported a less categorical approach, such as R (Malik) v Manchester Crown Court

[2008] EWHC 1362 (Admin); [2008] EMLR 19 and R v S (F) [2008] EWCA Crim 2177; [2009] 1 WLR 1489, as also did the dissenting judgment of Lawrence Collins LJ in C plc v P. Ultimately, the Commissioner preferred the preponderant view in the English cases, which (in his words) "distinguishes and (ultimately) discards Funke in favour of Saunders".

He then continued to set out the particulars of the relevant recent judgments on Article 6, before saying (at paragraph 58):

58. Considering the present case in the light of this body of law, the first notable feature is that there has been no determination of any "criminal charge" against Volaw or any of the other appellants, whether by way of criminal prosecution or otherwise. The present challenges under article 6 have been brought at the stage of the gathering of documentary material as part of an investigation into the possible commission of offences. As the Grand Chamber explained in Ibrahim, at para 253, the guarantees of article 6 are applicable from the moment that a criminal charge exists, "and may therefore be relevant during pre-trial proceedings if and in so far as the fairness of the trial is likely to be seriously prejudiced by an initial failure to comply with them" (emphasis supplied). In principle, therefore (and subject to exceptions), an examination of the compatibility of pre-trial conduct with article 6 will normally focus upon its effect on the fairness of the trial. In particular, as the European court has often stated, the right not to incriminate oneself is primarily concerned with the proof of guilt at trial: it "presupposes that the prosecution in a criminal case seek to prove their case without resort to evidence obtained through methods of coercion or oppression in defiance of the will of the accused" (Ibrahim, para 266; emphasis supplied). The privilege does not therefore act as a general prohibition on the use of compulsory powers to obtain documents or other forms of information at the stage of an investigation, even where a person has been charged with an offence within the meaning of article 6: "the right not to incriminate oneself is not absolute" (Ibrahim, para 269). As the court stated in Ibrahim, at para 269, "what is crucial in this context [ie in relation to compulsion to produce evidence] is the use to which evidence obtained under compulsion is put in the course of the criminal trial".

59. Secondly, although the reasoning and effect of the judgments in Funke v France, JB v Switzerland and Chambaz v Switzerland remain unclear, those judgments do not in any event appear to be germane to the present appeals. One would hesitate to conclude that the court intended in these cases to establish an absolute rule that the prosecution and punishment of a person

who refuses to provide incriminating real evidence in pre-trial investigations will contravene article 6. Such a rule would fatally undermine the court's acceptance in Saunders, at para 69, that a suspect can properly be required to provide other types of real evidence, such as samples of breath, blood, urine and DNA: a requirement which is normally underpinned by the threat of a sanction in the event of non-compliance. It may be that these judgments should be understood, consistently with the general approach adopted by the Grand Chamber in such cases as Jalloh v Germany, O'Halloran and Francis v United Kingdom and Ibrahim v United Kingdom, as reflecting the nature and degree of the compulsion or coercion used in order to obtain documents and information from the applicants (documents which might, in Funke at least, have been obtained by other, unobjectionable, means). Understood in that way, these cases might be fitted into the general pattern of later cases concerned with the use of oppressive methods of obtaining real evidence. Although that reasoning is not evident in the judgments in the Funke line of cases, it is nevertheless characteristic of the court to pay close attention to the facts of the cases coming before it, recognising differences of degree, and eschewing inflexible statements of principle. It is also characteristic of the court to recognise the need for a fair balance between the general interest of the community and the personal rights of the individual, the search for which balance it has described as being inherent in the whole of the Convention.

60. Whether or not that is how the Funke line of cases should be understood, they are in any event clearly distinguishable from the present appeals. They concerned situations in which the applicant was prosecuted and punished for his failure to produce self-incriminating evidence. That is not the situation in the present case.

It can, therefore, be seen there are plenty of potential difficulties in claiming incompatibility of Article 6 with a TIEA request. Lord Reed continued to consider the four factors set out in *Jalloh, O'Halloran* and *Ibrahim*. In relation to compulsion, he said (at paragraph 62):

62. Considering first the nature and degree of the compulsion used, Volaw (but none of the other corporate appellants, since they were not addressees of the notices) was subject to compulsion by virtue of the TIEA Notices and the 1991 Law Notice. The compulsion on Volaw consisted of the potential imposition of a fine for non-compliance. In the event that Volaw were to commit an offence under the 2008 Regulations, its officers might also be liable if they consented to, or connived at, the commission of the offence: regulation 16 (para 35 above). It is argued that the

> officers of Volaw were therefore also compelled to produce self-incriminating documents, although it has not been explained what role, if any, each of these unidentified individuals might have played in Volaw's provision of the documents in response to the notice. In the Board's view, however, none of them was compelled by the notices to produce the documents themselves, since (a) the notices were not addressed to them, and (b) the documents were not their documents, and were not in their possession. Nor were they compelled to participate in Volaw's production of the documents: that task could be delegated to other members of staff. Their only relevant obligation was not to consent to, or connive at, the commission of an offence by Volaw.
>
> 63. It is difficult to regard the compulsion arising from the service of the notices as falling within any of the three kinds of situations identified by the European court in para 267 of its Ibrahim judgment (para 43 above). In particular, the only situation mentioned there which concerned the obtaining of real evidence involved "physical or psychological pressure, often in the form of treatment which breaches article 3". It is difficult to regard the service of the notices in the present case as constituting such pressure. It is not comparable in any respect with the conduct with which the cases cited by the court (Jalloh, Magee and Gäfgen) were concerned. Nor is it comparable with the oppressive conduct of the authorities in the cases of Funke v France, JB v Switzerland and Chambaz v Switzerland, even if those cases were of any relevance in a situation where no prosecution for failure to provide the documents has taken place.

Lord Reed continued to consider the weight of public interest at paragraph 64, saying:

> 64. Considering next the weight of the public interest in the investigation and punishment of the offences at issue, the TIEA Notices were issued in order to assist in the investigation of possible tax offences under Norwegian law, in accordance with Jersey's obligations under the Jersey/Norway TIEA. The weight of the public interest in effective international co-operation in the investigation of possible tax avoidance and evasion cannot be doubted. As was explained at paras 24-25 above, international law has sought to respond to the increased possibilities of tax evasion and fraud consequent on the development of the international movement of persons, capital, goods and services, by improving mutual assistance between jurisdictions in relation to tax matters. This is a matter of particular importance in relation to global financial centres such

as Jersey. The present case, involving an individual taxpayer in Norway and numerous related companies and trusts based in a multitude of jurisdictions around the world, with their administration services provided by a financial services firm in Jersey, is an illustration of the circumstances which have led to the need for bilateral tax information exchange agreements such as the Jersey/Norway TIEA. It is only through the recovery of documentation from the financial services firm at the hub of the global network of companies and trusts that an effective investigation can be carried out. So far as the 1991 Law Notice is concerned, it was expressly issued in order to investigate "a suspected offence involving serious or complex fraud". The public interest in the investigation of offences of that character is a consideration of substantial weight.

65. It also has to be borne in mind that the notices were addressed to Volaw only because of its activities as a provider of administration services to the companies, trusts and individuals in question, and sought to recover documents containing factual information relating to the administration of those entities. Thus, each of the TIEA Notices relating to a company required Volaw to produce "all documents and records that Volaw holds which relate to [the company] (including, but not limited to, financial statements, postings reports, general ledger, bank accounts, payment instructions, statutory records, minute books; file notes, correspondence and trust documents) concerning the company's incorporation, administration, activities and operations, management, principals and directors, shareholders and shareholdings and beneficial ownership (including any subsidiaries)." The 1991 Law Notice required Volaw to produce documents relating to the internal affairs of the named companies: changes in the registered shareholders, records of dividends, loans and other payments to the registered shareholders, minutes of directors' and shareholders' meetings, and the like. There is a substantial public interest in maintaining the integrity of licensed providers of financial services. It is not unreasonable that they should be expected to co-operate with responsible investigations into possible tax offences or fraud involving their clients by producing information in their possession relating to their clients' affairs.

66. That is not to imply that the public interest in the investigation and punishment of tax evasion and corporate fraud, and in ensuring the integrity of providers of financial services, outweighs the value of the right not to incriminate oneself when that right crystallises at a trial. The public interest in these matters, important though it is, does not justify depriving

> defendants of a fair trial, conducted in accordance with the basic principles of a fair criminal procedure, as the judgment in *Saunders* demonstrates. But it may be a strong justification for requiring the provision of information and documents at the stage of pre-trial investigations, depending on such matters as the nature and potential significance of the information or documents in question, the use to which they may be put, and the existence of any procedural safeguards. Whether any or all of the documents can subsequently be used as evidence in the event of a trial is a separate question

In relation to the use to which the documents might be put, Lord Reed said:

> 67. Considering next the use to which the documents might be put, and the existence of any relevant safeguards in the procedure, it is again important to note that the present appeals concern pre-trial investigations. No documents have yet been produced, and it is impossible to predict what they might contain, or the use, if any, which the prosecution might seek (or, in relation to Norway, might have sought) to make of them at any trial. It has not been argued that the requirement to produce the documents specified in the notices would in itself prejudice the fairness of any trial which might subsequently be held (the argument, instead, is that a requirement to produce incriminating documents in the course of a criminal investigation prior to trial is sufficient in itself to violate article 6). Any documents produced to the Jersey authorities in compliance with the TIEA Notices would, until the Norwegian authorities abandoned their investigation, have been provided to them for their consideration, in accordance with the Jersey/Norway TIEA. In the event that any charges had subsequently been brought against Volaw in Norway and had proceeded to trial, and in the further event that the prosecution had sought to rely on any of the documents at such a trial, it would then have been open to Volaw to object to the admission of the evidence, on the ground that it had been obtained by the use of compulsory powers and its admission would violate their privilege against self-incrimination. The Norwegian courts would then have ruled on any such objection. Norway has ratified the ECHR. There is no reason why the courts of Jersey should seek to anticipate what might hypothetically occur in Norway following the production of the documents. The same considerations apply, mutatis mutandis, to the use at any trial in Jersey of documents produced in compliance with the 1991 Law Notice.
>
> 68. This is a convenient point at which to mention a point which the parties identified as one of the issues in the case: namely, the question whether the right not to incriminate oneself can apply

in relation to pre-trial investigations in one jurisdiction where any trial would take place in another. So far as the privilege under article 6 is concerned, Board is doubtful whether the question can be answered in categorical terms. It may be, as in other situations involving the application of article 6 in relation to foreign proceedings, that the answer depends on whether the applicant risks suffering a flagrant denial of justice in the requesting country (see, for example, *Othman v United Kingdom (Abu Qatada)* (2012) 55 EHRR 1, para 258). But it is unnecessary to decide the point, which does not yet appear to have been considered by the European court. All that need be said in the present case, where (a) the only potential incriminatory use of the documents which is contemplated would occur in trial proceedings, (b) those proceedings would take place in either Norway or Jersey, and (c) both those jurisdictions adhere to the Convention, is that it cannot be said (in the language of *Ibrahim*, at para 253) that the fairness of any trial is or was likely to be seriously prejudiced by the production of the documents in question at the pre-trial stage.

69. It is also relevant to bear in mind that, at any trial, the onus would be on the prosecution to establish the commission of an offence: offences which, so far as they concern tax evasion or fraud, would require proof of a dishonest intent. The notices did not call for any admission of liability: they simply requested documents containing objective factual information about the affairs of certain of Volaw's clients. The risk of the notices resulting in unreliable admissions of guilt is negligible.

Thus, the Privy Council found that there was no reason to conclude at that stage (i.e. when the notices had been given, but the matter had not progressed further) that Article 6 had been breached.

This does not mean that human rights are not relevant in the context of TIEAs; clearly they are. In particular Article 6 may be engaged in different circumstances, but consideration should also be given to Article 8 (right to respect for private and family life) as well as to domestic legislation, such as data protection legislation. In the context of a request from a jurisdiction that does not have equivalent human rights legislation to the ECHR, thought may also be given to the wider implications of providing information, and whether that may lead to a breach of one of the more basic human rights. Though this is relatively unlikely to arise in practice, it should be borne in mind where the circumstances of the case are particularly unusual.

Index